friend I could have!
Thanks for your
friendship, support and
fun.
 — Susan

GLOBAL AGEING IN THE TWENTY-FIRST CENTURY

Global Ageing in the Twenty-First Century
Challenges, Opportunities and Implications

Edited by

SUSAN A. McDANIEL
University of Lethbridge, Canada

ZACHARY ZIMMER
University of California at San Francisco, USA

ASHGATE

© Susan A. McDaniel and Zachary Zimmer 2013

All rights reserved. No part of this publication may be reproduced, stored in a retrieval system or transmitted in any form or by any means, electronic, mechanical, photocopying, recording or otherwise without the prior permission of the publisher.

Susan A. McDaniel and Zachary Zimmer have asserted their right under the Copyright, Designs and Patents Act, 1988, to be identified as the editors of this work.

Published by
Ashgate Publishing Limited
Wey Court East
Union Road
Farnham
Surrey, GU9 7PT
England

Ashgate Publishing Company
110 Cherry Street
Suite 3-1
Burlington, VT 05401-3818
USA

www.ashgate.com

British Library Cataloguing in Publication Data
Global ageing in the twenty-first century : challenges, opportunities and implications.
1. Population aging--Cross-cultural studies. 2. Aging--Cross-cultural studies. 3. Older people--Medical care--Cross-cultural studies. 4. Older people--Employment--Cross-cultural studies. 5. Older people--Economic conditions--Cross-cultural studies. 6. Intergenerational relations--Cross-cultural studies. 7. Older people--Government policy--Cross-cultural studies.
I. McDaniel, Susan A., 1946- II. Zimmer, Zachary.
305.2'6'09-dc23

Library of Congress Cataloging-in-Publication Data
McDaniel, Susan A., 1946-
  Global ageing in the twenty-first century: challenges, opportunities and implications / by Susan A. McDaniel and Zachary Zimmer.
       p. cm.
  Includes bibliographical references and index.
  ISBN 978-1-4094-3270-8 (hardback) -- ISBN 978-1-4094-3271-5 (ebook) 1. Aging--Social aspects. 2. Social history--21st century. I. Zimmer, Zachary. II. Title.
  HQ1061.M37613 2013
  305.26--dc23
                                                                                          2012026365

ISBN 9781409432708 (hbk)
ISBN 9781409432715 (ebk – PDF)
ISBN 9781472400055 (ebk – ePUB)

Printed and bound in Great Britain by the
MPG Books Group, UK.

Contents

List of Figures	vii
List of Tables	ix
Notes on Contributors	xiii
Preface and Acknowledgements	xix

1	Global Ageing in the Twenty-First Century: An Introduction *Zachary Zimmer and Susan McDaniel*	1
2	The Population Ageing Process in Global Perspective *François Héran*	13

PART I: HEALTHY AGEING AND HEALTH CARE

3	Ageing, Functional Disabilities and its Gender Dimensions: Results based on a Study in Delhi *Moneer Alam*	33
4	A Gendered Perspective on Well-Being in Later Life: Algeria, Lebanon and Palestine *Kristine J. Ajrouch, Kathryn M. Yount, Abla M. Sibai and Pia Roman*	49
5	A Global Perspective on Physiological Change with Age *Eileen Crimmins, Felicia Wheaton, Sarinnapha Vasunilashorn, Hiram Beltrán-Sánchez, Lu Zhang and Jung Ki Kim*	79
6	Religious Activity and Transitions in Functional Health and Mortality among Middle Aged and Older Adults in Taiwan *Mira M. Hidajat, Zachary Zimmer and Baai-Shyun Hurng*	105
7	Addressing Health Challenges of Ageing in sub-Saharan Africa: Policy Perspectives and Evidence Needs *Isabella Aboderin*	121
8	New Myths about Ageing: The Growth of Medical Knowledge and its Societal Consequences *Dorly J.H. Deeg*	139

PART II: AGEING WORKFORCE, RETIREMENT AND THE PROVISION OF PENSIONS

9   Population Ageing and its Global Challenges   159
Codrina Rada

10   Reimagining Old Age in Europe:
Effects of Changing Work and Retirement Patterns   175
Kathrin Komp

11   Risky Business: Ageing as an Information Technology Worker   195
Emily Jovic and Julie McMullin

PART III: SHIFTING INTERGENERATIONAL RELATIONS

12   Gender, Marital Status and Intergenerational Relations
in a Changing World   215
Sara Arber

13   The Cultural Context of Social Cohesion and Social Capital:
Exploring Filial Caregiving   235
Neena L. Chappell

14   Generational Differences in Caregiving and its Consequences   253
Janet Fast

15   Family Relations and the Experience of Loneliness
among Older Adults in Eastern Europe   267
Kim Korinek

16   Levels of Welfarism and Intergenerational Transfers within
the Family: Evidence from the Global Ageing Survey (GLAS)   291
George W. Leeson and Hafiz T.A. Khan

*   *   *

17   Conclusion:
Global Ageing in the Twenty-First Century – Where to From Here?   309
Susan McDaniel and Zachary Zimmer

Index   *319*

List of Figures

2.1	Relative change in the main age groups over the next decades in Germany	15
2.2	Relative change in the main age groups over the coming decades in France	17
2.3	Relative change in the main age groups over the next decades in Russia and the US	19
2.4	Percentage change in the main age groups over the next decades in China and North Africa	20
2.5	Share of working-age population in the US from 1950 to 2050, under the three variants projected by the UN Population Division (high, medium, low)	23
2.6	Share of working-age population (aged 20–59) in selected countries	23
2.7	Approximate period in which the share of the working-age population reached or will reach its peak in selected countries or sub-continents	25
5.1	Life expectancy at birth, 2011	81
5.2	Percent with high systolic blood pressure (≥ 140 mm Hg) by country and sex	84
5.3	Percent with diastolic blood pressure (≥ 90 mm Hg) by country and sex	85
5.4	Mean pulse pressure by country and sex	86
5.5	Percent overweight (body mass index ≥ 25 kg/m^2) by country and sex	88
5.6	Percent with high total cholesterol (≥ 240 mg/dl) by country and sex	90
5.7	Percent with low HDL cholesterol (< 40 mg/dl) by country and sex	91
5.8	Mean total/HDL cholesterol (mg/dl) ratio by country and sex	92
5.9	Percent with high glycosylated hemoglobin ($\geq 6.4\%$) by country and sex	93
6.1	Transitions between health states and mortality	111
8.1	Life expectancy from birth by birth cohort, the Netherlands	140

8.2	Life expectancy of those age 65+ by birth cohort, the Netherlands	141
8.3	Prevalence of chronic diseases in 65–85 year olds, 1992–2009	144
8.4	Prevalence of disability in 65–85 year olds, 1992–2009	144
8.5	Life expectancy from age 65 years with disease: Increase 1992–2002	145
9.1	Old-age dependency rates for 2000, 2025 and 2050 respectively	163
9.2	Economic dependency rates	165
9.3	Regional participation rates by age groups in 2000	167
9.4	Regional participation rates by gender in 2000	168
10.1	The effective retirement age in Europe, per geographical region (1970–2009)	178
10.2	The employment status of Europeans aged 50 to 65 years in 2006, by gender	181
10.3	Changes in the tripartite life-course model	185
12.1	Nature of inter-generational transfers between generations	217
12.2	Sex ratios (female/male) for five year age groups above age 60 across countries	225
12.3	Marital status by gender for people aged 65+ and 80+ in four countries	227
14.1	Distribution of care providers by age of caregiver and care receiver	256
14.2	Distribution of caregivers by generation and relationship	256
14.3	Consequences of caregiving	263

List of Tables

1.1	Observed estimates for 1970–75 TFR, observed and projected estimates for 1995–2000 TFR, and change statistics expressed as percentages, for the world, selected regions and selected countries	5
1.2	Population ageing statistics for the world, selected regions and selected countries	7
3.1	Percent reporting ADL difficulties by gender, place of residence and age	38
3.2	Measured grip, gait and self-balancing abilities by gender, place of residence and age group (%)	39
3.3	Self-reported difficulties in eating, bathing and dressing, and grip strength (scores: persons)	40
3.4	Count data regression results showing correlates of self-reported disabilities	42
3.5	List of variables for estimation of CDM and logistic regression models	45
3.6	Explained variables for estimation of CDM and logistic regression models	46
4.1	Socio-political and demographic background of the study countries	51
4.2	Descriptive statistics of the samples: Adults aged 65 years and older in Algeria, Lebanon and Tunisia	60
4.3	Family structure	62
4.4	Social relations	65
4.5	Socioeconomic status	67
4.6	Health and disability	68
5.1	Correlations between social indicators and biological measures	95
6.1	Sample composition (unweighted N, weighted %)	110
6.2	Descriptive statistics (weighted % or means)	111
6.3	Transitions between no ADL or IADL limitations, 1+ limitations, and mortality by home and public religious activity (unweighted N, weighted %)	113

8.1	Body Mass Index, waist circumference and physical activity, men and women ages 55–64 years in 1992 and 2002	142
8.2	Labor force participation at ages 55–64, the Netherlands, 1992–2010	149
8.3	Three trajectories of functional decline in 55–91 year olds observed across a period of six years	150
9.1	Population growth rates, selected world regions, percentage by age groups	161
9.2	Women as a percentage of population age-groups, world regions	162
9.3	Old-age dependency rates, world regions	164
9.4	Annual growth rate of labor force (15+) in percentages: 2000–2020, world regions	166
9.5	Required labor productivity growth	170
10.1	Average effective and average official retirement age in Europe, 2004–2009	180
10.2	How many retirees engage in paid work, in 2008	184
12.1	Expectation of life at birth and at age 65 by gender and country	222
12.2	Marital status distributions, and sex ratios of married and widowed, for aged 65+ and 80+, in Canada, France, Japan, Singapore and Turkey	228
12.3	Marriages of men and women aged 65 and over by country	230
13.1	Care provision by cultural group	245
13.2	Within group correlations between attitudes and behaviors	245
13.3	Multivariate analyses	246
14.1	Predictors of time spent on care tasks (hours/week of care: OLS regression coefficients)	258
14.2	Predictors of likelihood of participation in care tasks (logistic regression odds ratios)	260
14.3	Predictors of care-related health and social consequences (logistic regression odds ratios)	262
15.1	Basic demographic characteristics of the Bulgarian and Russian populations (2009)	273
15.2	Summary statistics for Bulgarian and Russian older adult heads of household, age 60 and older, 2004	277
15.3	Mean loneliness scale scores for Russian and Bulgarian heads of household, 60 and older, by sex, family structure and sociodemographic characteristics	278

15.4	OLS regression analysis: Predictors of loneliness in Russian and Bulgarian heads of household, age 60 and older, 2004	280
16.1	List of variables selected for the study	296
16.2	Odds ratios of significant parameters for the receipt of support by economy	298
16.3	Odds ratios of significant parameters for the provision of support by economy	300

Notes on Contributors

Isabella Aboderin holds a dual appointment as Senior Research Fellow at the African Population and Health Research Center (APHRC) in Nairobi, Kenya and Senior Research Fellow at the Oxford Institute of Population Ageing, University of Oxford, UK.

Kristine J. Ajrouch, PhD, is Professor of Sociology at Eastern Michigan University and Adjunct Research Professor in the Life Course Development Program at the Institute for Social Research, University of Michigan. Her primary research focus concerns the multi-dimensional area of social relations over the life course. Dr Ajrouch has studied, for over 15 years, Arab-Americans and Muslims in the United States. She recently initiated a research program focusing on family ties and ageing in the Middle East.

Moneer Alam, a PhD in economics, is Professor at the Institute of Economic Growth (Delhi). His fields of research include manpower planning and forecasting, labor market issues, health financing, catastrophic spending on healthcare, economic and health issues of ageing, etc. His two substantive contributions on ageing are *Ageing in India: Socio-economic and Health Dimensions* (Delhi: Academic Foundation, 2006) and *Demographics, Employment and Old Age Security: Emerging Trends and Challenges in South Asia* (eds Moneer Alam and Armando Barrientos, Delhi: Macmillan, 2010).

Sara Arber is Professor of Sociology and co-Director at the Centre for Research on Ageing and Gender (CRAG) at the University of Surrey, UK. She was President of the British Sociological Association (1999–2001). Sara has written over 200 journal articles on gender and ageing, inequalities in health and the sociology of sleep. Her books include *The Myth of Generational Conflict: Family and State in Ageing Societies*, *Connecting Gender and Ageing* and *Contemporary Grandparenting*.

Hiram Beltrán-Sánchez is an NIA Post-doctoral Fellow at the Andrus Gerontology Center at the University of Southern California. His research focuses on the study of health, health risk factors, morbidity and mortality patterns in the adult population both in the US and Mexico.

Neena L. Chappell, PhD, FRSC, Canada Research Chair in Social Gerontology, Tier 1, is a professor in the Department of Sociology and Centre on Aging at the University of Victoria, British Columbia, Canada. She has been conducting gerontological research for over 30 years and has established two university-based research centers on ageing (one at the University of Manitoba and one at the University of Victoria).

Eileen Crimmins, PhD is the AARP Professor of Gerontology at the University of Southern California where she is currently Director of the USC/UCLA Center on Biodemography and Population Health. She is also Director of the Multidisciplinary Training in Gerontology program. Professor Crimmins received her PhD in Demography at the University of Pennsylvania.

Dorly J.H. Deeg is Professor of Epidemiology of Aging in the EMGO-Institute for Health and Care Research, Department of Epidemiology and Biostatistics and Department of Psychiatry, VU University Medical Centre, Amsterdam, the Netherlands. She is Scientific Director of the Longitudinal Aging Study, Amsterdam and founding Editor-in-Chief of the *European Journal of Ageing*. Her research interests include health, disability and health and social care at older ages.

Janet Fast is a professor in the Department of Human Ecology at the University of Alberta. She is a family economist whose research addresses family, health and continuing care policy issues. Major themes are the economics of ageing and the paid and unpaid care work of family members. She currently co-leads an international and multidisciplinary research team investigating the intersection of work and care across the life course.

François Héran is with the French National Institute for Demographic Research (INED) (Director, 1999–2009). He served as Head of the Population Surveys at the French National Institute of Statistics (INSEE). He is the author of several reports: 'Demography and economy' (2002), 'Immigration, labour market, integration' (2002), 'Inequalities and discrimination' (2010) as well as a number of research articles. Recent books include *La Formation du couple* (2006, with Michel Bozon), *Le Temps des immigrés* (2007), *Figures de la parenté: une histoire critique de la raison structurale* (2009), and *Trente questions sur l'immigration* (2012).

Mira Hidajat is currently a post-doctoral fellow at the Institute of Public and International Affairs at the University of Utah. She received her PhD in Sociology and Demography from Pennsylvania State University. Her research interests include marital status disparities in healthy life expectancy and social and demographic disparities in ageing, disability and mortality in Asia and the United States.

Baai-Shyun Hurng is Director of the Population and Health Research Center, Bureau of Health Promotion, Taiwan. She has participated in a wide range of research related to health, including the Taiwan Longitudinal Study on Aging, a panel study of a representative sample of older Taiwanese that began in 1989. She is currently collaborating with Zachary Zimmer on a project that examines disability trajectories among older adults in Taiwan.

Emily Jovic completed a PhD at the University of Western Ontario, where she was also a graduate research assistant on the Workforce Aging in the New Economy (WANE) project. Emily is currently an adjunct research professor in the department of sociology at Western and she has been researching and publishing in the areas of work, learning, ageing, and the life course.

Hafiz T.A. Khan, PhD is a senior lecturer in the Department of Economics and International Development at Middlesex University London. He is also involved as a researcher at the Centre for Research into the Older Workforce (CROW), Middlesex University Business School and as a visiting fellow at the Oxford Institute of Population Ageing, University of Oxford. Mostly recently he worked with Dr George W. Leeson on The Global Ageing Survey (GLAS) at the University of Oxford. His research interests include the demography of populations ageing, social statistics, climate change, and elderly health.

Jung Ki Kim is a research associate professor at the Andrus Gerontology Center of the University of Southern California. She has researched health and health-related issues using large national and local datasets. Her research interests include works on socioeconomic status and biological risk, social support and health among older people and cross-country comparison of health status.

Kathrin Komp is a post-doctoral researcher at the Department of Sociology, Umea University, Sweden, and affiliate fellow of the program 'Future Leaders of Ageing Research in Europe'. She was previously a post-doctoral fellow, Prentice Institute, University of Lethbridge, Canada. Her research interests are on the effects of population ageing on welfare states, the changing structure of the life course and quantitative research methods. Recent publications include a co-edited volume, *Gerontology in the Era of the Third Age* (2011, Springer Publishing).

Kim Korinek is Associate Professor of Sociology and the Associate Director of the Asia Center at the University of Utah. Dr Korinek's research interests center upon the impacts of migration, migrant remittances and migration social relations upon intergenerational relations and family economies in origin societies, as well as upon migration's implications for health and socioeconomic mobility. She is especially interested in migration's effects upon Asian societies.

George Leeson is co-Director of the Oxford Institute of Population Ageing at the University of Oxford and Senior Research Fellow in the Department of Sociology at the University of Oxford. Dr Leeson's main research interests are in the socio-economic-demographic aspects of ageing populations, covering both demographic modelling of population development and the analysis of national and international data sets.

Susan McDaniel, Canada Research Chair in Global Population and Life Course, Prentice Institute, University of Lethbridge, Canada, has research interests in global population, life course, demographic ageing, generational relations, family change and social policy in international comparative perspective. She is the author of over 180 articles and book chapters, several books and research monographs. She has served as the editor of two journals, and currently serves on the editorial boards of 10 journals.

Julie McMullin is a professor in the Department of Sociology and Vice-Provost International at Western University, Canada. Her recent research examines social inequality in paid work, especially in relation to older workers. Her recent publications include: *Aging and Working in the New Economy: Changing Career Structures in Small IT Firms* (2010 with Victor Marshall); *Age, Gender, and Work: Small Information Technology Firms in the New Economy* (2011); and *Understanding Social Inequality: Class, Age, Gender, Ethnicity, and Race in Canada* (2010, 2nd edition).

Codrina Rada is an assistant professor in the Department of Economics at the University of Utah. Her research interests include the economics of pensions and ageing with a particular emphasis on questions of intergenerational transfers in the context of migration.

Pia Roman earned her MA in Sociology from Eastern Michigan University in 2010. She currently conducts health services research with the veteran population as part of the Veterans Administration Center for Clinical Management Research at the VA Healthcare System in Ann Arbor, Michigan. This research is conducted in partnership with The University of Michigan. Her primary research focus includes studying the impact of social interventions on personal health care practices.

Abla Sibai is Professor of Epidemiology at the Faculty of Health Sciences, American University of Beirut. Over the past 15 years, her research activities have been directed towards a better understanding of the demographic and epidemiologic transition in Lebanon and have led the way to placing older adult issues at the forefront on the national agenda and international scientific community. She is a co-founder and the current director of the newly established 'Center for Studies on Aging' in Lebanon and has published over 100 scholarly articles and book chapters.

Sarinnapha Vasunilashorn is a post-doctoral research associate in the Office of Population Research at Princeton University. She received her BSc in

Psychobiology from UCLA and PhD in Gerontology from USC. Her work aims to understand the fundamental processes that underlie ageing across populations by examining how biological indicators relate to a number of health and age-associated outcomes.

Felicia Wheaton is a pre-doctoral student at the Davis School of Gerontology at the University of Southern California. She received her BA in Integrative Biology and Anthropology at the University of California, Berkeley. Her research has examined how place and context are related to health outcomes by examining older adults in Mexico, the US and among the Tsimane of Bolivia.

Kathryn M. Yount, PhD is Associate Professor in Global Health and Sociology at EU. She is a leading social demographer of the family and family dynamics. She has directed or collaborated on more than 25 research grants from NIH, NSF, The World Bank, private foundations and Emory, to assess intergenerational relationships and transfers, parental investments in children and the impacts of investments in early childhood on health across the life course.

Lu Zhang is an undergraduate student at the University of Southern California, studying human development and ageing. She works on the 'China Health and Retirement Longitudinal Study' to examine the relationship between socioeconomic status and cardiovascular health outcomes in older adults. She is interested in the study of biomarkers and population ageing in developing nations.

Zachary Zimmer is Professor of Social and Behavioral Sciences at the University of California, San Francisco. He graduated with a PhD in Sociology from the University of Michigan in 1998. His research lies at the intersection of sociology, gerontology and demography. Zimmer studies older adults in developing countries, with particular interest in the links between socio-economic and demographic change and well-being of older persons. More specifically, some of his projects include studies of health inequalities in developing countries, the impact of the migration of adult children on older persons and the consequences of ageing in harsh environments such as extreme poverty. His work has appeared in a wide range of journals from across disciplines.

Preface and Acknowledgements

This volume began with several papers initially presented at the 2009 Rocco C. and Marion S. Siciliano Forum at the University of Utah entitled, 'Global Aging in the 21st Century: Challenges, Opportunities & Implications for the US'. It subsequently expanded to include many additional chapters, with the initial papers substantially updated and revised in chapter form. Both editors were faculty in the Institute for International and Public Affairs (IPIA), University of Utah at the time of the Siciliano Conference.

The annual Siciliano Forum examines some of the most pressing, least tractable current issues and provides uncommon opportunities for thoughtful deliberation of the public trust. The editors wish to thank Rocco and Marian Siciliano, the Siciliano family, and the organizers of the 2009 Siciliano Forum for their vision and support.

The editors also thank Dr J. Steven Ott, Director of the Institute of Public and International Affairs, and former Dean of the College of Social and Behavioral Sciences, University of Utah for his support of, and enthusiasm for, the work that went into the forum and the current volume. The editors appreciate Dr Ott's unwavering dedication in the face of difficult circumstances.

We further gratefully acknowledge the help and support of the following: Sheila Matson and Leanne Little, Administrative Assistants, Prentice Institute for Global Population and Economy, University of Lethbridge, for their tireless administrative support; Seong-gee Um and Sara Zella, Post-doctoral Fellows, and Germain Boco, Research Analyst at the Prentice Institute, for their generous assistance; Claire Jarvis and Jude Chillman of Ashgate Publishing for their interest in our book, their support and patience.

Chapter 1
Global Ageing in the Twenty-First Century: An Introduction

Zachary Zimmer and Susan McDaniel

The title of this volume implies a reality of which large numbers of demographers, economists, sociologists, geographers, policy-makers, and casual observers of global demographics are well aware. The world at this moment is experiencing an unprecedented change in its global age structure; a phenomenon commonly referred to as population ageing. Specifically, population ageing is a dynamic process wherein a growing proportion of people occupy the older range within an age structure. The definition of the specific age at which a person turns old is unimportant since population ageing is occurring regardless of the criteria that define old age, including criteria that may be cultural, political or practical.

It is not hyperbole to say that the ageing of the global population will be among the most important phenomena driving policy around the world over the next number of decades. What observers and interested parties do not always realize is that population ageing is taking place not only on a global level, and not only within certain countries, but it is occurring in nearly every country in the world, and certainly within every region of the planet. Population ageing is a phenomenon that is therefore shared across countries and regions that exist thousands of miles apart. It is shared across countries that may have little else in common. It is happening in rich parts of the world and poor parts of the world. It is occurring in countries that are less developed, with newly emerging economies and in countries with long standing advanced economies. It is occurring in countries that have a very small proportion of their population in old-age and in those that already have a large share of older people.

Interestingly, demographically speaking, the causes of population ageing are also generally similar regardless of the country. As will be outlined in more detail below, population ageing is primarily a function of reductions in fertility, or a decrease in the number of children that are born. It is secondarily a function of changes in mortality, with a reduction in the rate at which older adults die. But, while the causes are similar, the consequences and challenges that are faced by various countries differ enormously. One of the key factors that contribute to the consequences of population ageing is the speed at which it is taking place. It is extremely rapid in some countries and more modest in others.

While some consider population ageing a problem, we look at the phenomenon, as the title of this volume suggests, as generating challenges while also creating opportunities. Yet, the specific challenges and opportunities also vary considerably and are a function of many factors, including current and foreseeable economic conditions, current and foreseeable epidemiological realities and social circumstances that concern the elderly, possibly most notably norms and values surrounding intergenerational relations. Plus, there are region-specific circumstances that impact upon the challenges and opportunities created by population ageing. These include, among many others, the HIV/AIDS epidemic in Africa, the economic crisis in Europe, the change to a market economy in China and the migration of younger adults from rural to urban areas across many less developed countries. In short, while population ageing itself, and its demographic causes, are shared across the globe, the speed at which populations are ageing and the challenges and opportunities differ widely depending on a large number of social, demographic, epidemiological, economic and cultural circumstances that are unique to societies.

Thus, while population ageing is widely understood as an important demographic phenomenon worldwide, and is destined to have significant impacts on policy over the next several decades, because of a variety of conditions it is seen as an enormous concern in some places and of minor importance in others. For instance, countries in Europe have been long concerned about rising proportions of older adults in their populations. Conversations about how population ageing will impact on the future of social security have been taking place in the United States and Canada. Some societies in East Asia, such as Taiwan and Japan, have been intensively assessing policies to deal with their ageing populations. Others, such as countries in sub-Saharan Africa or South Asian countries like India, have been somewhat slower to respond to their changing demographics. Some of the reasons for this are explored in various chapters in this volume.

Why is the World Ageing?

Ansley Coale's 1964 article remains one of the most eloquent demographic explanations of why and how population age structures change (Coale 1964). As Coale states, '(w)hether a national population is young or old is mainly determined by the number of children women bear. When women bear many children, the population is young; when they bear few, the population is old' (1964: 48). Many more recent articles reiterate these ideas in somewhat greater detail (e.g., Kinsella and Phillips 2005; Powell 2010; Lee 2011). These authors explain that populations with no or relatively little migration that maintain constant age-specific fertility and mortality rates will, over time, develop a proportional unchanging age distribution, referred to in demographic terms as a 'stable' population. There are few examples of populations that are stable. However it is a basic theory that allows demographers to reconstruct historical populations. Today, global and all regional and national age structures are changing as a result of relatively rapid changes in rates of fertility and mortality, a phenomenon that is very recent in the history of human populations.

Recent declines in fertility are indeed the main driver of population ageing (Kinsella and Phillips 2005). Future population ageing will be a function of fertility declines expected to occur over the next several decades. The reason that fertility has such an enormous impact on ageing is that when a cohort characterized by high fertility and large family sizes move into old age, they are large in number compared to the following generations that are a product of lower fertility rates and thus smaller family sizes. An example in the western world is the baby boom, a period of high fertility experienced by western countries after World War II and continued into the early 1960s, after which fertility declined. Those born during the baby boom comprise a large proportion of the population relative to the cohort that followed. When they move into retirement age, the result will be a surge in the older population that will remain until the baby boomers themselves die out. Generally speaking, the greater the difference in fertility between generations, the more rapid will be the rate of population ageing. A cautionary note needs to be added for any country where population age structure is also influenced by in-migration. The United States and many other settler societies such as Australia and Canada, for example, would be experiencing much greater population ageing if it were not for in-migration of younger adults.

In the current era, extreme fertility declines over short periods of time are not unusual. Countries in East and Southeast Asia have witnessed sharp declines in fertility from highs of six to eight children per woman to well under two within a single generation. Countries in South and Latin America, such as Brazil and Mexico, have experienced similar changes over the same period. Eastern European countries did not begin with the same high fertility, but they have amongst the lowest fertility rates in the world today. Ukraine's fertility rate fell to about 1.1 children per woman in the early 2000s. Africa presents a different scenario. Fertility remains relatively high but is nonetheless falling. In Kenya, for example, fertility has fallen from highs of over eight children per woman in the 1960s to under five today, and further declines are expected.

Not all children born survive to an age where they begin to reproduce, and so population ageing if viewed as a long-term process will be tempered somewhat in countries that have or have had high infant mortality in the recent past. But, infant mortality has also been on the decline almost everywhere over the last 50 years. At first, declines in infant mortality make a population younger, since it increases the number of children entering a population. But, decline in infant mortality over time adds to population ageing since not only were women in the recent past having large numbers of children, but most if not all survived, unlike earlier generations. Thus the combination of infant mortality decline followed by fertility decline generates even more rapid ageing. An example is China where rapid declines in infant mortality occurred when fertility rates were still above five, and all five children had a high probability of surviving to old age. This high fertility cohort is beginning to move into older ages in China. But, their families are small in comparison, making this surviving elderly cohort even larger than had infant mortality not declined.

When and if fertility rates stabilize around the world, old-age mortality becomes a more important driver of population ageing. Taking Japan as an example, in 1960 a 60-year-old Japanese woman could expect to live about another 18 years (Statistics and Information Department – Minister's Secretariat – Ministry of Health Labour and Welfare 2012). At that time, women of 80 years and older, sometimes referred to as the oldest-old, constituted about 9% of the total female population 60 and older. By 2000, females turning 60 in Japan could expect to live an extra 27 years, to the ripe old age of 87, and the oldest-old constituted about 20% of the elderly female population. Clearly, the last several decades has seen the human race stretch the bounds of human longevity, and if this trend continues, mortality will have a larger impact on not only population ageing but also the distribution of age structure within the aged, with the oldest-old becoming a larger proportion of the elderly population. Still, the extent to which life expectancy, and especially life expectancy at old-age, will continue to increase is a subject of considerable debate and nothing can be taken for granted (Olshansky, Carnes and Cassel 1993; Wilmoth 2000; Bongaarts and Freeney 2002; Oeppen and Vaupel 2002). It is much easier to predict the impact of fertility on ageing since those who will turn old in the coming decades have already been born, as have their children. As such, what we know for sure is that the world will continue to grow older and older, and the challenges and opportunities associated with ageing populations will continue to be more and more in the public eye.

The Current State of Population Ageing

Thirty or forty years ago, it seemed that few in a position to project the future of demographic change expected that the world would witness the declines in fertility that has been achieved. Indeed, the 1960s was a time of very high fertility across the developing world, and importation of medical technology and improvements in public health was reducing infant mortality and adding to unprecedented growth in family sizes. The reasons behind the subsequent fertility decline in both the developed and less developed world are many, and in developing countries are often tied to notions of 'the demographic transition' and not within the scope of this chapter, but economic change, education, government policy and changes in values have all been hypothesized as motivating factors (Davis 1945; Hirschman 1994). It is enough at this time to point out that between 1970 and 1975 the global population was growing at about 2% per year, a rate that leads to a doubling in less than 35 years. Much attention at the time was focused on ways of reducing fertility as a way to halt overpopulation. It appears that in most countries these efforts were more successful than could have been imagined or anticipated.

To illustrate this empirically, Table 1.1 shows the Total Fertility Rate (TFR) for the world for the period 1995–2000 that was predicted about 20 years earlier

Table 1.1 Observed estimates for 1970–75 TFR, observed and projected estimates for 1995–2000 TFR, and change statistics expressed as percentages, for the world, selected regions and selected countries[1]

	Projection for TFR for 1995–2000 as assessed in 1973[2]	Observed TFR for 1995–2000[3]	The percent difference in observed versus predicted TFR for 1995–2000
World	3.28	2.79	-17.6
Africa	5.23	5.23	0.0
Europe	2.21	1.42	-55.9
Western Europe	2.09	1.52	-37.6
Eastern Europe	2.21	1.29	-71.6
East Asia	2.26	1.76	-28.1
Southeast Asia	3.73	2.65	-40.8
Latin America	3.87	2.73	-41.9
Australia	2.79	1.78	-56.6
Brazil	4.92	2.45	-100.8
China	2.46	1.80	-36.7
France	2.26	1.76	-28.1
India	4.10	3.31	-23.9
Indonesia	4.24	2.55	-66.4
Italy	2.26	1.22	-84.8
Japan	2.11	1.37	-54.1
Nigeria	6.17	5.99	-3.0
Poland	2.23	1.48	-51.0
Sweden	2.09	1.56	-34.0
Thailand	4.39	1.77	-147.9
United States	2.09	1.96	-6.7

Note: 1 = All projections based on medium variants; 2 = Source: (United Nations 1977); 3 = Source: (United Nations 2011).

in 1973 by the United Nations as well as the actual TFR that was observed for the period 1995–2000 as reported by the United Nations in 2011 (United Nations 1977; United Nations 2011). The third column compares the two numbers by showing the difference in the observed versus the projected TFR as a percent. Taking the world as an example, the TFR that was projected in 1973 to occur in 1995–2000 was 3.28 (the global TFR in 1973 was about 4.5). However, the observed TFR in 1995–2000 was actually 2.79. This represents a 17.6% underestimation in global fertility decline. With respect to regions, every region experienced a substantial fertility decline, and every region was expected to experience a decline. Still, with a few exceptions, the actual declines were much larger than anticipated. Even in places where fertility was already not much higher than replacement level, unexpected declines occurred, in some cases leading to currently extreme low fertility. Eastern Europe is a prime example, where fertility just over replacement level in the 1970s decreased to about 1.3 by the 1990s. Looking at individual countries provides a clearer idea of where fertility declines were most impressive and also most underestimated. The TFR in Thailand was expected to be a little greater than four children per woman, but in reality, it ended up being fewer than two, an underestimation of almost 150%. Developed countries, like Italy and Japan, had underestimations even though substantial declines were predicted, because the magnitude of the actual declines was not imaginable. Nigeria, and all of Africa, is one exception, with only moderate declines in fertility that pretty much matched expectations. Another exception is the United States where fertility barely declined over the period.

Table 1.1 is informative with respect to the degree to which fertility declined more than expected in most of the world, and therefore led to population ageing of a degree that was unanticipated. This surely may have led to some unpreparedness on the part of policy-makers. As noted above, mortality is also a factor and becomes more important when fertility stabilizes. Mortality declines over the period were also dramatic. Also noted, population ageing is a 'process' and is defined by the growth of the older population relative to the total population, not on the number of elderly within a population at a given time. Therefore, Japan is the 'oldest' country in the world by many measures, but it is not the fastest ageing. It is those countries and regions that are rapidly ageing that may face the most dramatic future challenges. Thus Table 1.2 looks at the world and the same set of regions and countries as Table 1.1, and presents a set of important population ageing statistics.

The first two columns indicate the current percent that are aged 60 and older and of those 60 and older, the percent that are 80 and older, which is to say the percent of elderly that constitute the oldest-old. The next two columns show the expected average annual growth rate in the 60 and older population expressed as a percent, over next 25 years, from 2010 to 2035. To provide some indication of how large these growth rates are, note that the global population is currently growing at a rate of about 1% per year. Population growth, like compounding interest in a bank, is exponential, and thus a 1% growth rate is not small. At this rate, it will take approximately 15 years to add an additional billion people to the global population. The final two columns show the impact of these growth rates on the actual population in 2035. The second to last column shows the expected percent that will be 60 and older in 2035, and the last column shows the percent of those 60 and older that will be 80 and older.

Taking the world as a whole, the current percentage age 60 and older is 11.0%. Of these people, 13.9%, or about 1 in 7.2, is old-old. The 60 and older population is, however, going to grow at an annual rate of 2.86%. The 80 and older population will be growing even faster, at 3.39. The result is that within 25 years the projected population 60 and older will be 18%, while 15.8% of these elders, or about 1 in 6.3, will be 80 and older.

Table 1.2 Population ageing statistics for the world, selected regions and selected countries

	% aged 60+ in 2010	Of those 60+ in 2010, % aged 80+	Expected average annual % growth in the 60+ population, 2010 to 2035	Expected average annual % growth in the 80+ population, 2010 to 2035	Projected % aged 60+ in 2035	Of those projected to be 60+ in 2035, % aged 80+
World	11.0	13.9	2.86	3.39	18.0	15.8
Africa	5.5	7.8	3.20	4.13	7.3	9.9
Europe	21.8	19.2	1.31	1.97	30.4	22.6
Western Europe	24.2	20.9	1.39	2.14	33.4	25.1
Eastern Europe	19.1	16.4	1.05	1.73	26.8	19.4
East Asia	14.0	12.9	3.02	4.01	29.0	16.5
Southeast Asia	8.3	10.3	3.89	6.06	17.9	17.8
Latin America	10.0	14.6	3.35	2.49	18.9	11.7
Australia	19.0	20.0	2.33	3.17	26.3	24.6
Brazil	10.3	14.4	3.43	4.30	21.1	17.9
China	12.3	11.0	3.41	4.43	28.0	14.2
France	23.0	23.4	1.49	2.16	30.0	27.7
India	7.6	8.8	3.40	4.37	13.7	11.2
Indonesia	8.2	8.8	3.93	4.90	18.3	11.2
Italy	26.5	22.1	1.33	1.74	37.0	24.4
Japan	30.5	20.7	0.74	2.75	39.5	34.3
Nigeria	5.3	7.2	2.75	3.68	5.8	9.0
Poland	19.2	17.7	1.44	2.60	28.4	23.7
Sweden	24.9	21.1	1.14	2.19	29.5	27.5
Thailand	12.9	13.0	3.17	4.00	26.8	16.0
United States	18.4	20.7	2.08	2.66	25.8	23.9

Source: United Nations 2011 (using medium estimates for projections).

The variation in this population ageing around the world can be seen immediately by looking at the expected growth rates. Africa, East Asia, Southeast Asia and Latin America will witness enormous increases of between 3 and 4% per annum. But, even countries in Europe, where fertility is low, will witness fairly sharp increases in older populations as larger cohorts move into old age. Southeast Asia is a particularly important region to look at as not only will there be a large increase in elderly, but the growth rate in the oldest-old is going to be over 6%. This is an astounding number that is destined to have enormous implications for the region. Looking at individual countries, Japan, with over 30% of its population already aged 60 and older, will see continued modest growth in its elderly population, although the gains in the oldest-old will be rapid. By 2035, almost 40% of Japan's population is expected to be 60 and older, and incredibly, about 1 in 3 of these people will be 80 and older. Brazil, China, India, Indonesia, South Korea and Thailand are the fastest ageing populations of the countries shown, and they will also see very rapid increases in their 80 and older populations. African countries like Nigeria will also see very rapid growth in its older population. Again, European countries like Italy, France, Poland and Sweden and the United States, are ageing at a somewhat more moderate rate, but these countries will still be ageing and will witness a very sizeable increase in their oldest-old population.

Challenges and Opportunities

The conclusion we come to by looking at the tables above is that every region and almost every country will experience very rapid population ageing over the next 25 years, mostly as a result of declines in fertility that were unexpected only a few decades ago. Even regions and countries that are already old will quickly become older, while developing countries, with enormous growth rates in 60+ and 80+ populations will begin to catch up. The subsequent chapter by Francois Héran will further examine the mechanisms behind population ageing and will explore the upcoming evolution of the phenomenon across a range of countries. Therefore, both this chapter and those that follow lead to questions that relate to these impending trends. What are the implications for Brazil as its older population doubles from 10% aged 60 and older to 20% over a short period of time? What are the consequences of China's increase from 12% aged 60 and older to 28%? China already has an enormously large net population of elderly. So too does India, and India's proportion age 60 and older will double as well within a couple of decades. What will be the impacts of this change in age structure in India on a country that is still emerging? What are the consequences of having one in four or even a greater ratio of elderly in the old-old category in currently developed countries like Australia, Canada, Italy, Japan, Sweden and the United States? Is the world ready for the challenge of this rapid population ageing, and possibly more important, can the world take advantage of opportunities that arise as population age structures change?

It would truly be impossible for one book to cover all possible issues related to global population ageing, even if focusing solely on demographic, economic and sociological perspectives, as the current volume does. We have therefore chosen three areas in which we believe the challenges and opportunities are extraordinary, and have solicited articles from a number of leading and emerging ageing scholars from around the world in order to provide new insights in these areas.

1) Healthy ageing and health care: It is hard to imagine any discussion of population ageing taking place without reference to health and health care. The

link between age and prevalence of health problems at the individual level is well established. It is simply the case that in every society that has experienced an epidemiological transition away from infectious and towards chronic disease as the leading causes of morbidity and mortality, the older we get the more prone we are to experiencing chronic disease (Omran 2005). What doubling the number of elderly within a society can do to the cost of health care is a question that is of utmost policy importance. Equally critical however is to understand current health situations among older adults around the world and how these have been changing over time so that we can prepare for the future.

Of course, variation in concerns surrounding health and health care will be driven, in large part, by current epidemiological, economic and social conditions in a society. In less developed countries, one challenge will be refocusing health care from a concentration on childhood and maternal health issues (which will still be a concern) to health issues for the aged. This in itself may require enormous changes and additions to human capital. In more developed countries, where older persons already constitute a large percent of the population, increased longevity may lead to increases in proportions that are disabled. This will depend upon whether longer life also equates with better health, or as has been frequently termed, whether we will experience a compression of morbidity (Jagger 2000), whereby we all age in more healthy states and then experience health problems in very late life The less compression of morbidity is a reality, the greater will be the challenges for ageing in developed countries.

Our section on health covers a wide part of the world, and addresses issues related to current health conditions, future implications and challenges. Alam provides findings from a small-scale survey of older adults in Delhi, India. Ajrouch and colleagues take us to the Middle East to examine health from a gendered point of view. This is particularly critical since women live longer than men and constitute a greater proportion of the elderly population as people live longer. Crimmins and colleagues provide an invaluably broad view of physiological changes by age across a large set of countries. This is one of the few expansive comparative looks at bio-indicators made possible by new availability of harmonized data. Hidajat and Zimmer tackle the issue of transitions in functional health by correlating it with religion, a health determinant that is often ignored but, as the chapter shows, of importance. Aboderin's particularly valuable contribution examines the policy issues of population ageing in sub-Saharan Africa, a region that is not often thought of as ageing. Yet this region faces numerous challenges due to its general poverty and HIV/AIDS pandemic. Finally, an insightful discussion by Deeg examines a number of myths about ageing and health, questioning at times the notion that longer life and better health go hand in hand, and backing up the discussion with data from the Longitudinal Aging Study Amsterdam.

2) Ageing workforce, retirement and the provision of pensions: It is a common perception that the developed world has become older during times of economic prosperity allowing those countries the opportunity to generously fund pensions,

while less developed countries are ageing without the resources necessary to financially support their older populations. In reality, the situation is more complex because financial challenges related to population ageing differ across social, political, historical terrains in addition to economic. Solutions to an ageing workforce range widely and include, among others, popular ideas such as increasing age of retirement, raising taxes to pay for a larger number of retired workers, and moving to more private pension schemes. Few have asked whether there are opportunities to be gained from an ageing workforce, and discussions of the implications of an ageing workforce in developing countries are rare.

The labor section of this volume has three contributions that focus attention on both positive and negative aspects of an ageing workforce. Rada examines labor and productivity in the developing and developed world in the face of population ageing. The variation in effects of ageing is examined, as are the impacts on shrinking workforces on the economic burden. Komp takes on Europe in its entirety by closely observing how work and retirement in that part of the world is changing due to the ageing of populations. Relying on qualitative interviews, Jovic and McMullin tackle the difficult challenge of older workers in the age of information technology.

3) Shifting intergenerational relations: One of the more challenging aspects of ageing populations worldwide is the potential threat to family norms and the notion of the family as the most obvious institution within which to provide care and support for older persons. Cowgill and Holmes (1972) were among the first to characterize the potential impacts of modernization on older adults, suggesting that changes in values towards westernization would alter intergenerational relations. Since then, a number of alternative theories, such as those focusing on altruism, family solidarity, modified extended family and new household economics have challenged the inevitability of a changing functional role for the family as populations age (Litwak 1960; Stark and Lucas 1988; Zimmer and Kwong 2003). A demographic perspective certainly makes the obvious point that an ageing population comes hand in hand with smaller family sizes and thus smaller networks upon which older persons can rely when in need. This would seem to be a negative consequence to population ageing. But, there are ways in which social cohesion can be maintained in the face of population ageing, and ageing can even present opportunities to families in various forms.

These issues are explored in a strong set of articles on shifting intergeneration relations. Chappell examines issues of filial piety referred to frequently among Confucian cultures, and provides an interesting comparison of Caucasian Canadians, Chinese Canadians and Hong Kong Chinese. Fast similarly examines caregiving determinants, drawing comparisons across generations. Korinek offers the only contribution in the volume focused on Eastern Europe. Using a rich data source, she looks at predictors of loneliness within a population that has amongst the lowest fertility rates in the world. Arber examines issues of gender and marital status among older persons and the implications for intergenerational relations.

This chapter is important because of the reality that increasing age tilts populations towards females and widows. Arber as well interrogates conceptual notions of intergenerational relations in a rapidly changing world. Leeson and Khan, drawing upon The Global Ageing Survey, a remarkable data set that captures attitudes and behaviors about later life in 21 countries, looks at predictors of support across a large cross-section of countries and draws out the similarities and differences about financial and personal care in generations.

In sum, this introduction has emphasized that ageing is a global fact and a reality that will impact on all human beings over the next number of decades. The phenomenon is too widespread to think otherwise. The extent of ageing now taking place was not anticipated 25 years ago, but is upon us, and is increasing at a rapid rate. We must understand the consequences of global population ageing as quickly as possible. Older persons who have contributed to society for their entire lives deserve this attention. Doing so has other wide reaching benefits besides those that are moral. It is our hope that the current volume adds new understanding to the consequences and implications of population ageing as related to health, work, and family and that this volume is a reminder that ageing is not a problem. It is a challenge that with the help of analyses and sound insights can present opportunities.

References

Bongaarts, J. and G. Freeney. 2002. How long do we live? *Population and Development Review* 24:271–91.

Coale, A.J. 1964. How a population ages or grows younger, in *Population: The Vital Revolution*, edited by R. Freedman. New York: Doubleday, 47–58.

Cowgill, D.O. and L.D. Holmes. 1972. *Aging and Modernization*. New York: Meredith Organization.

Davis, K. 1945. The world demographic transition. *Annals of the American Academy of Political and Social Science* 237:1–11.

Hirschman, C. 1994. Why fertility changes. *Annual Review of Sociology* 20:203–33.

Jagger, C. 2000. Compression or expansion of morbidity – what does the future hold? *Age and Ageing* 29:93–4.

Kinsella, K. and D.R. Phillips. 2005. Global aging: The challenge of success. *Population Bulletin* 60:1–40.

Lee, R. 2011. The outlook for population growth. *Science* 333:569–73.

Litwak, E. 1960. Geographic-mobility and extended family cohesion. *American Sociological Review* 25:385–94.

Oeppen, J. and J. Vaupel. 2002. Broken limits to life expectancy. *Science* 296:1029–31.

Olshansky, S.J., B.A. Carnes and C.K. Cassel. 1993. The aging of the human species. *Scientific American* 1:50–57.

Omran, A. 2005. The epidemiological transition: A theory of the epidemiology of population change. *The Milbank Quarterly* 83:731–57.

Powell, J.L. 2010. The power of global aging. *Ageing International* 35:1–14.

Stark, O. and R.E.B. Lucas. 1988. Migration, remittances and the family. *Economic Development and Cultural Change* 36:465–81.

Statistics and Information Department – Minister's Secretariat – Ministry of Health Labour and Welfare. 2012. Historical Statistics of Japan: http://www.stat.go.jp/english/data/chouki/02.htm, 2012. Accessed January 23, 2012.

United Nations. 1977. *World Population Prospects as Assessed in 1973*. New York: United Nations.

United Nations. 2011. *World Population Prospects: The 2010 Revision*. New York: United Nations.

Wilmoth, J.R. 2000. Demography of longevity: Past, present and future trends. *Experimental Gerontology* 35:1111–29.

Zimmer, Z. and J. Kwong. 2003. Family size and support of older adults in urban and rural China: Current effects and future implications. *Demography* 40:23–44.

Chapter 2
The Population Ageing Process in Global Perspective

François Héran

The aim of this chapter is to review the general definitions and concepts involved in population ageing from a demographic perspective. After reviewing the main mechanisms of population ageing, the chapter looks at how population ageing is liable to evolve over the coming decades. Data from across a range of countries are used to characterize differences in ageing and their implications.

The Four Mechanisms of Population Ageing

The ageing process gives rise to some confusion. Population ageing may be driven by four different mechanisms:

i) The first factor of population ageing operates at the top of the population pyramid. It is due to a steady increase in longevity. In most countries of the world, the rise in life expectancy observed since the 1970s will increase the height of the age pyramid within a few decades. This long-term trend is an important manifestation of the 'demographic transition', the transition from high birth and death rates to low birth and death rates as a country develops from a pre-industrial to an industrialized economy.

ii) The second factor of ageing operates at the bottom of the pyramid. It corresponds to the decline of fertility below the replacement level (i.e. fertility decreases at a faster pace than mortality). This is also a long-term trend associated with the classic demographic transition but it is strongly reinforced by the so-called 'second demographic transition', characterized by sub-replacement fertility, options to marriage for intimate unions, a disconnection between marriage and procreation, and no stationary population.

iii) A third factor corresponds to the after-effect of the baby boom, a strong but temporary increase in fertility that occurred in the past. Although generally mistaken for an expression of the second factor, this third phenomenon is substantially different. By growing older, the baby boomers form a bulge that gradually moves up to the top of the pyramid. In the beginning the baby boom rejuvenates the population. But after five or six decades it becomes a factor of ageing. Once the parenthesis of the baby boom is closed, fertility behavior returns to the general declining trend.

iv) For the record, a fourth factor of ageing is the selective emigration of young people. This has been observed in cases of sudden and massive emigration, such as in Albania in the 1990s.

How can we estimate the weight of each factor in the ageing process of the coming decades? The chapter shall be limited to the first three factors (the impact of selective emigration is not negligible but deserves a separate study). The data come from the World Population Prospects updated by the United Nations Population Division, and are updated every two years. The projections cover the years from 2000 to 2060. We will begin by relying on the central scenario which extrapolates from mortality trends observed in the last decades and assumes a general convergence towards a fertility rate of 1.8 children per woman (below the replacement level of 2.05).

A practical way to illustrate the dynamics of population ageing is to display the relative trends for different age groups on the same graph, a method inspired by Didier Blanchet (2002). Taking the example of Germany, as shown in Figure 2.1, the three solid lines show the trends for the three main age groups defined by the Population Division of the United Nations (UN): below 15 years, 15–64 years, 65 years and over. These age groups refer to broad categories with the middle group representing a let us a *potential* working population. The absolute numbers have been indexed to 0 in the starting year.

Under the central scenario established by the UN, the number of over-65s in Germany will increase by 75% between 2000 and 2035, while the middle and the youngest age groups will shrink by nearly 25%. Each change is already impressive in itself, but their divergence is even more striking. The widening gap between the upper and the lower curves offers a vivid image of the ageing process: it does not merely signify an increase in the number of older adults but an increase in the ratio between the older and younger generations (also measurable through the 'dependency ratio' or, conversely, the 'support ratio'). The graph also shows how the population ageing process can be broken down into its main components.

The upper part of the gap, above the zero growth line, illustrates the ageing process due to the increase in longevity (top-down ageing), plus the impact of the ageing baby boomers. The ageing process in Germany depends mainly on the gains in life expectancy accumulated in the last decades and, to a lesser extent, on the consequences of the baby boom, a past event that nobody can cancel out retrospectively. It accounts for approximately three-quarters of the prospective ageing process in Germany.

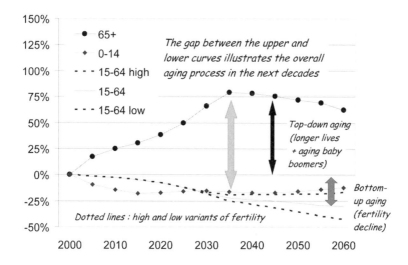

Figure 2.1 Relative change in the main age groups over the next decades in Germany
Source: Derived from UN Population Prospects, 2010.

The lower part of the gap, below the zero line, corresponds to the part of population ageing due to declining fertility (bottom-up ageing). Migration flows can partly offset this trend. In principle, this part of the ageing process can be modulated through appropriate family or migration policies.

The Most Reliable Component of Demographic Projection: The Future Number of Older Adults

Demographic projection raises challenges. Estimating trends in the number of older adults is by far the most reliable component of demographic projection since all persons who will reach the age of 65 within the next 50 years have already been born. Moreover, immigration is negligible at older ages. The impact of introducing mortality variants (for example a progressive convergence between men and women in the propensity to adopt risk behaviors) is significant but moderate. It will have only a minor upward or downward effect on the pace of increase in the elder population over the four or five next decades, which is due mainly to past gains in life expectancy.

Projecting the number of births is a more delicate operation. A part of the story is already known since we have a good idea of the number of women of childbearing age who will be living in the country over the next two decades. But the other part – the fertility behavior of future cohorts – remains unknown.

Regarding migration, demographers admit that there is no magic solution for making accurate predictions about its scale over the coming decades at the national level. There are numerous examples of sudden and unexpected large-scale migration flows in the recent past: Ecuadorians to Spain, Ukrainians to Portugal, Albanians to Italy and Greece.

Obviously, the degree of uncertainty of demographic projections is not merely technical. The first demographic transition yielded a universal model, based on the assumption of an inevitable return to a general equilibrium between birth and death rates. All countries were expected to follow the same trajectory, albeit with differences in timing. It was not until the 1980s that population scholars began to acknowledge the emergence of an unbalanced demographic regime with negative natural growth (more deaths than births), postponed unions, fertility rates below the replacement level and accelerated ageing. Van de Kaa and Lesthaeghe (1984) called this new phenomenon the 'second demographic transition'. The classic demographic transition (or first transition) was supposed to take us from one form of equilibrium to another: the decline in mortality would eventually follow the decline in fertility. However, in the second demographic transition which is progressively characterizing most countries of the globe, including China, this pattern no longer holds true. The new model is no longer based on the equilibrium assumption.

Limited Impact of Family Policy or Migration Policy on Population Ageing

Nonetheless, despite the uncertainty about future trends in the middle and lower age groups for the next 50 years, some firm conclusions remain valid. The best proof is the limited impact of the alternative scenarios. Building new scenarios to take account of uncertainty about fertility and migration levels barely modifies the trajectory of the younger groups, while the gap with the older group continues to widen over the years.

The two dotted lines in Figure 2.1 illustrate the respective impacts in Germany of the high and low fertility variants envisaged by the United Nations. Both are based on a strong hypothesis: plus or minus 0.5 children with respect to the fertility rate of the conservative scenario. While half a child may seem negligible, in demography it is not, especially if this deviation in fertility lasts for decades. Half a child is the same order of magnitude as the additional fertility generated by the baby boom in several European countries (in France, for example, it raised the fertility rate of the cohorts concerned from 2.5 children per woman to 3.0). In this case, the high variant envisaged by the UN demographers would mean that Germany will catch up with the French fertility level. However strong these hypotheses might be, they turn out to have very little impact on the age structure and the ageing process in Germany. The graph is quite explicit in this regard. The dotted lines will not deviate from the central scenario before 2035. While things may change in the distant future, no strong impact will be observed within the time horizon of the projections. Once again, the explanation is simple: the major factor of population ageing for a country such as Germany is the increase in life expectancy, the inexorable part of ageing.

Another alternative scenario could be a migration policy designed to encourage a constant inflow of young migrants. Combined with a rise in fertility, such a policy could halve the decline in the working-age population from 30% to just 15%, with major implications for the future of the German economy. Even so, neither a migration policy nor a family policy would be sufficient to close the widening gap between old and young. In practical terms, there is no way to close the gap between the upper curve and the lower curves: the bottom-up ageing process can be mitigated, but the top-down process driven by the continuous rise in life expectancy over recent decades is quite ineluctable.

This has an important consequence for policy-makers. As demonstrated in 2000 by the UN Report on Replacement Migration, the relative increase in the older population in the next decades will be so massive that it cannot possibly be offset by means of a pro-natalist policy or a policy designed to maintain a constant inflow of young migrants. A new baby boom only modifies the bottom of the age pyramid and young immigration can only make up retrospectively for low fertility 20 or 30 years earlier, while the impact on the apex of the pyramid is negligible, since the bulk of the ageing process in the coming decades will be the consequence of the rapid and constant increase in life expectancy over the last

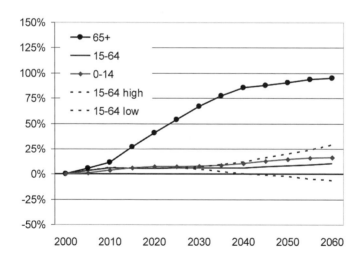

Figure 2.2 Relative change in the main age groups over the coming decades in France

Source: Derived from UN Population Prospects, 2010.

half century. Many policy-makers still imagine that they can use such policies to counter demographic ageing. Demographers can show them the error of their ways. In fact, the only potentially effective policies in this field are economic and social policies, acting on the employment rate of older workers, postponing the retirement age.

The German model also applies to a certain extent in central and southern Europe, while the United Kingdom, the Scandinavian countries and France (Figure 2.2, see page 17) are in a much more favorable situation, with a slight projected increase in the middle and young age groups. However, despite its remarkably higher fertility level by European standards (2.0 children per woman versus 1.5), France will not avoid the phenomenon of population ageing due to increased longevity. There is a French exception for fertility in Europe, but not for mortality or life expectancy.

Why the United States Will Experience More Population Ageing than Russia

In this regard, the comparison between Russia and the United States is highly instructive (Figure 2.3).

If we asked the general public, or even an assembly of academics, which of these two countries will undergo more population ageing in the next decades, most people would probably answer Russia because they spontaneously associate population ageing with economic challenges. However, the truth is the opposite. The share of the population aged 65 or over is currently around 13% in both Russia and the US. But if we take a dynamic point of view to evaluate the future rate of population ageing, the picture is quite different. Roughly speaking, the Russian graph moves closer to a balance between the upper and lower curves: relative population ageing seems to be equally shared between progress in longevity (at the top of pyramid) and sub-replacement fertility (at the bottom). This means that Russians have limited access to the privilege of population ageing because of their poor performance in life expectancy, which stands at just 63 years for men, i.e., nine years less than Poland, 12 years less than the US, 14 years less than Germany.

The demographic situation of the United States is quite different. It is a country that is likely to combine a rapid future increase in the number of older adults AND an impressive growth in its working-age population (much higher than in Europe). Various factors are contributing to the rapid growth of the American population: at one end, replacement level fertility rates combined with high immigration; at the other, steady progress in longevity (although still slower than that of Western Europe) plus the rising age of the large baby boom cohort. The American age pyramid is not only broad at the bottom but also increasing in height. In other words, demographic dynamism is compatible with population ageing. These two privileges are not true for the Russian population. An ageing America performs better than a declining Russia.

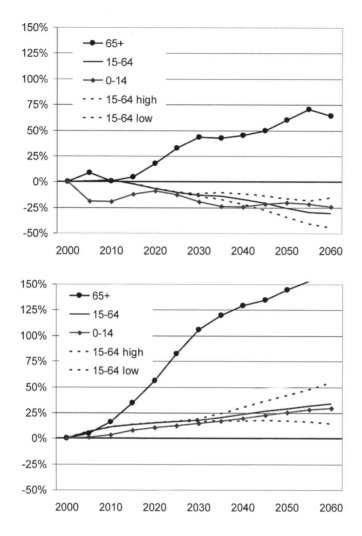

Figure 2.3 Relative change in the main age groups over the next decades in Russia and the US

Source: Derived from UN Population Prospects, 2010.

Graphs of this kind can illustrate both the share of the ageing process which operates at the top of the age pyramid (due to increased longevity and ageing baby boomers) and the share that operates at the bottom (due to declining fertility). They also reveal the inexorable component of ageing in contrast with the component amenable to change through appropriate policies. But these graphs do have their limits. They are ill-suited for less developed countries, where the population aged 65 and over is still small. Starting from a low level, the relative growth of this

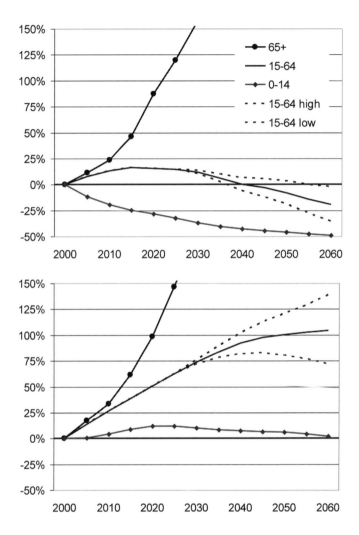

Figure 2.4 Percentage change in the main age groups over the next decades in China and North Africa

Source: Derived from UN Population Prospects, 2010.

age group is bound to accelerate in the next decades, with an anticipated five-fold increase. A slight change in the scale of our graphs is insufficient to follow this trend (see Figure 2.4). In China the three curves diverge more sharply: the decline in the number of children (already visible as a direct consequence of the one-child policy) is associated with a significant increase in the working-age population up to the 2020s, followed by a decrease (unless fertility increases again) and a spectacular increase in the elderly population. The 2010–2020 decade is favorable for the Chinese working population as the combined burden of the youngest and the oldest generations will not be too heavy. But the ageing process will continue at the top of pyramid as well at the bottom.

In India, as in North Africa, the ageing process will affect mainly the top of the pyramid, while sub-Saharan Africa will continue to rejuvenate its population due to its high fertility rates. But plotting the relative growth of the different age groups is not the best way to describe demographic trends in the emergent or developing countries. A more meaningful image can be given by graphs that highlight the potential importance of the demographic window.

The Opportunity Window or Demographic Bonus: An Indicator of a 'Favorable' Age Structure

The expressions 'demographic bonus', 'opportunity window' and 'demographic window' are synonyms (Bloom et al. 2003). An interesting indicator for less developed or emergent countries is the period in which the age structure is, in principle, most favorable for the economy: on the one hand, the share of the elderly in the overall population is still very low; while, on the other, a sharp decline in fertility is already beginning to reduce the proportion of children. In other words, the ageing process is already at work at the bottom of the pyramid but still limited at the top. This conjunction of factors alleviates the burden of the oldest and the youngest populations for the intermediate cohorts. The 'dependency' ratio is at its lowest. The existence of these demographic waves (Pool 2004) is a consequence of the demographic transition and, more precisely, of the time lag between mortality and fertility transitions. Other factors may induce significant variations in this general pattern, such as the impact of wars, the relative size of the baby boom cohorts, or the extent of migration flows.

Jacques Vallin has an interesting analysis of the demographic bonus for the years 1950 to 2050 (Vallin 2005). The age structure indicator is the share of the resident population belonging to the potential working-age group, ages 20–59. Data from the UN Population Division database cover a wide selection of countries. From 2000 onwards, Vallin uses the three UN projections, high, medium and low (depending on the speed of decline in mortality and fertility). The three variants have a visible impact on the size of the demographic bonus but leave its position in time unchanged. Vallin compares changes in the age structure indicator of each country with several patterns of the demographic transition. The first pattern is a very slow and early demographic transition beginning in the eighteenth century, as observed in France and the US. A second pattern provides a better fit with the trends observed in less developed countries: a steady increase in life expectancy in the years 1960–1985—from 58.5 years to 80 years—together with a steady decline in fertility from 6.8 children per woman down to 2.1.

First, if we consider countries with reliable demographic data covering the last two centuries, such as the UK and France, the phenomenon of demographic windows turns out to be not new. The working-age population (20–59) reached a first peak in both countries between 1920 and 1950, at around 55% of the total population, attributable in both cases to a narrowing at the base of the age pyramid. But the causes of this first demographic window were different. For France, it was due mainly to the birth deficit of the First World War (1.5 million fewer births), while for the UK it was the after-effect of a late but rapid fertility decline in the first decades of the twentieth century. It is noteworthy that this demographic opportunity served mainly to conduct (and eventually win) the Second World War. Assessing the use of this demographic bonus remains a tricky challenge.

The post-war baby boom put an end to this first opportunity by rejuvenating the age structure. But this seems self-contradictory. We can hardly say that the baby boom narrowed the range of opportunities rather than broadening it. In most countries of Western Europe the baby boom coincided with economic growth and massive immigration. The demographic bonus theory is somewhat paradoxical in this regard: it tends to interpret the baby boom as a burden rather than an opportunity. This is a short-sighted view. Taking a dynamic approach to the phenomenon, we realize that the burden is in fact an investment for the future. Once the baby-boomers reached adulthood, a new window of opportunity was opened, coinciding with the sharp decrease in mortality at older ages. Most Western countries are currently living in this new demographic window. In France and the UK, the share of the population aged 20–59 reached 54% in the year 2000. However, the window is rapidly closing now for France (owing to its increasing fertility rate), although it should close more progressively in UK over the coming years.

The same pattern can be observed in the US since the Second World War (Figure 2.5). The working-age population fluctuates in more or less the same way as it does in Western Europe. But its trajectory may diverge strongly in the next decades, depending on migration flows, fertility behavior and life expectancy trends. In the most favorable cases (not at all unrealistic), the US could prolong its present demographic bonus for decades, in strong contrast with Europe.

To what extent is the future evolution of the demographic bonus a good predictor of economic growth? A rigorous answer would require a time-series analysis connecting demographic facts with macro-economic indicators. At first sight, the staggering of the demographic bonus over time across countries seems to be consistent with their economic prosperity (Figure 2.6).

The emergence of Singapore as an economic power is consistent with its demographic bonus: the window has been wide open since 1975 and should stay so at least up to 2015, whatever the speculations on fertility and life expectancy. The same applies for Hong Kong and South Korea, with the peak shifted, respectively, to the years 2010 and 2015. Strikingly, the main emergent economies are opening their demographic window right now (China: 2010–2020), or will do so in the near future (Brazil: 2015–2025). Iran, Vietnam and Tunisia are following the same path.

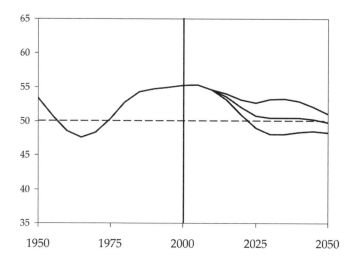

Figure 2.5 Share of working-age population in the US from 1950 to 2050, under the three variants projected by the UN Population Division (high, medium, low)

Source: Vallin, 2005.

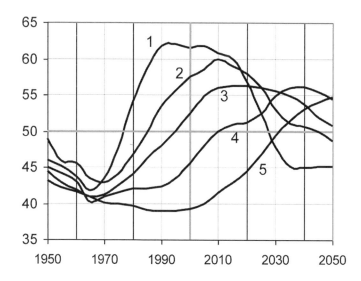

Figure 2.6 Share of working-age population (aged 20–59) in selected countries

Note: Singapore (1), China (2), Brazil (3), Egypt (4), Nigeria (5), from year 2000: UN projections (medium variant).
Source: Vallin, 2005.

In contrast, India will not benefit from the demographic bonus before 2030–2040 because of the persisting high fertility patterns in the Muslim states, in strong contrast with the Hindu states, especially the Dravidian peninsula. In Sri Lanka, Indonesia and Iran—to mention the larger countries only—the working-age population should peak in around 2025. The same obtains for the Philippines, Myanmar, Turkey or Algeria. All these countries illustrate the strong impact of demographic momentum. Despite a sharp fertility decline in recent decades, it will be a long time before this trend is converted into low birth rates; the annual number of births will remain high until the large cohorts of women of childbearing age born in the 1960s and 1970s reach the end of their reproductive lives. In Egypt, Kenya, South Africa, but also Bangladesh, the fertility decline is significant but too recent for the emergence of a favorable age structure before 2035–2045. It will occur even later for other demographic giants: around 2050 for Pakistan and 2060 for Nigeria (Figure 2.7).

Vallin closes the list with several sub-Saharan countries, Sudan, Ethiopia, Congo Democratic Republic and Niger. Due to the highest high fertility levels of the last decades, the percentage of working-age population in these populous and landlocked countries is at its lowest level since the 1950s. It should now begin to rise. But even under the controversial hypothesis of a steady fertility decline for the next 50 years, the opening of a favorable demographic window for these countries in the second half of the twenty first century remains out of reach.

Economic prosperity thus seems to go hand in hand with the proximity or remoteness of the demographic bonus. The nature of the correlation remains unclear. The less developed countries which entered the 'ageing transition' at an earlier date were also the first to reduce their fertility and promote education for both sexes. Economic development and the demographic bonus may share a common cause.

This observation should be extended to demographic indicators in general. By definition, the working-age population is a potential population. Its limits can be extended or restricted. Moreover, the exploitation of this potential depends on a number of political and social factors: the youth employment rate, older workers' employment rate, investments in education, the degree of gender equity, the selectivity of migration flows, the security climate, the quality of local and national governance, etc. But while demographers do not have the last word in the matter, they undoubtedly have the first. In spite of many uncertainties, demographic prospects help to define the backdrop of globalization and the world stage. They reveal not only the range of opportunities and possibilities but also the unequal capacities of the different countries to take advantage of them. This raises two questions: a technical question about the validity of use of an absolute age at which people are considered old (used so far), and an ethical or political question about the definition of the demographic good.

Singapore	1980–1990
Western Europe	1995
N./S. Europe	2000–2010
China	2010–2020
Brazil	2015–2025
Algeria	2020–2030
Mexico	2025–2035
India	2030–2040
Egypt	2035–2045
Nigeria	2050

Figure 2.7 Approximate period in which the share of the working-age population reached or will reach its peak in selected countries or sub-continents
Source: UN demographic prospects, analyzed in Vallin (2005).

Why Absolute Age Still Remains a Better Tool than Relative Age

A classic objection to the demographic approach to the ageing process is that the very nature of age has changed thanks to spectacular improvements in health. We all know that our parents looked mentally and physically older than we are at the same age. Given that, underlining the inexorable part of the ageing process due to the increase in life expectancy may seem to miss the point, since the reality of the population ageing is counterbalanced by a relative rejuvenating process. Why not measure population ageing with relative age instead of absolute age?

In fact, this is a recurrent concern among many demographers, and a recurrent failure too. In 1993, for example, a French historical demographer, Patrice Bourdelais, proposed to define relative age on the basis of disability-free life expectancy (by following, for example, changes in the age at which individuals still have 10 years to live in good health), an idea taken up more recently by Scherbov and Sanderson (2008). Gérard Calot, a director of INED in the years 1972–1992, made a different proposal. He suggested redefining individual age by its relative position in the age pyramid, taking a fractile close to the top of the pyramid (e.g. the age at which an individual is older than 80% of the population). He called this indicator 'homologous age' (Calot 1999).

These various endeavors may seem attractive because they defend a positive vision of the ageing process, running counter to the usual complaints of an 'old' society voting 'old' and consuming 'old' (a prejudice not confirmed by empirical research). But they have failed for a very simple reason: if age is indexed to life expectancy (disability-free or not) or to the shape of the age pyramid, age is merely replaced by life expectancy or age structure. In fact it is still useful to rely on an absolute definition of age, precisely to be able to measure the shift towards health improvement and greater well-being across age groups. The best way to measure a moving reality is not to use a moving yardstick. In any case, using relative age rather than the classic absolute age does not change the first-order truth of the inevitable ageing process. It is important to highlight the fact that this process is altogether inexorable and positive. As we saw from the comparison between Russia and the US, there is no need to change the definition of age to develop a positive vision of population ageing. Our judgment must derive from other considerations, such as the importance of top-down ageing (a positive phenomenon in itself) as compared with bottom-up ageing because of below-replacement fertility (which can be problematic).

Fewer Lives, Longer Lives, Better Lives: The Ethical Issue

Turning to the philosophical issue raised by the pioneers of demographic analysis, no demographer would venture to interpret demographic projections as a set of fatalistic or deterministic predictions. But this does not mean they are purely hypothetical. Robust conclusions can be drawn from demographic projections if the results stand up to the proof of alternative scenarios and clearly rank the strengths and the weaknesses of the different demographic situations. Within the ageing process, some inevitable mechanisms can be identified. For instance there is no way to cancel retrospectively the gains in life expectancy accrued in the last decades, no way either to act as if the baby boom never took place. But some mechanisms are still open to social or political action (such as future fertility or migration), provided we do not underestimate the necessary response time. Similarly, it would be naïve to ignore the impact of the age structures already accumulated in the age pyramid: demographic momentum contributes to shaping the probabilities of the demographic window. In other words, the field of opportunities is itself subject to numerous constraints.

Maybe the most striking paradox about determinism and human agency in the field of demography is the way in which the cumulative effects of past human interventions eventually create new constraints, and new inescapable realities, for subsequent generations. The progress in life expectancy is a good example. Considerable efforts have been devoted to reducing child and adult mortality. But we did not anticipate the consequences of this progress for the pension systems, the expense of the health sector, the balance between generations and other issues linked to population ageing. Nobody is to blame, since everybody took part in this collective preference for longer and better lives: the diseased, their kin, physicians, medical researchers, medical equipment engineers, policy-makers, etc. Ironically, the free and voluntary actions of all these actors have imposed a new set of unavoidable constraints on upcoming generations.

These considerations must be taken into account when seeking to predict in qualitative terms the rise or decline of well-being in our ageing societies. To put it simply, the ageing process is a demographic question but it does not call for demographic solutions. The only solution is to adapt our societies to this new situation, making the necessary social and economic reforms (mainly in terms of intergenerational solidarity, more employment for older workers and postponement of retirement age). The mobilization of social and economic forces to adapt the social system to ineluctable demographic change has nothing to do with fatalism or determinism: it provides scope for pro-active policy.

Our conception of 'demographic good' has evolved since the building of modern nation states. The goals have changed. The consolidation of the state in the Early Modern Period needed more lives to compensate for the inevitable death toll in the young ages. In the following centuries, the demographic transition revealed our collective preference for a qualitative objective, long before the elaboration of the human capital theory. We preferred to have fewer lives but longer lives and, possibly, better lives. More recently the option of lighter lives has emerged, based on the notion that current generations should reduce their ecological footprint for the sake of the generations to come. The old goals have not necessarily yielded to the new ones: population size, for example, still counts in the distribution of voting rights within the European Union institutions. We are now taking more seriously than ever the demographic weight of China and the huge domestic market it represents. We still admire the short but intense lives of the artists of the past. As a whole, however, the collective preference observed in most countries is for investment in quality rather than quantity.

Demographic indicators have evolved accordingly, starting with the concepts of positive natural growth (more births than deaths), rate of increase of the total population, then life expectancy, and disability-free life expectancy (or health expectancy). At the same time, the replacement rate has become the replacement rate in years lived. Instead of comparing the size of a cohort with the number of its children (for example how many girls born to 100 women of childbearing age will themselves reach childbearing age), the idea is to weight the number of persons by the number of years lived. For example, 90 girls can 'replace' 100 mothers if the life expectancy increases in the meantime by 10%. Taking into account the number of years lived (or the numbers of years left to live) may substantially change our assessment of human losses. For example, young people commit suicide less than the elderly but they sacrifice a higher number of years. Another example is the impact of Alzheimer's disease as compared with the impact of HIV/AIDS. If the rates are based on mere head counts, the Alzheimer's toll will be higher, but if it is weighted by the number of lost years the impact of HIV/AIDS will deserve much more attention.

In this last example, demographic analysis introduces three possible values of life: the number of lives, the length of life and the quality of life. But the relative importance of each variable (just think about the decisions taken by policy-makers in the health sector) is not merely a technical issue. It depends on ethical and political choices. Immanuel Kant, in his *Critique of Judgment* (2007 edition), considered that life has 'no price' but only 'dignity' (*Wardigkeit*). The value of your life, he said, does not depend on the bad or good things that *happen* to you but only from what you decide to do with your life. This does not abolish evil. But instead of looking for external responsibilities, you have to consider that evil is a spur for action. Ernst Cassirer has interpreted this theory as a radical attempt to bypass the Leibnitzian dilemma of theodicy (Cassirer 1945).

What are the consequences for current research in demography? In the light of Kantian ethics we should count every life as one, without weighting it with the number of years lived or lost. In practice, however, demographers stick to the ethical principle set up by Jeremy Bentham and John Stuart Mill for the hedonic calculus: 'each person is to count for one and no one for more than one' (Héran 2006). By construction, demographic indicators (such as total population, death rate, infant mortality, fertility rate, life expectancy, replacement rate ...) give the same weight to everybody, whatever their social influence, geographic distance or remoteness in time. This makes demography, from the outset, a comparative and neutral science. The results may be broken down into social or political strata but these variables remain exogenous, technically they do not enter into the construction of the demographic indicators.

However, this combination of Kantian and Benthamian approaches does not resolve the controversial issue of the qualitative value of life: is there a determined degree of disability or dependency beyond which one can consider that life is not worth living for lack of dignity? And if so, who will decide the matter? These ethical issues cannot be resolved by technical decisions. Demographers can nurture the debate, but they cannot provide the answers.

Acknowledgments

Language editing by Catriona Dutreuilh (INED).

References

Blanchet, D. 2002. Demographic trends and pensions: Fifteen years of debate. *Population & Societies*, 383, INED, October: 4.

Bloom D., Canning, D. and Sevilla, J. 2003. *The Demographic Dividend: A New Perspective on the Economic Consequences of Population Change*. Santa Monica, CA: RAND.

Bourdelais P. 1993. *L'Âge de la vieillesse, histoire du vieillissement de la population*. Paris: Odile Jacob (new ed. coll. 'poche' Opus, 1997).

Calot, G. and Sardon, J.-P. 1999. Les facteurs du vieillissement démographique. *Population*, 3:509–52.

Cassirer, E. 1945. Rousseau, Kant, Goethe, *Journal of the History of Ideas*, 6:483–501.

Héran, F. 2005. The world population over the next three centuries: Explosion, implosion or equilibrium? *Population and Societies*, 408.

Héran, F. 2006. Ethics and demography or Macrodemus and Microdemus in the country of ethicists. In *Demography: Analysis and Synthesis. A Treatise in Population Studies*, edited by G. Caselli, J. Vallin and G. Wunsch. Burlington, MA: Academic Press, 39–69.

Kant, I. 2007. *Critique of Judgement* (Kant 1724–1804). Oxford: Oxford University Press.

Landry, A. 1934. *La Révolution démographique*. Paris: Alcan (new ed. 1982, Paris: INED).

Pool, I. 2004. 'Demographic dividends', 'windows of opportunity' and development, CICRED Seminar on *Age-structural Transitions*, Paris, February 23–26, 2004. Available at: http://www.cicred.org/Eng/Seminars/Details/Seminars/Popwaves/PopwavesPool.pdf [accessed 3 February 2012].

Scherbov, S., Mamolo, M. and Lutz, W. 2008. Probabilistic population projections for the 27 EU Member States based on Eurostat assumptions, Working Paper, Vienna Institute of Demography.

Vallin, J. 2005. The demographic window: An opportunity to be seized. *Asian Population Studies*, 1(2):149–67.

PART I:
Healthy Ageing and Health Care

Chapter 3

Ageing, Functional Disabilities and its Gender Dimensions: Results based on a Study in Delhi

Moneer Alam

Despite being perceived as overwhelmingly young, India is rapidly ageing due to sustained decline infertility and increased life expectancies, especially at later ages (Alam 2006). With older adults constituting about 100 million in 2010 (UN World Population Prospects 2010 revisions), India is fast moving into a situation where elderly wellbeing and health pose serious challenges to current and future government planning.

From over 90 million in 2010, UN projections reveal that the number over age 60 will increase to 187.8 million by 2030. By 2050, this number will reach 323.1 million. This represents an astounding increase of about 350% within a short span of just 40 years. Projections also reveal considerable feminization of the elderly, with an increasing proportion of the older population being female. The fastest growing segment of the population over age 75 is women. A large percentage of older women will be widows. To many, these age structural changes may be regarded as the outcome of the country's socio-economic and health achievements. These successes however come with challenges(Kinsella 2000, Lloyd-Sherlock 2010), which require measures, mostly public, to ensure elderly health and wellbeing. This chapter is designed to highlight several issues relating to gender differentials in functional health of older adults in India with a focus on the Delhi municipal area.

In India, disability is officially defined by using pathology (Alam and Karan 2011). Dysfunctional health, caused by late-life diseases, senescence or frailty, is largely neglected. With a focus on functional health, some of the findings in this chapter may bring the issue of functional health of older adults to the center of the wider debate on ageing in India, including the urgency of examining functional health in policy including planning and financing of long term care services. In addition, this study examines the usability of health data generated by self-assessments. To be specific, the reliability of self-assessed health has long been questioned due to reporting biases (Sen 2002).This chapter provides evidence of the association between self-reports of functionality versus results based on task performance.

Cross-country analyses of functional health are rare in India and for that matter other South Asian countries. A few intra-country studies using cross-sectional data have demonstrated that older adults in the region remain largely susceptible to major diseases and have poor functional capabilities (Khetarpal 2003, Rahman and Barsky 2003, Alam and Mukherjee 2005, Alam 2006, World Bank 2008).[1] These studies raise many complex issues for families with elders and government health officials. Foremost among them perhaps is how to care for the functionally impaired, especially in countries like India where family structure is fast changing (Bali 2003, Niranjan, Sureender and Rao 1998), where there is large-scale migration (Jamuna 2000), rampant poverty (Alam 2009), and where there is a lack of public concern about the creation of necessary physical and financial means to access care for functionally dependents. Another major issue that sits against the backdrop of ongoing societal changes relates to the gender dimensions of functional impairments. A key issue to consider, for example, is whether elderly women are more functionally disabled than men? These issues are fast gaining importance in many ageing societies, and can no longer be neglected in India or elsewhere in South Asia, in large part due to the growing share of women elders and widows within the population.

The analysis to follow therefore attempts to explore a few of these issues with the help of a household survey in Delhi. The survey involved a specially designed protocol to record various details of sampled households including medically diagnosed diseases suffered by the elderly and their self-reported functional health. In addition, there was also a set of physical tests administered by a team of paramedics to make an objective assessment about functional strength and capabilities.[2] The survey was conducted in early 2005.

The remainder of this chapter is organized as follows. The next section briefly provides a few analytical concerns of the study and data. This is followed by a description of the sample population. Self-reported functional capabilities and the results obtained on the basis of physical capability tests are then summarized. A brief discussion on socio-economic correlates of functional health is provided. The chapter ends with some policy issues arising from the findings.

---

1 Based on a temporal analysis for 1961, 1973, 1981 and 1984–85, a study by Ahmed (1995) brings out detailed accounts of major disabilities suffered by the people in Pakistan. Interestingly, the study shows an over-time decline in the share of country's disabled population, apparently because of some definitional changes. As a whole, however, the study corroborates with our argument that individuals' age in South Asian countries is an important factor in disabilities (Ahmed 1995, Table 1).

2 The protocol was developed as part of a research grant provided by the Columbia University (Department of Sociomedical Sciences, Mailman School of Public Health) to study the ADL/IADL Statuses of the Elderly in India under its International Programme on 'Ageing and Health in Developing Countries'. For further details, see Alam 2005.

Data and Analysis

Studies on health in old age are constrained in India for several reasons. Notably,

1. lack of comprehensive data to study functional competencies of older persons in terms of basic or instrumental activities of daily living (BADL/IADL); and related
2. lack of well-designed measures of physical, mental or other forms of health which may be used to plan preventions and create geriatric support and rehabilitation infrastructure for elderly with functional problems.

These limitations have also constrained comparisons between results obtained from self-reported functional competence and observed measures of functional health. This study is partly a modest attempt to take some of these issues into consideration and examine the functional competence of a small sample using both self-rated and observed measures of functional health.

The survey includes major socio-economic characteristics and functional health, both self-rated and objectively tested. We began by asking the respondents to self-evaluate their abilities to perform BADLs/IADLs such as eating, drinking, bathing, dressing, toileting, cooking, transferring (getting in or out of bed/chair), walking within or outside the home, etc. Given doubts about the objectivity of self-reported health (Sen 2002), we decided to complement self-reported data by using a set of functional capability measurement tests designed to study (i) upper and lower extremity strength; (ii) body balancing ability; and (iii) physical movements. These tests are generally considered good indicators of functional health, so we presume the test outcomes—later converted into a set of scores assigned on the basis of physical performance help countercheck older respondent's own perceptions about their health. In addition, the tests may indicate risks of physical dependence among the old. They may also have some bearing on issues such as marketing of various insurance products, premiums, and need for specialized medical care (More, Wilcox and Hiris 1994, Severson et al. 1994).

Self-reported BADL/IADL capabilities[3] used to examine the disability include the following:

1. Eating/drinking
2. Dressing

---

3 As was described earlier, ADL/BADL denotes basic activities of daily living like eating, bathing, toileting, walking, transferring, etc. IADL or instrumental activities of daily living on the other hand refers to activities that requires a relatively better physical and mental conditions enabling individuals to perform physically more sustaining activities including shopping, keeping a tab on day to day expenditure or being able to do a bit more complex mental work like operating bank account, etc. Both of them also symbolize states of functional autonomy or dependence.

3. Bathing
4. Toileting or getting up from the toilet seat
5. Transferring (getting in or out of bed or chair)
6. Light household work like washing dishes/utensils/light cleaning
7. Walking 10–15 steps
8. Heavy household work like washing cloth or cleaning room
9. Cooking/preparing meals
10. Shopping for self and family
11. Walking (for about a quarter mile/km)
12. Lifting/raising both arms up over the head
13. Making telephone calls

A person expressing difficulty or needing assistance in performing a specific task was considered to have a disability or limitation.

Objective measurement of functional capabilities used the following physical tests:

1. **Grip strength (dominant hand)**
   Objective: to measure upper extremity strength
   Position: sitting with elbow in a bending position
   Outcome: equivalent weight recorded with the help of a hand dynamometer
2. **Timed gait**
   Objective and Time: 4-meter measured walk to judge leg strength (time recorded for complete course using a stop watch)
   Position: within or outside house/room without quad or ordinary cane
   Outcome: not attempted, attempted but not completed, completed
3. **Chair stands**
   Objective and Number: 5-time measure of leg strength and body balancing ability
   Position: without using any support and keeping feet remained on the floor
   Outcome: not attempted, attempted but not completed, completed
4. **Static side-by-side stand**
   Objective and Time: 10-second measure of body balancing ability (stop watch used)
   Position: standing with feet together and side by side, body movement allowed for maintaining body balance
   Outcome: not attempted, attempted but not completed, completed
5. **Static tandem stand**
   Objective and Time: 10-second measure of body balancing ability (stop watch used)
   Position: standing with heel of one foot in front and touching the toes of the other
   Outcome: not attempted, attempted but not completed, completed

The first three tests were applied to get an idea about physical (upper and lower extremity) strength of the older subjects, while the last two were used to approximate body balancing abilities.

Methodologically, the self-reported difficulties in ADLs are shown in terms of nominal (yes/no) scores. Ordinal scores (i.e., 0, 5 and 10) have however been used to analyze the physical performances of subjects. Taking grip strength test as illustration: 0 indicates the lowest performance level, and is scored by those whose grip strength falls short of mean grip strength minus SD.[4] A score of 5 indicates average performance (i.e., grip strength of a person lies somewhere between mean grip strength ± SD), and the highest score of 10 shows satisfactory performance and amounts to measured grip strength of an individual exceeding the mean + SD. These ordinal scores were also used to examine multinomial logit and count data models[5] which were conducted to identify socio-economic risk factors in functional disability and poor physical health.

Results

The sample was drawn from rural and urban areas of the National Capital Territory of Delhi with households as the primary data collection units. In all, a sample of 217 households was selected with at least one member aged 60 and above, with 115 households in rural areas and 102 in urban. Fifty three percent of the elders were women, about 21% were over age 75 and 52% were illiterate. Sixty percent were married and most of the others were widowed, with women being more likely to be widowed. About 41% report hypertension and 65% arthritis.

Self-reported and Performance Functionality

Disabilities reported in 13 functional domains are presented in Table 3.1.[6] The table shows that women and *older old* (≥75) have higher risks than men and those below 75. But, except for three functional domains—light household work, walking and telephoning—place of residence has no significant implications for disability risks.

---

4 It may as well be written as: 1/n (Σ measured grip strengths of n number of persons) − SD, where n = number of subjects participating in a particular test.

5 Both nominal and ordinal scale variables are mostly considered as qualitative or categorical variables. See Herndon (2006) for a more detailed discussion on scales and scaling techniques used to quantify outcomes.

6 Unfortunately, the degrees of disabilities—e.g. mild, severe or acute - may not be described with the help of available data.

Table 3.1 Percent reporting ADL difficulties by gender, place of residence and age

BADL/IADL domains	Respondents cross-classified by ...					
	Gender		Place of residence		Age group	
	Male	Female	Rural	Urban	60–74	75 +
1. Eating	45.5	47.0	44.7	48.1	41.2	63.8*
2. Dressing	12.9	20.1	17.8	15.5	14.0	24.1***
3. Bathing	14.4	23.5**	21.1	17.1	14.5	34.5*
4. Toileting	31.8	49.7*	42.1	40.3	35.7	60.3*
5. Transferring (chair/bed)	33.3	56.4*	44.1	47.3	43.0	55.2***
6. Light housework (dish washing)	60.6	55.0	52.6	63.6***	52.5	75.9*
7. Walking (10–15 steps)	15.2	29.5*	23.0	22.5	20.4	31.0***
8. Heavy housework (washing cloth)	81.8	75.2	79.6	76.7	76.0	86.2***
9. Preparing meal for own use	78.8	61.7*	68.4	71.3	67.0	79.3**
10. Shopping for self and family	30.3	47.0*	38.8	39.5	33.5	58.6*
11. Walking 200–250 yards	47.7	61.7**	49.3	62.0**	51.6	67.2**
12. Lifting both hands over head	28.8	40.3**	35.5	34.1	32.6	41.4*
13. Telephoning	31.8	52.3*	50.0	34.1*	39.4	53.4**

Note: * p<.001; ** p<.05; *** p<.01 by χ^2.

Table 3.2, which shows results of performance measures, does not intend to make a direct comparison with self-reported functional status. Yet an implicit objective *inter alia* is to see if both of these results drive similar inferences. Results of all five measurement tests are given in Table 3.2. The first two tests, grip strength and chair stands, who mean values. The next three are a representation of strength or endurance measured as: (i) full; (ii) partial; and (iii) not done. There are two important inferences arising from this table. One of these follows from the mean grip strengths. It appears from these values that the grip strength of the elders in our sample is lower than a comparable cohort of people from other countries or ethnic groups (Albert, Alam and Nizamuddin 2005). Many medical gerontologists consider grip strength as a good predictor of old age health including likely demand for medical care and hospital services. A possible inference may therefore be that the Indian elders are more susceptible to later life diseases causing pressure on medical infrastructure.

Table 3.2 Measured grip, gait and self-balancing abilities by gender, place of residence and age group (%)

	Male	Female	Rural	Urban	60–74	75+
Grip strength*						
Mean weight (in kgs)	14.4	8.8	11.9	10.9	11.8	10.1
SD	5.0	4.0	5.2	5.3	5.2	5.2
Participation	100.0	100.0	100.0	100.0	100.0	100.0
5-chair stands						
Mean time (in seconds)	15.1	16.1	15.9	15.2	15.7	14.8
SD	3.8	5.8	5.0	4.6	4.8	4.5
Participation	65.9	46.3	57.2	53.5	60.2	38.3
Failed/not done	34.1	53.7	42.8	46.5	39.8	61.7
Measured gait						
4 Meters	69.7	36.9	48.0	57.4	54.8	43.3
3 Meters	22.7	48.3	38.8	33.3	37.1	33.3
Participation	92.4	85.2	86.8	90.7	91.9	76.6
Failed/not done	7.6	14.8	13.2	9.3	8.1	23.4
Side-by-side stand						
Held for 10 seconds	84.8	74.5	80.3	78.3	82.4	68.3
<10 seconds	8.3	12.8	11.2	10.1	10.4	11.7
Participation	93.1	87.3	91.5	88.4	92.8	80.0
Failed/not done	6.8	12.8	8.6	11.6	7.2	20.0
Tandem stand						
Held for 10 seconds	33.3	21.5	25.0	29.5	30.3	15.0
<10 seconds	27.3	23.5	26.3	24.0	25.3	25.0
Participation	60.6	45.0	51.3	53.5	55.6	40.0
Failed/not done	39.4	55.0	48.7	46.5	44.3	60.0
N	132	149	152	129	221	60

Note: * Dominant hand and first trial; mean values declined moderately with each successive trial up to a total of four trials.

As expected, women register much lower grip strength (8.8 kg) with a smaller standard deviation. Between rural-urban and the two age categories, the former perform better in both the cases. Interestingly, however, the difference between the *older old* and others are only marginal. Women >75 often opted out completely (i.e., not done) or opted to lower targets. This is found for every test including gait, chair stands, tandem and side-by-side stands.

Partially, these results tend to validate the self-reported results summarized above. The results also support the reliability of self-reported data on functional disabilities and competence, although with a pinch of caution. We cross-tabulated the self-reports on eight critical BADLs/IADLs—eating, dressing, bathing, transferring, toileting, light and hard household work, walking 200–250 meters—against three performance measures including grip strength, chair stand and measured gait. Results are presented in Table 3.3.

Table 3.3 Self-reported difficulties in eating, bathing and dressing, and grip strength (scores: persons)

By yourself, do you have any difficulty in?	Grip index scores*			
	0	5	10	Total
Eating				
Yes	26.9	63.9	9.2	100.0
No	8.6	68.2	23.2	100.0
Total	17.1	66.2	16.7	100.0
Chi2(2)	18.513		Pr = 0.000	
Bathing				
Yes	40.7	53.7	5.6	100.0
No	11.5	69.2	19.4	100.0
Total	17.1	66.2	16.7	100.0
Chi2(2)	28.466		Pr = 0.000	
Dressing				
Yes	42.6	51.1	6.4	100.0
No	12.0	69.2	18.8	100.0
Total	17.1	66.2	16.7	100.0
Chi2(2)	26.998		Pr = 0.000	

Descriptive Statistics: Mean strength (kg.) = 11.4; SD = 5.3; Min = 0; Max = 23
* Grip strength index scores: 0 = < Mean—SD; 5 = Mean ± SD; 10 = > Mean + SD

By yourself, do you have any difficulty in?	Chair stand scores*			
	0	5	10	Total
Transferring (bed/chair)				
Yes	77.3	11.7	10.9	100.0
No	17.0	13.1	69.9	100.0
Total	44.5	12.5	43.1	100.0
Chi2(2)	113.500		Pr = 0.000	

Ageing, Functional Disabilities and its Gender Dimensions

By yourself, do you have any difficulty in?	Chair stand scores*			
	0	5	10	Total
Toileting				
Yes	71.6	13.8	14.7	100.0
No	25.5	11.5	63.0	100.0
Total	44.5	12.5	43.1	100.0
Chi2(2)	69.838		Pr = 0.000	

Descriptive Statistics: Mean time (second) = 4.9; SD = 4.7; Min = 0; Max 10
* Chair stand index scores as above

By yourself, do you have any difficulty in?	Measured gait: 3 and 4 meters			
	4 Meter	3 Meter	Not done	Total
Heavy HHDwork				
Yes	47.7	38.2	14.1	100.0
No	68.9	29.5	1.6	100.0
Chi2(2)	11.566		Pr = 0.003	
Shopping				
Yes	25.5	46.4	28.2	100.0
No	69.6	29.8	0.6	100.0
Chi2(2)	74.738		Pr = 0.000	
Walking up to 1/4 km				
Yes	32.9	47.7	19.4	100.0
No	76.2	22.2	1.6	100.0
Chi2(2)	56.631		Pr = 0.000	

Descriptive Statistics: Mean time = 2 seconds; SD = 0.686; Min = 1; Max 3
* Gait walk index scores as above

Clearly, findings indicate similarity between the self-reported and observed measures. The χ^2 tests are mostly significant at the 1% level. It may also be noticed that many of those reporting functional problems were ranked poorly in terms of performance test outcomes. Of the rest, some have either opted to go for a lower test target or have opted out altogether from the test.

Socioeconomic Correlates

A considerable body of literature now exists to show the role of socio-economic status (SES)in health outcomes of older individuals. Much of this literature has however been directed to the developed nations, although a shift in interest is slowly occurring (Rahman and Barsky 2003, Albert, Alam and Nizamuddin 2005,

Alam and Mukherjee 2005, Alam 2009). Table 3.4 presents a count data model (CDM) to identify socioeconomic risk factors. Appendix Table 3.5 defines all the variables used in our estimations. We tried to estimate a series of explanatory variables covering socio-economic conditions of the sample households and subjects, their physical health and a few instrumental factors like asset holdings, bank account or quality of life as demonstrated by the living space (or number of rooms) in a house. Not many of these variables have, however, helped to enhance explanatory power of the equations, implying that understanding the pathways of downward transition in functional health requires more sustained research and data collection.

Table 3.4 Count data regression results showing correlates of self-reported disabilities

Variables	Coefficient	Std. Error
Sex	0.081	0.045
income_rec~t	-0.091***	0.047
agegrp3	0.051***	0.025
Edu	-0.016	0.017
grand_child	-0.058	0.046
grip_index	-0.012	0.007
chair_index	-0.033*	0.005
timedgait_~x	-0.012**	0.005
_cons	1.129	0.077

Note: * p<0.001; ** p<0.01; *** p<0.05; Dependent variable = number of functional disabilities; No. of observations = 278; R^2 = 0.0342.

The table shows that the number of functional disabilities an individual reports increases with age, poverty (or lack of own source income), and sex. Women, for example, are apparently prone to a greater number of functional incapacitations than men. In addition, these risks may be higher among those suffering poor chair stand and measured gait strengths. In other words, apart from age, sex and income status of an individual, number of old age disabilities also bear a relationship with overall physical conditions—frailty, senescence and lower body strength. Another interesting observation stemming from these results is that persons with more self-reported disabilities also suffer from poor gait and chair stand weaknesses. Linkages between the self-reported and the observed measures of health are indicated.

Concluding Observations

India and many neighboring countries are witnessing significant improvements in population health parameters with increasing life expectancy and rapid growth in 60+ populations. This is particularly true for India where the projected population of elders is expected to increase from 92.7 million in 2010 to 187.8 million in 2030, and 323.1 million in 2050, i.e., almost a 3.5 times increase within a short span of next 40 years. Obviously, such a rapid increase in the old-age population, a majority of which comprises women and the older old, poses many serious challenges to India and its various institutions, particularly government. A great number of these challenges relate to old-age health and disabilities. While there are some traces of concern about these issues in the recent literature on old-age health in India and also in some other countries of South Asia, there are still many critical issues that remained largely neglected, particularly for lack of requisite information. Two of them, for example, include: (i) the gender and socioeconomic dimensions of later life functional health; and (ii) the appropriateness of self-reported health data, particularly on ability to perform basic activities of daily living (BADL). The latter is especially significant for countries where observed details on physical competence of older persons are almost non-existent. This study was mainly carried out to fill some of those gaps a survey conducted in the city state of Delhi.

A special survey protocol was designed to collect data from a group of respondents on their: (i) self-reported abilities to perform activities of daily living like eating, drinking, bathing, etc.; and (ii) physical strength based on a set of observed performance measures like grip strength, gait walk, etc. In addition to gender differentials in functional abilities, the two sets of information were also used to assess their conformities in terms of inferences drawn from both the measures. Both were also used to analyze the correlates of old age disabilities and poor physical performance.

Our results clearly reveal that older women are worse off with multiple disabilities reported in various domains of their daily activities. They as well score lower in observed physical strength tests. Widows are found to be the worst with very high prevalence of functional impairments. These results clearly suggest that old age health has several dimensions and policy guidelines need to recognize these dimensions and heterogeneities. Age enhances the risks of functional problems.

Moving to the ongoing debate on usability of self-reported health data, our results indicate its reliability, at least in cases of functional disabilities which are perhaps easier to identify and report. Both the observed as well as the self-reported health assessments were found to be mutually conforming. As far the correlates of poor functional health,widowhood turns out to be a very important pathway of downward transition in functional autonomy. Women outliving men is common in India and also in many other South Asian countries; this may soon become a central ageing issue in the region with considerable bearing on care providers, both medical and filial.

Financing of long term medical/nursing home care is another issue that needs serious attention by governments and health officials. Specific insurance policies may be developed to finance care requirements of senescent and functionally disabled. Governments may also consider subsidies to reduce prices of gadgets, appliances and support devices required by the disabled. Health hazardous businesses and ventures may be taxed to finance initiatives required by many of these upcoming heath issues. Further research and data collection on issues of ageing and dysfunctional health is strongly warranted, especially to design long term care and its financing mechanism.

Appendix

Table 3.5 List of variables for estimation of CDM and logistic regression models

Models	Explained variable	Explanatory variables
1. Count data regression (negative binomial)	Functional impairments (none, single and multiple)	Binary variables sex: male = 1, female = 0 agegrp2: > 75 = 1; < 75 = 0
2. Binary logit	Persons with 5 or more ADL disabilities = 1, others = 0	vegetarian: if veg. = 1, others = 0 occup_1: working for cash = 1; otherwise = 0 grand_child: grandchildren staying in the household = 1; otherwise = 0
	Persons with 2 to 4 ADL disabilities = 1, others = 0	d_widowed: widowed = 1; others = 0 d_edu: literate = 1; illiterate = 0
	Persons with single ADL disability = 0, others = 0	income_rec~t: recipients of own source income = 1, others = 0 arthritis: those reporting arthritis = 1, otherwise = 0
3. Multinomial logit regression (with 3 dependent outcomes)	Grip strength scores (0, 1, 2)	religion: Hindus = 1; others = 0 Continuous/discrete variables
	Chair stand scores (0, 1, 2)	agegrp3: age group 1 = 60–64 2 = 65–69
	Measured gait scores (0, 1, 2)	3 = 70 + religion
	The assumption of independence of irrelevant alternatives (IIA) was tested	1 = Hindu 2 = Muslim
	STATA 9 was used to estimate the models	3 = Sikh 4 = Christian marital: marital status 1 = married 2 = widowed 3 = separated 4 = never married edu: education 1 = illiterate 2 = literate (no formal schooling) 3 = up to 5th grade 4 = up to 10th grade 5 = up to higher secondary 6 = college level and above noperson: number of usual household members num_room: number of rooms 1 = single room house 2 = two-room residence 3 = more than two rooms grip_index: grip strength scores 0 = low 1 = medium 2 = high chair_index: chair stand scores 0 = low 1 = medium 2 = high timedgait_index: measured gait scores 0 = low 1 = medium 2 = high

Table 3.6 Explained variables for estimation of CDM and logistic regression models

Models	Explained variables
Count data regression model (negative binomial)	Functional impairments: none, single and multiple
Binary logit	Persons with 5 or more ADL disabilities = 1, others 0 Persons with 2 to 4 ADL disabilities = 1, others 0 Persons with single ADL disability = 0, others 0
Multinomial logit regression (with 3 dependent outcomes)	Grip Strength Scores (0, 1, 2) Chair Stand Scores (0, 1, 2) Measured Gait Scores (0, 1, 2)

The assumption of independence of irrelevant alternatives (IIA) was tested.
STATA 9 was used to estimate the models.

Explanatory variables used to estimate the CDM, binomial and multinomial logits are as follows:

Binary variables
sex: male = 1, female = 0; agegrp2: >75 = 1; <75 = 0; vegetarian: if veg. = 1, others = 0; occup_1: working for cash = 1; otherwise = 0; grand_child: grand children staying in the household = 1; otherwise = 0; d widowed: widowed = 1; others = 0; d_edu: literate = 1; illiterate = 0; income_rec~t: recipients of own source income = 1, others = 0; arthritis: those reporting arthritis = 1, otherwise = 0; religion: Hindus = 1; others = 0

Continuous and discrete variables
agegrp3: Age Group1 = 60–64, 2 = 65 – 69, 3 = 70+; Religion 1 = Hindu, 2 = Muslim, 3 = Sikh, 4 = Christian; marital: marital status, 1 = married, 2 = widowed, 3 = separated, 4 = never married; edu: education, 1 = Illiterate, 2 = Literate (no formal schooling), 3 = Up to 5th grade, 4 = up to 10th grade, 5 = up to higher secondary, 6 = College level and above; noperson: number of usual household members; num_room: number of rooms, 1 = single room house, 2 = two-room house, 3 = more than two rooms; grip_index: grip strength scores, 0 = low, 1 = medium, 2 = High; chair_index: chair stand scores, 0 = low, 1 = medium, 2 = High; timedgait_index: Measured gait scores, 0 = low, 1 = medium, 2 = High

References

Ahmed, T. 1995. The Population of Persons with Disabilities in Pakistan. *Asia-Pacific Population Journal*, 10(1), 39–62.

Alam, M. 2005. *South Asian Elderly: ADL and IADL Statuses of the Elderly in India – A Preliminary Investigation based on a Household Survey in Delhi*, April 2005, Mimeo.

Alam, M. 2006. *Ageing in India: Socio-economic and Health Dimensions*. Delhi: Academic Foundation.

Alam, M. 2009. Ageing, Socioeconomic Disparities and Health Outcomes: Some Evidence from Rural India. *Indian Journal of Human Development*, 3(1), 47–76.

Alam, M. and Karan, A. 2011. *Elderly Health in India: Dimension, Differentials and Determinants*, BKPAI Working Paper No. 3, United Nations Population Fund (UNFPA), New Delhi December 2011.

Alam, M. and Mukhejee, M. 2005. Ageing, Activities of Daily Living Disabilities and the Need for Public Health Initiatives: Some Evidence from a Household Survey in Delhi. *Asia-Pacific Population Journal*, 20(2), 47–76.

Albert, S.M. 2004. *Public Health and Ageing: An Introduction to Maximizing Function and Well-Being*. New York: Springer Publishing Company.

Albert, S.M., Alam, M. and Nizamuddin, M. 2005. Comparative Study of Functional Limitation and Disability in Old Age: Delhi and New York City. *Journal of Cross Cultural Gerontology*, 20, 231–41.

Bali, A.P. 2003. Family as Carer: The Changing Scenario, in *Ageing in India: Situation Analysis and Planning for the Future*, edited by A.B. Dey on behalf of the Ministry of Health and Family Welfare, and World Health Organization, 153–61.

Borooah, V.K. 2001. *Logit and Probit: Ordered and Multinomial Models (Quantitative Applications in Social Sciences)*, New Delhi/Thousand Oaks/London: Sage Publications.

Cameron, A.C. and Trivedi, P.K. 1986. Econometric Models based on Count Data: Comparison and Applications of Some Estimators and Tests. *Journal of Applied Econometrics*, 1, 29–53.

Chan, Y.H. 2005. Biostatistics 305, Multinomial Logistic Regression. *Singapore Medical Journal*, 46(6), 259–68.

Green, W.H. 2002. *Econometric Analysis*. Delhi: Pearson Education Press.

Herndon, R.M. 2006. *Handbook of Neuralgic Rating Scale*. New York: Demos Medical Publishing.

Jamuna, D. 2000. Ageing in India: Some Key Issues. *Ageing International*, 25(4), 16–31.

Khetarpal, K. 2003. Only Functionality Matters, in *Ageing in India: Situation Analysis and Planning for the Future*, edited by A.B. Dey on behalf of the Ministry of Health and Family Welfare, and World Health Organization, 79–84.

Kinsella, K. 2000. Demographic Dimensions of Global Ageing. *Journal of Family Issues*, 21(5), 541–58.

Lee, J. 1994. Odds Ratio or Relative Risk for Cross-sectional Data? *International Journal of Epidemiology*, 23, 201–12.

Lloyd-Sherlock, P. 2010. *Population Ageing and International Development: From Generalization to Evidence*. Bristol: Policy Press.

Long, J.S. 1997. *Regression Models for Categorical and Limited Dependent Variables: Advanced Quantitative Techniques in Social Sciences, Series No. 7*. New Delhi/Thousand Oaks/London: Sage Publications.

More, V., Wilcox,V., William, R. and Hiris, J. 1994. Functional Transitions among the Elderly: Patterns, Predictors and Related Hospital Use. *American Journal of Public Health*, 84, 1274–80.

Mujahid, G. and Siddhisena, K.A.P. 2009. *Demographic Prognosis for South Asia: A Future of Rapid Ageing*, Papers in Population Ageing No. 6, UNFPA – Asia and the Pacific Regional Office, Bangkok.

Newell, S.A., Girgis, A., Sanson-Fisher, R.W. and Savolainen, N.J. 1999. The Accuracy of Self-Reported Health Behaviors and Risk Factor Relating to Cancer and Cardiovascular Diseases in General Population: A Critical Review. *American Journal of Preventive Medicine*, 17(3), 211–29.

Niranjan, S., Sureender, S. and Rama Rao, G. 1998. Family Structure in India: Evidence from NFHS. *Demography India*, 27(2), 287–300.

Rahman, M.O. and Barsky, A.J. 2003. Self-Reported Health Among Older Bangladeshis: How Good a Health Indicator Is It? *The Gerontologist*, 43, 856–63.

Rimmer, J.H., David, B. and Pitetti, K.H. 1996. Research on Physical Activity and Disability: An Emerging National Priority, *Medicine & Science in Sports & Exercise*, 28(11), 1366–72.

Scott, M. 1997. *Applied Logistic Regression Analysis*. Quantitative Applications in Social Sciences Series. Thousand Oaks, CA: Sage Publications.

Sen, A.K. 2002. Health: Perception versus Observation. *British Medical Journal*, 324, 860–61.

Severson, M.A., Smith, G.E., Tangalos, E.G. et al. 1994. Pattern and Predictors of Institutionalization in Community-based Dementia Patients. *Journal of the American Geriatrics Society*, 42, 181–5.

Stone, R.I. 2000. *Long-Term Care for the Elderly with Disabilities: Current Policy, Emerging Trends, and Implications for the Twenty-First Century*. New York: Milbank Memorial Fund: http://bit.ly/Pyu8zT [accessed 30 August 2012].

Wagner, E.H., LaCroix, A.Z., Buchner, D.M. and Larson, E.B. 1992. Effects of Physical Activity on Health Status in Older Adults I: Observational Studies. *Annual Review of Public Health* (May)13, 451–68.

World Bank. 2008. *Sri Lanka – Addressing the Needs of an Ageing Population*. Report No. 43396-LK, Human Development Unit, South Asia Region, The World Bank.

World Population Prospects. The 2010 Revisions, Vol. II, Sex and Age Distribution of the World Population. Department of Economic and Social Affairs, Population Division: http://esa.un.org/wpp/unpp/panel_population.htm [accessed 30 August 2012].

Chapter 4
A Gendered Perspective on Well-Being in Later Life: Algeria, Lebanon and Palestine

Kristine J. Ajrouch, Kathryn M. Yount, Abla M. Sibai and Pia Roman

Population ageing is occurring rapidly in lower-income countries (Palloni, Pinto and Wong 2009), with the global share of adults 65 years or older expected to increase from 59% in 2000 to 71% in 2030 (Kinsella and Velkoff 2001). Declines in fertility and improvements in survival have led to rapid compositional changes, raising questions about the well-being of older adults. In this chapter, we view well-being as a comprehensive, multi-dimensional construct that includes: positive and negative engagements in family and social relations, a secure economic position and positive subjective and objective health status. Each dimension taps into key aspects of the quality of life in later life (Doyal and Gough 1991, George 2006). Older populations indeed are heterogeneous, living in diverse national contexts with marked differences in social, economic, and health conditions across subgroups. Gender inequalities are an area of global concern because women and men face unique social, economic, and health needs in later life (Knodel and Ofstedel 2003).

Demographic trends in Middle Eastern and North African (MENA) countries are consistent with global trends (Tabutin and Schoumaker 2005, Yount and Sibai 2009, Sibai, Tohme, Yount, Yamout and Kronfol, 2012); yet, population ageing in the region has received less attention than elsewhere. Moreover, older adults in several Middle Eastern countries have endured periods of high unemployment, declining economic conditions, and political instability and conflict, which likely create unusual contextual factors that may shape well-being in later life. Evidence for MENA countries, however, is largely based on sub national studies. This limitation is coupled with documented variability in gender and well-being *within* the Middle East (Ahmed 1992, Yount, Agree and Rebellon 2004, Offenhauer 2005, Yount and Agree 2005) and calls to account for the specific needs of older men and women (Knodel and Ofstedel 2003). In this chapter, we provide a comprehensive, comparative profile of well-being with regard to the family structure and social relations, socio-economic status and health of older women and men in national samples in Algeria, Lebanon and Palestine.[1] The subsequent sections proceed as

---

1 Throughout this chapter we use the terms Arab and MENA to reference the larger regions in which the study countries are located. Moreover, we refer to Palestine (comprised of the West Bank and the Gaza Strip, see Frisch 1998, Roy 1999, 2001, World

follows. First, we review the demographic and sociopolitical backgrounds of the countries under study. Second, we present a brief, theoretical discussion of gender, ageing and well-being, especially as it may apply to the Middle East. Finally, we offer a comparative analysis of gendered patterns with regard to well-being in later life in the three study settings.

Socio-political and Demographic Backgrounds of the Study Countries

The national socio-political and demographic context provides an important backdrop to gender, ageing and well-being in the three study countries (Table 4.1). Algeria, Lebanon and Palestine are three countries in the MENA region bordering the Mediterranean Sea. Algeria, located in northwestern Africa, is the largest Arab country in geographic and population size (2,381,741 km^2, 35 million population); whereas, Lebanon and Palestine are relatively small countries located in Western Asia (10,452 km^2, 4 million population; 6,020 km^2, 4 million population, respectively). The three countries share several similarities, including a common language and customs based on shared cultural values and principles. Yet, tremendous diversities also exist across these countries, reflecting differences in natural resources, economic systems, and in the timing, duration and nature of wars, political conflicts and occupations that may have variously contributed to shaping their socio-political priorities and demographic profiles.

Of particular consequence may be the unique experiences of political instabilities that mark the historical reality of each country. For example, Algeria's war for independence from France (1954–1962), in the end, led to selected legal reforms that granted women citizenship and equal rights to education (Turshen 2002). These reforms for women paled, however, in comparison to other countries in the Maghreb, such as Tunisia (Charrad 2001, 2007). Within 20 years, women in Algeria lost their rights, as the implementation of the "Family Code" in 1984 transformed women back to "minors," with no rights regarding marriage, divorce, education or work, or travel. Civil war in 1992 between Islamists and the Algerian government further affected families, as women struggled against crimes of war (Turshen 2002). New evidence suggests that women's low status in Algeria, with limited economic and political rights or resources, may derive from its status as an oil-producing nation (Ross 2008). Oil rich countries appear to develop economies that facilitate and reinforce a gendered division of labor (Olmsted 2005), with men earning high wages in the formal labor market and women working "invisibly" in unpaid, subsistence and domestic labor. Notably, the family structures in which men are the sole breadwinners may hamper

---

Bank 2010) as a country, though we acknowledge it has yet to be recognized as such by the United Nations. This approach facilitates our research goal to compare and contrast the "nationally" representative Palestinian population with those of Lebanon and Algeria.

Table 4.1 Socio-political and demographic background of the study countries

	Algeria	Lebanon	Palestine
Surface area (km^2)	2,381,741	10,452	6,020
Total population (thousands) (2011)[1]	35,980	4,259	4,152
Political instabilities	Independence war (1954–1962); Civil war (1992)	Civil war (1975–1990); Israeli occupation (1982–2000); Israeli war (summer 2006)	Israeli occupation (1948–present)
GDP per Capita ($US) (2010)[1]	4,473	9,284	1,820
Net overseas development assistance received per capita ($US) (2009)[2]	9	138	719
Urbanization (% urban population) (2010)[2]	66	87	72
Unemployment among youth (%) (2006-08)[2]	24.3	22.1	40.2
Adult (15+) Literacy Rate (2006-07)[2]	72.6	89.6	93.9
Life expectancy at birth (2010-2015)[1]			
Men	72	71	72
Women	75	75	75
Under 5 mortality rate per 1000 births (2010)[2]	36.0	22.1	22.3
Total fertility rate (2010)[2]	2.26	1.80	4.45
Percent above 60 years (2010)[1]			
Men	6	10	4
Women	8	11	5

Source: 1 = United Nations Statistics Division- Demographic and Social Statistics (http://unstats.un.org/unsd/demographic/products/socind/default.htm). See the following tabs for detailed data: Population / Health / Housing / Education / Work; 2 = World Bank, 2011 (http://databank.worldbank.org/ddp/home.do). Data tables may be located separately after entering the main site.

women's decision-making abilities, including those regarding their own health and health care (Zurayk, Sholkamy, Younis and Khattab 1997).

By comparison, Lebanon experienced a civil war from 1975 to 1990, the effects of which are identified as the most stressful socio-political event for older adults today (Sibai, Kanaan, Chaaya and Campbell 2007, Ajrouch, Abdulrahim and Antonucci 2010). Among middle-aged and older adults in Beirut, Lebanon during the civil war (1983–1993), men more often experienced any traumatic event (68% versus 63%) (Sibai, Fletcher and Armenian 2001). Men also more often experienced personal traumas (13% versus 4%), property losses (40% versus 30%) and displacement (29% versus 25%); whereas, women more often witnessed or heard about the traumas (31% versus 27%) and property losses (11% versus 7%) of other family members (Sibai et al. 2001). As such, these events affected men and women differently, with higher all-cause mortality among men than women. Moreover, the south of Lebanon was occupied from 1982 until 2000 and has experienced several waves of out migration among youth toward safer places and in search of opportunities for work. As a result, over 20% of older women are living alone in these areas (Sibai, Sen, Beydoun and Saxena 2004). During the summer 2006, Lebanon also faced a war with Israel, which led to the destruction of public infrastructures and private homes. Changing lifestyles stemming from war and political strife negatively affected the health of a large proportion of people for more than a decade (Sabbah, Le Vuitton, Droubi, Sabbah and Mercier 2007). The effect of war on women's position in Lebanon, however, has been described as emancipating. For instance, Shehadeh (1999) documents how the war ushered in a new era for women, showing their strength, resilience and capabilities. Reforms came into place including the repealing of a number of laws that before had viewed women as dependent, subservient and the property of their husband to giving women rights in purchasing land, insurance and starting a business (Shehadeh 1999). Though war led to many changes in women's rights and activities including increased pursuit of higher education and work outside the home, women continue to battle oppression and face discriminatory laws that limit their rights, especially once married (Shehadeh 2010).

Finally, Palestine has been occupied for more than 50 years, living with high levels of economic and political uncertainty (Khalidi 2007) and increasing risks of poverty because of Israeli restrictions on the mobility of Palestinians (Olmsted 2005, Mansour 2010). According to Olmsted (2005), such circumstances may inform gender patterns in family situations. For example, Olmsted reports that a higher percentage of older women (65 years or older) (2.7%) than same-aged men (0.7%) in Palestine reports having never married. Such gender differences may be attributed to an evolving patriarchal contract where women may not necessarily follow customary paths in part because of socio-economic and socio-political challenges in the occupied Palestinian territories along with expanding opportunities for women (Olmsted 2005). Moreover, as in many other countries (Zunzunegui, Minicuci, Blumstein, Noale, Deeg, Jylha, and Pedersen 2007), older women are more likely to live alone than older men. This pattern may reflect the tendency for men to marry women far younger than themselves, for women often to outlive men and for widowed men to remarry more often than widowed women (Olmsted 2011).

Whereas all three countries are considered low to middle income in the global stratification system (Firebaugh and Goesling 2004), economic conditions nevertheless vary across these countries. Amongst the three, Palestine has the lowest GDP per capita ($1,820), a figure that has changed little in the past 15 years (United Nations n.d.). Lebanon currently has the highest GDP ($9,284), but Algeria's GDP has almost doubled in the past two decades (United Nations n.d.), now reaching an estimated $4,473 per capita. Overall, levels of urbanization are on the rise in the three countries, with over two thirds of the populations in all three settings currently urbanized (Lebanon 87%, Palestine 72%, Algeria 66%) and the most rapid increase (of 14% in the past two decades) occurring in Algeria (World Bank n.d.). All countries have been economically dependent on wealthier countries for decades and more so now than in prior years. In fact, per capita overseas development assistance (ODA) has increased most dramatically in Palestine, from $719 in 1993 to $748 in 2009. In Lebanon, the per capita ODA more than tripled in the last 20 years, now reaching $138. Algeria has received the least overseas assistance, with its recent ODA per capita reaching a mere $9.1, ranging over the last two decades between $5 and $14 (World Bank n.d.).

Poor economic performance of some MENA countries has undermined opportunities for employment, which coupled with continued population growth has led to high levels of both unemployment and underemployment (Jabbour, Yamout, Hilal and Nehmeh 2012). The proportion unemployed is especially high among the youth and in poor and conflict-ridden areas of the region (Chaaban 2010). This circumstance has led to substantial waves of labor emigration,[2] including single men who emigrate for some number of years to save for the costs of marriage as well as young families seeking better opportunities for employment in other countries. In Algeria, youth migration has been rising particularly since 2000 as a result of the high rate of unemployment, especially among the most educated (Di Bartolomeo, Jaulin and Perrin 2011). Brain drain also is characteristic of Lebanon, where estimated rates of unemployment are high (22%) among youth (World Bank n.d). Palestine also has been facing the same challenge, although opportunities for employment recently have emerged with the increase of foreign investments (Hasan, AlAwlaqi, AlYaqout and AlGharaballi 2011). The implications of mass emigration are two-fold: reduced opportunities for intergenerational co-residence on one hand and on the other, increased opportunities for remittances to the country and the enhanced financial support of older parents.

Rates of literacy among adults (age 15 years and above) are surprisingly high in Palestine (93.9%) and are followed by those in Lebanon (89.6%) and then Algeria (72.6%) (World Bank n.d.). Life expectancy also is relatively high in all three countries, around 73 years (United Nations n.d.). For various geo-political reasons, notably to become the majority in their own community or

---

2 For instance, between 2000 and 2003, 39% of the Lebanese labor force and 14% of the Algerian one have opted for emigration (data not available for Palestinians) (Chaaban 2009).

against their rivalries, the total fertility rate in Palestine has been consistently high and is currently estimated at 4.45 births per woman of reproductive age, one of the highest in the region. By contrast, the total fertility rates in Lebanon and Algeria have been decreasing over the past few decades, reaching 1.80 and 2.26 births per woman, respectively. Currently, Lebanon has the highest percentage of older adults (at least 60 years of age) in the region, comprising 10% of the total population of men and 11% of the total population of women. Comparatively, older adults constitute somewhat smaller percentages of the total populations of men women, respectively, in Algeria (6% and 8%) and Palestine (4% and 5%). The low percentages of those at least 60 years of age in Palestine results primarily from the high rate of fertility.

Social experiences often have cumulative effects and ultimately may impinge on overall well-being depending on the various resources available to them (Elder and Liker 1982). On the one hand, surviving older adults may show resilience through socio-political instabilities (Douglass and McGadney-Douglass 2008, Greve and Bjorklund 2008), whereas on the other hand, they may exhibit diminished well-being. In sum, changing historical sociopolitical and demographic circumstances provide an important context for situating and interpreting the social, economic and health-related well-being of older men and women in the three contexts under comparison.

Gender, Ageing and Well-being in Middle East

At the same time that the Middle Eastern and North African (MENA) countries are accruing increasing absolute and relative numbers of older people, the systematic study of ageing and its correlates in this region continue to lag behind that of other regions of the world (Yount and Sibai 2009). A special consequence of population ageing involves changes in the links between gender and various indicators of well-being. Below we identify issues of theoretical interest concerning the nature of gender and ageing in the Middle East, with a particular focus on family and social relations, socio-economic conditions and disparities in health.

As in many other regions of the world, family relations constitute a key aspect of social relations in the MENA region. A considerable amount of research has examined the importance of social relations for well-being in the Western world (Durkheim 1951, Berkman and Syme 1979, Cohen and Syme 1985, Antonucci and Jackson 1987, House, Landis and Umberson 1988, Luescher and Pillemer 1998); yet, research from the West may not always apply in the MENA context. For instance, compared to men, women in the US are more "relationally oriented" in so far as they report having larger networks; however, women also appear to be both advantaged and burdened by these relationships, in that they report both relatively more support and more negativity in their relations (e.g., Antonucci, Akiyama and Lansford 1998). By contrast, family relations in Lebanon have been characterized by *patriarchal connectivity* (Joseph 1993) and this concept has been applied to family relations elsewhere in the Middle East (e.g., Yount, Cunningham, Engelman and Agree 2012). Specifically, Joseph has argued that men *and* women in Lebanese society are socialized to view themselves relationally. Families are *patriarchal* insofar as feminine and masculine selves are organized according to a gender and age hierarchy, in which the men and more senior women carry disproportionate privilege and power. *Connectivity* refers to an activity or intention to facilitate closeness, which includes the ability to anticipate the needs of another, answer for others and shape likes and dislikes in accordance with one another.

Joseph (1993) argues that men and older women expect to direct the lives of younger and especially younger female family members, through cultural entitlements that foster hierarchical relations between men and women, youth and elders. Younger and female members, who are expected to express their love and loyalty by serving, complying with and even anticipating the wishes of their elders, are seen as extensions of men and older adults. According to Joseph, in Lebanon, one's sense of self is grounded in social relations that play out as connectivity. This *patriarchal kin contract* describes age-gender-based rules of exchange. Ultimately, older men are thought to wield a large amount of control in social relations because of the cultural sanctions that allow men to direct the lives of women and youth. We extend this line of thinking to suggest that an older adult invests in in relations with younger people to whom s/he is connected for her/his well-being. Hence, men's sense of well-being may especially rest on their relations with women and younger adults, i.e., the extent to which women and younger adults fulfill their obligations according to the patriarchal kin contract.

Other work suggests that there may indeed be a gender cross-over effect concerning women's status and power in old age. The strong role of older women in families suggests that there are certain perceived (but not guaranteed) "benefits" for women to conform to the patriarchal kin contract, which motivate women to conform to the system to maximize their security, including in old age. In this way, women and especially those who are married mothers, invest heavily in their children (and sons) in the hopes of receiving dividends in old age (Kandiyoti 1988, Olmsted 2005, Yount 2005). Thus, the patriarchal system expects young women to be subservient, but the anticipated dividends in old age, if fulfilled, would provide a strong informal/familial safety net for those who marry and have children, especially if they bear sons. Older women in Arab societies who have invested in kin-keeping over the life course are observed to receive certain advantages over older men in co-residence and the financial support that they receive (Yount 2005, Yount et al. 2012).

The contribution of gender to differences in economic well-being between women and men will depend on the form and extent of gender inequality in a given context. Gender ideals may vary in how rigidly they are practiced across the MENA region (Yount 2012). Kandiyoti (1988) has attributed *crises of patriarchy* to economic changes that disrupt the gendered division of labor. Urbanization, industrialization, mass schooling and legal reforms also have altered gender relations in the region (Moghadam 2004, Charrad 2001, Fargues 2005, Tabutin and

Schoumaker 2005). The expansion of girls' schooling, however, may have been the most notable influence on gender relations, both within and across generations (e.g., Moghadam 2004, Fargues 2005). A comparison of school attainments in selected MENA countries show that such changes have contributed to increases, especially among women, in the mean age at first marriage and the proportion never married, as well as declines in the age gap between spouses (e.g., Fargues 2005, Tabutin and Schoumaker 2005). Yet, gender gaps favoring men in education and formal wage labor are large among today's older adults and may correlate with gender gaps in informal financial support from children (Yount and Sibai 2009).

Finally, disparities in health in the Middle East and Arab world may vary within and across nations. According to Yount (2012), inequities in the burden of disability and health are rooted in multiple hierarchies that distribute power unequally and affect the social conditions that are most proximate to individual health. One of those hierarchies involves the experiences of being female or male; these categories are socio-political in that maleness typically is favored, albeit in variable ways across space and time (Yount 2012). Gender's contribution to differences in health between women and men will depend on the form and extent of gender inequality in a given context. In settings where gender norms and hierarchies are more rigid, the influence of gender on health may be greater than in settings where these norms and structures are more flexible and thus where men's and women's lifestyles and roles are more similar. Substantial changes and variations in gender systems throughout the Middle East permit a comparative study of gender and health *within* the region (Moghadam 2004).

For the current countries under study, similarities in gender systems are present in the sense that family law is governed by religious law (Moghadam 2003), yet each country faces unique socio-political factors. Algeria is characterized by a highly gendered division of labor, with women pressured into domestic labor and men engaged in more wage-based work outside the home (Cheriet 2004, Jansen 2004, Houria 2007). Algerian women's formal workforce participation is extremely low. According to Houria (2007), less than one million women in a population of 14.5 million women participate in paid work (approximately 7%). In Lebanon, advancements have been gained since 1953 with several discriminatory laws toward women repealed or amended; yet, family as well as civil law still views a married woman as subordinate to her husband (Shehadeh 2010). Furthermore, patriarchal connectivity (Joseph 1993) pre-supposes a complex relationality between men and women, where gender and age shape family experiences over the life course with clear hierarchies in that men and older adults have authority over women and younger adults. In Palestine, difficulties arise in working to improve the status of women in the context of a decades-long military occupation including existing laws that do not provide sufficient protection for women from discrimination and unfair treatment (Shehada 2004, Rought-Brooks, Duaibis and Hussein 2010). The patriarchal contract in Palestine is thought to be evolving, where women slowly lose traditional safety nets provided by family because of occupation and the barriers that it brings (Olmsted 2005). In sum, diversities and commonalities characterize gender systems over the life course in Arab and Middle Eastern populations, necessitating comparative study of gender and well-being in the region.

Study Populations for Comparative Analysis

This study relies on an existing but under-used data source: the Pan Arab Project for Family Health (PAPFAM). PAPFAM obtained national samples of older adults in Algeria, Lebanon and Palestine by collaborating with key organizations and public agencies in each country. The Algerian sample (N = 3958; aged 60 years or older) was collected in 2002 in conjunction with the National Office of Statistics and Ministry of Health. The Lebanese sample (N = 1774; aged 65+) was collected in 2004 in conjunction with the Central Administration of Statistics and the Ministry of Social Affairs. The Palestinian sample (N = 1622; aged 60+) was collected in collaboration with the Palestinian Central Bureau of Statistics in 2006. Face-to-face interviews were carried out in which participants were asked about family and social relations, socio-demographic characteristics and economic conditions. Participants also were asked about personal disability and health status (with the latter subjective reports of functional limitations and self-rated health). Because the sample for Lebanon did not include those aged 60 to 64 years, only participants aged 65 years and older in Algeria (N = 2778) and Palestine (N = 1148) were included in the analysis. This decision facilitates comparisons across the three countries. Table 4.2 presents the overall indicators of interest by country.

Family Structure

Similar patterns in family structure were found in all three countries concerning gender, age and with regard to marital and widowed status, having children and living arrangements. In all three countries, approximately half of the sample was women (49.5% in Algeria; 48.9% in Lebanon and 57.8% in Palestine). The mean age of participants was around 73 years in all three countries. Patterns of marriage and widowhood differed to some extent across the study settings. Specifically, in both Algeria and Lebanon, approximately two thirds of participants were married (67.7% and 65.2%, respectively) and approximately one third were widowed (30.3% and 30.2%, respectively). In Palestine, however, slightly more than half were married (56.7%) and slightly less than half were widowed (40.2%). Relatively high rates of widowhood in Palestine may reflect protracted and ongoing occupation and conflict in Palestine, resulting in higher rates of conflict-related death among civilians in this setting than in the other study settings. A small minority in all three countries reported living alone; however, this percentage ranged from 2% in Algeria to 12% in Lebanon. Relatively high rates of emigration among youth in Lebanon may contribute to the higher rates of living alone, though wealth also may be a contributor (Tohme, Yount, Yassine,

Shideed and Sibai 2011). Almost all participants in each of the three countries reported having at least one child (95% or more).

Social Relations

Concerning the provision of support by elders to their family, variation concerning domestic support was minimal. Over one third of participants in Algeria and Palestine (37.2% and 34.2%, respectively) and close to 40% in Lebanon provided some sort of domestic support to their families, i.e., they reported helping any member of their family in his or her work or activity. More variation was found with regard to elders as a financial resource for the family: almost two thirds (61.5%) in Algeria reported that they financially supported either themselves and/ or others, whereas approximately half (49.1%) in Lebanon and one fourth (26.6%) in Palestine reported they care financially for themselves and/or others. These discrepancies may indicate variation in social security programs across countries (Yount and Sibai 2009). Although social insurance in Middle Eastern countries is limited and weak, the Algerian government subsidizes the minimum pension from employment (US Social Security Administration 2011).

The frequency of contact differed in all three countries. Less than one quarter (23.7%) of participants reported seeing their non-co-resident children daily in Algeria. On the other hand, over one half (56.5%) of participants reported seeing their children daily in Lebanon and close to half (44.6%) indicated that they see their children daily in Palestine. The lower contact frequency rate with children may reflect enormous geographical distance in Algeria or a trend towards residence of married children in the same neighborhoods as their parents, sometimes on different floors of the same building, in Lebanon and Palestine (Sibai et al. 2012).

Children's advice seeking and following were relatively high in all three countries, according to older adults. As for advice requested by their children, close to three quarters of older adults in Algeria reported that their children ask for advice (74.6%) and follow it (74.5%). A similar pattern was apparent in Lebanon where 77.8%reported that their children ask for advice; 82.2% reported that children follow it. The level was slightly lower in Palestine, where more than half (61.3%) reported that their children ask for advice and more than two thirds (69.1%) reported that their children follow the advice.

The percentage of elders who reported receiving financial support from children was high but variable across the study settings, with the lowest percentages in Algeria (49.0%) and the highest percentage in Lebanon (74.2%). Older adults in Palestine fell somewhere in the middle; two thirds (66.8%) reported financial support from their children. Variation may result from higher remittances in Lebanon and subsidized pensions in Algeria.

Overall, reports of negative family and non-family relations were low (scale ranges from 0–1) in Algeria and Lebanon. In Algeria, the mean index for negative family relations was 0.06 (SD = 0.16) and for negative non-family relations was 0.08 (SD = 0.19). In Lebanon, the mean index for negative relations was extremely low for family at 0.01 (SD = 0.07) and non-family at 0.02 (SD = 0.09). In Palestine, negative relations were reported as somewhat more prevalent. The mean index for negative family relations was 0.24 (SD = 0.35) and non-family relations was 0.35 (SD = 0.23). The relatively higher levels of negative relationships, both within and outside the family may reflect the added layer of stress and low social trust from protracted political instability and occupation.

Socio-economic Status

Socioeconomic patterns differed across the three countries concerning reports of literacy, source of income and income sufficiency. Rates of literacy were lowest among older adults in Algeria (12%), followed by those in Palestine (34.0%) and then Lebanon (56.3%). The fact that the Lebanese report the highest literacy rates and Algeria the lowest literacy rates may reflect contrasting historical experiences concerning education and the timing of the expansion of formal schooling in each country. For instance, Algeria, as part of the Maghreb, inherited widespread illiteracy from the colonial period, where the vast majority of the population was unable to read and write in any language (Bougroum, Diagne, Kissami and Tawil 2007). On the other hand, Lebanon's educational system boasts high-quality delivery, with greater public accountability than other countries in the region, regardless of per capita income (Worldbank n.d.). The fact that literacy rates are overall higher in Palestine than Algeria is somewhat surprising, given that on-going conflict has been associated with declines in education in other settings (Davies 2004). This discrepancy, therefore, could be a result of differential measurement error in reports of literacy across settings (Lloyd Behrman, Stromquist and Cohen 2005).

Concerning sources of income, not surprisingly the Algerians were most likely to report receiving income from a retirement or pension (52.7%), whereas the Lebanese and Palestinians most often reported children as their primary source of income (61.4% in Lebanon and 67.8% in Palestine). Interestingly, Lebanon reported much lower likelihoods of receiving income from social welfare programs than did Algeria and Palestine, possibly indicative of the weak government role in such programs (Dixon 2000).

Reports of income sufficiency varied across countries. Only one quarter (25.3%) of older adults in Algeria indicated that their income was sufficient; whereas, over half indicated that their income was sufficient in Lebanon (64.1%) and Palestine (57.1%). It may be that when family members, as opposed to pensions and retirement, are major sources of income, one reports more satisfaction with the amount, knowing the scarcity of other sources. Furthermore, the absolute level or amount of pension may be low, as it is in many Middle East countries and hence reliance on such a source not surprisingly results in high reports of income insufficiency.

Health Status

Similar patterns were found in all three countries concerning the prevalence of less than "good" self-rated health, but older adults in Palestine differed from those in Algeria and Lebanon regarding reports of functional limitation. Specifically, a large majority of participants in all three countries rated their own health as less than "good" (88.0% in Algeria; 78.8% in Lebanon; 85.0% in Palestine). Around one third of participants in Algeria (32.0%) and Lebanon (28.4%) reported experiencing some sort of functional limitation; whereas, in Palestine, more than two thirds indicated that they had some functional limitation (68.9%). It may be, for example, that Palestine's relatively poor economy or more protracted conflict once again explain this difference across settings, as poor economic conditions and armed conflict are associated with higher levels of mortality and higher prevalences of functional limitations (Murthy and Lakshminarayana 2006; Ruger and Kim 2006).

Table 4.2 Descriptive statistics of the samples: Adults aged 65 years and older in Algeria, Lebanon and Tunisia

	Algeria (N = 2,778)		Lebanon (N = 1,774)		Palestine (N = 1,148)	
	M (SD)	%	M (SD)	%	M (SD)	%
Demographic characteristics						
Gender (Woman = 1)		49.5		48.9		57.8
Age	72.68 (6.68)		73.25 (6.14)		73.66 (6.88)	
Family structure						
Marital status						
Married		67.7		65.2		56.7
Widowed		30.3		30.2		40.2
Living alone (ref: with family member)		2.0		12.0		11.2
Social relations						
Domestic support by elder (yes = 1)		37.2		41.1		34.2
Financial support by elder		61.5		49.1		26.6
Contact frequency – children visit						
Daily		23.7		56.5		44.6
Once a week		29.7		33.2		34.6
Once a month		18.3		3.9		11.8

	Algeria (N = 2,778)		Lebanon (N = 1,774)		Palestine (N = 1,148)	
	M (SD)	%	M (SD)	%	M (SD)	%
Contact frequency – children visit						
On occasions/when I feel sick		28.2		6.4		9.0
Informational support seeking – children (yes = 1)		74.6		77.8		61.3
Informational support received – children (yes = 1)		74.5		82.2		69.1
Financial support – children (yes = 1)		49.0		74.2		66.8
Filial obligations (yes = 1)		80.8		93.0		83.7
Relations with others						
Contact – others visit (yes = 1)		79.2		93.4		79.4
Negative relations – family (mean index 0–1)	.06 (.16)		.01 (.07)		.24 (.35)	
Negative relations – others (mean index 0–1)	.08 (.19)		.02 (.09)		.35 (.23)	
Socio-economic status						
Literate (yes = 1)		12.2		56.3		34.0
Income source – retirement/pension (yes = 1)		52.7		18.4		8.2
Income source – children (yes = 1)		30.9		61.4		67.78
Income source – social welfare (yes = 1)		22.1		2.5		20.4
Income source – work or property (yes = 1)		11.8		28.9		18.4
Income sufficient (yes = 1)		25.3		64.1		57.1
Disability and health status						
Self-rated health (good or better = 1)	.12 (.33)		.21 (.41)		.15 (.36)	
Any functional limitations (yes = 1)		32.0		28.4		68.9

Source: Authors' calculations of data from the Pan Arab Project for Family Health PAPFAM Surveys.

Patterns by Gender:
Do Men and Women Report Different Levels of Well-being?

Family Structure

Table 4.3 shows the distribution of selected family structure indicators, namely marital status and solitary living, among older men and women in Algeria, Lebanon and Palestine. Men were more than twice as likely as women to be married across all three countries. Concurrently, widowhood was significantly more common among older women than older men, albeit the percentage of those widowed was highest among Palestinian women. Living alone was approximately three times more common among older women than older men in the three countries.

Table 4.3 Family structure*

	Algeria		Lebanon		Palestine	
	N = 2,778		N = 1,774		N = 1,148	
	Male	Female	Male	Female	Male	Female
	$\bar{x}$ (SD)	$\bar{x}$ (SD)	$\bar{x}$ (SD)	$\bar{x}$ (SD)	$\bar{x}$ (SD)	$\bar{x}$ (SD)
Married	.92 (.27)	.43 (.50)	.86 (.35)	.44 (.50)	.86 (.34)	.35 (.49)
Widowed	.07 (.25)	.54 (.50)	.12 (.33)	.49 (.50)	.13 (.14)	.60 (.49)
Living alone	.01 (.08)	.03 (.18)	.07 (.25)	.18 (.38)	.05 (.21)	.16 (.37)

Note: * All results significant at p<.001.

Taken together, women were more disadvantaged than men in structural proxies for family support in all three countries. These findings corroborate those of prior research within (e.g., Yount 2005, Yount and Khadr 2008, Yount and Sibai 2009, Tohme et al. 2011) and outside (Iacovou 2000, Kinsella and Velkoff 2001) of the MENA region showing a greater propensity for older women to be widowed and to be living alone than older men.

Some differences with other MENA and non-MENA countries, however, are notable. Specifically, the higher percentages of older adults living alone in Lebanon and Palestine still are lower than those of most Western countries (Kramarow 1995, Mancunovich et al. 1995, Iacovou 2000, NIA 2007), replicate those observed in a few countries in the far east (Yi and Wang 2003, The Hong Kong Council of Social Services 2009), but exceed those in other Asian, African and Latin American countries (Bongaarts and Zimmer 2002, Frankenberg et al. 2002). Still, Lebanon and Palestine rank as the highest in the Middle East. In comparison, for example, 3.1% of men and 12.3% of women lived alone in Egypt in 2000 (Yount and Khadr 2008) and in Jordan, the percentage of older adults living alone did not exceed 6.1% (Mahasneh 2000). The low percentage of solitary living in Algeria is comparable to those observed in the oil-rich countries, such as Kuwait (0.3% of men and 1.9% of women) (Shah et al. 2002), where the norm of three-generation household still mostly prevails.

Not unlike gender gaps in marital life course trajectories outside of the MENA region (Lee and Palloni 1992, Westoff 2003, Anoshua and Kakoli 2009, Mba 2007), the varied marital histories of women and men within the MENA may account for differences in women's and men's living arrangements in later life. These circumstances include the higher life expectancy of women, their earlier widowhood and less frequent remarriage in case of widowhood or divorce (Olmsted 2011). In fact, in certain Arab countries, the higher rate of solitary living among older women compared to older men is accounted for entirely by women's higher propensity to be widowed (Yount and Sibai 2009). The relatively elevated proportion of widowhood among older Palestinian women, compared to the Algerian and Lebanese women, can also be attributed to poorer economic conditions, the longer history of elevated mortality among men associated with more protracted conflict, or other contextual differences across the three settings (Table 4.1).

Of all the various living arrangements, living alone is an intriguing category with respect to older adults in MENA countries. On the one hand, solitary living may signify financial and psychological independence. On the other hand, it may indicate social isolation and social deprivation. Studies of solitary living are especially relevant in the Middle East, given that older adults who live alone contradict the customary Arab arrangement of intergenerational co-residence and support, especially for women who become widowed. Because of high rates of patrilocal residence, blood marriage and quasi-co residence in the densely populated settings of the Middle East, intergenerational support tends to remain highly active (Yount et al. 2012). Therefore, further investigations are needed to determine the effects that living alone may have on the well-being of older adults in the Middle East, especially women among whom living alone is more common.

Social Relations

In this section, we address the topic of social relations with three groups of people: family, children and others including friends and neighbors (see Table 4.4). Social relations with family are examined in terms of support provided to the family by older persons and along the dimension of relationship quality. Social relations with children include attention to the frequency of contact, provision and extent of financial support and the practice of children seeking and listening to the advice of older parents. Finally, social relations with others are examined by discerning patterns related to visiting and relationship quality.

Support provided to the family, including the domestic and financial spheres, provides an opportunity to explore in what ways gender shapes the role of older adults as a resource within and across the three countries of study. One robust pattern evident in all three countries concerns the tendency for men to report providing financial support to families at over twice what women report. The widest gender gap was found in Algeria, where on average, 89% of men reported providing such support compared to 33% of women. In Lebanon and Palestine, a gender gap was present, though not as wide as found in Algeria. On average, 63% of men compared to 35% of women report providing financial support in Lebanon and 42% of men compared to 15% of women reporting that they provide financial support to their families in Palestine. The gender gap overall is not surprising, given the low rates of older women's documented wage work in these settings (Zurayk et al. 1997, Turshen 2002, UNIFEM 2004, Olmsted 2005) and elsewhere in the MENA region (Yount and Sibai 2009). The larger discrepancy in Algeria may reflect the fact that it is an oil-producing country and hence women's opportunity to work outside the home for wages is more limited (Olmsted 2005, Ross 2008). No statistically significant gender differences emerged concerning the provision of domestic support and indeed, rates were similar in all three countries. Our analyses do not, however, allow us to discern what types of domestic work are provided. For instance, it may be that women are more likely to provide help with cooking or child care, while men may provide assistance with manual labor, home projects, or economic activity such as bringing food from the market. Additionally, no statistically significant gender differences emerged with regard to negative relations with family, though the prevalence was higher among older Palestinians than among older Algerians and Lebanese. Being annoyed or disturbed at similar levels may reflect common organizational elements of family relations in Arabic-speaking countries, whereby men and women family members are intensely relational (e.g., Joseph 1993).

Relations with children are an important area of social relations, particularly within the context of weak states and weak social insurance systems (Yount and Sibai 2009). In such instances, children remain the main source of security in old age. Gendered patterns concerning the frequency of contact, financial support and whether or not children seek out and listen to the advice of older parents are areas where men and women may differ in the kinds of support exchanged with children. Though men and women are thought to be similarly relational in Arab culture (Joseph 1993), some dimensions may be expressed and experienced differently, especially those concerning instrumental aspects of relationships with children. Indeed, patterns in all three countries exhibit this tendency. Results showed no statistically significant difference by gender on contact frequency across all three countries, with men and women reporting children visit on average once a week. Although no gender gaps in receipt of financial support was reported among older Palestinians (69% of women; 64% of men), a significant difference was apparent in Algeria and Lebanon, with a higher percentage of women than men in Lebanon (81% of women; 68% of men) and Algeria (54% of women; 44% of men) reporting receipt of financial support from children (no time frame given). Financial support constitutes an instrumental dimension of support and so the presence of gender differences may signify the differential life experiences of men

Table 4.4 Social relations

	Algeria		Lebanon		Palestine	
	N = 2,778		N = 1,774		N = 1,148	
	Male	Female	Male	Female	Male	Female
	$\bar{x}$ (SD)	$\bar{x}$ (SD)	$\bar{x}$ (SD)	$\bar{x}$ (SD)	$\bar{x}$ (SD)	$\bar{x}$ (SD)
Family domestic support to	.35 (.48)	.40 (.49)*	.37 (.48)	.45 (.50)*	.30 (.46)	.37 (.48)*
Financial support to	.89 (.31)	.33 (.47)	.63 (.48)	.35 (.48)	.42 (.49)	.15 (.36)
Negative relations	.07 (.17)	.06 (.15)*	.02 (.07)	.01 (.07)*	.29 (.27)	.20 (.21)*
Children						
Contact frequency	2.47 (1.14)	2.51 (1.12)*	3.40 (.83)	3.40 (.85)*	3.19 (.91)	3.11 (.98)*
Financial support	.44 (.50)	.54 (.50)	.68 (.47)	.81 (.39)	.64 (.48)	.69 (.46)*
Informational support to	.75 (.43)	.74 (.44)*	.76 (.42)	.79 (.41)*	.67 (.47)	.57 (.50)*
Informational listened	.77 (.42)	.72 (.45)*	.83 (.38)	.81 (.39)*	.75 (.43)	.64 (.48)*
Others						
Visit	.82 (.39)	.77 (.42)	.94 (.24)	.93 (.25)*	.81 (.39)	.78 (.41)*
Negative relations	.09 (.21)	.06 (.16)	.02 (.10)	.02 (.08)*	.35 (.22)	.34 (.24)*

Note: * Not significant, otherwise all results significant p<.001.

and women. In other words, over the life course men are likely to earn money (and keep some portion of it), whereas women are not. The patriarchal contract permits women to expect from children (and children, especially sons, are furthermore taught to provide) financial support once the child has the means (Olmsted 2005). Women in Arab societies are thought to be generally advantaged over men in the informal economic exchanges that they receive in old age (Yount 2005). The lack of a gender difference in financial support in Palestine is notable and may be attributable to its long history of political instability, which often coincides with high levels of unemployment and economic and political uncertainty and substantial needs among both men and women for informal financial support (Olmsted 2005). Finally, results showed no significant gender difference in children's advice seeking and listening across all three countries. This finding may once again signify intensive intergenerational relations and common deference of children to older men and women within the family (Joseph 1993).

Finally, concerning relations with others, such as friends and neighbors, only in Algeria did gender differences emerge. Men in Algeria, on average, reported more visits (on average 82% of men; 77% of women) from others, but also more negative relations (on average 9% of men and 6% of women). Such differences, albeit small, may reflect that Algeria is an oil-producing country. Oil rich countries appear to develop economies that facilitate and reinforce a more gendered division of labor (Olmsted 2005), which may translate into less outside contact for women and hence less likelihood of visits and negativity from friends and neighbors. Interestingly, elders in Palestine reported the highest level of negative relations compared to the other two countries, but such negativity was experienced similarly by men and women. Again, this pattern may result from historical and on-going conflict in Palestine, which has resulted in high levels of economic and political uncertainty (Olmsted 2005). Elders in Lebanon reported the highest levels of visiting of all three countries, on average above 90% and the lowest levels (2%) of negative relations with others, regardless of gender.

Socio-economic Status

In this section we document socio-economic status (SES) including literacy, income sufficiency and income source. Table 4.5 presents an examination of SES, and offers insight into inequalities that mark the experience of older men and women across and within the three countries of interest.

Consistent with comparative studies of gender gaps in schooling among older adults in the MENA region (Yount and Sibai 2009), gender differences in literacy were a consistent pattern in all three countries here. Overwhelmingly, men reported 18% to 48% higher rates of literacy than did women. Such gaps in literacy likely resulted from historically divergent educational opportunities for boys and girls (Hammoud 2006), with boys benefitting first from the expansion of schooling (Yount and Sibai 2009).

Results showed a gender difference concerning income sufficiency in Algeria and Palestine. Compared to men, women consistently more often reported income sufficiency. This finding corroborates the sentiment that women in Arab societies are thought to be generally advantaged over men in the informal economic exchanges that they receive in old age (Yount 2005). Lebanon appears to be an exception, which may result from remittance activity related to high patterns of emigration among both men and women (Hourani 2005), which may level gender differences in old age as remittances are likely sent back to the family in general (as opposed to only mothers).

Finally, sources of income varied by gender in the expected ways. In all three countries, men more often reported receiving income from retirement/pension and work/properties than did women, though women reported a higher likelihood of receiving income from their children. Income from social welfare sources did not vary by gender with women and men just as likely to benefit from such sources.

Table 4.5 Socioeconomic status*

	Algeria		Lebanon		Palestine	
	N = 2,778		N = 1,774		N = 1,148	
	Male	Female	Male	Female	Male	Female
	$\bar{x}$ (SD)	$\bar{x}$ (SD)	$\bar{x}$ (SD)	$\bar{x}$ (SD)	$\bar{x}$ (SD)	$\bar{x}$ (SD)
Literacy	.21 (.41)	.03 (.18)	.70 (.46)	.42 (.49)	.62 (.49)	.14 (.35)
Sufficient income	.23 (.42)	.28 (.45)	.63 (.48)	.65 (.48)*	.51 (.50)	.62 (.49)
Sources of income						
Retirement/ pension	.71 (.46)	.34 (.47)	.23 (.42)	.14 (.34)	.14 (.34)	.04 (.20)
Children	.23 (.42)	.39 (.49)	.54 (.50)	.69 (.46)	.61 (.49)	.73 (.45)*
Work/ properties	.16 (.37)	.07 (.26)	.38 (.49)	.20 (.40)	.24 (.43)	.14 (.75)
Social welfare	.22 (.42)	.22 (.42)*	.02 (.15)	.03 (.16)*	.19 (.39)	.21 (.41)*

Note: * Not significant, otherwise all results significant p<.001.

Disability and Health

Table 4.6 shows the levels of self-rated health and activity limitations of older men and women in Algeria, Lebanon and Palestine. With the exception of activity limitations in the context of Algeria, all differences between women and men are significant. Moreover, all differences are in the expected direction, when compared to prior comparative studies in MENA countries (Yount and Sibai 2009). Specifically, older women report lower self-rated health than do older men, with men's self-rated health being twice as high as women's in Lebanon and Palestine. Gender gaps in scores for activities limitations are consistent with those for self-rated health, with older women reporting more activity limitations than older men, on average.

The high prevalence of functional disability among women reflects patterns in other Arab states (Yount and Sibai 2009). Studies have shown consistently that limitations in ADLs and IADLs are more prevalent in women than in men, but objective measures of functional limitations are lacking and women may tend to over-report such disabilities (Khadr and Yount forthcoming). Furthermore, in contrast to reported difficulties with ADLs, reported difficulties with IADLs are highly sensitive to gender roles and living conditions (Yount and Agree 2005, Zeki Al Hazzouri 2006). The correlates of disablement among men tend to be illiteracy (which may be correlated with occupation), the social and financial demands of raising a large number of daughters (Engelman et al. 2010),[3] as well as ill-health and unattended medical needs; whereas injury, living in poor settings and the biological demands of higher parity are correlated with disablement among women (Lamb 1997, Youssef 2005). Another cause of higher disability in older women than older men in Arab Middle-Eastern countries also may be women's higher rates of overweight and obesity (Khadr and Yount forthcoming). According to a recent review by Yount (2012), the prevalence of over-weight and obesity is higher among women than men in a majority of Arab settings and rates of obesity in adult women range from 20% to as much as 58%.

These findings corroborate those in other Arab Middle Eastern countries (Yount and Sibai 2009). In general, Arab countries have experienced a marked epidemiological transition, with non-communicable and degenerative diseases replacing communicable diseases as the leading causes of morbidity and mortality. Starting in the mid-to-late 1990s, epidemiological research in the Arab world shifted its focus to non-communicable diseases and mainly those of the circulatory system. Similarly, studies among older adults have focused on debilitating diseases such as musculoskeletal problems, hearing and vision problems and deterioration in activities of daily living (ADLs). Gender gaps in disability and health suggest a high degree of similarity in the three countries of interest.

Table 4.6 Health and disability*

	Algeria		Lebanon		Palestine	
	N = 2,778		N = 1,774		N = 1,148	
	Male	Female	Male	Female	Male	Female
	$\bar{x}$ (SD)	$\bar{x}$ (SD)	$\bar{x}$ (SD)	$\bar{x}$ (SD)	$\bar{x}$ (SD)	$\bar{x}$ (SD)
Self-rated health	15 (.35)	.09 (.29)	.28 (.45)	.14 (.35)	.20 (.40)	.11 (.31)
Activity limitations	.31 (.46)	.33 (.47)*	.25 (.44)	.32 (.47)	.61 (.49)	.74 (.44)

Note: * Not significant, otherwise all results significant p<.001.

---

3   In predominantly Arabic-speaking Muslim settings, fathers assume responsible for maintaining their children financially, typically until the children marry. Fathers also are responsible for maintaining a married daughter who becomes separated, divorced, or widowed from her husband.

Future Directions

Given the current and anticipated demographic trends characterizing MENA nations, countries in the region should consider planning to capitalize on the strengths as well as address the challenges associated with having an increasingly older population. Our focus on Algeria, Lebanon and Palestine allowed for a comparative analysis to understand better similarities concerning gender and well-being in the MENA region, as well as where differences arise. Value orientations, as well as longer life expectancies, decreasing birth rates, emigration, economic growth/stagnation and political stability/instability shape experiences of well-being, creating both challenges and opportunities. Below, we identify areas in need of future research with regard to each well-being dimension.

Family relations remain critical for all three countries in the absence of a strong welfare state. Our analysis shows that men are most likely to be married; whereas, women more often are widowed and living alone. The similar gender patterns across countries concerning marriage, widowhood and living alone point to the need for a deeper understanding of these structural proxies for family support (or its absence), especially for women. In particular, a better appreciation of quasi-co-residence and the enactment of intergenerational support across residence may help to interpret gender differences in family structures and, with longitudinal data providing insight into changes over time. For instance, there may be quite a bit more interaction between older adults and their children than indicated by co-residence. A child may be living in the next apartment or in the same building. Such arrangements facilitate transfers between generations (e.g., economic and/or instrumental support), as well as enable close relational ties that become activated in times of need. A focus on quasi-co-residence would permit more detailed insight about well-being among older adults with diverse living arrangements.

Relations both within the family and outside of it represent critical social capital for older adults in the MENA region. The fact men and women reported similarity across countries with regard to social relations (excluding financial support) corroborates the assumptions of patriarchal connectivity (Joseph 1993). That is, overall men and women are relational to similar degrees. Though quantity and prevalence may not vary by gender, future work should explore the nature of social relations in more detail. Our analysis also analyzed gender patterns in social relations with others, extending findings beyond the family context. Gender differences emerge only in Algeria where men report more negativity than women, suggesting factors unique to that country need to be better measured and tested. Indeed, social relations represent an important source of well-being, being a source of both emotional support and irritation. As noted by Sibai and colleagues (2004), strong community based affective ties characterize social relations in this region and so future research should strive to capture the nuance in relationships both within and outside of family, in the quest to uncover a more in-depth understanding of variations in social ties.

Gender gaps in various indicators of socio-economic status for the most part revealed patterns in an expected direction. Overwhelmingly, men reported higher literacy rates than did women and sources of income varied where men more often reported receiving income from retirement/pension and work/properties than did women, though women reported a higher likelihood of receiving income from their children. Later cohorts of women will most likely enter their later years with more education than the current cohort (Yount and Sibai 2009). Nevertheless, the current cohort of older adults may have needs for immediate assistance linked with fewer skills and lower levels of literacy. Furthermore, compared to men, women were more likely to report income sufficiency, except in Lebanon. The lack of gender difference in Lebanon may result from remittance activity related to high patterns of emigration among both men and women (Hourani 2005). Future directions in research would include a detailed focus on the large out-migration of young adults and better understanding the implications of remittances to older adults, especially if such remittances diminish gender gaps in later life as suggested in the Lebanese case.

Finally, gender gaps in health and disability, particularly older women's worse self-rated health and higher prevalence of activity limitations, corroborate findings for other Arab countries (Yount and Sibai 2009) and for other regions around the world (Crimmins, Kim and Sol-Auro 2010). However, some portion of older women's higher rates of activity limitations in the MENA region may result from their much higher rates of obesity than men (Yount 2012). Women's higher rates of obesity may stem from substantially more sedentary lifestyles that are associated with women's historical social roles and restrictions in their mobility (Batnitzky 2008). Aside from altering gender norms that socialize women to adopt more sedentary family roles, a focus on early lifestyle interventions may alleviate the burden of obesity and its sequelae in later life. For instance, promoting exercise, discouraging smoking and promoting a return to more customary diets that reduce high starchy foods may result in a curbing of unhealthy behaviors to reduce burden of disability in later life.

In sum, this chapter provides a comparative "baseline" from which researchers, practitioners and policy-makers can prioritize areas for further research and provide evidence for program planning and policy change, with particular focus on gendered experiences in later life.

References

Ahmed, L. (1992). *Women and Gender in Islam*. New Haven, CT: Yale University Press.

Ajrouch, K. J., Abdulrahim, S. and Antonucci, T. C. (2010). Interpersonal and Sociopolitical Stress over the Life Course. Presented at DIIFSD Conference/Workshop, Linking Research to Policy in the Middle East: Family Ties and Ageing, Beirut, Lebanon, October 19–21.

Anoshua, C. and Kakoli, R. (2009). Gender differences in living arrangements among older persons in India. *Journal of Asian and African Studies* 44(3): 259–77.

Antonucci, T. C. and Jackson, J. S. (1987). Social support, interpersonal efficacy, and health: A life course perspective. In Carstensen and Edelstein (eds) *Handbook of Clinical Gerontology*. Pergamon General Psychology Series, vol. 146, pp. 291–311. Elmsford, NY: Pergamon Press.

Antonucci, T. C., Akiyama, H. and Lansford, J. E. (1998). The negative effects of close social relations among older adults. *Family Relations*, 47, 379–84.

Batnitzky, A. (2008) Obesity and household roles: Gender and social class in Morocco. *Sociology of Health & Illness*, 30(3): 445–62.

Berkman, L. F. and Syme, S. L. (1979). Social networks, host resistance, and mortality: A nine-year follow-up study Alameda county residents. *American Journal of Epidemiology*, 109, 186–204.

Bongaarts, J. and Zimmer, Z. (2002). Living arrangements of older adults in the developing world: An analysis of demographic and health survey household surveys. *The Journal of Gerontology: Medical Sciences*, 57(3), 145–57.

Bougroum, M., Diagne, A. W., Kissami, A. and Tawil, S. (2007). Literacy Policies and Strategies in the Maghreb: Comparative Perspectives from Algeria, Mauritania and Morocco Research paper prepared for the UNESCO Regional Conferences in Support of Global Literacy, retrieved from http://unesdoc.unesco.org/images/0016/001611/161156e.pdf, accessed September 23, 2011.

Chaaban, J. (2010). Job creation in the Arab economies: Navigating through difficult waters, Arab Human Development Report Paper Series, No. 3. New York, NY: UNDP Regional Bureau for Arab States.

Charrad, M. (2001). *States and Women's Rights: The Making of Post-colonial Tunisia, Algeria, and Morocco*. Berkeley: University of California Press.

Charrad, M. (2007). Contexts, Concepts and Contentions: Gender Legislation in the Middle East. *Hawwa: Journal of Women in the Middle East and the Islamic World*, 5(1), 55–72.

Cheriet, B. (2004). Gender as a catalyst of social and political representations in Algeria. *The Journal of North African Studies*, 9(2), 93–101.

Cohen, S. and Syme, S. L. (1985). *Social Support and Health*. New York: Academic Press.

Crimmins, E. M., Kim, J. K. and Sole´-Auro´, A. (2010). Gender differences in health: Results from SHARE, ELSA and HRS. *European Journal of Public Health*, 21(1), 81–91.

Davies, L. (2004). *Education and Conflict: Complexity and Chaos*. New York, NY: Routledge

Di Bartolomeo, A., Jaulin, T. and Perrin, D. (2011). CARIM – Migration Profile Algeria. European University Institute.

Dixon, J. (2000). A global perspective on social security: Programs for the aged. *Journal of Ageing & Social Policy*, 11(1), 39–66.

Douglass, R. L. and McGadney-Douglass, B. F. (2008). The role of grandmothers and older women in the survival of children with Kwashiorkor in urban Accra, Ghana. *Research in Human Development*, 5(1), 1–18.

Doyal, L. and Gough, I. (1991). *Theory of Human Need*. Basingstoke: Palgrave Macmillan.

Durkheim, E. (1951). *Suicide*. New York: Free Press.

Elder, G. H. and Liker, J. K. (1982). Hard times in women's lives: Historical influences across forty years. *The American Journal of Sociology*, 88(2), 241–69.

Engelman, M., Agree, E. M., Yount, K. M. and Bishai, D. (2010). Parity and parents' health in later life: The gendered case of Ismailia, Egypt. *Population Studies*, 64(2), 165–78.

Fargues, P. (2005). Women in Arab countries: Challenging the patriarchal system? *Reproductive Health Matters*, 13(25), 43–8.

Firebaugh, G. and Goesling, B. (2004). Accounting for the recent decline in global income inequality. *American Journal of Sociology*, 110(2), 283–312.

Frankenberg, E., Chan, A. and Ofstedal, M.B. (2002). Stability and change in living arrangements in Indonesia, Singapore and Taiwan, 1993–99. *Population Studies*, 56(2), 201–13.

Frisch, H. (1998). *Countdown to Statehood: Palestinian State Formation in the West Bank and Gaza*. Albany, NY: State University of New York Press.

George, L. K. (2006). Perceived quality of life. In R. H. Binstock and L. K. George (eds) *Handbook of Ageing and the Social Sciences*, 6th edition. Amsterdam: Academic Press, 321–38.

Greve, W. and Bjorklund, D. F. (2008). The Nestor-Effect: Extending Evolutionary Developmental Psychology to a Lifespan Perspective. Paper presented at the biennial meetings of the International Society for the Study of Human Development, Wurzberg, Germany, July 13–17.

Hammoud, H. R. (2006). Illiteracy in the Arab World. Adult Education and Development 66. Retrieved from http://www.iiz-dvv.de/index.php?article_id=208&clang=1, accessed September 23, 2011.

Hasan, F., AlAwlaqi, A., AlYaqout, T. and AlGharaballi, T. (2011). *MENA Economic Overview*. Global Research-MENA.

Hourani, G. (2005). Emigration, Transnational Family Networks, and Remittances: Overview of the Situation in Lebanon. Retrieved from http://www.ndu.edu.lb/Lerc/publications/Emigration%20and%20Remittances-%20The%20Case%20of%20Lebanon.pdf, accessed September 23, 2011.

Houria, S. (2007). Education – work and gender in Algeria. *Africa Development*, 32(3), 121–30.

House, J. S., Landis, K. R. and Umberson, D. (1988). Social relationships and health. *Science*, 241, 540–45.

Iacovou, M. (2000). The Living Arrangements of Elderly Europeans. Working Paper 2000–09, Institute for Social and Economic Research, University of

Essex, Colchester, United Kingdom. Retrieved from http://www.iser.essex.ac.uk/pubs/workpaps/pdf/2000-09.pdf, accessed November 2008.

Jabbour, S., Yamout, R., Hilal, J. and Nehmeh, A. (2012). The Political, Economic and Social Context. In S. Jabbour, R. Giacaman, M. Khawaja and I. Nuwayhid (eds) *Public Health in the Arab World*. Cambridge, UK: Cambridge University Press, pp 21-34.

Jansen, W. (2004). The economy of religious merit: Women and ajr in Algeria. *The Journal of North African Studies*, 9(4), 1–17.

Joseph, S. (1993). Connectivity and Patriarchy among Urban Working-Class Arab Families in Lebanon. *Ethos*, 21(4), 452–84.

Kandiyoti, D. (1988). Bargaining with patriarchy. *Gender & Society*, 2, 274–90.

Khadr, Z. and Yount, K.M. (forthcoming). Reported Disability among Older Women and Men in Ismailia, Egypt. *Journal of Gerontology: Social Sciences*.

Khalidi, R. (2007). *The Iron Cage: The Story of the Palestinian Struggle for Statehood*. Boston, MA: Beacon Press.

Kinsella, K. and Velkoff, V.A. (2001). An Ageing World: 2001. US Census Bureau P95/01-1, US Government Printing Office, Washington DC. Washington, DC: US Government Printing Office.

Knodel, J. and Ofstedal, M.B. (2003). Gender and ageing in the developing world: Where are the men? *Population and Development Review*, 29(4), 677–98.

Kramarow, E. A. (1995). The elderly who live alone in the United States: Historical perspectives on household change. *Demography*, 32(3), 335–52.

Lamb, V. L. (1997). Gender differences in correlates of disablement among the elderly in Egypt. *Social Science and Medicine*, 45(1), 127–36.

Lee, Y. -J. and Palloni, A. (1992). Changes in the family status of elderly women in Korea. *Demography*, 29(1), 69–92.

Lloyd, C. B., Behrman, J. Stromquist, N.P. and Cohen, B. (eds.) *The Changing Transitions to Adulthood in Developing Countries: Selected Studies*. Washington, DC: National Academies Press.

Luescher, K. and Pillemer, K. (1998). Intergenerational ambivalence: A new approach to the study of parent-child relations in later life. *Journal of Marriage and the Family*, 60, 413–25.

Mahasneh, S. M. (2000). Survey of the health of the elderly in Jordan. *Medical Journal of Islamic Academy of Sciences*, 13(1), 39–48.

Mancunovich, D. J., Easterline, R. A., Crimmins, E. M. and Schaeffer, C. M. (1995). Echoes of the baby boom and bust: recent and prospective changes in living alone among elderly widows in the United States. *Demography*, 32(1), 17–28.

Mansour, H. (2010). The effects of labor supply shocks on labor market outcomes: Evidence from the Israeli–Palestinian conflict. *Labor Economics*, 17(6), 930–39.

Mba, C. J. (2007). Gender disparities in living arrangements of older people in Ghana: Evidence from the 2003 Ghana demographic and health survey. *Journal of International Women's Studies*, 9(1), 153–66.

Moghadam, V. (2004). Patriarchy in transition: Women and the changing family in the Middle East. *Journal of Comparative Family Studies*, 35, 137–62.

Moghadam, V. M. (2003). Engendering citizenship, feminizing civil society: The case of the Middle East and North Africa. *Women and Politics*, 25, 63–86.

Murthy, R. S. and Lakshminarayana, R. (2006). Mental health consequences of war: A brief review of research findings. *World Psychiatry*, 5(1), 25–30.

National Institute on Ageing, National Institutes of Health & US Department of Health and Human Services. (2007). Why population ageing matters: A global perspective. Retrieved from http://www.nia.nih.gov/research/publication/why-population-aging-matters-global-perspective, accessed August 30, 2012.

National_Reports/Arab%20States/Palestine.pdf, accessed November 23, 2011.

Offenhauer, P. (2005). *Women in Islamic Societies: A Selected Review of Social Scientific Literature.* Washington, DC: The Library of Congress. Retrieved from http://www.loc.gov/rr/frd/pdf-files/WomenIslamic_Societies.pdf, accessed December 26, 2006.

Olmsted, J. C. (2005). Gender, ageing, and the evolving patriarchal contract. *Feminist Economics*, 11(2), 53–78.

Olmsted, J. C. (2011). Norms, economic conditions and household formation: A case study of the Arab world. *This History of the Family*, 16, 401–15.

Palloni, A., Pinto, G. and Wong, R. (2009). Family support networks and population ageing. Paper presented at the seminar on family Support Networks and Population Ageing, Doha International Institute for Family Studies and Development, UNFPA and Institute for Policy Research, Northwestern University, Doha, Qatar, June 3–4.

Ross, M. L. (2008). Oil, Islam, and women. *American Political Science Review*, 102(1), 107–23.

Rought-Brooks, H., Duaibis, S. and Hussein, S. (2010). Palestinian women caught in the crossfire between occupation and patriarchy. *Feminist Formations*, 22(3), 124–45.

Roy, S. (1999). De-development revisited: Palestinian economy and society since Oslo. *Journal of Palestine Studies*, 28(3), 64–82.

Roy, S. (2001). Palestinian Society and Economy: The Continued Denial of Possibility. *Journal of Palestine Studies*, 30(4), 5–20.

Ruger, J. P. and Kim, H. J. (2006). Global health inequalities: An international comparison. *Journal of Epidemiology and Community Health*, 60(11), 928–36.

Sabbah, I., Le Vuitton, D. A., Droubi, N. et al. (2007). Morbidity and associated factors in rural and urban populations of South Lebanon: A cross-sectional community-based study of self-reported health in 2000. *Tropical Medicine and International Health*, 12(8), 907–19.

Shah, N. M., Yount, K. M., Shah, M. A. and Menon, I. (2002). Living arrangements of older women and men in Kuwait. *Journal of Cross-Cultural Gerontology*, 17(1), 37–55.

Shehada, N. Y. (2004). Uncodified justice: Women negotiating family law and customary practice in Palestine. *Development*, 47(1), 103–108.

Shehadeh, L. R. (ed.) (1999). *Women and War in Lebanon*. Gainsville, FL: University Press of Florida.

Shehadeh, L. R. (2010). Gender-relevant legal change in Lebanon. *Feminist Formations*, 22(3), 210–28.

Sibai, A. M., Fletcher, A. and Armenian, H. K. (2001). Variations in the impact of long-term wartime stressors on mortality among the middle-aged and older population in Beirut, Lebanon, 1983–1993. *American Journal of Epidemiology*, 154(2), 128–37.

Sibai, A. M., Kanaan, M. N., Chaaya, M. and Campbell, O. M. R. (2007). Mortality among married older adults in the suburbs of Beirut: Estimates from offspring data. *Bulletin World Health Organization*, 85, 482–6.

Sibai, A. M., Sen, K., Beydoun, M. and Saxena, P. (2004). Population ageing in Lebanon: Current status, future prospects and implications for policy. *Bulletin World Health Organization*, 82, 219–25.

Sibai, A.M., Tohme, R., Yount, K. et al. (2012). The older Arab – From veneration to vulnerability? In S. Jabbour, R. Giacaman, M. Khawaja and I. Nuwayhid (eds) *Public Health in the Arab World*. Cambridge, UK: Cambridge University Press, 264–75.

Tabutin, D. and Schoumaker, B. (2005). The demography of the Arab world and the Middle East from the 1950s to the 2000s. A survey of changes and a statistical assessment. *Population-E*, 60, 505–615.

The Hong Kong Council of Social Services. (2009). Elderly services in Hong Kong. Retrieved from www.hkcss.org.hk/download/folder/el/el_eng.doc, accessed August 30, 2012.

The World Bank. (2010). Country Brief. Retrieved from http://go.worldbank.org/Q8OGMLXI40, accessed December 14, 2011.

The World Bank. (2011). Data [by country]. Retrieved from http://data.worldbank.org/country/, accessed August 30, 2012.

The World Bank. (2011). *World Development Indicators: 2011*. Washington, DC: Green Press Initiative.

The World Bank. (n.d.). Why Some MENA Countries Did Better than Others. Retrieved from http://siteresources.worldbank.org/INTMENA/Resources/EDU_06-Chap06-Education.pdf, accessed September 23, 2011.

The World Bank. (n.d.) World Databank: World development indicators (WDI) & global development finance (GDF). Retrieved from http://databank.worldbank.org/ddp/home.do, accessed September 5, 2012.

Tohme, R.A., Yount, K.M., Yassine, S. et al. (2011). Socioeconomic resources and living arrangements of older adults in Lebanon: Who chooses to live alone? *Ageing & Society*, 30, 1–17.

Turshen, M. (2002). Algerian women in the Liberation Struggle and The Civil War: From active participants to passive victims? *Social Research: An International Quarterly*, 69(3), 889–911.

UNDP. (n.d.). The Millennium Development Goals in Lebanon. Retrieved from http://www.undp.org.lb/WhatWeDo/MDGs.cfm, accessed November 12, 2011.

UNIFEM. (2004). *Progress of Arab Women*. Amman, Jordan.
United Nations Data. (2008). *United Nations Statistics Division* [Country profile]. Retrieved from http://data.un.org/CountryProfile.aspx, accessed August 30, 2012.
United Nations Statistics Division. (n.d.) Demographic and Social Statistics. Retrieved from http://unstats.un.org/unsd/demographic/products/socind/default.htm, accessed September 5, 2012.
US Social Security Administration (2011). Social Security Programs Throughout the World: Africa, 2011. Research, Statistics and Policy analysis. Retrieved from https://www.socialsecurity.gov/policy/docs/progdesc/ssptw/2010-2011/africa/algeria.html, accessed August 28, 2012
Westoff, C. (2003). *Trends in Marriage and Early Childbearing in Developing Countries. DHS Comparative Reports 5*. Calverton, MD: ORC Macro.
World Stat. (2011). Retrieved from http://en.worldstat.info/, accessed August 30, 2012.
Yi, Z. and Wang, Z. (2003). Dynamics of family and elderly living arrangements in China: New lessons learned from the 2000 census. *The China Review*, 3(2), 95–119.
Yount, K. M. (2005). The patriarchal bargain and intergenerational co-residence in Egypt. *The Sociological Quarterly*, 46(1), 137–64.
Yount, K. M. (2012). Gender Disparities in Health. In S. Jabbour, R. Giacaman, M. Khawaja and I. Nuwayhid (eds) *Public Health in the Arab World*. Cambridge, UK: Cambridge University Press, 89–105.
Yount, K. M. and Agree, E. (2005). Differences in disability between older women and men in Egypt and Tunisia. *Demography*, 42(1), 169–87.
Yount, K. M. and Khadr, Z. (2008). Gender, social change and living arrangements among older Egyptians during the 1990s. *Population Research and Policy Review*, 27(1), 201–25.
Yount, K. M. and Sibai, A. M. (2009). Demography of Ageing in Arab Countries. In P. Uhlenberg (ed.) *International Handbook of Population Ageing*. Dordrecht, The Netherlands: Springer, 227–315.
Yount, K. M., Agree, E. and Rebellon, C. (2004). Gender and use of formal care among older adults in Egypt and Tunisia. *Social Science and Medicine*, 59, 2479–97.
Yount, K. M., Cunningham, S., Engelman, M. and Agree, E. (2012). Gender and Material Transfers between Older Parents and Children in Ismailia, Egypt. *Journal of Marriage and Family*, 74(1), 116–31.
Youssef, R. M. (2005). Comprehensive health assessment of senior citizens in Al-Karak governorate, Jordan. *East Mediterranean Health Journal*, 11(3), 334–48.
Zeki Al Hazzouri, A. G. (2006). Gender differences in reported physical disability among older adults in three underprivileged communities in the suburbs of Beirut. Unpublished Master's Thesis, American University of Beirut, Lebanon.

Zurayk, H., Sholkamy, H., Younis, N. and Khattab, H. (1997). Women's health problems in the Arab world: A holistic policy prospective. *International Journal of Gynecology & Obstetrics*, 58(1), 13–21.

Zunzunegui, M.V., Minicuci, N., Blumstein, T. et al. (2007). Gender differences in depressive symptoms among older adults: A cross-national comparison. The CLESA project. *Social Psychiatry and Psychiatric Epidemiology*, 42(3), 198–207.

Chapter 5
A Global Perspective on Physiological Change with Age

Eileen Crimmins, Felicia Wheaton, Sarinnapha Vasunilashorn, Hiram Beltrán-Sánchez, Lu Zhang and Jung Ki Kim

In Western countries, we think of certain physiological changes as part of normal "ageing." The idea that the levels of blood pressure and cholesterol rise, that weight increases, that functioning decreases is viewed as part of the ageing process. These physiological changes are monitored by physicians and health systems, and are associated with a significant portion of the use of prescription drugs. Physiological changes associated with age not only contribute to chronic disease, but also lead to disability, diminished quality of life and ultimately, mortality. Yet while ageing is inevitable, it is necessary to question whether the physiological changes we associate with ageing are the result of innate human biology and to what extent physiological age changes are shaped by the social environments in which we live.

In this chapter, we examine global differences in a number of markers of ageing to show that there are many patterns of physiological differences with age depending on environmental, cultural, economic, medical and historical circumstances. The observed differences highlight that what we regard as the ageing process is not consistent across countries and is very influenced by environmental circumstances. The differences that we observe suggest that these processes may be changing rapidly in much of the world and that much of what we have assumed to be normal physiological changes with ageing may reflect the environmental circumstances in modern Western or American society. These societies have undergone demographic and economic revolutions that are now ongoing in the rest of the world where newly ageing populations have lived through the entire economic and demographic transition.

Recently, a number of nationally representative surveys of ageing populations have added biomarkers to their data collections. The inclusion of measured physiology in social surveys allows for the comparison of markers of health which cannot be reported accurately by respondents in many circumstances. The ability to compare these measured indicators across societies allows us to make generalizations about ageing that have, heretofore, not been possible. To investigate whether physiological changes with age are universal, we examine age differences in a number of markers of physiological dysregulation associated with ageing across a range of populations including Japan, the United States (US), England, Taiwan, two provinces in China, Mexico, Indonesia and the Tsimane of

Bolivia. The synthesis of findings from different countries can lead to a deeper understanding of how physiological changes are shaped by social, economic and epidemiological factors. Different environmental contexts can serve as natural laboratories to explore how different combinations of macro-level and micro-level factors influence health in later life.

Data and Methods

Data Sources

We use data on measured biomarkers from recent surveys of national populations or extensive national sub populations to examine current age- and gender-specific patterns of blood pressure, body mass index, cholesterol and glycosylated hemoglobin (HbA1c). Data sets include the US National Health and Nutrition Examination Survey (NHANES) 2001–2006, the English Longitudinal Study of Ageing (ELSA 2004), the China Health and Retirement Longitudinal Pilot Study of two provinces Gansu and Zhejiang (CHARLS 2008), the Social Environment Biomarkers of Aging Study (SEBAS) in Taiwan (2000), the Indonesian Family Life Survey (IFLS 2007–2008), the Mexican Family Life Survey (MxFLS 2002), Mexico- National Health and Nutrition Survey (ENSANUT 2006),[1] Japanese National Health and Nutrition Survey (2004) and the Tsimane Health and Life History Project (2003–2007). For most populations, we have measures on adults age 20 and over, with the exception of China, England and Taiwan, where the sample includes individuals over age 50.

Our set of studies includes information from a wide range of countries at different stages of their demographic transitions; from the world's longest lived population – the Japanese – to a pretransitional short-lived foraging population in Bolivia – the Tsimane. In 2005, Japanese males and females lived on average 79 years and 85.7 years, respectively (Figure 5.1). At the other end of the continuum, the Tsimane are forager-farmers of the Bolivian Amazon with short adult life expectancy (42.6 years, estimated from 1950–1989) relative to other countries (Gurven et al. 2008). They represent a model for ageing in preindustrial human populations due to their high infectious morbidity and natural fertility (Walker et al. 2008), variable energy balance with high workloads and short life expectancies. After Japan, England has the next highest life expectancy. While life expectancy in Taiwan is now similar to that of the US (76 and 81 years for males and females, respectively), Taiwan has undergone a much more recent and rapid epidemiological and demographic transition. Mexico, China and Indonesia are countries that are in the process of rapid changes in nutrition and income accompanied by increases in life expectancy.

---

1 Figures 5.2, 5.2, 5.3, 5.4 and 5.5 use data from the MxFLS. Figures 5.6, 5.7 and 5.8 use data from ENSANUT.

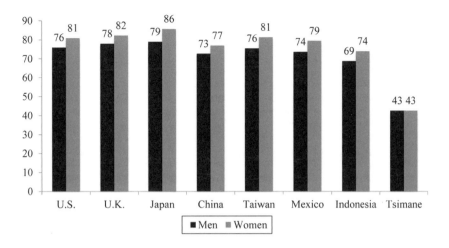

Figure 5.1 Life expectancy at birth, 2011
Note: Data from 1950–1989 calculated by Gurven et al. 2008.
Source: World Factbook, 2011 by CIA.

Measurement of Physiological Status

In large-scale population studies, the commonly collected biomarkers related to physiological ageing usually reflect cardiovascular functioning and metabolic indicators. The surveys we use have collected measured anthropometric indicators of height and weight, measured blood pressure from which we can elicit systolic blood pressure (SBP), diastolic blood pressure (DBP) and pulse pressure (PP), which is the difference between SBP and DBP. Pulse pressure reflects stiffness and inflammation in the blood vessels and some research has suggested that pulse pressure is a better indicator than either SBP or DBP of cardiovascular risk among the old (Blacher et al. 2000, Crimmins et al. 2008, Franklin et al. 2001).

Many studies that have collected blood samples have indicators of lipid levels including total cholesterol and high-density lipoprotein (HDL) cholesterol. Because most of these population samples do not have the subjects fast before collection, low-density lipoprotein (LDL) cholesterol is not recorded. We also examine the ratio of total cholesterol to HDL cholesterol as some research has suggested it is the ratio of the two, rather than the independent levels, that is important (Crimmins et al. 2008). A limited number of countries have information on HbA1c, which is an indicator of blood glucose concentration over the past few months. This can serve as an indicator of the presence of diabetes, prediabetes, or the control of diabetes among diabetics.

In each country, we examine the average level of markers or the percent (prevalence) of the population above the clinically determined level for defining risk for age-sex groups within a population (See Figures for definitions). For the measure of pulse pressure and the ratio measure of total/HDL cholesterol we show levels by age rather than percent elevated. We also examine the links between prevalence of risk levels of these markers and life expectancy, urbanization and per capita gross domestic product in these populations.

Age Differences in Physiological Markers

While we are interested in physiological change with age, we examine cross-sectional differences in physiological markers by age. Longitudinal data, which in most cases we do not have, would be required to look at individual change with age. We are cognizant that while age differences may be due to changes in physiology with age, they could also result from cohort differences in physiology or to differential survival of the most physiologically healthy into the oldest ages. Many physiological measures change in a predictable manner with age, others are less predictable; some biomarkers increase or decrease with age, while others follow a U-shaped pattern with respect to age differences (Glei et al. 2011). In the following sections we examine each set of markers in turn; first the cardiovascular markers and then the metabolic indicators.

Blood Pressure

Normal arterial ageing, including thickening and stiffening of arterial walls, leads to an increase in systolic blood pressure with age, even in the absence of cardiovascular disease (Finch 2007). Between age 20 and 80, systolic blood pressure has been shown to increase by about 22% (O'Rourke and Nichols 2005); however, not all research indicates that blood pressure increases in populations throughout the age range. Examination of age differences in SBP in the US population shows that increases in SBP occur in middle age but that in old age the level of SBP in the population plateaus (Crimmins et al. 2006). A longitudinal study by Glei and colleagues (2011), studying people age 45 and over in Taiwan, found little age-related increase in SBP over 6 years, which they attribute to the period effect of increased use of anti-hypertensive medication.

In contrast, diastolic blood pressure is thought to follow an inverse U-shape with age (Franklin et al. 1997). Diastolic blood pressure has been observed to increase until age 55 and then decrease after age 60 (Yashin et al. 2006). As DBP decreases at older ages and SBP continues to increase, there is generally an age-related increase in the prevalence of high pulse pressure (Skumick, Aladjem and Aviv 2010). The age changes may not be the same among all groups in the population; at the younger years DBP among women is lower than that of men, but it increases more rapidly with age (Yashin et al. 2006) and in the US high blood pressure among older adults over age 70 is greater among women than men (Kim et al. 2006). Average pulse pressure has been shown to more than double between age 20 and 80 (O'Rourke and Nichols 2005).

Blood pressure varies across countries and has been shown to change over time within countries. Generally, in comparison to industrialized populations, traditional populations and less urbanized societies have lower levels of blood pressure, less increase in blood pressure with age and lower rates of hypertension (Gurven et al. 2009, Ostfeld and D'Atri 1977, Page 1976, Pavan et al. 1997, Poulter and Sever 1994, Waldron et al. 1982). It is clear, however, that a number of characteristics contribute to variability in blood pressure across populations including salt intake and culture (Waldron et al. 1982). It has been suggested that the link between industrialization and blood pressure may result from changes in social organization and structure that accompany industrialization (Carvalho et al. 1985, Cassel 1975, Epstein and Eckoff 1967, Lowenstein 1961, Marmot 1980, McGarvey and Baker 1979, Patrick et al. 1983, Prior and Stanhope 1980, Waldron et al. 1982). Overall levels of blood pressure and its increase with age, have been shown to be higher in people with more involvement in money economy, greater economic competition and more contact with individuals of different beliefs and cultures (Cooper et al. 1997, Waldron et al. 1982).

Figures 5.2 and 5.3 show the prevalence of men and women with hypertensive levels of SBP and DBP. Mexico, Indonesia and Japan have the highest prevalence of hypertension, while the US has relatively low hypertension, which is at least partly related to extensive use of medication to control blood pressure in the US (Crimmins et al. 2010). The Tsimane have almost no high systolic blood pressure even at older ages. More generally it has been reported that arterial disease is much lower in the Tsimane than among US adults (Gurven et al. 2009, Vasunilashorn et al. 2010). Countries with higher prevalence of high SBP (Figure 5.2) also have a higher prevalence of high DBP (Figure 5.3). High-risk levels of DBP are more common in Mexico, Indonesia, Japan and Taiwan than in the US or England or among the Tsimane (Figure 5.3).

If we did not include the Tsimane in our comparison, we might conclude that the substantial increase in high SBP was universal. However, the fact that high blood pressure is rare among the Tsimane suggests that contextual, social and dietary factors also play an important role. Also, some of the highest prevalences of high systolic and diastolic blood pressure in both sexes are observed in Mexico and Indonesia, countries with relatively low levels of income compared to the US, Japan and England. Both countries have undergone rapid epidemiologic and nutrition transitions in the past several decades and these risk factors seem to be more prevalent at younger ages than in more developed countries. Finally, there appears to be variation between countries not only in the absolute prevalence of high systolic and diastolic blood pressure at a given age, but also substantial variation in the shape and inflection points of the age trends.

Mean pulse pressure with age increases in all countries and the pattern of increase with age are quite similar across countries (Figure 5.4). At the younger ages, the differences across countries are quite small but they increase with age and are quite large at the oldest ages. The countries with high pulse pressure include Indonesia and Mexico; on the other hand, the Tsimane have relatively low pulse pressure.

Men

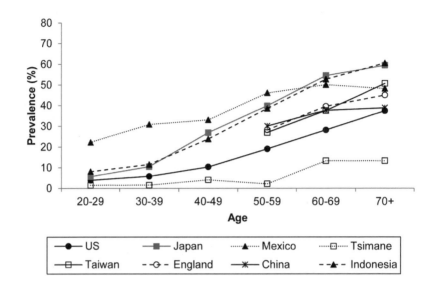

Women

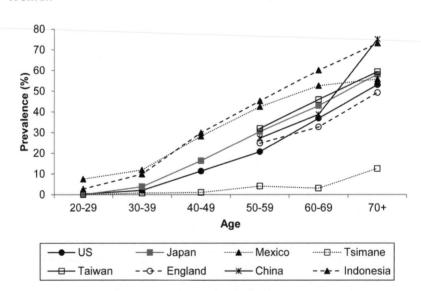

Figure 5.2 Percent with high systolic blood pressure ($\geq$ 140 mm Hg) by country and sex

A Global Perspective on Physiological Change with Age

Men

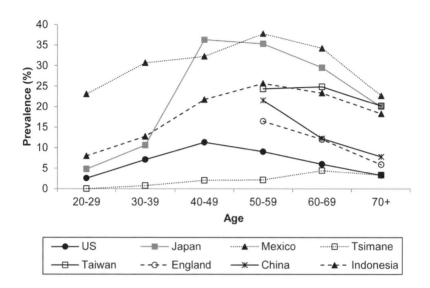

Women

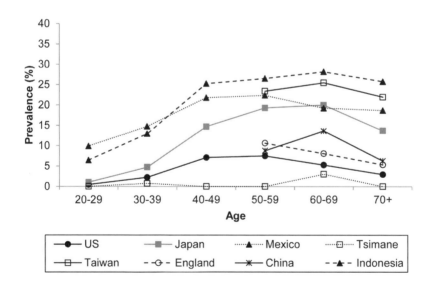

Figure 5.3 Percent with diastolic blood pressure (≥ 90 mm Hg) by country and sex

Men

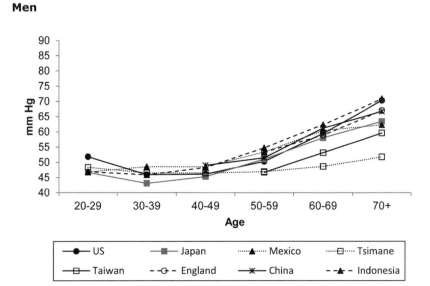

Women

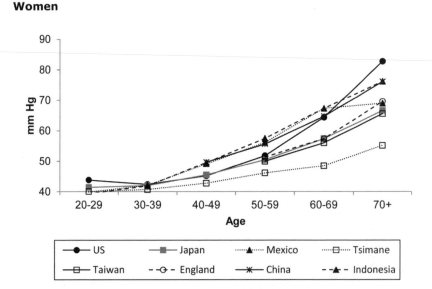

Figure 5.4 Mean pulse pressure by country and sex

Body Mass Index

In general, body mass index (BMI) and the prevalence of overweight and obesity in populations have been found to increase until about 60 years of age, after which weight tends to decline (Seidell et al. 2000). Most studies on BMI changes with age are cross-sectional and therefore, while this pattern may be due to age changes, cohort differences in BMI and selective survival of those with lower BMI could also explain the observed lower BMI level at older ages. Several studies have in fact documented that later cohorts have a higher BMI at a given age compared to older cohorts at the same age (Juhaeri et al. 2003, Nooyens et al. 2008, Sheehan et al. 2003). There is also evidence that links obesity in early and mid life to earlier mortality (Lewis et al. 2009). For example, results from a life-table analysis of data from the Framingham Heart Study show that at age 40, obese non-smokers had a life expectancy of about 6 to 7 years shorter than those who were not obese (Peters et al. 2003). Lower survival among the obese could help explain the suggestion that cross-sectional studies underestimate the association between BMI and mortality (Nooyens et al. 2008).

BMI has been shown to be lower in traditional than in industrialized populations and to increase with gross domestic product (GDP) (Pavan et al. 1997, Strauss and Thomas 2007). It has also been shown to have increased over time in most countries. Many studies, from Africa and Asia to the Americas and Europe, have observed increasing numbers of overweight and obese individuals. These increases have been associated with dietary changes occurring across geography, culture and stage of development (Galal 2002, Kosulwat 2002, McHiza and Steyn 2011, Misra et al. 2011, Misra, Singhai and Khurana 2010, Pomerleau et al. 2003, Popkin 2010, Rivera et al. 2002, Neila et al. 2011). The rise in urban living, international trade and global economic integration has brought wide availability of cheap processed food, fast food, sweeteners and edible oils. Concurrent improvements in standard of living and household income, especially among rapidly developing nations, have resulted in personal dietary changes including the reduction of vegetable and fruit consumption and the increase in animal-sourced foods (Misra et al. 2011, Popkin 2001, 2008, Popkin, Lu and Zhai 2002).

The prevalence of overweight (BMI^3 25kg/m^2) by age group, sex and country is shown in Figure 5.5. In most country populations, it appears that BMI increases until middle age, i.e. about age 45 and then decreases later in life. There are clearly two groups of countries in Figure 5.5. People in Mexico, the US and England are far more likely to be overweight than in the other countries. On the other hand, the prevalence of overweight is relatively low in the Asian countries and among the Tsimane. Japanese women are particularly unlikely to be overweight although the prevalence has a faster increase with age than in any other country. Among men, Indonesians are the least likely to be overweight across all ages.

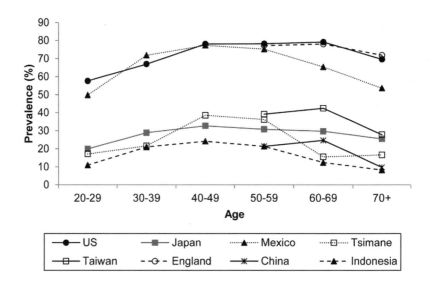
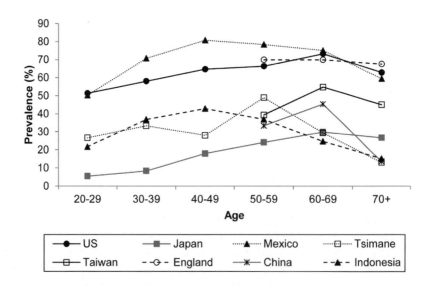

Figure 5.5 Percent overweight (body mass index ≥ 25 kg/m²) by country and sex

Cholesterol

Total cholesterol has been recognized as having an inverted U pattern with age in both cross-sectional and longitudinal studies. Studies based on the US show that total cholesterol tends to increase until approximately age 50 among men and age 60 among women (Schubert et al. 2005). In women, total cholesterol then plateaus until about age 70 after which it declines, while in men, total cholesterol begins to decline at age 50 and declines at an accelerating rate after age 70 (Yashin et al. 2006).

National differences in total cholesterol may be linked to both diet and epidemiological conditions. Increases in calorie intake, particularly intake of saturated fats, have been associated with higher cholesterol levels (Clarke et al. 1997, Mattson, Erikson and Kligman 1972). In subsistence populations, where food containing high saturated fats is less available than in modern societies, cholesterol levels are lower (Expert Panel on Detection Evaluation and Treatment of High Blood Cholesterol in Adults 2001, Gurven et al. 2009, Lindeberg et al. 2003, Pauletto et al. 1996, Pavan et al. 1997). While in general, cholesterol levels among the global ageing population are rising, this escalation is most drastic among rapidly developing nations due to increases in high-fat diets. Less developed nations are experiencing growing cholesterol levels in highly urbanized areas, while these levels have general stabilized or dropped in developed nations due to greater health education and awareness of the effects of diet (Deaton et al. 2011, Levenson, Skerret and Gaziano 2002). The Tsimane, who still have high levels of infection in their population, should have relatively low levels of cholesterol as infection typically lowers both total cholesterol and high density lipoprotein (HDL) cholesterol (Finch 2007, Vasunilashorn et al. 2010).

Measured high total cholesterol is highest among English men and Chinese and English women (Figure 5.6). It is exceptionally low, or almost non-existent, among the Tsimane. The other countries have roughly similar levels although Indonesia and Taiwan are on the low side. The US has moderate values; however, it is important to note that the US is the country where measured cholesterol is most likely to be reduced by the use of drugs. Young Japanese women have very low levels of high cholesterol but the increase with age is sharp in this group. For men, most of the increase with age in total cholesterol occurs before age 40–49; for women, the increase continues to older years as shown in earlier literature (Kim et al. 2006).

National differences in low HDL cholesterol are not the same for women and men (Figure 5.7). In Indonesia, men have very high prevalence of low HDL cholesterol; Japan, China and England have low levels. Among women, Mexico, Indonesia and the Tsimane are quite high in adverse levels of HDL. HDL is the lipid we expect to be more related to infection and this may be more true for women than for men. Among women, adverse levels of HDL cholesterol are low in the US, Japan and China. There is no pattern of increase with age in adverse levels of HDL cholesterol in any of the countries.

90 *Global Ageing in the Twenty-First Century*

Men

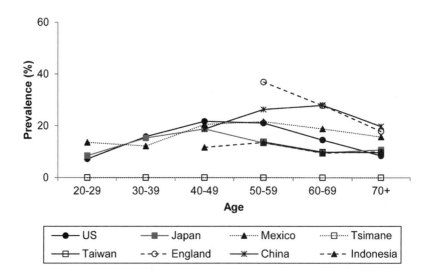

Women

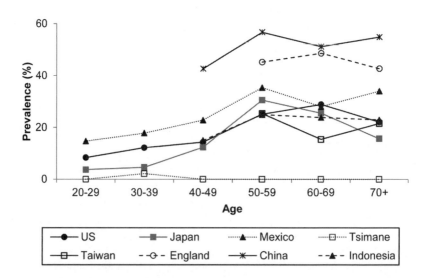

Figure 5.6 Percent with high total cholesterol (≥ 240 mg/dl) by country and sex

A Global Perspective on Physiological Change with Age 91

Men

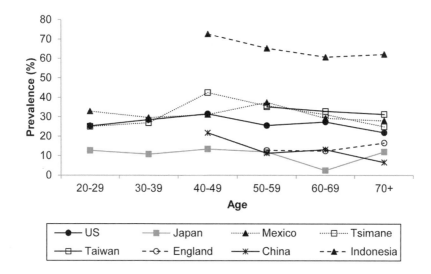

Women

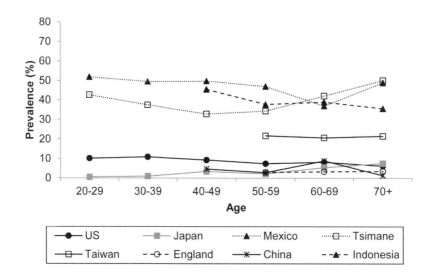

Figure 5.7 Percent with low HDL cholesterol (< 40 mg/dl) by country and sex

Men

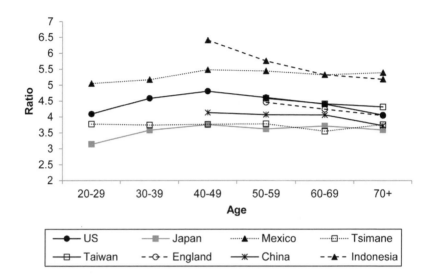

Women

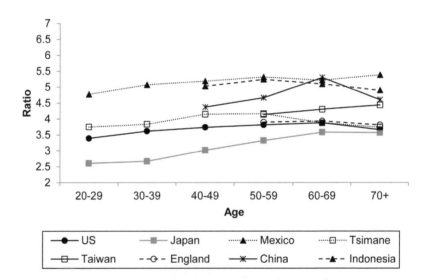

Figure 5.8 Mean total/HDL cholesterol (mg/dl) ratio by country and sex

Men

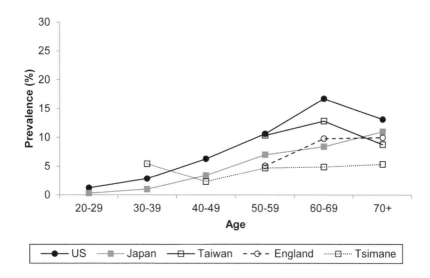

Women

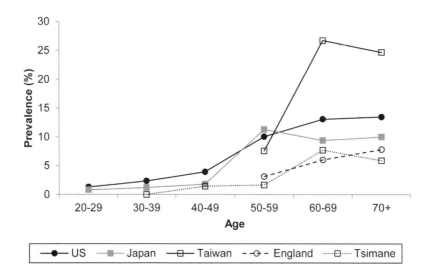

Figure 5.9 Percent with high glycosylated hemoglobin (≥ 6.4%) by country and sex

We also present the ratio of total to HDL cholesterol (Figure 5.8). There is little pattern of age change in this ratio, except among Japanese women. The age pattern for total/HDL cholesterol is more similar across all countries than the patterns observed for the independent measures of total cholesterol (Figure 5.6) and HDL cholesterol (Figure 5.7). The ratio is, however, particularly high among Indonesians and Mexicans.

Glycosylated Hemoglobin (HbA1c)

The prevalence of diabetes mellitus increases with age, at least up to the older ages, and many studies find a positive association between age and blood glucose and HbA1c (Chiu, Martinez and Chu 2005, Pani et al. 2008, Yashin et al. 2006). National differences in insulin regulation may also arise from diet and weight differences. Insulin regulation may be affected by increasing weight and increasing food consumption. Increases in diabetes have been noted in many countries undergoing industrialization (Zheng et al. 2009). The prevalence of type 2 diabetes has surged across older populations worldwide (Jia et al. 2002, Misra, Singhai and Khurana 2010, Rivera et al. 2002).

We have information on HbA1c from only five populations: the US, Japan, Taiwan, England and the Tsimane. The Tsimane generally have very low prevalence of elevated HbA1c (Figure 5.9). English women also have relatively low levels. Countries with high adverse levels of HbA1c also differ for men and women. The United States and Taiwan are high for men; among women, Taiwan is exceptionally high particularly at older ages.

Social Indicators

We hypothesized that physiological changes with age are not only the result of biological ageing, but are also influenced by social processes that vary considerably across countries. We examine correlations between country-level indicators of social and economic development and the average prevalence or level of each of the biomarkers discussed above for the 50–59 age group by sex. We choose to examine the rates for those aged 50 to 59 because biological risk at these ages tends to have risen from values found among younger age groups, yet selective mortality is not as extensive as that which has occurred among older age groups. Correlations were not calculated for the prevalence of high HbA1c because this measure was only collected in five of the eight studies. The Tsimane were excluded from the correlations because they are an extreme outlier in terms of life expectancy and data are not available on the other social indicators.

To examine the association between social factors and biological measures in the fifth decade, we employ the following country-level indicators: life expectancy, per capita gross domestic product and percent urban (CIA 2011). Higher levels of these indicators signify greater development and a later stage in demographic and epidemiologic transition.

In general, the correlations in Table 5.1 suggest that life expectancy is negatively associated with most measures of biological risk, although the relationship appears stronger for some measures than others. For instance, there is a fairly high negative correlation between life expectancy and the prevalence of low HDL cholesterol, particularly in men ($r = -0.77$) and the ratio of total to HDL cholesterol in both men and women ($r = -0.74$ and $r = -0.85$, respectively). Among women, mean pulse pressure and prevalence of high SBP are negatively correlated with life expectancy, but this relationship is much weaker among men. The exception to the negative relationships is the positive relationship between life expectancy and the percent overweight among men ($r = 0.42$).

Table 5.1 Correlations between social indicators and biological measures

	Life expectancy	GDP	Urban
Men			
Prevalence of high SBP	-0.25	-0.62	-0.23
Prevalence of high DBP	-0.07	-0.45	-0.17
Mean pulse pressure	-0.41	-0.58	-0.31
Prevalence of overweight	0.42	0.53	0.93
Prevalence of high total cholesterol	0.26	0.08	0.38
Prevalence of low HDL cholesterol	-0.77	-0.44	-0.36
Ratio of total/HDL cholesterol	-0.74	-0.47	-0.12
Prevalence of high SBP or medication	**0.07**	**-0.12**	**0.31**
N	7	7	6
Women			
Prevalence of high SBP	-0.52	-0.72	-0.43
Prevalence of high DBP	-0.21	-0.39	-0.33
Mean pulse pressure	-0.87	-0.90	-0.63
Prevalence of overweight	0.02	0.22	0.76
Prevalence of high total cholesterol	-0.11	-0.36	-0.20
Prevalence of low HDL cholesterol	-0.52	-0.52	-0.11
Ratio of total/HDL cholesterol	-0.85	-0.84	-0.43
Prevalence of high SBP or medication	**-0.36**	**-0.18**	**0.06**
N	7	7	6

Note: GDP = gross domestic product; % Urban = percent living in an urban area; SBP = systolic blood pressure; DBP = diastolic blood pressure; PP = pulse pressure; HDL = high density lipoprotein.

Most markers of cardiovascular and metabolic dysfunction are also negatively correlated with per capita GDP and proportion of the population that is urban, with the exception of prevalence of overweight, which is positively associated with all country-level social indicators. In particular, higher GDP is associated with a lower prevalence of high SBP and lower mean pulse pressure and ratio of total to HDL cholesterol. In general, the correlations between urbanization and most measures are weaker than those found for GDP. However, greater urbanization is strongly correlated with higher prevalence of overweight.

It is interesting that the percent urban relates to the biological indicators somewhat differently than the other measures. Overweight, hypertension, high cholesterol, diabetes and other risk factors appear to be more prevalent in urban settings, at least in developing countries (Beltrán-Sánchez et al. 2011, Njelekela et al. 2003, Sobngwi et al. 2004, Yang et al. 2010). The association between urbanization, globalization and health is thought to be, at least in part, due to changes in diet and physical activity (Popkin 1999, Rivera 2002, 2004). The rapid urbanization now occurring with increasing life expectancy may be changing the links between the epidemiological transition and the rise in overweight.

Health Care Systems

Health care system features likely contribute to differences in physiological ageing across countries due to differences in treatment and control of some biological risk factors. In contexts where infectious diseases are still highly prevalent, health care systems may be more oriented toward treating infectious disease than toward the prevention and management of chronic conditions. In the face of rising chronic disease prevalence, health care systems in many lower-income countries are financially and structurally poorly equipped to meet the health needs of a rapidly ageing population. Substantial variation exists between countries in rates of awareness, treatment and control of chronic conditions. These tend to be higher in more developed countries (Ong et al. 2007, 2008) compared with less developed countries (Blondin and Lewis 2007, Porapakkham, Pattaraarchachai and Aekplakorn 2008, Rampal et al. 2008).

Awareness, treatment and control of biological risk factors depend in part on access to health care. In countries with national health systems or universal coverage, fewer barriers exist for health care services such as blood pressure and cholesterol screenings. In other countries, access to care is often conditional on having health insurance due to the high costs of out-of-pocket care. In Mexico, for example, health insurance coverage was highly associated with medication use for hypertension (Maurer 2008). In the US, compared with insured individuals, uninsured diabetics and those with high cholesterol were significantly less likely to have been diagnosed and uninsured individuals with hypertension were less likely to achieve control of their high blood pressure (Wilper et al. 2009). Globally, there are high proportions of those with elevated risk factors who are unaware of their condition, even in developed countries. Thus, health care systems that facilitate access to health services and emphasize preventative care and screenings can help reduce the levels of biological risk.

This is true in the countries we investigate here. There are three countries for which we have information on the use of medication to control hypertension: the US, England and Japan. If we define hypertension as either measured high or using medication and recompute the correlations between the percent having high SBP among those aged 50–59 and the life expectancy, GDP and percent urban, the size of the correlations is considerably reduced, indicating that much of the relationship came from the differences caused by the use of drugs to control measured hypertension in rich countries. In rich countries, people have their hypertension diagnosed and treated so the measured levels are lower than they would be otherwise.

Conclusion

This analysis provides, for the first time, an examination of the age differences in multiple bio-indicators across a number of countries, which span the range of development and life expectancy. The availability of harmonized data has made this type of cross-country comparison possible. Of particular significance in this study is the use of measured risk factors such as weight, blood pressure and cholesterol, which provide more accurate assessments of the underlying physiological status of the population than self-reported indicators. It becomes apparent that there is considerable heterogeneity in the pattern of age-related physiological changes between countries and across indicators. Some indicators, such as high systolic and diastolic blood pressure, mean pulse pressure and high glycosylated hemoglobin, show a clear pattern of differences across ages that imply change with age.

The prevalence of high SBP increases with age, while high DBP increases until middle-age and levels off or decreases. The exceptions to these patterns are the Tsimane of Bolivia, who show little change in either measure with age, calling into question whether age changes in blood pressure are universal. At any given age, countries also differ considerably in the prevalence of high blood pressure, suggesting that non-age related factors such as diet, economic conditions, level of development and access to health care and antihypertensives may be more important than age per se. Mean pulse pressure appears to rise with age and shows less variation between countries. Glycosylated hemoglobin also rises with age, particularly in the United States.

On the other hand, several biomarkers do not appear to change with age in any regular pattern. Cholesterol levels and overweight levels are not strongly related to age in most of these countries. Certainly there are higher levels of risk for these measures after the beginning of adulthood but these occur long before what one would consider old age. Large differences in levels of risk at any given age, however, suggest that environmental factors are of greater importance than age.

The variability in level of physiological dysregulation across countries is not random. For example, the Tsimane have minimal levels of risk from all of these indicators. Japan and Taiwan have low levels of overweight but high prevalence of high systolic and diastolic blood pressure. Mexico and Indonesia have a high prevalence of high systolic and diastolic blood pressure, high total cholesterol, low HDL cholesterol and high mean total/HDL ratio. However, Mexico has a much higher prevalence of overweight compared to Indonesia. England and the US have very high prevalence of overweight but appear to do fairly well in terms of blood pressure, HDL cholesterol and the ratio of total/HDL cholesterol, which may be due to the widespread use of medications for these risk factors. However, these countries differ in the prevalence of high total cholesterol, which is much more common in England and high glycosylated hemoglobin, which is more prevalent in the US. Meanwhile, China appears to have intermediate levels of most biomarkers. These differences seem to be patterned in part by the economic status and level of urbanization of each country.

Some of the biomarkers vary with economic status but not all markers vary in the same way. Countries with high levels of SBP and pulse pressure, and low levels of HDL cholesterol appear to be poorer, with lower life expectancy and lower GDP. On the other hand, overweight and high cholesterol tend to be more common in more urban societies. Further studies that examine longitudinal change with age will more clearly illustrate the individual biological changes with age across these very different populations and better clarify the links between change in biomarkers and individual and community level factors.

References

Banks, J., Marmot, M., Oldfield, Z. and Smith, J.P. 2006. Disease and disadvantage in the United States and in England. *JAMA*, 295(17), 2037–45.

Beltrán-Sánchez, H., Thomas, D., Teruel, G. and Crimmins, E. 2011. Links between childhood and adult social circumstances and obesity and hypertension in the Mexican Population. *Aging and Health*, 23(7), 1141–65.

Blacher, J., Staessen, J.A., Girerd, X. et al. 2000. Pulse pressure not mean pressure determines cardiovascular risk in older hypertensive patients. *Archives of Internal Medicine*, 160(8), 1085–9.

Blondin, N. and Lewis, J. 2007. Prevalence, awareness, treatment and control of hypertension in a rural Nicaraguan sample. *Journal of Human Hypertension*, 21(10), 815–17.

Carvalho, J.J.M., Lima, J.A.C., Carvalho, J.V. et al. 1985. Blood pressure is directly related to the degree of acculturation among primitive Yanomamo Indians. *Circulation*, 72(1181), 296.

Cassel, J. 1975. Studies of hypertension in migrants, in *The Epidemiology and Control of Hypertension*, edited by O. Paul. New York: Stratton Intercontinental Medical Book Corp, 41–61.

Chiu, K.C., Martinez, D.S. and Chu, A. 2005. Comparison of the relationship of age and beta cell function in three ethnic groups. *Clinical Endocrinology*, 62(3), 296–302.

CIA. 2011. *The World Factbook*. [Online]. Available at: https://www.cia.gov/library/publications/the-world-factbook/ [accessed: 31 October 2011].

Clarke, R., Frost, C., Collins, R. et al. 1997. Dietary lipids and blood cholesterol: Quantitative meta-analysis of metabolic ward studies. *British Medical Journal*, 314(7074), 112–17.

Cooper, R., Rotimi, C., Ataman, S. et al. 1997. The prevalence of hypertension in seven populations of West African origin. *American Journal of Public Health*, 87(2), 160–68.

Crimmins, E.M., Garcia, K. and Kim, J.K. 2010. Are International Differences in Health Similar to International Differences in Life-Expectancy? in *International Differences in Mortality at Older Ages: Dimensions and Sources*, edited by E.M. Crimmins, S.H. Preston and B. Cohen. Washington, DC: National Research Council. Panel on Understanding Divergent Trends in Longevity in High-Income Countries.

Crimmins, E.M., Johnston, M., Hayward, M. and Seeman, T. 2006. Age differences in allostatic load: An index of frailty, in *Longer Life and Healthy Aging*, edited by Z. Yi, E.M. Crimmins, Y. Carriére, et al. Dordrecht, Netherlands: Springer, 111–26.

Crimmins, E.M., Vasunilashorn, S., Kim, J. and Alley, D.E. 2008 Biomarkers of aging in human populations. *Advances in Clinical Chemistry*, 46, 161–215.

Deaton, C., Froelicher, E.S., Wu, L.H. et al. 2011. The global burden of cardiovascular disease. *Journal of Cardiovascular Nursing*, 26(45), S5–14.

Epstein, F.H. and Eckoff, R.D. 1967. The epidemiology of high blood pressure: geographic distribution and etiologic factors, in *The Epidemiology of Hypertension*, edited by J. Stamler, R. Stamler and T.M. Pullman. New York: Grune & Stratton, 155–66.

Expert Panel on Detection, Evaluation, and Treatment of High Blood Cholesterol in Adults. 2001. Executive summary of the Third Report of The National Cholesterol Education Program (NCEP) (Adult Treatment Panel III). *Journal of the American Medical Association*, 285(19), 2486–97.

Finch, C.E. 2007. *The Biology of Human Longevity*. San Diego: Academic Press.

Franklin, S.S., Gustin, W., Wong, N.D. et al. 1997. Hemodynamic patterns of age-related changes in blood pressure: The Framingham Heart Study. *Circulation*, 96(1), 308–15.

Franklin, S.S., Larson, M.G., Kahn, S.A. et al. 2001. Does the relation of blood pressure to coronary heart disease risk change with aging?: The Framingham Heart Study. *Circulation*, 103(9), 1245–9.

Galal, O.M. 2002. The nutrition transition in Egypt: Obesity, undernutrition and the food consumption context. *Public Health Nutrition*, 5(1A), 141–8.

Glei, D.A., Goldman, N., Lin, Y.H. and Weinstein, M. 2011. Age-related changes in biomarkers: Longitudinal data from a population-based sample. *Research on Aging*, 33(3), 312–26.

Gurven, M., Kaplan, H., Winking, J. et al. 2008. Aging and inflammation in two epidemiological worlds. *Journal of Gerontology: Medical Sciences*, 63A(2), 196–9.

Gurven, M., Kaplan, H., Winking, J. et al. 2009. Inflammation and infection do not promote arterial aging and cardiovascular disease risk factors among lean horticulturalists. *PLoS ONE*, 4(8), e6590.

Jia, W., Xiang, K., Chen, L. et al. 2002. Epidemiological study on obesity and its comorbidities in urban Chinese older than 20 years of age in Shanghai, China. *Obesity Reviews*, 3(3), 157–65.

Juhaeri, J.S., Jones, D.W. and Arnett, D. 2003. Associations of aging and birth cohort with body mass index in a biethnic cohort. *Obesity*, 11(3), 426–33.

Kim, J.K., Alley, D., Seeman, T. et al. 2006. Recent changes in cardiovascular risk factors among women and men. *Journal of Women's Health*, 15(6), 734–40.

Kosulwat, V. 2002. The nutrition and health transition in Thailand. *Public Health Nutrition*, 5(1A), 183–9.

Levenson, J.W., Skerrett, P.J. and Gaziano, J.M. 2002. Reducing the global burden of cardiovascular disease: The role of risk factors. *Preventive Cardiology*, 5(4), 188–99.

Lewis, C.E., McTigue, K.M., Burke, L.E. et al. 2009. Mortality, health outcomes, and body mass index in the overweight range. *Circulation*, 119(25), 3263–71.

Lindeberg, S., Ahren, B., Nilsson, A. et al. 2003. Determinants of serum triglycerides and high-density lipoprotein cholesterol in traditional Trobriand Islanders: The Kitava Study. *Scandinavian Journal of Clinical and Laboratory Investigation*, 63(2), 175–80.

Lowenstein, F.W. 1961. Blood pressure in relation to age and sex in the tropics and subtropics. *Lancet*, 277(7173), 389–92.

Marmot, M.G. 1980. Affluence, urbanization and coronary heart disease, in *Disease and Urbanization*, edited by E.J. Clegg and J.P. Garlick. London: Taylor & Francis, 127–44.

Mattson, F.H., Erikson, B.A. and Kligman, A.M. 1972. Effect of dietary cholesterol on serum cholesterol in man. *American Journal of Clinical Nutrition*, 25(6), 589–94.

Maurer, J. 2008. Assessing horizontal equity in medication treatment among elderly Mexicans: Which socioeconomic determinants matter most? *Health Economics*, 17(10), 1153–69.

McGarvey, S.T. and Baker, P.T. 1979. The effects of modernization and migration on Samoan blood pressure. *Human Biology*, 51(4), 467–79.

Misra, A., Singhai, N. and Khurana, L. 2010. Obesity, the metabolic syndrome, and type 2 diabetes in developing countries: Role of dietary fats and oils. *Journal of the American College of Nutrition*, 29(3 Suppl), 389s–301s.

Misra, A., Singhal, N., Sivakumar, B. et al. 2011. Nutrition transition in India: Secular trends in dietary intake and their relationship to diet-related non-communicable diseases. *Journal of Diabetes*. [Epub ahead of print].

Njelekela, M., Sato, T., Nara, Y. et al. 2003. Nutritional variation and cardiovascular disease risk factors in Tanzania: Rural-urban difference. *South African Medical Journal*, 93(4), 295–9.

Nooyens, A.C.J., Visscher, T.L.S., Verschuren, W.M.M. et al. 2008. Age, period and cohort effects on body weight and body mass index in adults: The Doetinchem Cohort Study. *Public Health Nutrition*, 12(6), 862–70.

Ong, K.L., Cheung, B.M.Y., Man, Y.B. et al. 2007. Prevalence, awareness, treatment, and control of hypertension among United States adults 1999–2004. *Hypertension*, 49(1), 69–75.

Ong, K.L., Cheung, B.M.Y., Wong, L.Y.F. et al. 2008. Prevalence, treatment, and control of diagnosed diabetes in the US national health and nutrition examination survey 1999–2004. *Annals of Epidemiology*, 18(3), 222–9.

O'Rourke, M.F. and Nichols, W.W. 2005. Aortic diameter, aortic stiffness, and wave reflection increase with age and isolated systolic hypertension. *Hypertension*, 45(4), 652–8.

Ostfeld, A.M. and D'Atri, D.A. 1977. Rapid sociocultural change and high blood pressure. *Advances in Psychosomatic Medicine*, 9, 20.

Page, L. 1976. Epidemiologic evidence on the etiology of human hypertension and its possible prevention. *American Heart Journal*, 91(4), 527–34.

Pani, L.N., Korenda, L., Meigs, J.B. et al. 2008. Effect of aging on A1c levels in individuals without diabetes. *Diabetes Care*, 31(10), 1991–1996.

Patrick, R.C., Prior, I.M., Smith, J.C. et al. 1983. The relationship between blood pressure and modernity among Panopeans. *International Journal of Epidemiology*, 12(1), 36–44.

Pauletto, P., Puato, M., Caroli, M.G. et al. 1996. Blood pressure and atherogenic lipoprotein profiles of fish-diet and vegetarian villagers in Tanzania: The Lugalawa study. *Lancet*, 348(9030), 784–8.

Pavan, L., Casiglia, E., Pauletto, P. et al. 1997. Blood pressure, serum cholesterol and nutritional state in Tanzania and in the Amazon: Comparison with an Italian population. *Journal of Hypertension*, 15(10), 1083–90.

Peters, A., Barendregt, J.J., Willekens, F. et al. 2003. Obesity in adulthood and its consequences for life expectancy: A life-table analysis. *Annals of Internal Medicine*, 138(1), 124–32.

Pomerleau, J., Mckee, M., Lobstein, T. and Knai, C. 2003. The burden of disease attributable to nutrition in Europe. *Public Health Nutrition*, 6(5), 453–61.

Popkin, B.M. 1999. Urbanization, lifestyle changes and the nutrition transition. *World Development*, 27(11), 1905–16.

Popkin, B.M. 2001. Nutrition in transition: The changing global nutrition challenge. *Asia Pacific Journal of Clinical Nutrition*, 10(S1), S13–18.

Popkin, B.M. 2008. Will China's nutrition transition overwhelm its health care system and slow economic growth? *Disease & Demography*, 27(4), 1064–76.

Popkin, B.M. 2010. Recent dynamics suggest selected countries catching up to US obesity. *American Journal of Clinical Nutrition*, 91(1), S284–8.

Popkin, B.M., Lu, B. and Zhai, F. 2002. Understanding the nutrition transition: Measuring rapid dietary changes in transitional countries. *Public Health Nutrition*, 5(6a), 947–53.

Porapakkham, Y., Pattaraarchachai, J. and Aekplakorn, W. 2008. Prevalence, awareness, treatment and control of hypertension and diabetes mellitus among the elderly: The 2004 national health examination survey III, Thailand. *Singapore Medical Journal*, 49(11), 868–73.

Poulter, N.R. and Sever, P.S. 1994. Blood pressure in other populations, in *Textbook of Hypertension*, edited by J.D. Swales. Oxford: Blackwell Science Ltd., 22–45.

Prior, I.A.M. and Stanhope, J.M. 1980. Blood pressure patterns, salt use, and migration in the Pacific, in *The Epidemiology of Arterial Blood Pressure: Developments in Cardiovascular Medicine*, vol. 8, edited by H. Kesteloot and J.V. Joosen. The Hague: Martinus Nijhoff, 243–62.

Rampal, L., Rampal, S., Azhar, M. and Rahman, A. 2008. Prevalence, awareness, treatment and control of hypertension in Malaysia: A national study of 16,440 subjects. *Public Health*, 122(1), 11–18.

Rivera, J.A., Barquera, S., Campirano, F. et al. 2002. Epidemiological and nutritional transition in Mexico: Rapid increase of non-communicable chronic disease and obesity. *Public Health Nutrition*, 5(1A), 113–22.

Rivera, J.A., Barquera, S., Gonzalez-Cossio, T. et al. 2004. Nutrition transition in Mexico and in other Latin American Countries. *Nutrition Reviews*, 62(s2), S149–57.

Schubert, C.M., Rogers, N.L., Remsberg, K.E. et al. 2005. Lipids, lipoproteins, lifestyle, adiposity and fat-free mass during middle age: The Fels Longitudinal Study. *International Journal of Obesity*, 30(2), 251–60.

Seidell, J.C., Visscher, T.L.S., Schürch, B. and Scrimshaw, N.S. 2000. Body weight and weight change and their health implications for the elderly. Paper to the Impact of Human Aging on Energy and Protein Metabolism and Requirements: Proceedings of an IDECG Workshop, Boston, USA, May 3–6, 1999.

Sheehan, T.J., DuBrava, S., DeChello, L.M. and Fang, Z. 2003. Rates of weight change for black and white Americans over a twenty year period. *International Journal of Obesity*, 27(4), 498–504.

Skumich, J.H., Aladjem, M. and Aviv, A. 2010. Sex differences in pulse pressure trends with age are cross-cultural. *Hypertension*, 55(1), 40–47.

Sobngwi, E., Mbanya, J.C., Unwin, N.C. et al. 2004. Exposure over the life course to an urban environment and its relation with obesity, diabetes, and hypertension in rural and urban Cameroon. *International Journal of Epidemiology*, 33(4), 769–76.

Strauss, J. and Thomas, D. 2007. Health over the Life Course, in *Handbook of Development Economics*, vol. 4, edited by T.P. Schultz and J. Strauss. Amsterdam: North-Holland, 3375–474.

Vasunilashorn, S., Crimmins, E.M., Kim, J.K. et al. 2010. Blood lipids, infection, and inflammatory markers in Tsimane of Bolivia. *American Journal of Human Biology*, 22(6), 731–40.

Vieira-Filho, J.P.B. 1978. O diabetes mellitus entre os índios dos Estados Unidos do Brasil. *Revista de Antropologia*, 21, 53–60.

Waldron, I., Nowotarski, M., Ferimer, M. et al. 1982. Cross-cultural variation in blood pressure: a quantitative analysis of the relationships of blood pressure to cultural characteristics, salt consumption, and body weight. *Social Science and Medicine*, 16(4), 419–30.

Walker, R.S., Gurven, M., Burger, O. and Hamilton, M.J. 2008. The trade-off between number and size of offspring in humans and other primates. *Proceedings of the Royal Society B: Biological Sciences*, 275(1636), 827–33.

Wilper, A.P., Woolhandler, S., Lasser, K.E. et al. 2009. Hypertension, diabetes, and elevated cholesterol among insured and uninsured US adults. *Health Affairs*, 28(6), 1151–9.

Yang, W., Lu, J., Weng, J. et al. 2010. Prevalence of diabetes among men and women in China. *New England Journal of Medicine*, 362(12), 1090–101.

Yashin, A.I., Akushevich, I.V., Arbeev, K.G. et al. 2006. Insights on aging and exceptional longevity from longitudinal data: Novel findings from the Framingham Heart Study. *Age*, 28(4), 363–74.

Zheng, Y., Stein, R., Kwan, T. et al. 2009. Evolving cardiovascular disease prevalence, mortality, risk factors, and the metabolic syndrome in China. *Clinical Cardiology*, 32(9), 491–7.

Zulfa, A., Zandile, M. and Nelia, S. 2011. Diet and mortality rates in Sub-Saharan Africa: Stages in the nutrition transition. *BMC Public Health*, 11(1), 801. [Epub ahead of print].

Chapter 6
Religious Activity and Transitions in Functional Health and Mortality among Middle Aged and Older Adults in Taiwan

Mira M. Hidajat, Zachary Zimmer and Baai-Shyun Hurng

Although religious activity has been found to be an important predictor of life expectancy and disability onset among elderly persons in the West (Hummer et al. 1999), little research has examined the nature of the religion-health/mortality relationship in Asian countries. Insights from the Western studies point to health behaviors and psychosocial factors (such as through social interactions) as mechanism by which religiosity influences health and mortality. Additionally, there has been evidence that religious practices reduce stress and have cognitive benefits. However, an East Asian setting such as Taiwan, the setting of the current chapter, has a very different religious landscape, which is dominated by Buddhism and Daoism. While these religions do have their festivals and celebrations, overall they are very personal meditative types of endeavors and, in comparison to Western religions, are less focused on public meetings and interpersonal associations. Thus, it may not be possible to generalize results from US or other western based studies to Eastern religious settings. In this chapter, we examine the association between private and public religious practice and transitions in disability and mortality among elderly Taiwanese using a nationally representative longitudinal dataset. We begin however with a look at the current ageing situation in Taiwan.

Background

Ageing in Taiwan

As a function of drastic fertility declines over the course of a single generation, Taiwan is among the world's most rapidly ageing societies. Taiwan's Total Fertility Rate, which was about seven children per woman in 1950, and about two and a half in 1980, fell below one child per woman in 2010, giving Taiwan among the lowest fertility rates in the world (Taiwan Government Information Office 2010). As a result of the introduction of fewer young individuals into the population, the elderly, as a proportion, has grown. The percentage of Taiwan's population aged 65 and older, for instance, was a little over 2% in 1950, a little over 4% in 1980 and about 10% in 2010. It is expected, however, to reach over 20% by 2027 and over 30% by 2042 (Council for Economic Planning and Development 2011).

The decline in fertility in Taiwan has been accompanied by declines in mortality that is almost equally as dramatic (Government of Taiwan 2011). Life expectancy at birth, which was resembled most developing and underdeveloped countries four or five decades ago, is now on par with the world's most developed countries. A female born in Taiwan in 2011 can expect to live over 82 years and a 60 year old female can expect to live over 25 more years. These figures are very close to those found in the United States. Furthermore, the health and life expectancy of older adults in Taiwan may have been greatly affected by Taiwan's introduction of a Universal Health Insurance Program in 1995 (Zimmer, Martin and Lin 2005). Evidence exists that the greater access afforded elders through this program may have decreased old-age mortality. The impact on old-age morbidity is less certain.

As a final note, it is interesting to observe that Taiwan is one of the only societies in the world today where elderly males outnumber elderly females. This is the result of mass in-migration of 'Mainlanders' – soldiers that fled to the island after China's revolution in the late 1940s (Zimmer et al. 2005). These soldiers, mostly unmarried males, were apt to receive jobs in the government sector after the establishment of Taiwan as an independent entity from Mainland China. Working in the government sector gave them certain privileges, including better life-long health care than the rest of the population. Today 'Mainlanders' remain a homogenous group with better health outcomes than the rest of the population. Since they impact on health and mortality rates, any analysis of health and ageing in Taiwan needs to recognize this group.

Religious Activity, Mortality and Disability

We move on now to discuss the subject of the current analysis – the link between religion and health in older adults. In general, studies on the relationship between participation in religious activities in the public sphere and mortality comprise the bulk of the research on religion and mortality. This approach has garnered consistent evidence showing that higher frequency of attendance at religious institutions is associated with lower mortality. Strawbridge et al. (1997) used the Alameda County study that followed roughly 6,500 people aged 21 to from 1965 to 1994 and found that those who were frequent religious attendees had higher survival than those who were not but that the benefit was higher for women than for men. Other studies (Koenig et al. 1999, Musick et al. 2004, Bagiella et al. 2005, LaCour et al. 2006) also found that those who attended religious services more frequently had higher survival than those who had lower religious attendance net of controls. Hummer et al. (1999) found a gradient in frequency of religious attendance in relation to risk of death that persists even after controlling for demographic and socioeconomic factors, health behaviors, social support, and health status. They found that those who attend religious services more than once per week to have about seven years higher life expectancy at age 20 than those who never attend.

Research on religious practice at home or in the private sphere has been sparse and results tend to be less consistent. Some studies found support for positive effect of private religious activity on longevity (Ellison 1991, Helm et al. 2000) while others find no relationship (Markides 1983, Koenig et al. 1999, Musick et al. 2004), and yet others find that the association depends on initial health status (Helm et al. 2000). Furthermore, there has also been inconsistency in how private religious practice is measured. For example, Helm et al. (2000) used indicators such as prayer, meditation, and Bible study while Krause (1998) stratified the concept of private religious practice into several dimensions such as non-organizational religiosity (reading the Bible, watching religious programs on radio or TV) and religious coping (finding support from God in times of crises, prayer, seeking divine guidance for decision-making). Other studies use religious coping to represent private religious activity (Oxman et al. 1995, Koenig et al. 1999, Pargement et al. 2001).

The benefits of religious activity extend beyond longevity to other health outcomes such as functional health. Park et al. (2008) found that elderly persons who go to more frequent religious activities have lower prevalence of ADLs and IADLs. They also reported slower increase in severity among more religious persons and faster increase among less religious persons. Other studies found lower incidence of functional limitations among religious persons even after controls (Idler and Kasl 1997, Benjamins 2004, Berges et al. 2010). Although most studies find positive effects of religious activity on functional health, one study found no relationship between religious attendance and functional limitations (Kelley-Moore and Ferraro 2001).

Religion and Health in East Asia

The religious landscape of East Asia in general and Taiwan in particular is very different from the US and other European countries. Unlike Mainland China, Taiwan has been reported to have very high levels of religious freedom and social hostilities or religious-based discrimination are virtually nonexistent (Pew Forum on Religious and Public Life 2009, US Department of State 2010), similar to countries in Europe and the US. This promotes the growth of a diverse religious landscape with 1,684 religious groups having officially registered with the Taiwanese government (Taiwan Ministry of the Interior 2010). Nevertheless, Taiwan is predominated by Eastern religions such as Buddhism and Daoism. The Taiwanese government estimated that adherents of these groups comprise 43% and 40% of the population respectively (Taiwan Ministry of the Interior 2006). Some religious practices of Buddhism in Taiwan can be said to be health-oriented with activities like meditation, eating a vegetarian diet, as well as spiritual activities like chanting. There are also humanitarian efforts through volunteerism and charitable organizations as well as religious outreach through missionary work, publication of religious materials, and establishment of educational institutions and media outlets. Daoist practices involve social rituals such as sacrificial offerings, fasting, and festival celebrations as well as individualistic practice like religious study. Through its core philosophy, Daoism emphasizes a lifestyle of compassion, moderation, and humility.

The rest of the population self-identify with a diverse set of non-mutually exclusive religions/spiritual beliefs that range from traditional Chinese folk religions/beliefs such as ancestor and deity worship to organized religions with influences from outside East Asia such as Islam and Christianity, while a large segment do not self-identify with any particular religion.

Few studies to date have examined religion, health and mortality in East Asia. Among those that do, the results are mixed. Some find support for the association between religion and health/mortality while others do not. A study from Taiwan by Yeager et al. (2006), which also used the same dataset that we use in this chapter, found that religious attendance (public but not private) had a statistically significant effect on mortality even after controlling for demographic factors, health behaviors, health status, and social support. They found that compared to those who never attend religious services, elderly Taiwanese persons who attend sometimes have reduced risk in mortality, and the risk is reduced even further for those who attend often. Those who rarely attend religious services have similar risk to those who never attend. However, the association between religious activity and mobility limitations disappeared after controlling for a number of possible intervening covariates.

Studies from China found that higher frequencies of religious participation are associated with lower mortality, but one study found the association only exists among women and individuals with poor health status at baseline (Zhang 2008) while another study (Zeng et al. 2011) found the association in both sexes and for the most religious group, the association persisted after controlling for health behaviors and conditions.

Studies from Japan also found mixed results. Several studies report higher religiosity to be associated with fewer reports of hypertension (Krause et al. 2002) and better self-reported health rating (Krause et al. 1999). Ogata et al. (1984) analyzed a sample of male Zen priests from Eastern and Western Japan with a 23-year mortality follow-up and found that this group had lower mortality than the general Japanese population. However, the study could not rule out several selection factors based on initial health status and socioeconomic factors, as Zen priests must have had college education and successfully pass intense physical and mental training prior to ordination into the priesthood. A study of the laity in two community samples in Japan with a seven-year follow-up found no protective effect of religion from mortality (Iwasaki et al. 2002).

Contribution of the Current Chapter

The current chapter contains an empirical analysis that will contribute to the literature in religion, health, and mortality in several ways. First, we examine transitions in functional status and mortality, examining outcomes as a function of baseline status. While mortality is an important health outcome for obvious reasons, functional outcomes, such as the ability to conduct various daily activities, is equally critical due to the link with formal and informal health care needs. Therefore, associations between religiosity and functional status outcomes can be vital for the determination of policy within an ageing society such as Taiwan. Second, since one core difference between Judeo-Christian and Eastern religions is in the type of religious practice (or how religious worship is conducted), we use two indicators of religious practice that reflect these differences, namely public (such as worshipping in a temple/church) and private/home practice (such as praying) to compare how the association between religion and health/mortality differ by the type of religious activity, and whether differential strength in the association by type of religious activity that has been found in the west is also found in Taiwan. Third, improving on a previous study (Yeager et al. 2006), we extend the analysis to more recent data collected in 2007.

Data and Methods

The data come from 'The Survey of Health and Living Status of the Middle Aged and Elderly in Taiwan. The survey begun in 1989 by the Taiwan Provincial Institute of Family Planning (which later became the Bureau of Health Promotion of the Taiwan Department of Health) and the University of Michigan, with support from the Taiwan government and the US National Institute on Aging. The initial respondents were representative of the nine percent of Taiwan's population in 1989 that was aged 60 and older and living in either the community or institutions. Follow-ups have been conducted in 1993, 1996, 1999, 2003 and 2007. A second survey cohort of 2,462 people ages 50 to 67 were added in 1996 and were re-interviewed in subsequent waves. The current baseline data is the 1999 wave, which was the first since 1989 to include questions on religiosity, but unlike the 1989 data has consistent follow-up measures of functional health.

The dataset for this study is divided into two time segments each with a baseline and follow-up measure: 1999 to 2003 and 2003 to 2007. The first segment includes 4,263 observations, and the second includes 3,362 observations, with baseline and outcome functional status and mortality information. For the analysis, these two segments are pooled to provide a total sample size of 7,625 observations (see Table 6.1). From 1999–2003, 7.5% of the sample died while from 2003–2007, another 9.6% died. The mean age of the sample is 66.6 years old (standard deviation = 8.7 years).

Table 6.1 Sample composition (unweighted N, weighted %)

	1999		2003		2007	
	N	%	N	%	N	%
Alive	4439	100.0	3503	92.5	2740	90.4
Dead	0	0.0	760	7.5	622	9.6
Total (non-missing)	4439	100.0	4263	100.0	3362	100.0
Missing	**0**		**176**		**141**	

We consider two measures of disability as indicators of functional health. These measures are based on a common conceptualization of the disablement process, suggesting that disability is the outcome of physical functioning limitations but specifically speaks to the capacity to conduct tasks necessary for daily living (Verbrugge and Jette 1984). We use Activities in Daily Living (ADLs) and Instrumental Activities of Daily Living (IADLs), which are defined as measures of disability in common disability frameworks. These measures were originally developed for rehabilitation patients in a clinical setting to mark the milestone of independent self-care (Katz 1963). ADLs include items that pertain to self-maintenance, such as bathing and dressing. IADLs include items that pertain to maintenance of one's physical environment, such as cooking and cleaning. Self-reported measures of disability, such as used in this study, have been found to be as accurate as diagnosing comorbidity using medical records (Katz et al. 1996). We define a person as having an ADL or IADL limitation if they report one or more difficulties across a series of consistently measure items included in the three surveys. In our analysis, we consider transitions between having no ADL or IADL limitations to having any limitation or death. Transition between the no limitation and any limitation states can be bi-directional; one can experience an onset or recovery from a limitation.

Religious activities are measured as private (home) religious activity and public (church/temple) attendance. The main religious activity question was, 'Please tell me how often you do each activity'. Home religious activity was measured from the question, 'At home, pray, burn incense, worship gods or Buddha'. Church/temple attendance was measured from the question, 'Go to church or temple to worship'. Table 6.2 presents the descriptive information for the independent variables. We find that about half of the sample (51.5%) engages in home religious activity often while only 18.4% participates in church/temple worship with the same frequency. About a quarter of the sample performs home religious activity sometimes or rarely while most respondents (57%) engage in church/temple activity at this frequency. About 10% of the sample never participated in home religious activity or church/temple activities. We do not include information on religious affiliation in our analysis because the focus of our study is on level of religious activity. However,

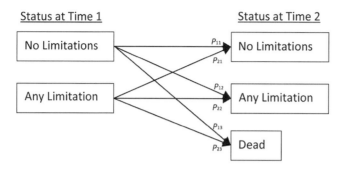

Figure 6.1 Transitions between health states and mortality

we would like to note that the religious affiliation composition of our sample is similar to data from the Taiwanese government; about half of our sample identifies as Taoists while a third identify as Buddhists, 14% have no religious affiliation, and about 5% identify as either Christian, Catholic, Yi-Guan Dau, or Other.

Table 6.2 Descriptive statistics (weighted % or means)

	N = 4,439
Private religious activity	
Often	51.5
Sometimes	15.0
Rarely	10.5
Never	9.3
No religious affiliation	13.7*
Total	**100.0**
Public religious activity	
Often	18.4
Sometimes	37.3
Rarely	19.7
Never	10.8
No religious affiliation	13.8*
Total	**100.0**

Note: * Respondents with no religious affiliation are excluded from the analysis.

Results

We descriptively examine functional and mortality transitions by frequency of religious activity (see Table 6.3). Table 6.3 provides weighted percentages and unweighted numbers of transitions. The upper panel of Table 6.3 displays results for ADL disability. As expected, the overall ADL results show that respondents who begin a period without ADL limitations are less likely to die and more likely to remain functionally healthy at follow-up. For instance, 83% of those without limitations with respect to ADLs remain without at the end of the observation period compared to only about 15% of those that began the period Inactive.

Results that cross-tabulate outcome health status with home religious activity show that respondents with higher frequencies of home religious activities, which are activities such as praying or worshipping god or Buddha, are able remain free of ADL limitations over time, have lower proportions of deaths, and become disabled less often than those who with lower frequencies or never do these activities. For instance, the percent remaining free of limitations is 84.5% for those that are often engaged in home religious activity, and fall under 80% for those that rarely or never engage in home religious activity. With respect to death, 9.3% of the often group die compared to 12.8% of the rarely group and 12.5% of the never group.

The differences are even greater for those who initially had ADL limitations. Quite amazingly, 20.7% that are engaged in home religious activity often improve to being free of ADL limitations by the end of the observation period in comparison to only 4.1% of those that engage in these activities never. There is also a very large difference in the percent dying, 46% of those that engage in home activity often and initially had ADL limitations die compared to 60.5% of those that engage in the activity never. Additionally, there are fairly clear gradients with the higher level of religious activity relating to better outcomes regardless of initial ADL status. These findings suggest that among those who had limitations at baseline, not engaging in home religious activities relates to not recovering from ADL disability and dying at a higher rate. However, the proportion of the sample that remains disabled does not differ by level of home religious activity. Taken together, these findings suggest that respondents who had ADL limitations and never engage in any home religious activity tend not to recover from their disability and instead die at a higher proportion than others in the sample.

Findings with respect to public religious activities are similar. For instance, for those that have no ADL limitations at baseline, the chances of remaining disability-free are highest for those who often engage in public religious activity and lowest for those that never engage, with a clear gradient effect as engagement decreases in frequency. Similar conclusions can be made with respect to becoming disabled or dying from the disability-free state. For those beginning the observation period with an ADL disability, there is a very clear association with greater frequency of activity translating into a greater probability of recovery and a lower probability of death.

Table 6.3 Transitions between no ADL or IADL limitations, 1+ limitations, and mortality by home and public religious activity (unweighted N, weighted %)

Status at Time 1		No limitations				One or more limitations			
Status at Time 2	N	No limit.	1+ limit.	Dead	Total	N	No limit.	1+ limit.	Dead	Total
Panel A. ADL										
Total	5800	83.0	6.8	10.2	100.0	686	15.2	32.8	52.0	100.0
Home										
Often	3629	84.5	6.2	9.3	100.0	271	20.7	33.3	46.0	100.0
Sometimes	967	82.4	6.9	10.7	100.0	106	19.7	31.2	49.1	100.0
Rarely	682	78.4	8.8	12.8	100.0	126	15.7	28.9	55.4	100.0
Never	522	79.2	8.3	12.5	100.0	183	4.1	35.4	60.5	100.0
Public										
Often	1328	84.7	6.2	9.1	100.0	81	32.2	27.3	40.5	100.0
Sometimes	2552	84.9	6.1	9.0	100.0	168	15.1	38.7	46.2	100.0
Rarely	1300	80.9	7.6	11.5	100.0	180	15.8	26.9	57.3	100.0
Never	620	74.8	9.3	15.9	100.0	257	9.0	34.4	56.6	100.0
Panel B. IADL										
Total	3776	69.6	24.0	6.4	100.0	2710	18.3	54.5	27.2	100.0
Home										
Often	2391	69.2	24.7	6.1	100.0	1509	22.2	55.6	22.2	100.0
Sometimes	659	72.3	20.8	6.9	100.0	414	15.6	56.9	27.5	100.0
Rarely	407	69.7	23.1	7.2	100.0	401	10.6	55.6	33.7	100.0
Never	319	67.0	26.0	7.0	100.0	386	12.6	46.3	41.1	100.0
Public										
Often	881	67.8	25.5	6.7	100.0	528	26.8	54.4	18.8	100.0
Sometimes	1740	71.4	23.2	5.5	100.0	980	20.1	56.7	23.2	100.0
Rarely	813	70.9	21.9	7.2	100.0	667	14.8	55.2	29.9	100.0
Never	342	61.9	29.7	8.4	100.0	535	9.4	49.3	41.3	100.0

The second panel of Table 6.3 presents findings on IADL limitations and mortality. The overall IADL results indicate that those who initially do not have IADL limitations tend to remain without throughout the observation period. On the other hand, those who began the observation period with one or more IADL limitations have higher rates of death than those without IADL limitations and have low recovery rates from IADL disability. When we examine how these trends differ by religious activity, we see that those who never participate in any religious activity, home or public, have the worst health outcomes compared to any other group in the study. Among those who participate in religious activities, we see no gradient in health outcome by frequency of activity. This means that higher frequencies of religious activity are not associated with better health outcomes, unlike the findings on ADL limitations where we do see a clear gradient. For those who started the observation period with one or more IADL limitations, however, we still see a gradient in religious activity for the recovery transition and the dying transition. Some similarities to the ADL findings above were found. Respondents with IADL disabilities who never engage in any religious activity tend to have much lower proportions of recovery and higher proportions of death compared to respondents who engage in any religious activity.

On balance, the results show a clear gradient impact of both home and public religious activity and remaining free of disability, improving from having a disability and not dying. Improvements from the state of having limitations are a little less clear.

Conclusion

The association between religious activity and health/mortality has been studied widely in the US and Europe where the religious landscape largely consists of religions like Christianity and Judaism whose main modes of worship focuses on public/social activities such as church/temple attendance. In this analysis, we set out to examine how the association between religious activity and transitions in functional health/mortality would play out in a setting like Taiwan, a country with levels of religious freedom and diversity that are similar to the US but with has a different religious landscape and composition. Generally we find evidence that religious activities in the public sphere as well as at home have some positive associations with transitions in health and mortality, lowering risks of disability onset and death as well as increasing risks for recovery from disability. These associations are clear in descriptive findings, persist across home and public activity, and are fairly consistent across two disability measures, ADLs and IADLs. In addition, there are clear gradients, with the greater the level of activity the greater the benefit.

There are small variations depending on the specific disability outcome as well as the type of religious activity. There is a clear gradient in functional health and mortality outcomes by frequency of home religious activity for respondents who have no ADL limitations. Those who have the highest level of home religious activity (i.e. often) have the best outcomes and those who have the lowest level (i.e. never) have the worst outcomes. The gradient is not as clear when we examine IADL limitations. Differences in ADL and IADL findings may reflect the differing domains of disability measured by each indicator. ADL items measure fundamental self-care, are closely tied to loss of physical functioning and indicate a more severe level of disability than IADL items, which measure one's ability to live independently in society. Comparing between home and public religious activities, our findings suggest that the latter seems to associate with disability and mortality transitions more strongly than the earlier. These findings are consistent with previous studies reviewed above showing that public religious activities have stronger protective effects from mortality.

In addition to the analysis shown here, we ran multivariate models that control for social and demographic factors that have been shown in previous studies to influence the association between religion and health/mortality such as age, sex, education, marital status, and previous health status. Although we found positive effects of religious activity on functional health and survival similar to the analysis shown above, most of the coefficients did not reach statistical significance. We speculate that this is due to small sample size.

Several mechanisms that link religious activity and health/mortality have been suggested by previous studies (Hummer et al. 2004). First, religion is thought to influence health and mortality through social regulation of behavior that may have beneficial effects on health and mortality. Many religious groups have teachings that promote healthy lifestyles through such things as prohibition of drug use, smoking, excessive (or any) alcohol consumption, or eating certain foods such as meat, or avoidance of engaging in risky sexual behaviors. Some religious groups also have pacifist teachings that promote peaceful lifestyles such as avoidance in participating in any acts of violence or using weapons. There may also be organized sporting events or outdoor activities that promote an active lifestyle. In addition to positive encouragement to follow a healthy lifestyle, similar to other social norms, there may be sanctions for breaking these norms from the wider religious community such as excommunication from the religious group. These consequences may increase the incentive to quit smoking, drug use, etc. or never take them up in the first place. In this case, health behaviors could be considered as either mediating factors or selection factors for the relationship between religious activities and mortality (Idler 2004). Evidence for health behaviors as mediating factors show that the effect of religion on mortality is reduced with the introduction of health behavior variables (Strawbridge 1997).

Another pathway through which religion influences health and mortality is through the social support networks accessible to religious adherents through their participation in religious activities. These social networks have been found to be helpful in times of need in providing emotional support (Ellison and George 1994). Participation in activities provides a sense of belonging and social identity, which is associated with better mental health (Krause and Wulff 2005, Schwartz et al. 2003). Religious groups also often promote the formation and maintenance of a stable marital relationship. Church influence on social network through marriage is indirect but important because marriage provides strong social support for spouses (Waite and Lehrer 2003). These functions have been shown to serve as moderating factors for the relationship between religion and mortality, as when social support variables are introduced to the model, the effect of religion on mortality declines (Strawbridge 1997).

Moreover, previous research has found that religious activities such as church attendance and spiritual practices such as transcendental and mindfulness meditation, yoga, and Zen-based relaxation stimulate positive physiological responses (For a review of the literature, see Seeman et al. 2003). This is a moderating factor that particularly speaks to our population. Although initially research on the association between religious/spiritual activities and physiological responses focused on a single indicator such as blood pressure, there is evidence that these activities are associated with numerous indicators and multiple systems such as lower blood pressure, better lipid profiles, better immune functioning, lower cholesterol, lower stress hormone levels, less oxidative stress, less stress hormone reactivity, reduction in anxiety and depression, reduction in carpal tunnel syndrome, and increased activity in the areas of the brain involved in attention and control of the autonomic nervous system. Taken together, previous studies suggest that religious/spiritual activities may produce positive physiological responses. However, Seeman et al. (2003) caution that there may be a publication bias against studies that finds negative or no effect of religion on physiological responses. Further research needs to be done to overcome the methodological limitations of current studies such as limited sample sizes, and other aspects of religion beyond frequency of church attendance and meditations.

Our conclusion is that there appears to be few differences found in links between religion and health in Taiwan versus the West, at least at the descriptive level. In Taiwan, those who are religious and begin healthy are more likely to end up healthy and not die. If they begin with disability, the more religious are more likely to recover and not die. However, our division of home and public religious activity does lead to some potential hypotheses for further testing. In Taiwan, those who are more religious have better transitions regardless of where they practice. In the West, the majority of religious practice is expressed in public rather than home activity. Our study suggests that the meditative activities that are often centerpiece of religion as practiced in the East may be equally beneficial, suggesting mechanisms other than social support as being the key explanatory factors that link religion and good health. This clearly sets up the need for more testing of home versus public effects and the different ways in which each type of practice leads to better health.

References

Bagiella, E., Hong, V. and Sloan, R.P. 2005. Religious attendance as a predictor of survival in the EPESE cohorts. *International Journal of Epidemiology* 34(2), 443–51.

Benjamins, M.R., Musick, M.A., Gold, D.T. and George, L.K. 2003. Age-related declines in activity level: The relationship between chronic illness and religious activities. *Journals of Gerontology Series B: Psychological and Social Sciences* 58(6), 377–85.

Berges, I.-M., Kuo, Y.-F., Peek, M.K. and Markides, K.S. 2010. Religious involvement and physical functioning among older Mexican Americans. *Hallym International Journal of Aging* 12(1), 1–10.

Council for Economic Planning and Development. 2011. Population Projections for Taiwan: http://www.cepd.gov.tw/encontent/m1.aspx?sNo=0001457 [accessed December 22, 2011].

Davidson, R.J., Kabat-Zinn, J., Schumacher, J. et al. 2002. Alterations in brain and immune function produced my mindfulness meditation. *American Psychosomatic Society* 65, 564–70.

Ellison, C.G. 1991. Religious involvement and subjective well-being. *Journal of Health and Social Behavior* 32(1), 80–99.

Ellison, C.G. and Levin, J.S. 1998. The religion-health connection: Evidence, theory, and future directions. *Health Education Behavior* 25(6), 700–20.

Government of Taiwan. 2011. Life Tables for Republic of China: http://sowf.moi.gov.tw/stat/english/elife/elist.htm [accessed December 24, 2011].

Helm, H.M., Hays, J.C., Flint, E.P. et al. 2000. Does private religious activity prolong survival? A six-year follow-up study of 3,851 older adults. *Journals of Gerontology Series A: Biological and Medical Science* 55(7), M400–5.

Hummer, R.A. 2005. Commentary: Understanding religious involvement and mortality risk in the United States. *International Journal of Epidemiology* 34(2), 452–3.

Hummer, R.A., Ellison, C.G., Rogers, R.G. et al. 2004. Religious involvement and adult mortality in the United States: Review and perspective. *Southern Medical Journal* 97(12), 1223–30.

Hummer, R.A., Rogers, R.G., Nam, C.B. and Ellison, C.G. 1999. Religious involvement and U.S. adult mortality. *Demography* 36(2), 273 85.

Idler, E.L. and Kasl, S.V. 1997. Religion among disabled and nondisabled persons: Cross-sectional patterns in health practices, social activities, and well-being. *Journals of Gerontology Series B: Psychological and Social Sciences* 52(6), S294–305.

Iwasaki, M., Otani, T., Sunaga, R. et al. 2002. Social networks and mortality based on the komo-ise cohort study in Japan. *International Journal of Epidemiology* 31(6), 1208–18.

Kabat-Zinn, J. 2003. Mindfulness-based interventions in context: Past, present and future. *Clinical Psychology* 10(2), 144–56.

Katz, J.N., Chang, L.C., Sangha, O. et al. 1996. Can comorbidity be measured by questionnaire rather than medical record review? *Medical Care* 34(1), 73–84.

Katz, S. 1983. Assessing self-maintenance: Activities of daily living, mobility, and instrumental activities of daily living. *Journal of the American Geriatric Society* 31, 721–7.

Kelley-Moore, J.A. and Ferraro, K.F. 2001. Functional limitations and religious service attendance in later life: Barrier and/or benefit mechanism? *Journals of Gerontology Series B: Psychological and Social Sciences* 56(6), S365–73.

Koenig, H.G., Hays, J.C., Larson, D.B. et al. 1999. Does religious attendance prolong survival? A six-year follow-up study of 3,968 older adults. *Journals of Gerontology Series A: Biological and Medical Sciences* 54(7), M370–76.

Krause, N. 1998. Stressors in highly valued roles, religious coping, and mortality. *Psychology and Aging* 13(2), 242–53.

Krause, N., Ingersoll-Dayton, B., Liang, J. and Sugisawa, H. 1999. Religion, social support, and health among the Japanese elderly. *Journal of Health and Social Behavior* 40, 405–21.

Krause, N., Liang, J., Shaw, B.A. et al. 2002. Religion, death of a loved one, and hypertension among older adults in Japan. *Journals of Gerontology Series B: Psychological and Social Sciences* 57(2), S96–107.

La Cour, P., Avlund, K. and Schultz-Larsen, K. 2006. Religion and survival in a secular Region: A twenty year follow-up of 734 Danish adults born in 1914. *Social Science and Medicine* 62(1), 157–64.

Markides, K.S. 1983. Aging, religiosity, and adjustment: A longitudinal analysis. *Journals of Gerontology Series A: Life Sciences and Medicine* 38(5), 621–5.

Musick, M.A., House, J.S. and Williams, D.R. 2004. Attendance at religious services and mortality in a national sample. *Journal of Health and Social Behavior* 45(2), 198–213.

Ogata, M., Ikeda, M. and Kuratsune, M. 1984. Mortality among Japanese Zen priests. *Journal of Epidemiology and Community Health* 38(2), 161–6.

Oman, D., Kurata, J.H., Strawbridge, W.J. and Cohen, R.D. 2002. Religious attendance and cause of death over 31 years. *International Journal of Psychiatry in Medicine* 32(1), 69–89.

Oxman, T.E., Freeman, D.H. and Manheimer, E.D. 1995. Lack of social participation or religious strength and comfort risk factors for death after cardiac surgery in the elderly. *Psychosomatic Medicine* 57, 5–15.

Pargament, K.I., Koenig, H.G., Tarakeshwar, N. and Hahn, J. 2001. Religious struggle as a predictor of mortality among medically ill elderly patients: A 2-year longitudinal study. *Archives of Internal Medicine* 161(15), 1881–5.

Park, N.S., Klemmack, D.L., Roff, L.L. et al. 2008. Religiousness and longitudinal trajectories in elders' functional status. *Research on Aging* 30(3), 279–98.

Pew Forum on Religious and Public Life. 2009. *Global restrictions on religion*. Washington, DC.

Strawbridge, W.J., Cohen, R.D., Shema, S.J. and Kaplan, G.A. 1997. Frequent attendance at religious services and mortality over 28 years. *American Journal of Public Health* 87(6), 957–61.

Taiwan Government Information Office. 2010. The Republic of China Yearbook 2010: http://www.gio.gov.tw/taiwan-website/5-gp/yearbook/contents.htm [accessed on November 16, 2011].

Taiwan Ministry of the Interior. 2006. Taiwan Yearbook 2006: http://www.gio.gov.tw/taiwan- website/5-gp/yearbook/22Religion.htm [accessed on November 16, 2011].

US Department of State. 2010. International Religious Freedom Report 2010: http://www.state.gov/g/drl/rls/irf/2010/148895.htm [accessed on November 16, 2011].

Verbrugge, L.M. and Jette, A.M. 1984. The disablement process. *Social Science and Medicine* 38(12), 1–14.

Yeager, D.M., Glei, D.A., Au, M. et al. 2006. Religious involvement and health outcomes among older persons in Taiwan. *Social Science and Medicine* 63(8), 2228–41.

Zeng, Y., Gu, D. and George, L. 2011. Association of religious participation with mortality among Chinese old adults. *Research on Aging* 33(1), 51–83.

Zhang, W. 2008. Religious participation and mortality risk among the oldest old in China. *Journals of Gerontology Series B: Psychological and Social Sciences* 63(5), S293–7.

Zimmer, Z., Martin, L.G. and Lin, H.-S. 2005. Determinants of old-age mortality in Taiwan. *Social Science and Medicine* 60(2), 457–70.

Chapter 7
Addressing Health Challenges of Ageing in sub-Saharan Africa: Policy Perspectives and Evidence Needs

Isabella Aboderin

Debate on policy challenges associated with the health of older populations in sub-Saharan Africa (SSA) has intensified in recent years, centring on a concern about older persons' vulnerability to ill-health and their exclusion from health services. Despite international policy calls and formal expressions of commitment on the part of SSA governments, comprehensive policy action has remained scant. The impasse reflects a lack of political will and an uncertainty about required policy approaches, engendered by weaknesses in existing policy frameworks and wide gaps in understanding of old age-related health in the region. Based on a critical review of relevant SSA and international scientific, policy and development literature this chapter pinpoints key perspectives and evidence needs for advancing health care policies and provisions on ageing and health in SSA.

Background

International debate on the policy challenges associated with the health of ageing populations in sub-Saharan Africa (SSA) has intensified in recent years, based on two key points of departure. The first are current demographic projections, which (though tenuous, given the absence of reliable vital registration systems in most SSA countries (Velkoff and Kowal 2006) show SSA to have the fastest growing older population of any world region. While the share of persons aged 60 and over[1] will remain much lower than elsewhere (increasing from presently 5 percent to only 8.3 percent by 2050), their absolute number will see the sharpest rises globally: from 43.1 million in 2010 to 163 million by 2050 (UNPD 2011). Second is SSA's status as the poorest and 'least developed' major world region (World Bank 2011, UNDP 2011), which implies that the ageing of its populations

---

1   The United Nations' definition of 'old age' as 60 years and over is becoming increasingly entrenched in the international discourse. Readers should bear in mind the limitations of this definition, however, including its questionable appropriateness for African settings.

is largely unfolding in contexts of widespread economic strain (Aboderin and Ferreira 2009).

Against this backdrop, the discourse on challenges of ageing and health in SSA centers not, as it does in industrialized countries, on queries about expected trends in old age morbidity, mortality and disability and the sustainability of existing health and care systems (Robine and Michel 2004, Ofstedal et al. 2007, Martin et al. 2010). The focus, rather, are concerns about a heightened vulnerability of older persons to detrimental health outcomes – in two respects. On one level, older populations in SSA are deemed to be at particularly high risk of ill-health and disability from age-related chronic non-communicable disease (CNCD), due to a lifetime of exposure to conditions of deprivation and a growing prevalence of modifiable CNCD risk factors (Aboderin and Ferreira 2009). On a second level, older persons are believed to suffer from a lack access to even basic health care – suggesting an element of age-related exclusion from such services (Kalache, Aboderin and Hoskins 2002, HAI 2008, Aboderin and Ferreira 2009, Lloyd-Sherlock 2010).

The concerns are supported by a still limited but growing body of evidence, notably from studies such as the Ibadan Study of Ageing, the World Health Organization (WHO) Study on Adult Health and Ageing (SAGE) (Kowal et al. 2010, WHO 2011a) as well as a volume of work on aspects of chronic non-communicable diseases (CNCD), which show the following (see Aboderin 2011 for overview):

1. Sizeable proportions of older persons suffer from malnutrition, often multiple physical and mental CNCD (such as musculo-skeletal and cardiovascular conditions, impaired vision or hearing, depression and dementia) and consequent impaired health and function.
2. Within the older population, levels of ill-health and impaired function clearly vary between sociodemographic (e.g., gender, rural/urban, socioeconomic) groups. Evidence suggests a consistently higher risk of disability, depression, dementia as well as self-reported poor health and function among older women compared to men, as well as an association of urban residence to greater levels of hypertension, impaired function and depression. Findings on relationships of socioeconomic status (SES) to health outcomes, however, are less clear. A number of studies suggest – as in industrialized countries – an association of poorer general health or functioning to lower socio-economic groups (SES) (Kuate-Defo 2006, Biritwum, 2010, Gómez-Olivé et al. 2010, Phaswana-Mafuya, Peltzer and Gómez-Olivé 2010). Others find no such relationship (Kyobutungi, Egondi and Ezeh 2010, Mwanyangala et al. 2010) or, in the case of specific illness, find a greater prevalence among higher SES groups (Gureje, Kola and Afolabi 2007). Similarly, while most existing evidence suggests an association of urban residence to greater levels of ill-health or disability (see Aboderin 2008 for review), others find the reverse (Biritwum 2010).

3. In adult populations as a whole, there is a considerable prevalence of CVD and diabetes and major CNCD risk factors, in particular hypertension, but also dyslipidemia, obesity, alcohol and tobacco use.
4. The prevalence of CNCD and risk factors varies across countries as well as between sociodemographic groups. Clearly emerging patterns include a consistently higher prevalence of hypertension, as well as diabetes and obesity in urban compared to rural areas.
5. Older persons and adults with CNCD often lack access to required curative, preventive or diagnostic health services.
6. Older persons may have systematically less access to health care than younger age groups.
7. Health and functional impairments may significantly impact on older persons' quality of life, as well as their ability to sustain their livelihoods (Ahenkora 1999, Mohatle and de Graft Agyarko 1999, Spitzer and Mabeyo 2011, Aboderin, unpublished data).
8. In most SSA countries (with the exception of South Africa) the only long term care option available to functionally dependent older persons is informal caregiving provided by family members. While a systematic, large-scale assessment is yet to be undertaken, all indications point to extensive and profound inadequacies in such care, reflecting either an unavailability of carers or their lack of skills, capacity and resources. The inadequacies impact gravely not only on the extent to which even basic care needs remain unmet but also, ultimately, on the dignity of older care recipients and the well-being of carers (Aboderin and Hoffman 2011).

Policy Challenges

In response to the concerns, two international frameworks, the 2002 United Nations Madrid International Plan of Action on Ageing (MIPAA) (UN 2002) and the 2003 African Union Policy Framework and Plan of Action on Ageing (AU-Plan) (AU/HAI 2003), urge the development of strategies to enhance health service provision for Africa's older persons as a way to realize their right to health and to encourage their valuable contributions to families and societies. The Plans call for two main types of measures: 1) multi-faceted health promotion strategies to prevent disease and disability among successive cohorts of older persons; and 2) policies to ensure full access to adequate curative and rehabilitative care for older persons who already suffer from disease or disability. Such responses, as MIPAA and AU-Plan assert, are to be forged as part of core national health and development agendas and to serve the ultimate goal of enhancing older persons' quality of life (Aboderin and Ferreira 2009).

The recommendations, echoed in a recent United Nations report on the right to health of older persons (UN 2011a), overlap with intensifying calls on Africa's governments to address the countries' rising burden of CNCD, in particular cardiovascular disease (CVD), chronic lung disease (CLD), diabetes and cancers, which overwhelmingly affect adults in their middle and older ages (Amuyunzu-Nyamongo 2010, de Graft Aikins et al. 2010). The calls are part of an intensifying global movement on NCD, encapsulated in the political declaration adopted at the recent UN high level meeting on NCD (UN 2011b).

As signatories to MIPAA and AU Plan and further spurred by CNCD agenda, SSA countries formally acknowledge the need for policy responses on old age-related health needs. Collectively, African governments propose action to address these needs in the African Union Africa Health Strategy 2007–2013 (AU 2007). Individual states (including, for example, Burundi, Kenya, Nigeria, Senegal, South Africa and Tanzania) pledge relevant measures as part of national health sector plans and, in some cases, broader national policy frameworks on ageing (Aboderin and Gachuhi 2007).

Typically, countries propose (to varying extent) one or both of two kinds of responses: 1) steps to develop preventive and/or curative primary health care services for major CNCD and, in some cases (e.g., Kenya) other degenerative diseases (KMOH 2005); and/or 2) social protection measures to redress the exclusion of older persons (and other vulnerable groups) from health services, by removing financial barriers. Thus, Kenya's National Health Sector Strategic Plan II 2005–2012 (NHSSP II), for example, proposes:

> Various measures ... to improve financial access to health services, specifically for the financially vulnerable and the very poor: the elderly, street children and orphans, single mothers, and patients with chronic diseases like TB, HIV/AIDS, diabetes, etc. (KMOH 2005: 12)

Impasse in National Policy Action

However, despite such pledges, little comprehensive policy action has ensued. All indications are that SSA health services remain largely or partially unresponsive to CNDC broadly and older persons' health needs specifically. This includes the few countries – specifically Senegal and South Africa – that have implemented broad fee exemptions for older persons (WHO 2006, Aboderin 2008, Clausen and Wilson 2010, NDOH 2011).

The reasons for the policy impasse have not yet been formally investigated. However recent joint analyses by health policy, practice and research stakeholders from several SSA countries point to three implicated factors: 1) long delays in or obstructions to the enactment of drafted policies, as is the case, for example, with Nigeria's National Policy on Ageing (2008); 2) loose policy formulation that is unable to guide detailed program design; and 3) compromised implementation due to insufficient budget allocation or other capacity limitations (Aboderin and Gachuhi 2007, Aboderin 2008).

The three impediments are symptomatic of a persisting uncertainty of SSA policy-makers and planners in two regards. First, is a continued lack of conviction that action on old age-related health should be a priority within a context of myriad pressing public health and development challenges. A seemingly typical stance of legislators and central planning or finance ministries is that national budgets have no capacity to sustain the realization of policies for older persons. Such policies, as opposed to programmes on essential health needs of children, youth and younger-age adults, are seen as an obstruction, or at best as irrelevant, to core national development interests. Second, decision-makers lack clarity about what specific measures are needed to effectively ensure the health of older adults. An example are provisions on older persons in Kenya's NHSSP II whose translation has been hindered, among others, by a lack of insight into what exactly older persons' priority health needs and access problems are, and how health or other sectors should appropriately respond to them (Aboderin and Gachuhi 2007, Aboderin 2008).

What underlies the uncertainties are weaknesses in both the existing policy frameworks and the evidence base upon which policy-makers can build.

Weaknesses in Policy Frameworks

At the level of policy frameworks, the key messages and recommendations contained in the ageing-specific policy frameworks, MIPAA and AU Plan, have often remained unnoticed in, or marginal to mainstream policy discussions in SSA countries (Aboderin 2011b). At the same time, the more prominent, and potentially much more influential global and national NCD agenda, fails to sufficiently expound the specific needs of older persons (who constitute a majority of NCD sufferers), in three key respects.

First, it contains no mention of, or provision on particular health care access problems of older persons especially in poor countries. Second, the agenda's focus on the four NCD causing the greatest mortality burden, (CVD, CLD, Cancer and Diabetes) provides little scope for responses on other chronic diseases, such as dementia, musculo-skeletal conditions or vision impairments, which while not major causes of death, have immense impacts on the lives and livelihoods of older persons. Third, and lastly, the NCD agenda provides little, if any, direction regarding urgently needed responses on long term care for older persons.

Evidence Gaps

Despite the fair body of accumulated evidence that has illuminated the contours of old age-related health challenges in SSA, critical gaps remain in understanding of both 1) the scope, determinants and impacts of unmet old age-related health needs in SSA societies; and 2) the nature and causes of major deficiencies in service provision for them.

Overcoming the Policy Impasse

Overcoming the policy impasse will require concerted efforts, both conceptual – to merge mainstream NCD agendas with core aspects of MIPAA and AU-Plan recommendations on older persons' health – and empirical. A new, systematic, research effort on ageing and health is needed to address the current knowledge gaps impeding policy action in this area. The need for such further inquiry has been clearly recognized in recent reviews, as well as the AU Plan and MIPAA, and the associated UN Research Agenda on Ageing for the Twenty-first century (Cohen and Menken 2006, UN/IAGG 2008). However, the frameworks provide limited guidance on what specific evidence is required as a priority in SSA and what broad approaches should inform its generation. This includes an omission to underscore the importance of building synergy between inquiry on ageing and the international research agenda on CNCD (Daar et al. 2007, WHO 2011b).

Building on the above, the remainder of this chapter attempts to distil the kinds of evidence and perspectives that are essential for advancing policy and practice on ageing and health in SSA.

The two basic tasks for research are to generate information that can 1) strengthen the case on why SSA governments should address old age-related health needs as a priority; and 2) clarify what forms such action should take. A starting point for pinpointing what evidence is needed for the first task, is to appreciate three health systems imperatives that SSA health policy-makers will need to take into account when deciding on action, namely: 1) acute resource constraints; 2) a priority focus on attaining the Millennium Development Goals (MDGs); and 3) the objective of achieving equity in health care.

Acute Resource Constraints

SSA's public health sectors face acute resource pressures, which follow decades of under investment and are compounded by a 'triple burden' of persisting infectious and rising chronic disease as well as injury and trauma. Despite government and donor pledges to increase health spending, national health services remain limited by major shortfalls in infrastructural, financial, medical and/or human capacity (AU 2007, WHO 2010, WHO 2011c).

Priority Focus on Millennium Development Goals

Within the context of constrained resources, SSA health sector strategies give priority to the provision of services to achieve the health-related MDGs 4, 5 and 6 – that is, to reduce the rates of child and maternal mortality, HIV/AIDS, malaria and tuberculosis (TB) (for all of which SSA has the highest rates globally) (UN, 2011c). In so doing, the strategies form an integral part of countries' overall Poverty

Reduction Strategies (PRS),[2] which seek to attain all eight MDGs (Handley et al. 2009, IMF 2011). Kenya's NHSSP II, for example, states:

> The Government of Kenya is determined to ... ensure that the health sector plays its essential role in the realization of the Kenyan Economic Recovery Strategy for Wealth and Employment Creation (ERS) ... As a signatory of the Millennium Declaration with its internationally defined Millennium Development Goals (MDGs), Kenya has expressed its commitment to reach these targets in the remaining ten years ... The NHSSP II is an integral part of ERS, from which it is derived. (KMOH 2005: 5)

The preference given to services for maternal and child health, malaria, TB and HIV/AIDS is reinforced by the often heavy reliance of SSA health systems on donor aid – which is overwhelmingly earmarked for MDG-related programmes (ADB 2006).

Equity in Health Care as a Major Objective

In addition to a focus on the MDGs, SSA health sector strategies and overarching national development plans typically assert a fundamental objective of achieving equity in health care. For example, Nigeria's revised national health policy is directly based on:

---

2 PRS are central to present development efforts in most SSA countries. They go by different names such as the 'Economic Recovery Strategy for Wealth and Employment Creation (ERSWEC) in Kenya' or the 'National Economic Empowerment and Development Strategy (NEEDS)' in Nigeria. Each strategy stipulates a framework for macroeconomic, structural and social policies that a respective country will pursue, ultimately, to achieve the MDGs. The eight MDGs and their associated targets, as set out in the UN Millennium Declaration, form the core of the international community's development agenda for poor world regions, including SSA. The targets, to be achieved by 2015, are to:

- Halve the proportion of people whose income is less than $1 a day and the proportion that suffers from hunger.
- Attain universal primary education in all countries.
- Eliminate gender disparity in primary and secondary education and at all levels of education.
- Reduce mortality by two-thirds among children younger than five years.
- Reduce the maternal mortality ratio by three-quarters.
- Halt and begin to reverse the spread of HIV/AIDS, and the incidence of malaria and other major diseases.
- Halve the proportion of people without access to safe drinking water, and by 2020, achieve significant improvement in the lives of at least 100 million slum dwellers.
- Develop a global partnership for development.

"The principle of social justice and equity and ... ideals of freedom and opportunity" and the goal of "equity in health care and in health for all Nigerians". (NFMOH 2005: 4)

The emphasis on health equity reflects growing international recognition of its importance as a prerequisite not only for social justice but also for effective development (World Bank 2006, WHO 2008, UNDP 2011). The equity perspective, together with health systems' resource constraints and a core emphasis on the MDGs points to three principal kinds of evidence that are needed to reinforce the argument on why policy action on old age-related health should be pursued.

Challenges for Research I: Strengthening the Case for Action

Magnitude of the Problem

A first area of evidence required to strengthen the case for action is data to quantify the extent of the 'problem' of old age-related ill-health in individual countries – both in absolute and relative terms. National indices and regional league tables are needed on 1) the prevalence of CNCD, disability, and CNCD risk factors in the middle – and older aged population; and 2) levels of basic service provision for them, together with data on the share of national health service loads caused by such conditions. Such evidence will likely raise political will to act on old age-related health – just as SSA governments are spurred to action on maternal, child health and major infectious diseases by regular publication (for example in Human Development, or MDG reports) of country-level data and rankings of mortality rates from, and service provision for, these conditions. Building on the proposed global monitoring framework for NCD proposed by the WHO (WHO 2011d) – together with developing a body on 'ageing and health' modelled on the WHO Information and Accountability Commission on Women and Children's Health' would constitute expedient approaches to drive and compel routine reporting on old age related health indicators.

In a few countries, useful data to furnish initial national indicators are being generated by monitoring surveys such as those using the WHO STEPS approach to 1) risk factor; and/or 2) stroke surveillance (WHO 2011e), and/or are expected to emerge from completed rounds of the WHO SAGE study. Further primary data generation is inevitable, however, and should build on an expansion of routine national surveys (such as Demographic and Health Surveys, or Multiple Indicator Cluster Surveys) already undertaken by most SSA countries to monitor core development and health trends (Aboderin 2011c).

A prerequisite for such efforts is a refinement of currently available survey measures of health in SSA adult populations. Focus is required on shortcomings of commonly used 1) self-reporting indicators of disease; 2) self-ratings of symptoms or function; and 3) quality of life (QOL) scales. The first two measures presuppose knowledge that respondents could only derive from their own health literacy or formal diagnoses by medical services. Both are far from given in SSA settings, especially among older, rural, or poor adults. Items requiring respondents' self-ratings of symptoms or levels of function – as for example in SAGE 'health state descriptions' or Instrumental Activities of Daily Living (IADL) scales, can be limited in two respects. First, queried functions, such as, for example, difficulty with climbing stairs or concentrating on a task for 10 minutes, may be neither meaningful nor elicit accurate information in rural or illiterate older populations. Second, while respondent ratings may capture actual health states among literate older adults in countries with advanced health systems (Kuhn, Rahman and Menken 2006), their effectiveness remains less clear for older persons in SSA contexts, who may have very different conceptions of health and function in old age as well as of 'complaints' about them. Unfortunately, we know very little about such conceptions at present. Thus, while some advances are being made with the use of anchoring vignettes as in the WHO SAGE study, careful qualitative work – as well as triangulation with health examination and biomarker data – is required to illuminate meanings and relevance of older adults' evaluations of their health and function in SSA settings.

Impacts on 'Development'

A second kind of evidence necessary to bolster the case for action on old age-related ill-health and disability, is careful documentation of the extent to which such conditions impact negatively on countries' social and economic development – in particular on progress toward achieving the MDGs and other salient development objectives. Analysis should specifically consider MDG-related areas, such as child well-being and HIV/AIDS, as well as productivity broadly, to which middle aged and older persons in SSA are known to contribute substantially, by virtue of their intergenerational family and economic roles, in particular in agricultural production (Ahenkora 1999, Mohatle and De Graft Agyarko 1999, Aboderin and Ferreira 2009).

Research to examine the development 'costs' of old age related ill-health and disability may usefully build on approaches being developed for assessing the broad economic costs or socioeconomic consequences of CNDC (WEF 2011).

Age-related Inequities in Health Care Access

A final, critical kind of evidence needed to raise political will to act on older persons' health is firm data on the extent to which older persons indeed have systematically less access to health care than do younger age-groups. A latent potential for such age-related access inequities certainly exists within a health systems context that combines acute resource constraints with a categorical priority focus on developing services for younger, MDG-related groups (children, mothers, malaria, TB and AIDS sufferers). However, no robust evidence exists thus far of possible age-related disparities in health care access. Similarly, (old)age has been largely overlooked as a potentially important factor in the intensifying debate on access inequities. Perhaps tellingly it is also omitted in the conceptual framework of the WHO Commission on Social Determinants of Health (WHO 2008). Studies to date have focused mainly on household-level disparities by socioeconomic or rural/urban status; or individual (including intrahousehold), level differences by gender or children's age. With one or two exceptions, no research has directly examined the role of (old) age as a determinant of differential health care access (Sauerborn, Berman and Nougtara 1996, McIntyre 2004).

Efforts to illuminate potential age-related access inequities – given difficulties in defining and operationalizing this concept (Oliver and Mossialos 2004) – require three types of evidence. First, are nationally representative data on patterns of health service utilization and receipt of appropriate care for existing need in the older compared to younger age population. Second are health systems analyses to establish the relative availability (and, where appropriate, affordability) of basic services (diagnostic tests, medicines, equipment, skilled staff) for old-age-related conditions, compared to service provision for essential health needs of younger age groups. Third are qualitative explorations of key factors shaping relative service utilization and care receipt among young and old within households and families. Recent conceptual developments regarding social exclusion in old age, globalization and social determinants of health (Phillipson 2006, Scharf et al. 2001, Labonté and Schrecker 2007) can then be drawn on to illuminate and theorize age–related disparities and their individual/family, local-, national- and global-level drivers.

Challenges for Research II: 'Clarifying Approaches'

Having strengthened the case for action on old-age-related health, research is needed to clarify what practical approaches are likely to be most effective and appropriate for 1) enhancing access to care for old age-related ill-health; and 2) preventing the development of such conditions in the first place. Two key areas require investigation to this end.

Determinants of Access to Health Care

First, is the development of a sound understanding of major demand and 'supply-side' factors at micro and macro levels that presently combine to impede access to adequate care for older persons and those with CNCD. Indications of some of these factors are provided by a number of small-scale, qualitative studies on care seeking among older people or diabetes sufferers, analyses of the availability and cost of essential CNCD drugs, and general examinations of impacts of user-fee or quality changes on health service utilization in SSA countries (see Aboderin 2011a for overview). The findings point to negative impacts of physical and logistical access difficulties, financial barriers related to service fees and/or transport costs and a perceived lack of quality (or unavailability altogether) of requisite services in the public sector. Beyond this, however, no systematic, country-level evidence exists.

Although some recent SSA health systems and policy research has sought to examine determinants of health care utilization in detail, the focus has been on MDG-related service areas, specifically malaria, HIV/TB, and maternal and child care (see Aboderin 2011a). Similar investigations on care services for old age-related ill-health are urgently needed. The 'Health Access and Livelihood' framework (Obrist et al. 2007) provides a useful starting point for and can be further refined by such research.

Social Determinants of Health at Older Ages

The major evidence required for identifying apposite strategies to prevent ill-health and disability in older ages is an understanding of the social mechanisms that act over the life course to engender them. The direct behavioral and biological CNCD risk factors are, of course, well recognized (UN 2011b). Much less is known, however, about the social processes and causal pathways that give rise to them in SSA settings. As indicated above, a small number of studies have explored, and found, basic social patterns of specific diseases or health and function broadly by gender, rural/urban or socio-economic status in older SSA adult populations. However, the evidence is neither comprehensive nor consistent. Also lacking – in contrast to burgeoning research in developed and other developing world regions (McMunn et al. 2006, Smith and Golman 2007, Nguyen et al. 2008, WHO 2008, Zimmer 2008), are further investigations of the actual social determinants that cause ill-health at older ages in Africa. Such inquiry needs to be fostered and should actively examine the relevance for SSA of theoretical and empirical insights generated by research in other world regions. A focus should be notions on 1) timing and effects of impacts including ideas about an accumulation of social and health (dis)advantage over the life course (Ferraro and Shippee 2009); and 2) key social exposures negatively shaping adult health, such as direct impacts of work (Crystal 2006); material deprivation; stress, lack of control and unhappiness; lack of social support; and infectious disease (Marmot and Wilkinson 2006, WHO 2008, Monteverde, Noronha and Palloni 2009).

A most immediate need, however, is for enhanced research on the basic social patterns of health and disease in older adult populations in SSA. A prerequisite for this (in addition to refining measures of health status as discussed above) is the forging of more incisive indicators of rural/urban, economic and social status than currently exist.

Measures of Rural/Urban Status

As others have noted (Kinra 2004), there is a need to move beyond current simple comparisons of rural and urban residents, to accurately capture individuals' lifetime exposure to urban or rural environments. Major issues to be considered in this respect include, first, difficulties of obtaining accurate chronological recall of previous life phases, including birth dates, due to a widespread lack of formal education and birth certificates among current older cohorts in the SSA context. This may be tackled through the use of prompts on locally relevant historical events (Ogunniyi and Osuntokun 1993) and a focus on broad life stages (early childhood, adolescence, early adulthood, middle age, old age). Second, are frequent country and time-period variations in the classification criteria used to define 'rural' and 'urban' areas in surveys. These necessitate careful reflection on the ways in which particular criteria relate to key exposures ascribed to rural and urban contexts. Last is the importance of distinguishing exposures to urban environments resulting from in-migration as opposed to urbanization of a previously 'rural' place of residence – as impacts on health will likely be different (Kinra 2004).

Measures of Economic Status

Improving measurement of economic status of (older) adults in SSA requires the development of sound individual-level indicators to replace presently used household-based markers such as wealth indices based on household assets, per capita income or expenditure. Besides general doubts about the value of income and assets as gauges of household economic well-being in SSA settings (Falkingham and Namazie 2002, EGPS 2006), such indicators overlook the critical factor of how resources are allocated between individual household members (Aboderin and Ferreira 2009). Subjective measures of individual economic well-being, as employed in recent US and Latin American research (Nguyen et al. 2008, Blazer, Sachs-Ericsson and Hybels 2005, 2007), may be useful alternatives and should be explored. In addition, there is a need for retrospective indicators, as developed for example in the SHARELIFE study conducted in Europe, which can capture earlier life economic well-being of middle-aged or older adults.

Measures of Social Status

Thus far, social status has received little, if any, active consideration in investigations on the social patterns of health in older ages in SSA. The significance of this omission is indicated by evidence from the developed world of a clear link between lower social status and worse health outcomes, mediated by maladaptive chronic stress responses and/or risk behaviors and engendered by feelings of lack of control, insecurity, hopelessness or hostility (Marmot and Wilkinson 2006). One may reasonably assume that similar processes also play a role in shaping (older) adults' health in SSA societies – and their investigation is imperative.

However, measures of social status, based on occupational and educational class as used in industrialized countries (McMunn 2006), are unlikely to be suitable for this purpose, given a broad lack of formal education especially among older cohorts, and the predominance of informal, unstructured labor markets in SSA. Development of appropriate indicators of social status should be a priority and must begin with qualitative explorations of the criteria through which social hierarchies and prestige in earlier and later adult life are constructed in African settings.

Conclusion

This chapter has described the present impasse in policy action on ageing and health in SSA and pinpointed major impediments underlying it – namely a lack of political will and/or clarity about what concrete programs to fashion, which largely reflect decision-makers' dearth of understanding of the scope, determinants and impacts of old age-related health needs. Building on an appreciation of the present health systems context in SSA, the paper highlights the need for a merging of NCD and ageing policy agendas for SSA and for five key areas of evidence in order to (a) strengthen the case for action on the health of older populations; and (b) clarify what forms it should take. If realized, systematic research on the five areas: 1) the magnitude of the problem; 2) its impacts on progress in development; 3) the possible existence of age-related inequities in health care access; 4) determinants of access to health care; and 5) social determinants of health and function at older ages – carries a real potential to advance policy and practice in SSA. This will need to be complemented by rigorous evaluations of the effectiveness of existing programmes designed to improve health care utilization or CNCD prevention or management among older SSA populations. Beyond a potential policy impact, SSA research on the above areas can serve to advance scientific debate on issues of ageing and health globally – in particular if analyses embrace a comparative international perspective. A first step towards the fostering of such a perspective is increased exchange and joint reflection between SSA scholars and those working on other world regions. The chapter hopes to make a contribution to this.

References

Aboderin, I. (2011a) Understanding and Advancing the Health of Older Populations in sub-Saharan Africa: Policy Perspectives and Evidence Needs. *Public Health Reviews* 32: 357–76.

Aboderin, I. (2011b) Understanding our ageing world assessment of national level implementation of the Madrid International Plan of Action on Ageing (MIPAA) in the Africa region. Consultancy report submitted to HelpAge International/ UNFPA.

Aboderin, I. (2011c) Advancing evidence generation on older persons in sub-Saharan africa. Paper presented at the 7th World Ageing and Generations Congress, St. Gallen, Switzerland, 29 August – 1 September 2011.

Aboderin, I. (2008) Advancing health service provision for older persons and age-related non-communicable disease in sub-Saharan Africa: Identifying key information and training needs. AFRAN Policy-Research Dialogue Series, Report 01–2008. Oxford Institute of Ageing.

Aboderin, I. and Ferreira, M. (2009) Linking ageing to development agendas in sub-Saharan Africa: Challenges and approaches. *Journal of Population Ageing* 1, 51–73.

Aboderin, I. and Gachuhi, M. (2007) First East African policy-research dialogue on ageing. Identifying information gaps. AFRAN Policy-Research Dialogue Series, Report 01–2007. African Research on Ageing Network. Oxford Institute of Ageing.

Aboderin, I. and Hoffman, J. (2011) Caregiving in contexts of poverty in sub-Saharan Africa: critical perspectives on debates and realities. Keynote paper presented at the Festival of International Conferences on Caregiving, Disability, Aging and Technology. Toronto, June 5–8, 2011.

African Development Bank (ADB) (2006) *African development report 2006. Aid, debt relief and development in Africa*. Oxford: Oxford University Press.

African Union (AU) (2007) *Africa health strategy 2007–2013*. Addis Ababa: African Union.

African Union/HelpAge International (AU/HAI) (2003) Policy framework and plan of action on ageing. Nairobi: HAI Africa Regional Development Centre.

Ahenkora, K. (1999) *The contribution of older people to development*. The Ghana study. UK: HelpAge International.

Amuyunzu-Nyamongo, M. (2010) Need for a multi-factorial, multi-sectorial and multi-disciplinary approach to NCD prevention and control in Africa. *Global Health Promotion*. 1757–9759, suppl. 31–2.

Biritwum, R. (2010) Patterns in disability and frailty of older adults: Evidence from SAGE. Paper presented at the World Health Organization SAGE Ageing and Health Meeting, June 2–4, 2010.

Blazer, D.G., Sachs-Ericsson, N., Hybels, C.F. (2005) Perceptions of unmet basic needs as a predictor of mortality among community-dwelling older adults. *American Journal of Public Health* 95, 299–304.

Blazer, D.G., Sachs-Ericsson, N., Hybels, C.F. (2007) Perceptions of unmet basic needs as a predictor of depressive symptoms among community-dwelling older adults. *Journal of Gerontology Biological Sciences and Medical Sciences* 62, 191–5.

Clausen, T. and Wilson, A.O. (2010) Twenty-five years of expectation. Where are the services for older people with mental illness in Africa? *International Psychiatry* 7, 32–4.

Cohen, B. and Menken, J. (2006) Report – Aging in sub-Saharan Africa: Recommendations for furthering research, in B Cohen and J Menken (eds)

Aging in sub-Saharan Africa: Recommendations for furthering research. Washington, DC: The National Academies Press, 7–45.

Crystal, S. (2006) Dynamics of late-life inequality: Modeling the interplay of health disparities, economic resources and public policies, in J. Baars, D. Dannefer, C. Phillipson and A. Walker (eds) *Aging, globalization and inequality*. Amityville, NY: Baywood, 205–14.

Daar, A.S., Singer, P.A., Persad, D.L. et al. (2007) Grand challenges in chronic non-communicable diseases. *Nature* 450, 494–6.

De-Graft Aikins, A., Unwin, N., Agyemang, C. et al. (2010) Tackling Africa's chronic disease burden: From the local to the global. *Global Health* 6, 5.

Expert Group on Poverty Statistics (EGPS). Compendium of best practices in poverty measurement (2006). Available from: http://www.ibge.gov.br/poverty/pdf/rio_group_compendium.pdf (accessed 8 February 2011).

Falkingham, J. and Namazie, C. (2002) *Measuring health and poverty. A review of approaches to identifying the poor*. London: DFID Health Systems Resource Centre, Department for International Development (DFID).

Ferraro, K. and Shippee, T.P. (2009) Aging and cumulative inequality: How does inequality get under the skin? *Gerontologist* 49, 333–43.

Gómez-Olivé, F.X., Thorogood, M., Clark, B.D. et al. (2010) Assessing health and well-being among older people in rural South Africa. *Global Health Action* S2, 23–35.

Gureje, O., Kola, L. and Afolabi, E. (2007) Epidemiology of major depressive disorder in elderly Nigerians in the Ibadan Study of Ageing: A community-based survey. *Lancet* 370(9591), 957–64.

Handley, G., Higgins, K., Sharma, B. et al. (2009) Poverty and poverty reduction in sub-Saharan Africa: An overview of the issues. Overseas Development Institute (ODI) Working Paper 299, London: ODI.

HelpAge International (HAI) (2008) *Older people in Africa. A forgotten generation.* London: HelpAge International.

International Monetary Fund (IMF) (2011) The IMF and the millennium development goals. IMF fact sheet. Available from: http://www.imf.org/external/np/exr/facts/mdg.htm (accessed 1 November 2011).

Kalache, A., Aboderin, I. and Hoskins, I. (2002) Compression of morbidity and active ageing: Key priorities for public health policy. *Bull World Health Organ* 80, 243–4.

Kenya Ministry of Health (KMOH) (2005) National Health Sector Strategic Plan II 2005–2012. Nairobi, Kenya.

Kinra, S. (2004) Commentary: Beyond rural-urban comparisons: Towards a life course approach to understanding health effects of urbanization. *International Journal of Epidemiology* 33, 777–8.

Kowal, P., Kahn, K., Ng, N. et al. (2010) Ageing and adult health status in eight lower-income countries: The INDEPTH WHO-SAGE Collaboration. *Global Health Action*, suppl 2, 11–22.

Kuate-Defo, B. (2006) Interactions between socioeconomic status and living arrangements in predicting gender-specific health status among the elderly in Cameroon, in B. Cohen and J. Menken (eds) *Aging in sub-Saharan Africa: Recommendations for furthering research*. Washington, DC: The National Academies Press, pp. 276–313.

Kuhn, R., Rahman, O., Menken, J. (2006) Survey measures of health: How well do self- reported and observed indicators measure health and predict mortality, in B. Cohen and J. Menken (eds) *Aging in sub-Saharan Africa: Recommendations for furthering research*. Washington, DC: The National Academies Press, pp. 314–42.

Kyobutungi, C., Egondi, T., Ezeh, A. (2010) The health and well-being of older people in Nairobi's slums. *Global Health Action* S2, 45–53.

Labonté, R. and Schrecker, T. (2007) Globalization and social determinants of health: Introduction and methodological background (Part 1 of 3). *Global Health* 3, 5–15.

Lloyd-Sherlock, P. (2010) *Population ageing and development. From generalisation to evidence*. Bristol: Policy Press.

Marmot, M. and Wilkinson, R.G. (eds) (2006) *Social determinants of health*. Oxford: Oxford University Press.

Martin, L.G., Freedman, V.A., Schoeni, R.F. and Andreski, P.M. (2010) Trends in disability and related chronic conditions among people aged fifty to sixty-four. *Health Affairs* 29, 725–31.

McIntyre, D. (2004) Health policy and older people in Africa, in P. Lloyd-Sherlock (ed.) *Living longer. Ageing, development and social protection*. London and New York: Zed Books, pp. 160–83.

Mohatle, T. and deGraft Agyarko, R. (1999) *The contribution of older people to development. The South Africa study*. London: HelpAge International.

Monteverde, M., Noronha, K. and Palloni, A. (2009) Effect of early conditions on disability among the elderly in Latin America and the Caribbean. *Population Studies* 63, 21–35.

Mwanyangala, M.A., Mayombana, C., Urassa, H. et al. (2010) Health status and quality of life among older adults in rural Tanzania. *Global Health Action* S2, 36–44.

National Department of Health, South Africa (NDOH) (2011) South African Declaration on the Prevention of NCD.

Nguyen, C.T., Couture, M.-C., Alvarado, B.E. and Zunzunegui, M.-V. (2008) Life course socioeconomic disadvantage and cognitive function among the elderly population of seven capitals in Latin America and the Caribbean. *Journal of Aging and Health* 20, 347–62.

Nigeria Federal Ministry of Health (NFMOH) (2005) Revised national health policy. Abuja, Nigeria: Federal Ministry of Health.

Obrist, B., Iteba, N., Lengeler, C. et al. (2007) Access to health care in contexts of livelihood insecurity: A framework for analysis and action. *PLoS Medicine* 4, 1584–8.

Ofstedal, M.B., Zimmer, Z., Hermalin, A. et al. (2007) Short-term trends in functional limitation and disability among older Asians: A comparison of five Asian settings. *Journal of Cross Cultural Gerontology* 22, 243–61.

Ogunniyi, A.O. and Osuntokun, B.O. (1993) Determination of ages of elderly Nigerians through historical events: Validation of Ajayi-Igun. *West African Journal of Medicine* 12, 189–90.

Oliver, A. and Mossialos, E. (2004) Equity of access to health care: Outlining the foundations for action. *Journal of Epidemiology and Community Health* 58, 655–8.

Phaswana-Mafuya, N., Peltzer, K. and Gomez-Olive, F.X. (2010) Health and health service utilization in South Africa: Evidence from SAGE. Paper presented at the World Health Organization SAGE Ageing and Health Meeting, June 2–4, 2010.

Phillipson, C. (2006) Aging and globalization: Issues for critical gerontology and political economy, in J. Baars, D. Dannefer, C. Phillipson and A. Walker (eds) *Aging, globalization and inequality*. Amityville, NY: Baywood, pp. 43–58.

Robine, J.M. and Michel, J.P. (2004) Looking forward to a general theory on population aging. *Journal of Gerontology Medical Sciences* 59A, 590–7.

Sauerborn, R., Berman, P. and Nougtara, A. (1996) Age bias but no gender bias in the intra- household resource allocation for health care in rural Burkina Faso. *Health Transition Reviews* 6, 131–45.

Scharf, T., Phillipson, C., Kingston, P. and Smith, A.E. (2001) Social exclusion and older people: Exploring the connections. *Education and Ageing* 16, 303–20.

Spitzer, H. and Mabeyo, Z.M. (2011) *In search of protection. Older people and their fight for survival in Tanzania*. Klagenfurt, Austria: Drava.

United Nations (UN) (2002) *Madrid International Plan of Action on Ageing (MIPAA)*. New York, NY: United Nations.

United Nations (UN) (2011a) Thematic study on the realization of the right to health of older persons by the Special Rapporteur on the right of everyone to the enjoyment of the highest attainable standard of physical and mental health. Anand Grover. United Nations, Official Document A/HRC/18/37. Available from: http://ap.ohchr.org/documents/dpage_e.aspx?m=100 (accessed 28 October 2011).

United Nations (UN) (2011b) Political declaration of the High-level Meeting of the General Assembly on the Prevention and Control of Non-communicable Diseases. United Nations Official Document A/66/LI. Available from: http://www.un.org/en/ga/ncdmeeting2011/ (accessed 28 October 2011).

United Nations (UN) (2011c) Millennium Development Goals. Available from: http://www.un.org/millenniumgoals/ (accessed 1 November 2011).

United Nations Development Programme (UNDP) (2011) *Human development report 2011. Sustainability and equity. A better future for all*. New York, NY: Palgrave Macmillan.

United Nations Population Division (UNPD) (2011) World population prospects: The 2010 revision. Available from: http://esa.un.org/unpp/ (accessed 30 October 2011).

United Nations/International Association of Gerontology and Geriatrics (UN/IAGG) (2008) *Research agenda on ageing for the 21st century*. New York, NY: United Nations.

Velkoff, V.A. and Kowal, P.R. (2007) *Population ageing in sub-Saharan Africa: Demographic dimensions 2006*. US Census Bureau, Current Population Reports, P 95/07-1. Washington, DC: US Government Printing office.

World Bank (2005) *World development report 2006: Equity and development*. Washington, DC: World Bank.

World Bank (2011) Country classification. Available from: http:// go.worldbank.org/K2CKM78CC0 (accessed 28 October 2011).

World Economic Forum (WEF) (2011) *The global economic burden of non-communicable diseases*. Geneva: WEF.

World Health Organization (WHO) (2006) *The health of the people. The African regional health report*. Brazzaville: WHO Regional Office for Africa.

World Health Organization (WHO) (2008) *Closing the gap in a generation: Health equity through action on the social determinants of health. Final Report of the Commission on Social Determinants of Health*. Geneva: WHO.

World Health Organization (WHO) (2010) *World health report 2010. Health systems financing. The path to universal coverage*. Geneva: WHO.

World Health Organization (WHO) (2011a) WHO Study on global AGEing and adult health (SAGE). Available from: http://www.who.int/healthinfo/systems/sage/en/index.html. (accessed 8 November 2011)

World Health Organization (WHO) (2011b) *A prioritized research agenda for prevention and control of noncommunicable diseases*. Geneva: WHO.

World Health Organization (WHO) (2011c) *World health statistics 2011*. Geneva: WHO.

World Health Organization (WHO) (2011d) *Targets to monitor progress in reducing the burden of noncommunicable diseases. Recommendations from a WHO technical working group on noncommunicable disease targets*. Geneva: WHO.

World Health Organization (WHO) (2011e) STEPwise approach to surveillance. Available from: http://www.who.int/chp/steps/en/ (accessed 1 November 2011).

Zimmer, Z. (2008) Poverty, wealth inequality and health among older adults in rural Cambodia. *Social Science and Medicine* 66, 57–71.

Chapter 8

New Myths about Ageing: The Growth of Medical Knowledge and its Societal Consequences

Dorly J.H. Deeg

It is only since the last century that older people are considered as a separate group in society. Since then, the representation of old age and older people was predominantly negative. A Dutch saying expresses this succinctly: Old age comes with infirmities. Until recently, this saying represented western society's general view of ageing. Older people were not only frail and sick, they also were a marginal group in a society that emphasizes youth and youthfulness (Butler 1980, 1990). If an older individual appeared on television, without exception s/he was living in a nursing home. Grey hair, clothes of a drab color, somber environment, washed-out look. From an older person nothing could be expected that could contribute to society. On the contrary, the slowly but surely increasing number of older individuals was seen as a threat for society, because the cost of care and pensions would reach unsustainable heights. And older persons themselves did nothing to counteract this threat.

The picture in the previous paragraph is sketched in the past tense. Studies of the popular press in Finland and the US show that the image of ageing has turned positive since the turn of the century (Rozanova 2010, Lumme-Sandt 2011). Also in the Netherlands since the 1990s, the media promote images such as the Zwitserleven feeling[1] and the Bertolli older adult.[2] Life after retirement has been depicted as the 'second adolescence' (Knipscheer 2005). Older people are assumed to go on holiday four times a year, to become internet-wise by following computer courses, and to manage their own care utilization. And of course, older people might as well work a few years longer to compensate for the growth of costs. The representation of older age seems essentially changed. The view of older age is so positive that there does not seem a limit to its joys. Have old myths about ageing (Van der Maas 1982, Lupien and Wan 2004) indeed replaced new myths?

---

1 Zwitserleven is a life insurance company whose advertisements show healthy older people e.g. on a big motorbike.

2 Bertolli is a brand of margarine based on olive oil, advertised showing older people dancing.

Also in the area of health care – which is not unconnected to societal change – positive views have gained predominance, as evidenced by the advocacy to apply cholesterol-lowering drugs in older patients and the rise of anti-ageing medicine (Jacobson 2006, Joyce and Loe 2010). In this contribution, I will discuss four of these positive views, which I will term new myths:

- Increasing longevity implies living increasingly healthy (Fries 2003);
- Increasing longevity implies ageing with fewer chronic diseases, limitations, and depressive symptoms (Christensen et al. 2009);
- Future generations of older people will be healthier (Gilleard and Higgs 1998)
- In old age, health decline is the same for everyone (Palmore 1999).

I will contrast these myths to empirical data from the Netherlands, a western country that may serve as exemplary for the developments discussed.

Myth 1: Longer Life because of Healthier Living

The first myth is related to an uncontestable fact: life expectancy in developed countries continues to increase. I will first show how this increase is realized in the Netherlands.

Figure 8.1 shows the development of life expectancy at birth since 1861, the year from which mortality statistics are deemed to be reliable.

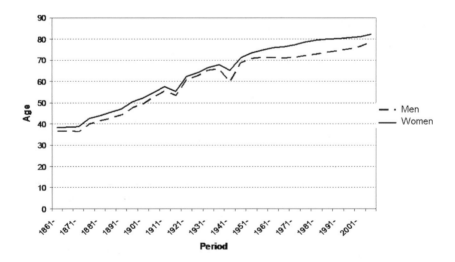

Figure 8.1 Life expectancy from birth by birth cohort, the Netherlands
Source: Netherlands Interdisciplinary Demographic Institute.

We can see that in the Netherlands, life expectancy started to increase from 1870. In 1900, life expectancy of both men and women was around 45 years. In first decades of the twentieth century, life expectancy rose quickly, so that in 1940 – at the start of World War II – it had increased by 20 years. This rise was similar for men and women. After a dip during World War II, life expectancy continued to rise until 1990 for women, whereas for men, life expectancy stagnated. Since 1990, men's life expectancy is catching up and is increasing faster than women's. In all, like in other developed countries, life expectancy in the Netherlands has increased substantially.

Explanations for this increase are different across historic periods. In the second half of the nineteenth century, the period in which life expectancy started increasing, the increase could be attributed to the decrease of mortality in newborns and infants (Omran 1971). Mortality in this age group has decreased to a now practically unchangeable minimum. In the first half of the twentieth century, also mortality of older children and young adults started to decline. In the second half, mortality up to adult ages became so low that not much improvement seemed possible (Olshansky and Ault 1986). Nevertheless, life expectancy continues to increase. This must, then, be attributed to a decline in mortality at older ages.

In Figure 8.2, it can be seen that life expectancy from age 65 has indeed increased since 1861 – for those who reached the age of 65. However, this increase is very modest. Between 1861 and 1940 it totaled just over two years for both men and women. Although we do see an accelerated increase in women after World War II, in men we observe even a decline until 1970. Similarly to life expectancy from birth, we see that men are catching up since the new millennium, so that

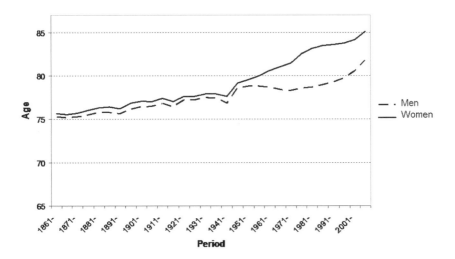

Figure 8.2 Life expectancy of those age 65+ by birth cohort, the Netherlands
Source: Netherlands Interdisciplinary Demographic Institute.

they now have an additional five years of life expectancy as compared to 1861 – provided they survive until age 65. In all likelihood, life expectancy from age 65 will continue to increase in the near future.

An often forwarded explanation for the increase in life expectancy, also among the older population, is the supposed improvement in health habits (Fries 2003). This explanation fits nicely in the current time and age, in which much value is laid upon a healthy lifestyle and individual responsibility for it (Angus and Reeve 2006). However, we have to do with a myth, because there is no empirical support for this explanation. In Table 8.1 the 10-year trend in health habits is demonstrated using data from the Longitudinal Aging Study Amsterdam (LASA) for the age group of 55–64 years – the age group that is on the verge of becoming older adults (Visser et al. 2005).

Table 8.1 Body Mass Index, waist circumference and physical activity, men and women ages 55–64 years in 1992 and 2002

	Men		Women	
	1992	2002	1992	2002
N	396	426	438	473
	%	%	%	%
Body Mass Index category†				
Obesity	9.5	18.4	20.5	27.5
Overweight	55.0	56.1	42.9	39.1
Normal weight	35.5	25.5**	36.7	33.4
High-risk waist circumference‡	32.3	40.2*	61.8	68.0
Sports participation	60.7	58.2	64.2	60.6
Netherlands norm healthy activity#	82.5	69.1*	91.8	75.2**

Note: * $p<0.05$; ** $p<0.01$ between same-sex samples 1992 en 2002, adjusted for age and education; † Obesity BMI ≤ 30 kg/m^2, overweight 25 ≤ BMI < 30 kg/m^2, normal weight BMI < 25 kg/m^2; ‡ For men > 102 cm, for women > 88 cm; # Minimally 30 minutes a day moderately intensive physical activity, every day of the week.
Source: Longitudinal Aging Study Amsterdam (Visser et al. 2005).

In both men and women, the prevalence of overweight and obesity increased between 1992–93 and 2002–03. In 1992, only 9.5% of men and 20.5 of women were obese, whereas in 2002 the prevalence had increased to 18.4% in men and 27.5% in women. Also, the average waist circumference, and thus the percentage of 55–64 year olds with a high-risk waist circumference, increased – especially in men. These changes in obesity and waist circumference remain practically unchanged after additional adjustment for physical activity, smoking behavior, and alcohol consumption.

More than half of 55–64 year olds practiced one or more sports, and this percentage remained the same over the 10-year period. However, men who practiced a sport spent significantly less time on their sports. In addition, the percentage of persons complying with the Netherlands Norm for Healthy Activity (defined as 30 minutes of moderate activity each day, for five days a week) decreased in both men and women.

The substantial increase in obesity and the decline in physical activity in middle and older age have also been reported for other countries for the same period (Leveille, Wee and Iezzoni 2005, Alley et al. 2007). These findings demonstrate clearly that the increase in life expectancy since 1992 has little to do with an improvement in health habits.

Myth 2: Longer Life therefore Less Diseases and Disabilities

There is no doubt that life expectancy is directly related to health status. After all, the large majority of mortality is due to diseases. Not surprisingly, the increase in life expectancy is often explained with the claim that the population's health is increasing (Christensen et al. 2009). This explanation represents a myth. It completely ignores the empirical fact that in all western countries, the prevalence of chronic diseases is increasing (Crimmins and Beltrán-Sánchez 2011).

For the Netherlands, the National Institute for Public Health and the Environment had made projections of the prevalence of single chronic diseases for the year 2025. It expects a rise of over 30% in absolute prevalence for heart diseases, diabetes, lung diseases and osteo-arthritis (NIPHE 2010). These are projections for the population of all ages. We have shown that the recent gain in life expectancy is concentrated in the ages 65 and over. It might be possible that in this age range, the prevalence of diseases is not increasing. Based on data from LASA, Figure 8.3 shows changes in the prevalence of several highly prevalent chronic diseases among 65–85 year olds during the period 1992–2009. In general, a rise in prevalence is observed. The increases are greater than 10% for heart diseases, diabetes, cancer, and joint disorders. Thus, also for the older population, a substantial increase in the prevalence of chronic diseases is seen. It is not likely that this increasing trend will stop.

Chronic diseases are often accompanied by functional limitations and disability, especially when they reach a more severe phase. Following the course of a chronic disease, we will first encounter mild limitations in bodily functions, and later on, severe limitations and disability, making people dependent on help in daily activities of living (Verbrugge and Jette 1994). Improvements in the treatment of chronic diseases can delay the onset of limitations, but so far no cure exists for the major chronic conditions. Thus, when the prevalence of chronic diseases increases, it is likely that the prevalence of limitations and disability increases – unless the treatment of diseases improves to such an extent that the onset of limitations is delayed by such a period that it compensates the increase in disease prevalence. In

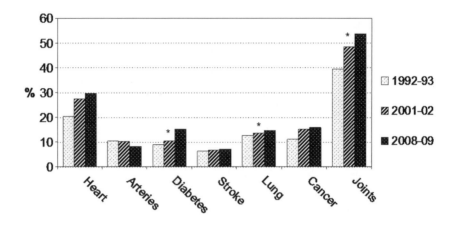

Figure 8.3 Prevalence of chronic diseases in 65–85 year olds, 1992–2009
Note: * Expected increase >10% through 2020 (Netherlands Institute for Public Health and the Environment 2006).
Source: Longitudinal Aging Study Amsterdam.

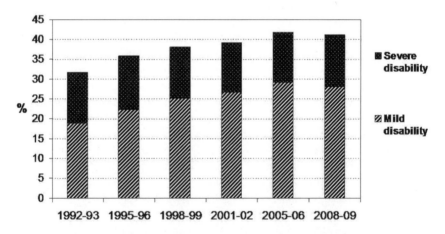

Figure 8.4 Prevalence of disability in 65–85 year olds, 1992–2009
Source: Longitudinal Aging Study Amsterdam.

a recent OECD report, in many western countries an increase in the prevalence of severe disability was observed, but in equally many western countries a decline in this prevalence is seen (Lafortune et al. 2007). In the Netherlands, we observe an increase in mild disability, while severe disability is declining (Puts et al. 2008). Figure 8.4 shows both developments for the period from 1992 to 2009. The data so far, therefore, do not warrant the conclusion that the increase in life expectancy is concomitant to an increase in the older population's health.

Life Expectancy in the Chronically Ill

Do we then have to go back to the old myth that old age comes with infirmities? Certainly, but its implications are not as negative as they seem at first sight. The rise in the number of older people with chronic conditions has not come about unwittingly. In fact, during the past decades much effort is spent to reach just this (Van der Maas 1982). It may just be the case that life expectancy is increasing at older ages, *especially* among chronically ill people.

To address this hypothesis, data are needed that allow specific study of the development of life expectancy in chronically ill people. This is possible using data from two LASA cohorts nine years apart, and calculating life expectancies based on mortality observed from 1992–93 to 1996 and from 2001–02 to 2005 using a life table approach for specific disease groups (Figure 8.5). On the left in this figure, it can be seen that for the total population at age 65, life expectancy has increased with 2.6 years in just nine years' time, from 14.8 to 17.4 years. The other bars in Figure 8.5 show the life expectancy of people with specific diseases that are associated with increased mortality. Of course, life expectancy for these disease groups is shorter than average. Nevertheless, for most disease groups we observe a substantial increase of over three years in life expectancy between 1992–93 and 2001–02. Cancer constitutes an exception showing an increase of 'only' one year.

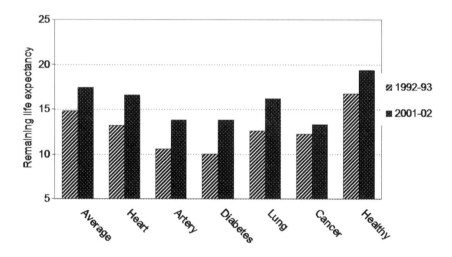

Figure 8.5 Life expectancy from age 65 years with disease: Increase 1992–2002

Source: Longitudinal Aging Study Amsterdam; three-year mortality follow-up from 1992 and 2002.

On the right, it is shown that for life expectancy in people without diseases the nine-year increase is only relatively modest.

Why has life expectancy increased so much more for chronically ill than for healthy older people? Let us review how the existence of a chronic disease is determined. This is done by one or more physicians who establish a diagnosis. This diagnosis, however, does not mark the beginning of the disease, but is only a confirmation of its presence. With improving diagnostic methods, this confirmation can be obtained in an ever earlier stage of the disease. 'Case finding' is an important goal in health care. The earlier the stage of the disease, the milder its treatment can be. When the application of mild methods of treatment also improves, the progress of the disease can be made to slow down, and the diseased person does not necessarily become limited by his or her disease. Thus, the extra increase in life expectancy in the chronically ill is due to the enormous improvement in diagnostics and treatment options – in short, to the advancement of medical care (Bunker 2001). This advancement is based on many decades of effort and dedication, and now we experience its benefits.

Quality of Life: Disability

It may be noted that many readers will find the term 'benefits' out of place in this context. Many older people live a life that has been robbed of quality because they have been limited in their range of activities. Moreover, advancement of diagnostics and treatment are not the same for every chronic condition or are not applied with the same amount of success.

A major indicator of quality of life is the extent of disability in activities of daily living. An important question is to what extent chronic diseases are linked to disability. For the period 1987–2001 in the Netherlands, Puts et al. (2008) reported changes in the association between chronic diseases and severe disability. However, these changes differed across diseases. For some, traditionally life threatening diseases (heart disease, diabetes), the extent of severe disability had decreased, whereas for non-life threatening diseases (back disorders, osteo-arthritis) it had increased.

Notably, heart disease seems to make a positive exception both regarding its increased associated life expectancy and its decreased association with disability. This implies that the living conditions for heart disease patients have improved considerably. Why is heart disease such an exception? Of old, a myocardial infarction was life-threatening if not fatal, and in the longer run, other heart diseases were fatal as well. Treatment of heart diseases can in fact be considered as crisis management, and is characterized by a measure of heroism: lives are saved – and by doing so, living conditions of heart patients are improved. Bypass and angioplastic surgery, however, were not instantaneously successful. It took decades of trial and error to reach this point.

In addition to positive developments, the study of changes in the associations of chronic diseases with disability also demonstrates that new problems have emerged that demand a solution. Arthritis patients suffer more disability. This may be related to another emerging problem due to the longer life expectancy with most diseases: the longer one lives with one disease, the greater the chance of getting another disease. Thus, although generally arthritis is no cause of death, arthritis patients are likely to live longer with their disease because mortality of other diseases has been pushed back.

There is still much room for improvement in medical care and cure. It should be a priority for the next decade to spend as much effort on improving the living conditions of older people with chronic diseases as has been spent on improving the treatment of heart disease. This will make a strong appeal to our creativity in increasing pertinent scientific evidence to support medical cure and care. This is the more urgent when keeping in mind that not only the prevalence of single diseases, but also multimorbidity will increase in the years to come, further complicating cure and care (Meinow et al. 2006). In our efforts, let us no longer exclusively focus on life saving heroism. Let us consider the living conditions of older people themselves. This should imply that more attention is needed to push back disability. In addition, we should not forget mental health, because this is a strong determinant of quality of life.

Quality of Life: Depressive Complaints

From longitudinal research in the context of LASA, chronic diseases have been shown to be strongly associated with depressive symptoms, here for convenience indicated by 'depression' (Bisschop et al 2004). Similar to disability, chronic diseases differ in their association with depression. The strongest associations with depression exist for joint disorders, stroke and lung disease, followed by cancer and heart disease. From LASA data no support is obtained for an association of diabetes and depression, provided that comorbidity is taken into account (Pouwer et al. 2003). In addition to the strength of the association, the mechanism behind the association with depression appears to differ across chronic conditions. The association of stroke with depression has been largely attributed to the extent of disability. For other diseases, disability plays a much smaller role in the explanation of their association with depression. A further point that should be noted is the importance of the duration of the disease. For recently diagnosed diseases, the association with depression is not as strong as for diseases that have been present for a longer period (i.e., three or more years). Thus, depressive complaints seem to increase with the duration of a disease.

The recognition of depression by health care professionals has been reported to be poor (Helmes and Duggan 2001). As an explanation it has been forwarded that depressive symptoms are often masked by somatic diseases so that neither health care professionals nor older depressed persons themselves realize that a depression is underlying the somatic problems (Van Exel et al. 2000). In light of the increase in life expectancy with diseases, this implies that it is eminently important to pay attention to depressive complaints in older people with somatic diseases.

I hope I have presented compelling arguments for the statement that the continued increase in life expectancy does not automatically imply that the health of the older population is improving. On the contrary, I have shown that life expectancy increases much faster in older people with chronic diseases than in those without chronic diseases. As a society, we have to learn to live with higher prevalence of chronic diseases. Moreover, I have presented evidence that the additional years of life for many chronic diseases are accompanied by mild disability, for some diseases by severe disability, and again for many diseases by depressive complaints. I now would like to dismiss the claim that older people are becoming increasingly healthy to the realm of New Myths.

Myth 3: Future Generations of Older People Will be Healthier

In the previous paragraphs I have focused on the ages 65 and over. What about the age group that precedes these years, the so-called younger old-aged 55–64? These are the older people of the future. Will they be healthier than their predecessors? Much can be said in favor of a positive answer. They had a better life, because they grew up in more favorable economic and social conditions that provided them with better chances in life. These better chances should be likely to extend towards health in older age, especially because they helped create a proactive self-image (Gilleard and Higgs 1998). Unfortunately, in the Netherlands we observe the same trends in this age group as in the age group 65 and over, although of course the prevalence of diseases and disability are lower (Hoogendijk et al. 2008, Van de Kamp et al. 2008). We observe a rising prevalence of chronic conditions in both genders, and in women a rise in the prevalence of disability and depressive complaints. In the United States, where until recently a persistent decline in disability was observed, exactly in these younger-old a reversal of the declining trend in disability is reported (Martin et al. 2010).

A completely different trend is seen in labor participation in the age group 55–64 years. In the Netherlands, since the early 1990s a clear increase in labor participation is noted for both men and women. After a decrease during the 1980s, between 1992 and 2010 labor participation of men rose from 37.5% to 61.2%. In women, labor participation at all ages has been much lower than in men historically. However, also in women labor participation increased substantially from 1992 to 2010: from 11.0% to 36.1% (Statistics Netherlands 2011). The observed increase started in 1995, the year in which Dutch economy started booming. No doubt, the favorable economic situation in the mid 1990s and the concomitant government regulations to attract or maintain older workers in the labor market, contributed to the observed increase in labor participation. Nevertheless, the increasing trend persisted after the crisis year 2008. This makes it likely that the economic necessity to continue working became an increasingly important factor in labor participation (Proper, Deeg and Van der Beek 2009).

Table 8.2 Labor force participation at ages 55–64, the Netherlands, 1992–2010

	1992	1996	2001	2006	2010
Men	37.5	39.2	45.7	53.1	61.2
Women	11.0	13.7	19.5	27.5	36.2

Source: Statistics Netherlands (http://statline.cbs.nl).

Failing health in the age group 55–64 years does not necessarily exclude people from labor market participation. However, this requires specific measures. It is an important task for both research and policy to examine how the labor market potential can be increased by realizing a better fit between the work conditions and the capacity of workers in this age group. This endeavor seems more fruitful than attempts – observed in several countries including the Netherlands – to force a higher retirement age through financial sanctions.

Diversity: Beyond Myths

Perhaps one of the most tenacious myths is that old age is the same for everyone (Peterson 1994, Palmore 1999). Whether the myth is negative, like in 'old age comes with infirmity', or positive, like in 'old age comes with wisdom', it assumes that all older people can be lumped together. But is not the condition for existence of any myth about a population segment that this segment is homogeneous? As gerontologists, we know that ageing implies something different for everyone. Ageing is a diversity issue (Weaver 1999). It is now a matter of transforming this knowledge into relevant measures.

When I search my own conscience as a researcher of ageing, I acknowledge that too much research produces 'average' truths. We should focus much more on heterogeneity (Dressel et al. 1997). With insights into the heterogeneity of ageing, we can equip policy and practice to take measures that are tailored to the needs of specific groups. Research in which different groups are distinguished, according to demographic characteristics or health status, has been termed diversity sensitive or intersectional research (Bekker et al. 2005). This type of research in not easy; it is a challenge to carry it out to satisfaction (Moerman and Van Mens-Verhulst 2004). It is perhaps an even greater challenge to implement its results into practice (Celik et al. 2007, Bekker and Van Mens-Verhulst 2007). Below, I give one example that shows the power of diversity conscious research.

I have argued that we have to learn to live with higher prevalence of diseases. The disease burden of chronic diseases largely stems from functional limitations and disability. It is therefore crucial to prevent or delay the onset and deterioration of disability – in short, to slow down functional decline. To be able to do this, insight is needed into determinants of functional decline. Two well-known social determinants of disability are a low level of education and the absence of a partner or spouse (Huisman et al. 2005, Kriegsman et al. 1997). Older persons with a low level of education generally have a lower standard of living as well as less knowledge about where and how services can be obtained. Older persons who lose their partner often fall back to a lower living standard and lack the direct support from the partner, which may increase their vulnerability in both social and psychological respect. Empirical research shows that these two social determinants are associated with functional decline, regardless of age, gender and the particular chronic diseases present (Deeg 2005).

Functional decline may follow different courses over time. Some people become gradually more disabled, other people experience a substantial decline within a short period of time. Ferrucci and colleagues (1996) distinguish a progressive and a catastrophic trajectory. When the catastrophic decline takes place shortly before death, it is termed 'terminal drop' (Riegel and Riegel 1972). In fact, this is the ideal trajectory: it involves a maximum proportion of life without disability (Fries 1980). In research and practice, it should therefore be endeavored to decrease the number of people with a progressive trajectory. In designing measures, it is of practical importance to know which groups of older people experience a progressive trajectory.

For data on functional decline, we resort once more to LASA. Table 8.3 shows the six-year course of disability in the older Dutch population, summarized into three trajectories: one trajectory without any disability (53%), a catastrophic trajectory (24%), and a progressive trajectory (23%) (Deeg 2005). When trajectories are distinguished according to level of education and partner status, only 16% of the higher educated and 16% of the older adults who have a partner turn out to experience a progressive trajectory. In contrast, a progressive trajectory is experienced by as many as 33% of the lower educated and 38% of the older adults without a partner. Furthermore, an interaction of both social determinants is observed: among older adults without a partner, 47% of the lower educated

Table 8.3 Three trajectories of functional decline in 55–91 year olds observed across a period of six years

	Total	Education		Partner	
		Low	High	No	Yes
Stable no disability	53%	41%	63%	37%	62%
Catastrophic increase	23%	26%	21%	25%	22%
Progressive increase	24%	33%	16%	36%	16%

Source: Longitudinal Aging Study Amsterdam (Deeg 2005).

against 26% of the higher educated experience a progressive trajectory, whereas among older adults who have a partner, these percentages are only 21% and 12%, respectively.

This example is illustrative of diversity sensitive research. To the question 'which group of older people benefit most from measures to prevent progressive decline?', the answer is: those without a partner and with a low level of education.

Conclusion

I started this chapter by stating that ageing is a relatively new societal phenomenon, and even more recent is the common distinction of the older population as a separate group – sometimes indicated with the term 'seniors'. With the distinction of a separate group, myths about this group tend to be formed, a number of which are strengthened by the growth of medical knowledge. Successively, I discussed three myths: 1) Longer life expectancy is based on healthier living; 2) Longer life expectancy implies ageing with fewer chronic diseases, limitations, and depressive symptoms; 3) Future cohorts of older people will be healthier. I have shown that these myths do not hold up in the face of empirical data on trends in health in the Netherlands. These trends are exemplary for other western countries as evidenced by recent publications. On the contrary, the longer lives of older people are characterized by more diseases, disabilities and depressive complaints. This is true for the ages of 65 and over as well as for the 'younger-old' aged 55–64 years, who constitute the older population of the future. Finally, by introducing the notion of diversity, I addressed the 'mother of myths' that all older people experience the same health declines. Using longitudinal data, I showed that socially advantaged elders who had higher education and who have a partner, are less likely to experience a trajectory of progressive functional decline than their less advantaged counterparts. The empirical findings presented help raise awareness of myths, which in turn help to improve policy and practice, so that ultimately quality of life of older people is improved.

Acknowledgement

The Longitudinal Aging Study Amsterdam (LASA) is funded largely by the Ministry of Welfare, Health and Sports of the Netherlands.

References

Alley, D.E. and Chang, V.W. 2007. The changing relationship of obesity and disability, 1988–2004. *Journal of the American Medical Association* 55, 2020–27.

Angus, J. and Reeve, P. 2006. Ageism: A threat to 'ageing well' in the 21st century. *Journal of Applied Gerontology* 25, 137–52.
Bekker, M.H.J. and Van Mens-Verhulst, J. 2007. Anxiety disorders: Sex differences in prevalence, degree, and background, but gender-neutral treatment. *Gender Medicine* 4B, S178–93.
Bekker, M., Van Vliet, K., Klinge, I. et al. 2005. Een aanzet tot richtlijnen voor diversiteitsbewust gezondheid(szorg)onderzoek [A proposal for guidelines for diversity-sensitive research in health and health care]. *Tijdschrift voor Genderstudies* 2, 36–43.
Bisschop, M.I, Kriegsman, D.M.W., Deeg, D.J.H. et al. 2004. The longitudinal relation between chronic diseases and depression in older persons in the community: The Longitudinal Aging Study Amsterdam. *Journal of Clinical Epidemiology* 57, 187–94.
Bunker, J. 2001. Medicine matters after all. Measuring the benefits of medical care, a healthy lifestyle, and a just social environment. *Nuffield Trust Series* no. 15, London.
Butler, R.N. 1980. Ageism – a foreword. *Journal of Social Issues* 36, 8–11.
Butler, R.N. 1990. A disease called ageism. *Journal of the American Geriatrics Society* 38, 178–80.
Celik, H., Abma, T., Widdershoven, G. et al. 2007. Implementation of diversity in healthcare practices: Barriers and opportunities. *Patient Education and Counseling* 71, 65–71.
Christensen, K., Doblhammer, G., Rau, R. and Vaupel, J.W. 2009. Ageing populations: The challenges ahead. *Lancet* 374, 1196–208.
Crimmins, E.M. and Beltrán-Sánchez, H. 2011. Mortality and morbidity trends: Is there compression of morbidity? *Journals of Gerontology B Social Sciences* 66, 75-86.
Deeg, D.J.H. 2005. Longitudinal characterization of course types of functional limitations. *Disability and Rehabilitation* 27, 253–61.
Deeg, D.J.H. 2005. The development of physical and mental health from late midlife to early old age, in *Middle Adulthood: A Lifespan Perspective*, edited by S.L. Willis and M. Martin. London: Sage, 209–41.
Deeg, D.J.H. and Westendorp-de Serière, M. (Red). 1994. *Autonomy and wellbeing in the aging population I: Report from the Longitudinal Aging Study Amsterdam 1992–1993*. Amsterdam: VU University Press.
Dressel, P., Minkler, M. and Yen, I. 1997. Gender, race, class, and aging: Advances and opportunities. *International Journal of Health Services* 27, 579–600.
Ekamper, P. 2008. Vergrijzende EU onderzoekt toekomstige arbeidsmarkt [Aging European Union studies future labor market]. *Demos, Bulletin about Population and Society* 24(9), 11–12.
Ferrucci, L., Guralnik, J.M., Simonsick, E. et al. 1996. Progressive versus catastrophic disability: A longitudinal view of the disablement process. *Journals of Gerontology: Medical Sciences* 51A, M123–30.

Fries, J.F. 1980. Aging, natural death, and the compression of morbidity. *New England Journal of Medicine* 80, 245–50.

Fries, J.F. 2003. Measuring and monitoring success in compressing morbidity. *Annals of Internal Medicine* 139, 455–9.

Gilleard, C. and Higgs, P. 1998. Ageing and the limiting conditions of the body. *Sociological Research*. [Online] 3(4), 4. Available at: http://www.socresonline.org.uk/3/4/4.html [accessed: 20 December 2011].

Helmes, E. and Duggan, G.M. 2001. Assessment of depression in older adult males by general practitioners. Ageism, physical problems and treatment. *Australian Family Physician* 30, 291–94.

Hoogendijk, E., Broese van Groenou, M., Van Tilburg, T. and Deeg, D. 2008. Educational differences in functional limitations: Comparisons of 55–65-year-olds in the Netherlands in 1992 and 2002. *International Journal of Public Health* 53, 281–9.

Huisman, M., Kunst, A., Deeg, D. et al. 2005. Educational inequalities in the prevalence and incidence of disability in Italy and the Netherlands were observed. *Journal of Clinical Epidemiology* 58, 1058–63.

Jacobson, T.A. 2006. Overcoming 'ageism' bias in the treatment of hypercholesterolaemia – a review of safety issues with statins in the elderly. *Drug Safety* 29, 421–48.

Joyce, K. and Loe, M. 2010. A sociological approach to ageing, technology and health. *Sociology of Health & Illness* 32, 171–80.

Knipscheer, C.P.M. 2005. *De tweede adolescentie* [The second adolescence]. Retirement lecture. Amsterdam, the Netherlands, 14 October 2005.

Kriegsman, D.M.W., van Eijk, J.T.M., Penninx, B.W.J.H. et al. 1997. Does family support buffer the impact of specific chronic diseases on mobility in community-dwelling elderly? *Disability and Rehabilitation* 19, 71–83.

Lafortune, G., Balestat, G. and the Disability Study Expert Group Members. 2007. *Trends in severe disability among elderly people: assessing the evidence in 12 OECD countries and the future implication.* OECD Health Working Papers No. 26 Paris. [Online]. Available at: http://ideas.repec.org/p/oec/elsaad/26-en.html [accessed: 30 March 2007].

Leveille, S.G., Wee, C.C. and Iezzoni, L.I. 2005. Trends in obesity and arthritis among baby boomers and their predecessors, 1971–2002. *American Journal of Public Health* 95, 1607–13.

Lumme-Sandt, K. 2011. Images of ageing in a 50+ magazine. *Journal of Aging Studies* 25, 45–51.

Lupien, S.J. and Wan, N. 2004. Successful ageing: From cell to self. *Philosophical Transactions of the Royal Society of London Series B-Biological Sciences* 359, 1413–26.

Martin, L.G., Freedman, V.A., Schoeni, R.F. and Andreski, P.M. 2010. Trends in disability and related chronic conditions among people ages fifty to sixty-four. *Health Affairs* 29, 725–31.

Meinow, B., Parker, M., Kareholt, I. and Thorslund, M. 2006. Complex health problems in the oldest old in Sweden 1992–2002. *European Journal of Ageing* 3, 98–106.

Moerman, C.J. and Van Mens-Verhulst, J. 1994. Gender-sensitive epidemiological research: Suggestions for a gender-sensitive approach towards problem definition, data collection and analysis in epidemiological research. *Psychology, Health and Medicine* 9, 41–52.

Netherlands Health Council. 2008. *Ouderdom komt met gebreken* [Old age comes with infirmities]. Advies 2008/1. The Hague: Netherlands Health Council.

Netherlands Institute for Public Health and the Environment. 2010. *Public Health Future Forecast 2010*. Bilthoven, the Netherlands: Netherlands Institute for Public Health and the Environment.

Olshansky, J.S. and Ault, A.B. 1986. The fourth stage of the epidemiologic transition: The age of delayed degenerative diseases. *The Milbank Quarterly* 64, 355–91.

Omran, A.R. 1971. The epidemiologic transition. A theory of the epidemiology of population change. *The Milbank Memorial Fund Quarterly* 49, 509–38.

Palmore, E.B. 1999. *Ageism: Negative and Positive*. New York: Springer Publishing Company.

Peterson, M. 1994. Physical aspects of aging – is there such a thing as normal. *Geriatrics* 49, 45–9.

Pouwer, F., Beekman, A.T.F., Nijpels, G. et al. 2003. Rates and risks for comorbid depression in patients with type II diabetes mellitus: Results from a community-based study. *Diabetologia* 46, 892–8.

Proper, K.I., Deeg, D.J.H. and Van der Beek, A.J. 2009. Challenges at work and financial rewards to stimulate longer workforce participation. *Human Resources for Health* Aug(11/7), 70.

Puts, M.T., Deeg, D.J., Hoeymans, N. et al. 2008. Changes in the prevalence of chronic disease and the association with disability in the older Dutch population between 1987 and 2001. *Age and Ageing* 37, 187–93.

Riegel, K.F. and Riegel, R.M. 1972. Development, drop, death. *Developmental Psychology* 6, 306–19.

Rozanova, J. 2010. Discourse of successful aging in The Globe & Mail: Insights from critical gerontology. *Journal of Aging Studies* 24, 213–22.

Statistics Netherlands. 2011. http://statline.cbs.nl [accessed 30 October 2011].

Van de Kamp, K., Braam, A.W. and Deeg, D.J.H. 2008. Verschuiving van de ervaren gezondheid van 55–64-jarigen tussen 1992/'93 en 2002/'03. Verklarende factoren [Shift in the self-perceived health of 55–64-year olds between 1992/'93 and 2002/'03. Explanatory factors]. *Tijdschrift voor Gerontologie en Geriatrie* 39, 182–92.

Van der Maas, P.J. 1982. Mythen over vergrijzing en volksgezondheid [Myths about population aging and public health]. *Tijdschrift voor Sociale Geneeskunde* 60, 711–21.

Van Exel, E., Stek, M.L., Deeg, D.J.H. and Beekman, A.T.F. 2000. The implication of selection bias in clinical studies of late life depression: An empirical approach. *International Journal of Geriatric Psychiatry* 15, 499–2.

Verbrugge, L.M. and Jette, A. 1994. The disablement process. *Social Science and Medicine* 38, 1–14.

Visser, M., Pluijm, S.M.F., van der Horst, M.H.L. et al. 2005. Leefstijl van 55–64-jarige Nederlanders minder gezond in 2002/'03 dan in 1992/'03 [Lifestyle of Dutch people aged 55–64 years less healthy in 2002/'03 than in 1992/'93]. *Nederlands Tijdschrift voor de Geneeskunde* 149/31, 2973–8.

Weaver, J.W. 1999. Gerontology education: A new paradigm for the 21st century. *Educational Gerontology* 25, 479–90.

PART II:
Ageing Workforce, Retirement and the Provision of Pensions

Chapter 9
Population Ageing and its Global Challenges

Codrina Rada

Population ageing is taking place at an accelerated rate across the world. United Nations World Population Prospects predict the world's share of individuals 65 and over relative to working age individuals to increase to 25 percent by 2050 from about 10 percent in 2000.

While the ageing process differs among countries and regions, its effects are expected to be felt everywhere. Developing countries, many of which lack a formal income-security system for old-age, are experiencing the fastest growth in the number of older individuals. This reality is likely to coerce the political and economic establishment into introducing some form of income provision for old age – an extremely difficult task given the size of informal employment in developing economies. The rise in old-age dependency rates to unprecedented levels and the slowdown in the expansion of the labor supply could exercise labor cost pressures in industrialized countries, and test financial sustainability of existing pension systems. Should labor shortages materialize, it remains unclear what will be the exact consequences on economic performance. Firms may try to move some of their production units to countries where ageing is not as pronounced (and therefore the labor is cheaper). Alternatively, policy can encourage labor migration from younger countries or provide incentive to retain older people in the workforce. More important, firms may try to bypass the issue of a lower labor supply by spending considerable efforts to raise labor productivity and therefore produce the same amount of output with fewer workers. One crucial point I argue in this chapter is that investment in labor productivity presents a sustainable solution to potential labor supply constraints brought about by the ageing process in developed economies.

A second aspect I take issue with concerns methodologies across and within disciplines to quantify and assess population ageing. For demographers population ageing implies an increase in the median age of a population, whereas the economist thinks of it in terms of a higher share of older to the working age individuals. Even across societies ageing or the concept of old age is often perceived in different ways (United Nations 2007). As a result views on what constitutes population ageing or its magnitude remain relatively fluid.

The analysis I provide in this chapter traces some of the conclusions made by the United Nations report on *Development in an Ageing World* (United Nations 2007). The chapter starts with a simple account of population growth by age-group and gender. Next, the chapter contrasts indicators of old-age and economic

160   Global Ageing in the Twenty-First Century

dependency rates followed by an analysis of labor participation rates for different demographic groups. Calculations of labor productivities required to sustain an ageing labor force shed light on some of the real challenges brought about by the global ageing process. An overview of these indicators provides a basis for countries and regions comparisons. This multifaceted approach also allows for a more thorough account of population ageing in different parts of the world and hence might provide a suitable platform to assess national but also world-wide policies. The chapter concludes with few general policy recommendations.

Regional Demographic Trends

Judging by Table 9.1 population ageing is indeed becoming a global phenomenon in the twenty-first century. The upcoming demographic changes, although not uniform do follow similar trends across regions. The young-age population, defined here as 0–14, will decline over the second quarter of this century in all regions besides Africa and Northern America. The expansion of working-age population is expected to decelerate rapidly everywhere but in Africa, while the number of those 65 or older continues to grow strongly across the board. Although deemed as young in terms of median age statistics, Africa, Asia and Latin America and the Caribbean are seeing their older populations increasing at a rapid pace. The number of people over 65 years of age are projected to grow throughout 2000–2050 at about 2.5 percent or more annually in these regions which amounts to an overall increase of 140 percent by 2030 (National Institute on Aging 2007). At the same time, today's ageing regions, Northern America and Europe, will eventually see a slower rise of older populations as they transition to a new demographic steady-state. Overall, the fact is that while developed regions have the largest share of older population (see Table 9.3 below), the fastest growth in the actual number of elderly is taking take place in developing nations.

A world level comparison of annual growth rates by age-groups for the first and second quarter of the century replicates trends observed at the regional level. The world's young population will fall in absolute terms, while the working age population will grow at a slower rate. The only age group that is projected to record robust growth is the older population which will add individuals at a rate of 2.3 percent during 2050–2025, thus reinforcing the view that ageing is a phenomenon present in most of the world.

Statistics on gender distribution by age-groups in Table 9.2, provide additional insights into the global ageing process. Differences in life expectancy for men and women have resulted in higher shares of older women in all regions. The most dramatic outcome is observed in Eastern Europe where women accounted for 66 percent of the population that was 65 and older in 2000, and for a staggering 69 percent of those 70 and above. Hence, we expect to see not only an older world, but a world with an older population that tends to have more women than men. These stylized facts on ageing and gender urge us to re-think labor force policies and

Table 9.1 Population growth rates, selected world regions, percentage by age groups[1]

Regions	2000–2025				2025–2050			
	0–14	15–64	65+	70+	0–14	15–64	65+	70+
Africa	1.50	2.56	3.20	3.34	0.32	1.81	3.59	3.70
sub-Saharan Africa	1.69	2.72	3.11	3.29	0.40	2.01	3.55	3.58
Asia	-0.23	1.28	3.28	3.52	-0.54	0.20	2.64	3.02
Eastern Asia	-0.90	0.49	3.11	3.48	-0.76	-0.60	1.91	2.35
Latin America	-0.49	1.33	3.48	3.54	-0.66	0.09	2.83	3.20
South America	-0.53	1.29	3.52	3.56	-0.61	0.05	2.75	3.11
Northern America	0.28	0.70	2.48	2.25	0.16	0.34	1.21	1.60
Europe	-0.55	-0.21	1.39	1.47	-0.27	-0.63	0.89	1.21
Eastern Europe	-1.02	-0.58	1.08	1.03	-0.63	-0.96	0.69	0.94
Southern Europe	-0.15	0.11	1.45	1.68	-0.07	-0.74	1.34	1.69
Western Europe	-0.46	-0.14	1.71	1.83	-0.13	-0.50	0.72	1.09
World	0.13	1.26	2.80	2.89	-0.26	0.44	2.35	2.66

the provision of safety nets such as old-age income and health care. As discussed in the next section women are considerably behind men when it comes to labor force participation rates. The two effects combined, higher share of women in older age and significantly lower participation rates, suggest significant economic and welfare payoffs to measures that specifically target the female labor force. A successful approach to raise women participation has the potential to bring relief to labor supply shortages, while at the same time guarantee an old-age income and protection from poverty. The latter point is especially important since overall poverty among older women is already more pronounced compared to older men (United Nations 2007).

With this context in mind it is no surprise that population ageing has become a regular item on policy agendas in many countries. Nonetheless, it remains a contentious issue especially among economists who lead debates about how much of a financial burden the older population is expected to be for the coming decades; and consequently, to what extent to proceed with reforms that target public or defined-benefit pension schemes. From the economic viewpoint population ageing becomes a challenge when dependency rates – calculated as the ratio between the dependent population and the economically active population – rise enough to force a change in how the economy provides for its dependent population. In practical terms, this boils down to either changes in the current distribution of income through taxation, or to a decline in benefits promised to retirees. At first

---

1 Unless specified, all data for figures and tables come from United Nations Population Prospects Database, 2008.

Table 9.2 Women as a percentage of population age-groups, world regions

Regions	2000			2025			2050		
	14–64	of 65+	of 70+	14–64	of 65+	of 70+	14–64	of 65+	of 70+
Africa	0.50	0.55	0.56	0.50	0.55	0.57	0.50	0.54	0.56
sub-Saharan Africa	0.51	0.55	0.56	0.50	0.56	0.57	0.50	0.54	0.55
Asia	0.49	0.54	0.55	0.49	0.54	0.55	0.48	0.55	0.56
Eastern Asia	0.49	0.54	0.56	0.48	0.54	0.55	0.47	0.55	0.56
Latin America	0.51	0.56	0.57	0.51	0.56	0.57	0.50	0.57	0.58
South America	0.51	0.56	0.58	0.50	0.57	0.58	0.50	0.57	0.58
Northern America	0.50	0.58	0.60	0.49	0.55	0.56	0.49	0.54	0.56
Europe	0.51	0.62	0.64	0.50	0.59	0.61	0.49	0.58	0.59
Eastern Europe	0.51	0.66	0.69	0.51	0.64	0.67	0.50	0.62	0.65
Southern Europe	0.50	0.58	0.60	0.49	0.57	0.58	0.49	0.55	0.56
Western Europe	0.50	0.61	0.64	0.50	0.56	0.58	0.49	0.56	0.57
World	0.49	0.56	0.58	0.49	0.55	0.57	0.49	0.55	0.57

glance, a comparison of old-age dependency rates for upcoming decades may legitimize some of the fears concerning the implications of population ageing. Figures 9.1 (a) through (c) provide a snapshot of old-age dependency rates for years 2000, 2025 and 2050 respectively. It is indeed the case that dependency rates are increasing in all regions over the next four decades.

Table 9.3 (see page 164) complements Figure 9.1 with additional numbers for few selected countries. The ageing process is especially pronounced in the industrialized countries and regions (Europe, Northern America, and Eastern Asia) but also in some developing countries such as China and several large Latin American countries. Japan stands out among all countries. Its population ageing is expected to put to test the ability of the economy to provide for its older citizens. Based on the numbers in Table 9.3, there was one Japanese over 65 years of age for every four working age individuals in 2000. By 2050 for every three workers there will be two individuals 65 or older.

The doomsday scenarios for public pension systems in the wake of baby-boomers retirement in the industrialized world, especially the United States, is based on numbers as those presented in Table 9.3. Advocates of private pension accounts and defined-contribution schemes have promoted them as a viable solution to the economic problems caused by population ageing. However, a switch to a private pension system is not necessarily going to ensure the security of old-age income since the level of pensions remains a function of how well the economy is performing (Rada 2011). One thing such a reform would do is privatize risk by shifting the responsibility for old-age income from the society to the individual (Barr 2002). The recent financial crisis has in fact signaled the danger of a strategy that makes retirement income rely entirely on the performance of financial markets.

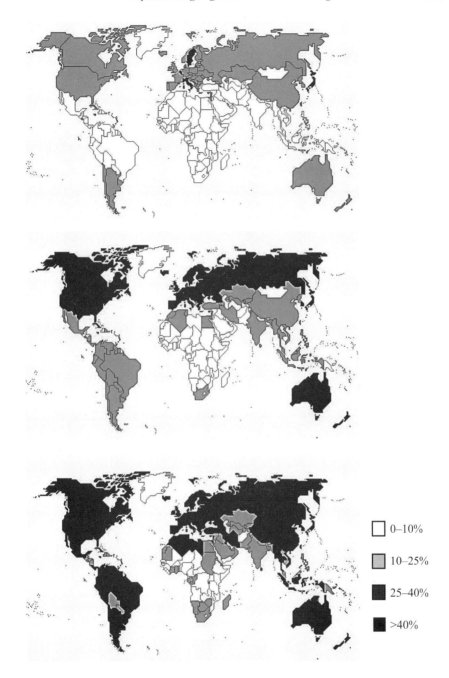

Figure 9.1 Old-age dependency rates for 2000, 2025 and 2050 respectively

Table 9.3 Old-age dependency rates, world regions

Regions	2000	2025	2050
Africa	0.06	0.07	0.11
Sub-Saharan Africa	0.06	0.06	0.09
Asia	0.09	0.15	0.27
Eastern Asia	0.11	0.22	0.40
China	0.10	0.19	0.38
India	0.07	0.11	0.20
Japan	0.25	0.50	0.74
Latin America and the Caribbean	0.09	0.16	0.31
South America	0.09	0.16	0.31
Argentina	0.16	0.20	0.30
Brazil	0.08	0.16	0.36
Northern America	0.19	0.29	0.36
Europe	0.19	0.29	0.36
Eastern Europe	0.19	0.28	0.43
Western Europe	0.24	0.38	0.51
France	0.25	0.37	0.47
Germany	0.24	0.40	0.59
United Kingdom	0.24	0.31	0.38
Southern Europe	0.25	0.34	0.58
Italy	0.27	0.39	0.62
World	0.11	0.16	0.25

If we place the debate in a historical perspective we learn that economies around the world have, in the past, successfully accommodated similar levels of dependency rates as those projected for upcoming decades. Figure 9.2, for example, compares regional economic dependency rates for 1980, 2000 and projections for 2020. The economic dependency rate measures the support that the current workforce must provide to the dependent population. It is calculated as a ratio of all dependents – young, old and the potentially economically inactive – to the economically active population. Outside of Northern America, economic dependency rates for 2020 are not expected to depart significantly from levels recorded in the 1980s. Lack of data on the economically active population beyond 2020 can be overcome by looking at the ratio of young and old to the working-age population, an indicator known as the overall dependency rate. This way of assessing dependency rates rests on two very strong assumptions – that all working age individuals are part of the labor force and that no individual over 65 is economically active – and therefore must be interpreted with caution. Overall dependency rates will increase between 25 to 50 percent by 2050 in Northern America, Europe and East Asia, as compared to 2000. A subsequent section of this chapter confronts this increase in overall dependency rates by suggesting

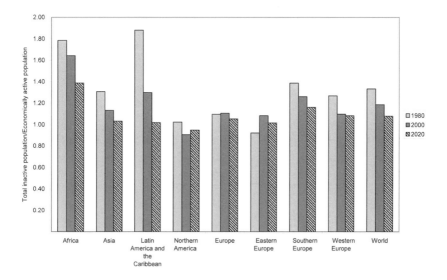

Figure 9.2 Economic dependency rates
Source: International Labour Organization, "LABORSTA: economic active population estimates and projections" 2008.

labor productivity growth as a mechanism to accommodate a larger dependent population. In the meantime we explore in more detail dynamics of labor force participation. Specifically, we point out that important reserves of labor exist in many so-called older countries and that the policy should focus on facilitating participation in the labor markets by working age individuals that remain outside the job market.

Population Ageing: Implications for the Labor Force

The analysis of demographic trends presented so far emphasizes the decline in the expansion of working age individuals for all regions. However, there is not a one to one relationship between the growth of working-age population and the growth of the labor force. By definition the labor force or the economically active population, includes all individuals who are 16 years of age or older, who are currently employed or are actively looking for employment. The decision of each individual to participate or not in the labor force determines the difference between growth rates of working-age population and of the labor force respectively. Estimates for the rate of expansion of economically active populations in Table 9.4 are from the International Labor Organization (ILO). These data take into account all individuals who are part of the labor force including those over 65 years of age. A first thing to notice is the contrast in labor force patterns for women and for men.

In all regions women dominate and sometimes by a significant margin. In other words, these projections *assume* that women will expand their participation in the labor force from their currently much lower levels of participation (see Figure 9.4, page 168). Such a behavior on the part of the female population can compensate for the overall slowdown in the working-age population. A closer look at the data also shows that these projections assume little or no increase in the current participation rates for those 65 and over. This working assumption provides some space for policies that encourage healthy individuals to remain in the labor force beyond 65 years of age.

Table 9.4 Annual growth rate of labor force (15+) in percentages: 2000–2020, world regions

Regions	Total	Men	Women
Africa	2.73	2.51	3.04
Asia	1.33	1.30	1.37
Eastern Asia	0.52	0.48	0.57
Latin America and the Caribbean	1.82	1.43	2.40
South America	1.88	1.51	2.39
Northern America	0.81	0.75	0.89
Europe	0.08	-0.13	0.33
Eastern Europe	-0.34	-0.46	-0.20
Southern Europe	0.50	0.10	1.04
Western Europe	0.22	-0.06	0.56

Source: International Labour Organization, "LABORSTA: economic active population estimates and projections" 2008.

In fact, as observed in Figure 9.3 participation in the labor market follows an interesting dynamic across age-groups as well as across regions. As expected, rates peak for individuals 25 to 50 years old in all regions. Developed regions record the highest participation rates for these age groups, at over 80 percent or more. Lower participation rates at older ages is the rule across all regions, but Europe stands out with its sudden shift towards significantly lower numbers for individuals over 50 years of age. ILO statistics show that in 2000 only 54 percent of individuals in the 55–59 age-group were active in the labor market in Europe compared to 84 percent for the 45–49 age group. Moving to the 60–64 age bracket, only one in four individuals is economically active, while the same ratio is one for every two individuals for the other regions. This result is partially due to earlier statutory retirement age that applies in most European countries. The political economy of retirement in Europe is a complicated one. Europe has an ageing population, very low fertility rates and generous public pension schemes. At the same time

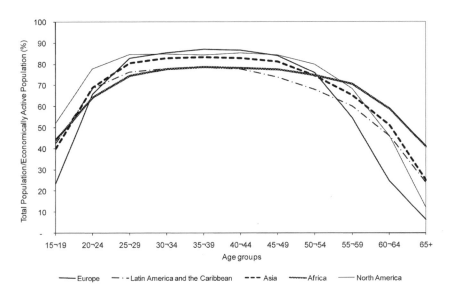

Figure 9.3 Regional participation rates by age groups in 2000
Source: International Labour Organization, "LABORSTA: economic active population estimates and projections" 2008.

unemployment rates in the region, especially in large economies such as Germany or Italy, have been stubbornly high for the past decades. Hence, a trade-off appears between the financial needs of the pension system that can be eased through an increase in the retirement age, and the pool of available jobs. Without additional efforts to increase the demand for labor, either private or public, an increase in the retirement age would create a larger labor force and may only contribute to Europe's high unemployment rates which range from 6 percent in Germany to almost 11 percent in Italy. Instead, policy can provide better results if the focus is on the current unemployed or reserve labor which, if put to work, would make a sizable contribution to the public pension system. It is therefore not clear that in the end a rise in the retirement age would provide significant benefits to Europe's economic and fiscal situation. While such an approach would alleviate pressures from pensions it can easily contribute to rising costs with unemployment.

Workforce related policies should be sensitive also to patterns in participation rates by gender. Figure 9.4 depicts a striking difference in the labor market presence between men and women. Historically, participations rates are considerably lower for women compared to men in the developing regions due to the traditional role taken by women as the main caretaker of the household and children. Another factor that has led women to reduce labor market participation is the lack of access to formal labor markets. It is surprising, however, that differential patterns in participation rates by gender appear so strongly in the developed regions of

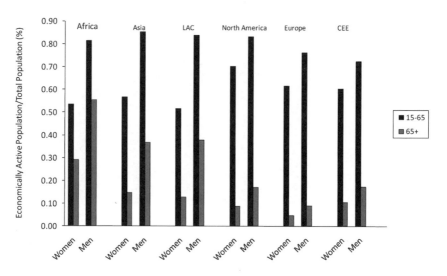

Figure 9.4 Regional participation rates by gender in 2000
Source: International Labour Organization, "LABORSTA: economic active population estimates and projections" 2008.

Europe and Northern America where integration of women in the labor market has long been underway. On average, women tend to record participation rates that are about 25 and 15 percentage points lower than those of men of the same age in the developing and developed countries respectively. This difference narrows somewhat for those over 65 in advanced economies, but continues to remain high in the less developed world.

Population Ageing and Productivity Growth

We can draw two main conclusions from the previous two sections. First, population is ageing in all regions of the world albeit in different dimensions: the largest share of older population is expected in developed economies, while developing countries will see the fastest rise in the number of elderly. Second, the composition and dynamics of the labor force in most developed economies indicates significant reserves of labor that could presumably compensate for the decline in growth rates of working-age population.

This section addresses the question of economic sustainability of population ageing especially in industrialized economies. I introduce productivity growth as a crucial variable in the analysis. For many developing countries which lack any formal social security program productivity growth *per se* may not be enough. Formalization of employment and the introduction of a safety net system for old-age are necessary to ensure adequate income security for a growing number of elderly. These conditions require deep changes in the basic structure of developing countries' economies. A transfer of labor from informal, low-pay jobs to formal, high-productivity, high-pay jobs is imperative for the viability of any social security system. Structural transformation of this sort requires sustainable economic growth (Rada and Taylor 2006, Rada 2007). Hence, output growth is a first necessary step to ensure that an economy can manage successfully its rising old-age dependency rates. In the words of the former Federal Reserves' Chairman, Alan Greenspan: 'The real resources available to fund pension benefits depend on the economy's long-term growth rate, which in its simplest terms is determined by the growth rate of labor employed plus the growth rate of the productivity of that labor' (Greenspan 2003). The following analysis concentrates primarily on the case of developed economies and makes only side references to economic conditions in the developing world.

Stimulating labor productivity growth can be one solution to the decline in the growth rate of labor supply in the industrialized economies over the next few decades. A rise in productivity translates into an increase in the number of available *effective* workers (Palley 1998). In simple terms let real output, X, be given by:

$$X = \varepsilon_L L \tag{1}$$

where L is the amount of labor, and ε_L is labor productivity or output per worker. In growth rates, relation (1) becomes:

$$\hat{X} = \hat{\varepsilon}_L + \hat{L} \tag{2}$$

Output growth results from an increase in productivity and/or from more labor input. In addition, it is straightforward that output growth per capita undergoes the same dynamic as the rate of growth of aggregate output. If we subtract the rate of population growth, n, from both sides of equation (2) we obtain:

$$\hat{X} - n = (\hat{\varepsilon}_L + \hat{L}) - n \tag{3}$$

Based on the decomposition in equation (3) we can simulate the required productivity growth necessary to sustain an annual GDP per capita growth of 2 percent, which is a reasonable trend in GDP per capita for a developed economy. Results for few selected industrialized economies and one developing country, India, are presented in Table 9.5.

Among more developed economies Japan has to achieve an annual 2.6 percent growth in labor productivity in order to compensate for the decline in its labor force. Next is the US with 2.5 percent per year. Despite the fact that the US is not going to age as fast as its industrialized counterparts, it expects a more rapid population growth which acts as a drag on GDP per capita. Simulations for Germany and Italy assume significant improvements in employment and labor force participation rates. Finally, the numbers for India are calculated such that

Table 9.5 Required labor productivity growth

Labor productivity	Germany*	Italy	US	India	Japan
Fold Increase 1960–2000	2.63	3.33	1.94	2.60	4.82
Annual growth 1960–2000	2.6%	3.1%	1.7%	2.4%	4.0%
Fold Increase 2000–2050	3.01	3.17	2.93	6.60	3.60
Annual growth 2000–2050	2.2%	2.3%	2.5%	3.8%	2.6%

Note: * West Germany only for 1960–1997; a) Unemployment rates are in line with estimates from WESP 2007. For India, Japan and the US unemployment rates are kept at 4 percent, while for Italy and Germany unemployment rates decline from 11 percent and respectively in 2000 to 4 percent by 2035/30; b) GDP per capita for India increases at 4 percent annually instead of 2 percent as for the rest.
Source: World Development Indicators 2006 database for GDP per capita and employment. UN World Population Prospects 2008 database for statistics on demographic changes. International Labor Organization, 'LABORSTA: economic active population estimates and projections' 2008.

GDP per capita grows annually at 4 percent, a reasonable assumption since the Indian economy starts from much lower levels of income per capita.

Comparing these simulation results with historical records on labor productivity, growth rates in range of 2–2.5 percent for developed economies are certainly attainable although maintaining such growth on an annual basis over several decades is not necessarily a trivial (United Nations 2007). Taking the data in Table 9.5 at their face value, we may also say that labor supply constraints are not as dire as most of the economic literature implies. This is certainly the case for the US where higher immigration and fertility rates could ease to some extent labor supply shortages. Arguments supporting the assumption that the economy is below its full capacity can be brought forward also for Germany and Italy where higher unemployment rates and low participation rates especially among those 50 and older, point to little or no labor supply constraints for now. On the other hand, Japan is more likely to reach (if it hasn't done so already) its limits in terms of labor supply. In Japan's case a more aggressive stand towards stimulating productivity growth and labor force participation at older ages should therefore be a priority for economic policy.

The expected rise in the average age of the workforce has raised concerns about the prospects for labor productivity increases. The research on the relationship between age and productivity or job performance remains inconclusive (OECD 1998, World Bank 2007, Ovseiko 2008). Several studies present some evidence that suggests a decline in labor productivity with age. Results tend to depend on the type of occupation and skill sets, which suggests that any efforts to maintain or improve productivity among older workers must target specific jobs and skills (World Bank 2007, Schaie 1994). It is difficult, however, to pinpoint the sectors and professions on which training and educational policy should focus. This is because the types of goods and services that will be demanded and therefore produced in the future may be changing to reflect the presence of a larger share of older population in overall consumption. Very few studies have explored the relation between population ageing and changes in patterns of aggregate demand (Luhrman 2008, Borsch-Supan 2003). Using data on consumption behavior for UK households, Luhrman (2008) finds that under certain conditions older households tend to consume more services, especially health care, relative to younger households. If production turns out to be biased towards services, then measures to raise productivity must rely less on capital building and more on job training in information and communication technologies. The findings by Luhrman (2008), even if under strong assumptions, should be tested for other economies. Household surveys provide the necessary information we can use to learn and forecast changes in aggregate demand and help to prepare better for the needs of older populations.

Conclusions and Some Policy Considerations

The intent in this chapter has been, first, to compare current and upcoming demographic changes for broadly defined regions with a focus on implications for the labor force. Several conclusions emerged. First, the expansion of working age populations will slow down in all regions but Africa. Europe is the only region where an actual decline in the labor force will take place. Countries such as Japan will see as well a shrinking labor force but outside Europe an absolute decline in the labor force will tend to be regionally scattered. Second, old-age dependency rates will go up in most countries and regions. However, if we take into account the entire dependent population, young and old, dependency rates will, at least until 2020, not be higher than those seen in the 1980s. Third, an account of population ageing must not ignore differential rates of growth for men and women populations. Significant differences in life expectancy, especially in the emerging economies, will bring about a larger share of older women. This process is going to further impact labor force polices as well as health and income security strategies.

Next, this chapter advances the argument that population ageing will not exercise a labor constraint on the economic system as large as some of the economics literature predicts. To back this claim I first show that many rapidly ageing countries in fact do have some reserves of labor which, given the right policy approach, can ease labor supply shortages. In the first place, much lower participation rates among women indicate significant leeway for policies that target the working-age population. The decline in participation rates after 50 years of age in many economies, but especially in Europe, suggest that policies should take an active role in encouraging the workforce to stay economically active at older age. Finally, advances in life expectancy and in the number of healthy years means that many individuals reaching retirement age may want in fact to remain economically active. Policy should support such behavior on the part of workers and it should dissuade employers from engaging in discrimination practices against older workers.

The last and most important point I am making in this chapter is that dealing successfully with the economic 'burden' of population ageing depends on the ability of the economy to stimulate innovation and labor productivity growth. Hence, economists should base their calculations of dependency rates on the *effective* number of workers and not simply on the number of workers. As future workers become more productive, output is expected to increase which means a larger pool of goods and services that can be distributed among members of a society becomes available. This is the first and necessary condition for accommodating an ageing population. This is not to say that redistribution of output will happen free of economic and political challenges. On the contrary, policies that control income distribution will have to be done in a way that will not hurt incentives to further economic activity (Rada 2011).

References

Barr, Nicholas (2002), Reforming pensions: Myths, truths, and policy choices. *International Social Security Review*, 55(2), 3–36.

Borsch-Supan, Axel (2003), Labor Market Effects of Population Aging, *LABOUR*, CEIS, Fondazione Giacomo Brodolini and Blackwell Publishing Ltd, vol. 17 (SpecialIs), 5 44, 8.

Chawla, Mukesh, Gordon Betcherman and Arup Banerji (2007), *From Red to Gray: The Third Transtion of Aging Populations in Eastern Europe and Former Soviet Union.* World Bank.

Greenspan, Alan (2003), Excerpt from statement by Alan Greenspan before the Special Committee on Aging, United States Senate: http://fraser.stlouisfed.org/historicaldocs/ag03/download/29169/Greenspan_20030227.pdf.

Luhrmann, Melanie (2008), *Effects of Population Ageing on Aggregated UK Consumer Demand.* [Mimeo] Institute for Fiscal Studies, London.

National Institute on Aging (2007), *Why Population Aging Matters: A Global Perspective*. Washington, DC: National Institute on Aging.

OECD (Organization for Economic Co-operation and Development) (1998), Maintaining Prosperity in an Ageing Society: The OECD Study on the Policy Implications of Ageing, Working Paper AWP 4.1. Paris: OECD.

Ovseiko, Pavel (2008), *Ageing Workforces*. Oxford: Oxford Institute of Ageing.

Palley, Thomas I. (1998), The Economics of Social Security: An Old Keynesian Perspective. *Journal of Post Keynesian Economics*, 21(Fall), No. 1.

Rada, Codrina (2007), Stagnation or transformation of a dual economy through endogenous productivity growth. *Cambridge Journal of Economics*, 31(5), 711–40.

Rada, Codrina (2009), Introducing Demographic Changes in a Model of Economic Growth and Income Distribution. Department of Economics Working Papers Series, 2009_01, University of Utah.

Rada, Codrina (2011), Social Security Tax and Endogenous Technical Change in an Economy with an Aging Population. Department of Economics Working Papers Series, 2011_04, University of Utah.

Rada, Codrina and Lance Taylor (2006), Empty Sources of Growth Accounting, and Empirical Replacements à la Kaldor with Some Beef, *Structural Change and Economic Dynamics*, 17(3), 486–500.

Schaie, Warner K.K.W. (1994), The course of adult intellectual development. *American Psychologist*, 49(4), 304–13.

United Nations (2007), Development in an Ageing World. World Economic and Social Survey, Department of Economic and Social Affairs. New York: United Nations.

Chapter 10
Reimagining Old Age in Europe: Effects of Changing Work and Retirement Patterns

Kathrin Komp

Europe is grey. Europe has been the oldest continent in the world for several decades – and it is still ageing (United Nations 2011b). Europeans could expect to live until age 66 in the 1950s, until age 74 in the beginning of the twenty-first century, and to a life expectancy of 82 years in 2050 (United Nations 2011a). This remarkable demographic profile attracts the attention of scholars, policy-makers, entrepreneurs, the public and the media. Population ageing is a pressing issue in Europe and it also is widely discussed. What are the consequences of population ageing for European countries? And how should Europeans best react to their ageing populations? The answers to these questions largely depend on how old age is viewed. A negative view on old age draws attention to challenges associated with population ageing; a positive view, in contrast, highlights the possibilities ageing populations hold.

As the European population ages, its image undergoes changes. Europe's older population is shedding its traditional image, characterized by the need for support and protection (Johnson, Conrad and Thomson 1989). Instead, this population group is beginning to be seen as heterogeneous, with one part keeping the traditional image and the other part adopting an image that is characterized by capability (Carr and Komp 2011). Corporations, policy-makers, and researchers already picked up on this change, incorporating it into many of their activities. Policy-makers, for example, have been addressing older peoples' capabilities through reforms that strengthen older people's workforce participation, and through programs supporting older volunteers (Baldock 1999, Arza and Kohli 2008). While society slowly starts to accommodate this new image of old age, another shift in the image of old age is already dawning at the horizon. This second shift will bring the image of old age closer to its traditional form, to need for support and protection.

The changing image of old age is a symptom of a larger redefinition process of old age that is ongoing in Europe. Changing work and retirement patterns are important drivers of this redefinition. Consequently, this chapter begins by explaining the mechanisms through which work and retirement shape the understanding and image of old age in Europe. Then, it will outline changes in European work and retirement patterns during the last decades. Subsequently, it will discuss how these changes influence the understanding and image of old age. Finally, it will critically reflect on the implications of these changes for a greying Europe.

How Can Work and Retirement Shape Old Age?

In early twenty-first-century Europe, the understanding and image of old age are closely tied to paid work. In fact, paid work plays such a crucial role, that European societies are sometimes labeled 'work societies' (e.g., Kohli 1988, Phillipson 2004). In work societies, paid work is not only a source of income, it also shapes areas beyond income. For example, workforce participation determines a person's social status and his or her access to social insurance schemes (Shaw et al. 2007). The influences of paid work accumulate over the life course to shape old age, e.g. an individual's financial situation, life-style, and health status (O'Rand 1996). Moreover, paid work shapes the structure of the life course – and with it the understanding and image of old age.

For a long time, paid work split the life course into three distinctive parts: youth, middle age, and old age (e.g., Henretta and Lee 1996, Kohli 1988, 2007). Following this logic, youth represents the years prior to labor force participation. During those formative years, young people experience their initial socialization and education. They are acquiring the skills they need to participate in the labor force. In this sense, we can view youth as the preparation for paid work (Settersten and Mayer 1997). When one's youth ends, middle age sets in. Middle age is the time that people spend working for pay. In work societies, these years are considered the productive years of life, during which people contribute to the economy (Ekerdt 1986, Riley and Riley 1994). Upon retiring from paid work, people enter the last part of their lives: old age. In contrast to youth and middle age, this last part of life is not defined by characteristic activities. Instead, it is defined as the absence from paid work. This definition based on a lack of activity gives old age an image of lacking and defect (Minkler and Holstein 2008, Gilleard and Higgs 2010). The common justification for such a lack of activity is presumed age-related deterioration of health, which renders physical activities more difficult (Suanet, Broese van Groenou and Braam 2009).

The tripartite life course model, just described, establishes a clear and direct link between the end of paid work, retirement, and the image of old age. In this model, retirement from paid work heralds the onset of old age. We can, therefore, consider retirement as a marker to tell us who is old and who is not old.

The signaling function of retirement is particularly well-pronounced in Europe, because in contrast to, for example, the United States and Canada, most European countries retain mandatory retirement. A mandatory retirement age forces people out of the labor market at a certain age. It thereby regulates the activities of individuals, and ties ideas about the activities and capabilities of individuals to chronological age. Mandatory retirement thus contributes to the institutionalization of the life course (Kohli 2007). Consequently, the tri-partite life course model becomes more accurate and easy to interpret. Indicators that are based on the tripartite life course model, such as dependency ratios, likewise become more accurate.

Can the Tripartite Life-course Model Capture Old Age Today?

Lately scholars have started to criticize and deconstruct this tripartite life-course model. They argue that even though the model has merits, it does not sufficiently capture the complexity of contemporary life courses. Among other things, they point out that retirement does not necessarily coincide with the end of paid work and that people might transition in and out of paid work several times.

Currently, we notice an increasing gap between retirement and the end of paid work in Europe for two reasons. First, people sometimes withdraw from paid work before the traditional retirement age. Individuals might, for example, take such a step because they cannot find a suitable position within their field, or because generous pension schemes provide them with this opportunity (Schils 2008, Schroder, Hofacker and Muller-Camen 2009). Consequently, retirement might not coincide with a complete withdrawal from paid work. Second, older people might want to continue working after retirement to, for example, supplement their pension benefits with wages. This can be necessary for older people who have made smaller contributions to pension schemes because of previous unemployment spells, or who have lost retirement savings due to unstable financial markets and economic crises (Esping-Andersen 1996, Butrica, Smith and Toder 2009). As a consequence, the discrepancy between retirement and the withdrawal from paid work might further increase.

Another recent phenomenon in Europe is that people sometimes transition in and out of paid work several times. Such multiple transitions can be caused by, for example, multiple spells of unemployment that interrupt working careers (Shorrocks 2009). Another possible cause is that individuals realize that they have insufficient income upon retirement and therefore start to work again (Dendinger, Adams and Jacobson 2005). As a consequence of the multiple transitions, borders between life-phases become fuzzy. Individuals might no longer clearly belong to one life-phase, but instead occupy a space between life-phases. This could impact their identity. Moreover, the existence of spaces in between life phases will water down the previously clear image of life phases, such as old age.

This criticism of the tripartite life course model casts doubt on the supposed link between paid work, retirement, and old age. The link becomes ambiguous, and the definition of old age loses some of its sharpness. As a consequence, we must realign our understanding and image of old age. Interestingly, the changing work and retirement pattern in Europe does not only challenge the traditional image of old age, but also contributes to the redefinition of old age. The following sections of this chapter will describe changes in the work and retirement pattern in Europe and explain how those changes affect the understanding and image of old age.

The Changing Work and Retirement Pattern in Europe

During the past few decades, the Europeans took up new practices when it came to the end of their working lives and their transition into retirement. The two most common changes were an early transition into retirement and a lack of workforce participation in advance of retirement. Currently, a third practice also becomes important: the possibility of working after retirement.

The Retirement Age

In the late twentieth century, the retirement trend in Europe changed. Until the end of the twentieth century, Europeans were retiring at an increasingly earlier age. However, the effective retirement age eventually stabilized and, in some countries, even started to increase again. In the future, we can expect the effective retirement age to increase even further.

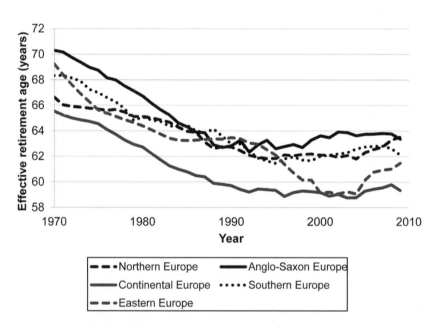

Figure 10.1 The effective retirement age in Europe, per geographical region (1970–2009)

Source: Author's own calculations based on Organisation for Economic Co-operation and Development, 2011a.

Figure 10.1 shows the evolution of the effective retirement age in Europe between 1970 and 2009.[1] This figure shows that Europeans in Anglo-Saxon countries retire at a comparatively late age, and that the citizens of Continental Europe retire at a comparatively early age. The citizens of Northern, Southern, and Eastern Europe retire at an age that lies generally between that of Anglo-Saxon and Continental Europe. Finally, this figure shows that the trend towards an increasingly earlier retirement changed in the early 1990s across Europe, except in Eastern Europe, where the change occurred one decade later.

The changes in the effective retirement age in Europe are remarkable, considering that they occur before the mandatory retirement age. They, therewith, underline that the mandatory retirement age is not the only factor shaping when people withdraw from paid work. Moreover, they indicate that the mandatory retirement age might be a less suitable indicator for when people withdraw from paid work and, therewith, for when old age begins.

Several factors played together to allow Europeans to retire increasingly early and to then create a reversal in this trend. In the late twentieth century, Europeans could retire early because expanding welfare states provided financial security for old age. Those welfare state provisions 'pulled' older workers out of the labor market (Hemerijck 2009). At the same time, high unemployment rates left especially older workers without work. Lack of work opportunities sometimes 'pushed' older workers into early retirement (Myles 2002). High unemployment rates developed, for example, in Continental Europe, where structural unemployment emerged (Bussemaker and Van Kersbergen 1999), and in Eastern Europe, where the collapse of communism ended the employment guarantee (Haggard and Kaufman 2009). However, the economic crises of the previous decades eroded public budgets and thus the capability of European welfare states to finance early retirement for much longer. At the same time, population ageing increased the number of pensioners in Europe, which put additional pressure on pension schemes. Consequently, European policy-makers strengthened their efforts to delay retirement (Hemerijck 2009). They did this by raising the mandatory retirement age and by preventing early retirement (OECD 2006, Kohli and Arza 2011). Those reform efforts visibly increased the effective retirement age in Europe from the 1990s on.

The effective retirement age in Europe will probably continue to increase in the near future for two reasons. First, the effective retirement age is still below the current mandatory retirement age in most European countries, in particular in Continental Europe and among women throughout Europe (see Table 10.1). Recent reforms preventing early retirement, therefore, still have room to develop effects. Second, policy-makers continue to implement new reforms that prevent

---

1 The OECD dataset includes suitable data for the following countries: Denmark, Finland, Norway, and Sweden (Northern Europe); Ireland, and the United Kingdom (Anglo-Saxon Europe); Greece, Italy, Portugal, and Spain (Southern Europe); Austria, Belgium, France, Luxembourg, and the Netherlands (Continental Europe); and Estonia, Hungary, and Poland (Eastern Europe).

early retirement and that raise the mandatory retirement age. For example, in 2007 the German government decided to increase the retirement age from 65 to 67 years (International Social Security Association 2007). Another example, in 2010 and 2011, the Danes heatedly discussed reform plans to hinder early retirement (Jyllands-Posten 16.05.2011). These reform efforts will probably delay retirement in Europe even further in the coming years.

Table 10.1 Average effective and average official retirement age in Europe, 2004–2009

	Men		Women	
	Effective retirement age	Mandatory retirement age	Effective retirement age	Mandatory retirement age
Northern-Europe	64.2	65.5	62.8	65.5
Anglo-Saxon Europe	63.8	65.5	62.9	63
Southern Europe	62.9	65	61.3	62.5
Eastern Europe	62.6	63.3	60.3	61
Continental Europe	59.3	64	59.4	63

Source: Author's own calculations, based on Organization for Economic Co-operation and Development, 2011b.

Workforce Participation before Retirement

The tripartite life course model suggests that people work until they retire. However, in Europe we can often observe that people abstain from paid work for some time before they retire. Important reasons for such non-participation in paid work are unemployment, poor health, and the need to provide care to kin. Retirement and labor market policies in Europe make it possible to abstain from paid work for these reasons.

Figure 10.2 provides an overview of the employment status of Europeans aged 50 to 65 years in 2006. This age range includes the years directly below the mandatory retirement age in most European countries in the early twenty-first century (OECD 2006). The figure shows that men in this age group mainly use four categories to describe their employment status. Two of these categories, 'working' and 'retired', are captured by the tripartite life-course model. However, the other two categories, 'unemployed' and 'disabled', are not captured by the model, which classifies individuals between age 50 and 65 as they are either working or retired. Unemployed Europeans often receive unemployment benefits or unemployment pensions to compensate for their lack of income. Like unemployed Europeans, disabled Europeans might receive a pension, the disability pension, to compensate for their lack of employment income (OECD 2006). However, Hinrichs (2000)

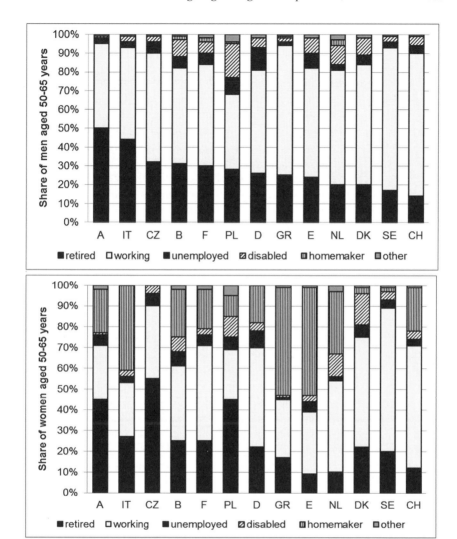

Figure 10.2 The employment status of Europeans aged 50 to 65 years in 2006, by gender

Note: Country abbreviations: A = Austria; IT = Italy; CZ = Czech Republic; B = Belgium; F = France; PL = Poland; D = Germany; GR = Greece; E = Spain; NL = The Netherlands; DK = Denmark; SE = Sweden; CH = Switzerland

Source: Author's own calculations with data from the Survey of Health, Ageing and Retirement in Europe.

and the OECD (2006, 2011c) note that some individuals use these pensions and benefits to withdraw early from the labor market, even before they qualify for early retirement pensions.

Women in the same age range mainly describe their employment status as either 'working', 'retired' or 'homemaker'. Being a homemaker is another activity that is not captured by the tripartite life course model, as it is an activity that takes place outside the work-centered perspective on which the model is based. The concentration of homemakers among women is a sign of the gender-specific distribution of household tasks. It is still mainly women who carry out household chores and unpaid care work within families, which sometimes prompts them to either abandon a job they already hold or not to take up a paid position at all (Lewis and Campbell 2007, Lewis, Campbell and Huerta 2008). Particularly Continental European countries, such as Germany and Austria, designed their social security systems to facilitate women's activity as homemakers. They did this by making some social rights of working men transferrable to their stay-at-home wives. Researchers, consequently, pointed out that those social security arrangements followed the ideal of a male breadwinner, female homemaker model (Pfau-Effinger 2004a, 2004b).

In addition to gender-differences, Figure 10.2 also highlights country differences in the employment status of Europeans aged 50 to 65 years. It shows that the Swiss and the Swedes in this age group are particularly likely to work. It also shows that Austrians, Italian men, and Czech and Polish women in this age group are particularly likely to be retired. Moreover, it reveals that especially Polish men and Danish women in this age group describe themselves as 'disabled'. The figure also highlights that unemployment is particularly common in Germany. Finally, this figure shows that especially Southern and Continental European women describe themselves as 'homemakers'.

Policy-makers and researchers recognize that Europeans are often un- or non-employed before they retire, and they consider this situation problematic for the economy, for welfare states, and for older people themselves. The economy is affected because many European countries experience a labor shortage, which would be alleviated if un- and non-employment in old age decreased (Van Dalen, Henkens and Schippers 2009). Welfare states have to foot the bill for un- and non-employment in old age because those who do not work do not contribute to pay-as-you-go-financed pension schemes, but they do collect unemployment benefits (Esping-Andersen et al. 2002). Older people, finally, might book financial losses because they miss out on wages and possibly accumulate fewer rights to pension benefits (Brown, Orszag and Snower 2008, Hoff 2008).

To increase the workforce participation before retirement, European policy-makers have introduced several programs and policy reforms. These programs and reforms, for example, strive to adapt workplaces to the needs of older people by adjusting the working hours. This way, older Europeans can more easily remain in employment when their physical capabilities decline (Naegele and Walker 2006). Moreover, policy-makers attempt to make it easier for women to combine paid work and family care. The goal is to keep women in the labor market even when they decide to raise children, or care for family members (Gordon, Whelan-Berry and Hamilton 2007, Hokenstad and Roberts 2011). Another goal of the political programs and reforms is to encourage life-long learning, that is learning throughout the entire life course. Through life-long learning people can stay in touch with e.g. technological developments, which increases their employability in old age (Lamb, Brady and Lohman 2009, Stenfors-Hayes, Griffith and Ogunleye 2008). Consequently, the unemployed rate among individuals nearing retirement might decline.

Taken together, these reforms could increase the workforce participation before retirement. Consequently, retirement might become a better marker for the end of paid work again, which might help to re-establish a clear-cut definition for the onset of old age.

Workforce Participation after Retirement

After decades of discussing early retirement, researchers and policy-makers in Europe are now paying more attention to the possibility of working after the current retirement age. On the one hand, they consider the option of increasing the mandatory retirement age in order to extend the working life of Europeans. On the other hand, they also discuss the option of working for pay while being retired.

The mandatory retirement age was the focus of many reforms in Europe during the late twentieth and early twenty-first century, with most reforms promoting delayed retirement. For example, in 2007 the German government increased the retirement age from 65 to 67 years (International Social Security Association 2007). Another example, in 2010 the French government presented a draft pension reform that raised the mandatory retirement age from 60 to 62 years (International Social Security Association 2011). The goals behind these reforms are to facilitate the financial sustainability of public pension schemes and to ensure a sufficient pension level for retirees (Hinrichs 2000, Komp and Van Tilburg 2010).

Paid work after retirement became more relevant in the wake of the recent economic crises. Because of the economic crises, some older people have lost their retirement savings. Moreover, public, private and occupational pension schemes now often have to work with tighter budgets (Hemerijck, Knapen and Van Doorne 2009, Komp, Van Tilburg and Broese van Groenou 2010). These developments lower the income of European pensioners and may force some of them to work for pay after retiring. This would follow a trend that is already evident in the United States. In the US, many pensioners lost their retirement savings that were invested in 401K plans when the stock market crashed, leading them to return to work to generate income (Bass 2011).

At the moment, however, few European retirees work for pay. In 2008, for example, only one in every 50 European retirees did so (see Table 10.2). This number is even lower in e.g. France, Latvia, and Spain. It is higher in e.g. Romania, the Ukraine and the Netherlands. In Romania, about one in every twenty retirees works for pay. Because of the economic crisis and the improving health of the older Europeans population, we can expect to see these numbers increase in the future. This change will make retirement age less suitable as an indicator for the absence from paid work. Moreover, old age will be more strongly characterized by activity and productive engagement than ever before.

Table 10.2 How many retirees engage in paid work, in 2008

Percentage	Countries
5–5.9%	Romania
4–4.9%	Ukraine
3–3.9%	Czech Republic, The Netherlands, Switzerland
2–2.9%	Hungary, Norway, Sweden
1–1.9%	Belgium, Croatia, Cyprus, Germany, Denmark, Finland, Greece, Ireland, Russia, Slovakia, Turkey, United Kingdom
Below 1%	Estonia, France, Latvia, Poland, Portugal, Slovenia, Spain

Source: Author's own calculations, using data from the European Social Survey.

A 'New' Old Age in Europe

The rising mandatory retirement age, and the increasing workforce participation before and after retirement redefine old age in Europe. These developments are changing ideas about the onset and the image of old age. Consequently, we may need to modify the tripartite life course model to capture those changes.

When introducing modifications to accommodate changes in the work and retirement pattern, we also need to introduce modifications to accommodate another kind of fundamental change: the expanding life-expectancy. Since the beginning of the twentieth century, the life-expectancy of Europeans increased rapidly due to improving health. In fact, improving health is one of the main reasons why Europeans are capable of working until a later age. Consequently, the tripartite life course model should reflect the fact that old age continues until a later age and that an increasing number of older people are healthy (Laslett 1989, Settersten and Mayer 1997).

Figure 10.3 illustrates how the tripartite life-course model can be adapted to capture the changing character of old age in Europe. The original model is displayed at the top of the figure. In this model, old age starts with retirement and the simultaneously occurring withdrawal from paid work. Old age, therefore, takes on an image of inactivity. Due to the changes in the work and retirement pattern in Europe, however, both the onset and the image of old age have to be redefined.

The current situation in Europe can be captured with an adapted model, as it is displayed in the middle of Figure 10.3. The adapted model captures the changing work and retirement pattern, the increasing life expectancy, and the increasing

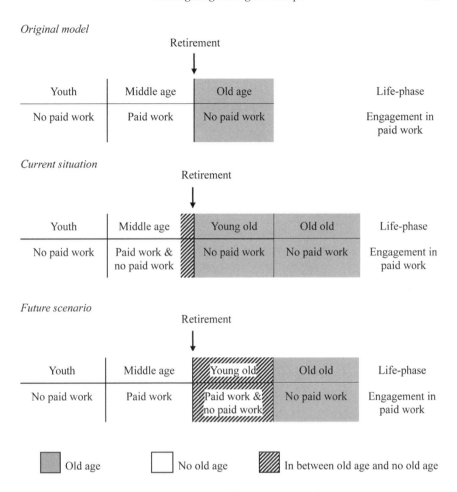

Figure 10.3 Changes in the tripartite life-course model

healthy life expectancy. It does this through two major changes. First, the adapted model shows a fuzzy boundary between middle and old age. During the years leading to retirement, many Europeans do not work, but instead experience a spell of unemployment, disability, or simply engage as homemakers. This aligns middle age with old age to some degree, in that an abstention from paid work occurs in both life phases. As a consequence, the onset of old age becomes fuzzy in that it now occurs during a transitional period between the withdrawal from paid work and retirement. It, therewith, occurs at some point at or before the mandatory retirement age, which can be earlier than the original tripartite life-course model suggests.

Second, the adapted model consists of four life-phases instead of three. The additional life-phase results from a split of old age into a phase of being 'young old' and a phase of being 'old old'. The phase of being 'old old' in the adapted life-course model largely corresponds to the phase of old age in the tripartite life-course model. The phase of being 'young old', however, has been newly inserted into the model to capture the increasing healthy life expectancy. Those additional healthy life years are nowadays also enjoyed by retirees, which were originally assumed to be in poor health. The term 'young old' captures this paradoxical situation: Like younger individuals, the young old are healthy; Like older individuals, on the other hand, the young old already withdrew from paid work. Some researchers conclude that this specific situation can be seen as the crown of life, as it allows individuals to pursue activities of their choice (Laslett 1989, Carr and Komp 2011).

Taken together, we can see two different types of older Europeans today. The first average older person of today's Europe is younger than the one portrayed by the original tripartite life-course mode. This individual may be uncertain of his or her status as an older person, and instead wonder whether he or she should not be considered middle aged instead. He or she will also be healthier and more active than older people were just some decades ago. Consequently, this individual sparks discussions on the potential of old age and on the idea that older people represent an untapped resource to the labor market. The second average older person of today's Europe is the opposite of the active and healthy older individual just described. He or she is of a higher chronological age than older people used to become just some decades ago. However, like the older people of previous decades, also this individual is in poor health and engages is only few activities.

In the future, our understanding of old age will continue to change. It is very likely that we are about to witness another turn of perspective which brings the current ideas of old age closer back to their traditional form. In other words, the idea of old age will probably gravitate towards the need for support and protection again. The bottom part of Figure 10.3 depicts how the typical life course in Europe could look after this second turn of perspective.

The second turn of perspective is triggered by the increasing mandatory retirement age and by increasing workforce participation before and after retirement. Both of these developments point to a chronologically later beginning to old age, possibly even after age 65. Unfortunately, these developments fail to re-establish a clear boarder between middle age and old age. Retirement and the withdrawal from paid work will still occur at different ages, which means that the border between middle age and old age will remain blurred. The difference, however, is that this fuzzy border will now be located in the years directly following retirement – instead of the years directly preceding it.

The shift of the onset of old age beyond the mandatory retirement age affects how we characterize older people. More particularly, this shift influences how we characterize the young old, while it leaves the characterization of the old-old untouched. As a consequence of the shift, individuals start to be considered to be young old from a higher chronological age on. This delayed onset of old age shortens the time individuals spend being young old. Moreover, the young old will be more likely to work for pay in the future. This activity strengthens their connection with the labor market and, thereby, links their identity more closely to the one of middle-agers. In the future, the young old might therefore not consider themselves to be old, but instead see themselves as individuals in the last stages of middle-age. As a consequence, the idea of old age might narrow down to the phase of being 'old old'. Old age might thus return to its image of poor health, need, and inactivity.

Implications for Greying Europe

Europe is greying and while it does so, the meaning of old age is changing. From an initial understanding of older people as frail and deserving of inactivity, this meaning changed to one of capable individuals who choose inactivity. In the future, we can expect yet another change leading to us back to an understanding of older people as frail individuals.

The changes in the understanding of old age have far-reaching consequences. These changes affect older people, society as a whole, policy-makers, and researchers. Older people experience the effects of these changes in their daily lives. They are caught in the middle of the redefinition of old age and advance the redefinition process every day with their interactions. Today's older people are therefore the first agents to act on the new understanding of old age and to propagate it in their social and economic environments, such as their families and the market (for an explanation of the mechanism, see Neugarten 1974).

Society sees the changing understanding of old age reflected in the degree of social cohesion and intergenerational tension. The current idea of older people as an untapped resource decreases social cohesion and increases intergenerational tensions in Europe. European welfare states have undergone a period of retrenchment and restructuring since the 1980s, during which policy-makers have tried to identify and tap new resources (Hemerijck 2009). Policy-makers have strived to encourage their citizens to take more responsibility for themselves and their well-being and to contribute to the welfare of their countries where possible (Esping-Andersen et al. 2002). Considering these efforts, the view of older people as an untapped resource has become quite popular. This view sometimes leads to the conclusion that inactivity in old age in unfair for other population groups, a conclusion which threatens social cohesion and increases intergenerational tensions (Komp 2011, Minkler and Holstein 2008). In the future, however, when the image of old age becomes more closely tied to the ideas of need and frailty again, social tensions should subside again.

Policy-makers have to account for the changing understanding of old age in their actions. On the one hand, the characteristics of old age determine what old age policies are needed. Frail older people, for example, need health care, whereas capable older people will be more responsive to active ageing policies (Binstock 2005, Komp 2011). On the other hand, the image of old age determines which old age policies people accept and which policies they protest. For example, the existence of a mandatory retirement age in Europe gives older Europeans a sense of entitlement to pensions and leisure in old age; it brings them into a situation where they feel they have contributed their proper share to the economy and the community and deserve freedom from labor market obligations (Kohli 1991, Svallfors 2008). When Europeans began to withdraw from the labor market at an increasingly younger age, this feeling of entitlement also set in at an ever younger age. As a consequence, governmental efforts to keep older Europeans in the labor market until a later age have met with protest. For example, the Dutch protested a reform proposal to raise the mandatory retirement age in 2009 and the French protested similar reform plans in 2010 (BBC 24.06.2010, Trouw 20.09.2009).

Researchers, finally, have to accommodate the changing definition and image of old age in studies on old age and on population ageing. Gerontologists need to consider the definition of old age when they decide which individuals to include in their studies (Hooyman and Kiyak 2008). Life-course scholars need to pay attention to the different stages of old age when they describe how the lives of individuals progress (Aisenbrey and Fasang 2010). Scholars in e.g. demography and political science, finally, need to consider changes in the life course model when they describe how population ageing progresses. Dependency ratios, which are central indicators for measuring the progress of population ageing, are based on the idea of a tripartite life-course with crisp boundaries between the life-phases (Calasanti and Bonanno 1986, Brucker 2008). Due to the emergence of a new life-phase and the blurring of boundaries between the life-phases, this indicator loses some of its informative value.

Although the considerations presented in this chapter can inform scientific, political and public discussion, we should nevertheless keep their limitations in mind. After all, these considerations are based on a model, meaning an abstraction from reality. The life situations of individuals are usually more complex than the ones depicted in models, which means that we should not draw conclusions on specific individuals from the model. Moreover, the tripartite life course model is criticized on several grounds, not only on the grounds of the changing work and retirement patterns and the increasing life expectancy. For example, researchers also suggest that workforce participation is not the only activity that structures a life course (Calasanti 1993); that people might not experience life-phases in the order suggested by the tripartite life course model (Hammer 2007); and that the current life course encompasses more than just three or four life phases (e.g. Laslett 1989, Maier, De Graaf and Frericks 2007, Jones 2009). Finally, the considerations in this chapter only scratch the surface of within- and between-country differences in the definition of old age. Europe is a heterogeneous continent and this chapter can only give the interested reader a first, rough impression of changes in the definition and image of old age in Europe. Future studies still need to further explore differences between European countries, e.g. due to different types of welfare states, and within European countries, e.g. regarding gender and socio-economic status.

In conclusion, this chapter underlines that the labor market and retirement reforms which were recently implemented in Europe have more extensive consequences than often suggested. These reforms not only affect the labor market, pension schemes, and older people's economic situation – they affect society's understanding of old age. In other words, retirement reforms and labor market developments contribute to a re-definition and re-imagination of old age. European societies are still in the process of adapting to the latest change in the understanding of old age, which characterizes the first part of old age as an untapped resource. However, we can already detect the emergence of a second turn in the understanding of old age, which brings the understanding back to its original image of need and frailty. The next decades will show how European societies and older individuals adapt to this re-imagination process of old age.

Acknowledgements

I wrote part of this chapter during my employment at the Prentice Institute for Global Population and Economy, University of Lethbridge, Canada. I would like to thank the Prentice Institute for the support in writing this chapter. I, moreover, wish to thank Jani Erola, Jari Kannisto, Elina Lappalainen and Elena Wiegand for their helpful comments and suggestions regarding this chapter.

References

Aisenbrey, S. and Fasang, A.E. 2010. New life for old ideas: The 'second wave' of sequence analysis bringing the 'course' back into the life course. *Sociological Methods and Research* 38(3), 420–62.

Arza, C. and Kohli, M. (eds) 2008. *Pension Reform in Europe. Politics, Policies and Outcomes.* Oxon: Routledge.

Baldock, C.V. 1999. Seniors as volunteers: An international perspective on policy. *Ageing and Society* 19(5), 581–602.

Bass, S. 2011. From retirement to 'productive aging' and back to work again, in *Gerontology in the Era of the Third Age: Implications and Next Steps*, edited by D. Carr and K. Komp. New York: Springer, 169–88.

BBC 2010. *France Strike over Pension Age Reform.* [Online, 24 June]. Available at: www.bbc.co.uk/news/10401929 [accessed: 28 September 2010].

Binstock, R. 2005. The contemporary politics of old age policies, in *The New Politics of Old Age Policies*, edited by R.B. Hudson. Baltimore: Johns Hopkins University Press, 265–93.

Brown, A.J.G., Orszag, J.M. and Snower, D.J. 2008. Unemployment accounts and employment incentives. *European Journal of Political Economy* 24(3), 587–604.

Brucker, E. 2008. Employment population age-share differences: An international comparison of the economic impact of population aging. *Journal of Aging and Social Policy* 21(1), 17–30.

Bussemaker, J. and Van Kersbergen, K. 1999. Contemporary social-capitalist welfare states and gender inequality, in *Gender and Welfare State Regimes*, edited by D. Sainsbury. Oxford: Oxford University Press, 15–46.

Butrica, B.A., Smith, K.E. and Toder, E.J. 2009. What the 2008 stock market crash means for retirement security. *The Retirement Policy Program Discussion Paper 09–03*. Washington, DC: The Urban Institute.

Calasanti, T. 1993. Bringing in diversity: Toward an inclusive theory of retirement. *Journal of Aging Studies* 7(2), 133–50.

Calasanti, T. and Bonanno, A. 1986. The social creation of dependence, dependency ratios, and the elderly in the United States: A critical analysis. *Social Science and Medicine* 23(12), 1229–36.

Carr, D. and Komp, K. 2011. *Gerontology in the Era of the Third Age*. New York: Springer.

Dendinger, V.M., Adams, G.A. and Jacobson J.D. 2005. Reasons for working and their relationship to retirement attitudes, job satisfaction and occupational self-efficacy of bridge employees. *The International Journal of Aging and Human Development* 61(1), 21–35.

Ekerdt, D.J. 1986. The busy ethic: Moral continuity between work and retirement. *The Gerontologist* 26(3), 239–44.

Esping-Andersen, G. 1996. *Welfare States in Transition*. London: Sage.

Esping-Andersen, G., Gallie, D., Hemerick, A. and Myles, J. 2002. *Why We Need a New Welfare State*. New York: Oxford University Press.

Gilleard, C. and Higgs, P. 2010. Aging without agency: Theorizing the fourth age. *Aging and Mental Health* 14(2), 121–8.

Gordon, J.R., Whelan-Berry, K.S. and Hamilton, E.A. 2007. The relationship among work–family conflict and enhancement, organizational work–family culture, and work outcomes for older working women. *Journal of Occupation Health Psychology* 12(4), 350–64.

Haggard, S. and Kaufman, R.R. 2009. How regions differ. *Journal of Democracy* 20(4), 64–78.

Hammer, T. 2007. Labour market integration of unemployed youth from a lifecourse perspective: The case of Norway. *International Journal of Social Welfare* 16(3), 249–57.

Hemerijck, A. 2009. In search of a new welfare state in Europe: An international perspective, in *The Welfare State in Post-Industrial Society. A Global Perspective*, edited by J. Powell and Joe Hendricks. Heidelberg: Springer, 71–98.

Hemerijck, A., Knapen, B. and Van Doorne, E. (eds) 2009. *Aftershocks. Economic Crisis and Institutional Choice*. Amsterdam: Amsterdam University Press.

Henretta, J.C. and Lee, H. 1996. Cohort differences in men's late-life labor force participation. *Work and Occupations* 23(2), 214–35.

Hinrichs, K. 2000. Elephants on the move: Patterns of public pension reform in OECD countries. *European Review* 8(3), 353–78.
Hoff, A. 2008. Tackling poverty and social exclusion of older people – lessons from Europe. Oxford Institute of Ageing Working Paper 308. Oxford: Oxford Institute of Ageing.
Hokenstad, M.J.T. Jr. and Roberts, A.R. 2011. International policy on ageing and older persons: Implications for social work practice. *International Social Work* 54(3), 330–43.
Hooyman, N.R. and Kiyak, H.A. 2008. *Social Gerontology: A Multidisciplinary Perspective*. Boston: Allyn & Bacon.
International Social Security Association 2011. *France: Presentation of Draft Pension Reforms*. [Online]. Available at: www.issa.int/ssd_fetch/dt/2536/en [accessed: 15 June 2011].
International Social Security Association 2007. *Germany: Increase in Pensionable Age to 67*. [Online]. Available at: www.issa.int/ssd_fetch/dt/1719/en [accessed: 15 June 2011].
Johnson, P., Conrad, C. and Thomson, D. (eds) 1989. *Workers versus Pensioners: Intergenerational Justice in an Ageing World*. Manchester, New York: Manchester University Press.
Jones, G. 2009. *Youth*. Cambridge: Polity Press.
Jyllands-Posten 2011. *3F-formand: S og SF bør ikke satse alt på efterløn* [EF-President: S and SF Should Not Bet Everything on Retirement]. [Online, 16 May]. Available at: jp.dk/indland/indland_politik/article2433009.ece [accessed: 16 May 2011].
Kohli, M. 1988. Ageing as a challenge for sociological theory. *Ageing and Society* 8(4), 367–94.
Kohli, M. 1991. Retirement and the moral economy: A historical interpretation of the German case, in *Critical Perspectives on Aging: The Political and Moral Economy of Growing Old*, edited by M. Minkler and C.L. Estes. Amityville, NY: Baywood Publishing, 273–92.
Kohli, M. 2007. The institutionalization of the life course: Looking back to look ahead. *Research in Human Development*, 4(3–4), 253–71.
Kohli, M. and Arza, C. 2011. The political economy of pension reform in Europe, in *Handbook of Ageing and the Social Sciences*, edited by R.H. Binstock and L.K. George. London: Elsevier Academic Press, 251–64.
Komp, K. 2011. The political economy of the third age, in *Gerontology in the Era of the Third Age*, edited by D. Carr and K. Komp. New York: Springer, 51–66.
Komp, K. and Van Tilburg, T. 2010. Ageing societies and the welfare state: Where the inter-generational contract is not breached. *International Journal of Ageing and Later Life* 5(1), 7–11.
Komp, K., Van Tilburg, T. and Broese van Groenou, M. 2010. Paid work between age 60 and 70 years in Europe: A matter of socio-economic status? *International Journal of Ageing and Later Life* 5(1), 45–75.

Lamb, F.F., Brady, E.M. and Lohman, C. 2009. Lifelong resiliency learning: A strength-based synergy for gerontological social work. *Journal of Gerontological Social Work* 52(7), 713–28.

Laslett, P. 1989. *A Fresh Map of Life: The Emergence of the Third Age*. Basingstoke: Macmillan.

Lewis, J. and Campbell, M. 2007. UK work/family balance policies and gender equality, 1997–2005. *Social Politics* 14(1), 4–30.

Lewis, J., Campbell, M. and Huerta, C. 2008. Patterns of paid and unpaid work in Western Europe: Gender, commodification, preferences and the implications for policy. *Journal of European Social Policy* 18(1), 21–37.

Maier, R., De Graaf, W. and Frericks, P. 2007. Policy for the 'peak hour' of life: Lessons from the new Dutch life course saving scheme. *European Societies* 9(3), 339–58.

Minkler, M. and Holstein, M. 2008. From civil rights to … civic engagement? Concerns of two older critical gerontologists about a 'new social movement' and what it portends. *Journal of Aging Studies* 22(2), 196–204.

Myles, J. 2002. A new social contract for the elderly? in *Why We Need a New Welfare State*, edited by G. Esping-Andersen, D. Gallie, A. Hemerijckand J. Myles. Oxford: Oxford University Press, 130–72.

Naegele, G. and Walker, A. 2006. *A Guide to Good Practice in Age Management*. Dublin: European Foundation for the Improvement of Living and Working Conditions.

Neugarten, B.L. 1974. Age groups in American society and the rise of the young old. *Annals of the American Academy of Political and Social Science* 415(1), 187–98.

O'Rand, A.M. 1996. The precious and the precocious: Understanding cumulative disadvantage and cumulative advantage over the life course. *The Gerontologist* 36(2), 230–38.

Organization for Economic Co-operation and Development (OECD) 2006. *Ageing and Employment Policies: Live Longer, Work Longer*. Paris: OECD.

Organization for Economic Co-operation and Development (OECD) 2011a. *Average Effective Age of Retirement in 1970–2009 in OECD Countries*. [Online]. Available at: www.oecd.org/document/54/0,3746,en_2649_34747_39371887_1_1_1_1,00.html [accessed on: 8 June 2011].

Organization for Economic Co-operation and Development (OECD) 2011b. *Average Effective Age of Retirement versus the Official Age, 2004–2009*. [Online]. Available at: www.oecd.org/document/54/0,3746,en_2649_34747_39371887_1_1_1_1,00.html [accessed on: 8 June 2011].

Organization for Economic Co-operation and Development (OECD) 2011c. *Pensions at a Glance 2011. Retirement-Income Systems in OECD and G20 countries*. Paris: OECD.

Pfau-Effinger, B. 2004a. *Development and Culture of Welfare States and Women's Employment in Europe*. Aldershot: Ashgate.

Pfau-Effinger, B. 2004b. Socio-historical paths of the male breadwinner model – an explanation of cross-national differences. *The British Journal of Sociology* 55(3), 377–99.
Phillipson, C. 2004. Work and retirement transitions: Changing sociological and social policy contexts. *Social Policy and Society* 3(2), 155–62.
Riley, M.W. and Riley, J.W. Jr. 1994. Structural lag: Past and future, in *Age and Structural Lag. Society's Failure to Provide Meaningful Opportunities in Work, Family and Leisure*, edited by M.W. Riley, R.L. Kahn and A. Foner. New York: John Wiley & Sons, 15–36.
Schils, T. 2008. Early retirement in Germany, the Netherlands, and the United Kingdom: A longitudinal analysis of individual factors and institutional regimes. *European Sociological Review* 24(3), 315–29.
Schroder, H., Hofacker, D. and Muller-Camen, M. 2009. HRM and the employment of older workers: Germany and Britain compared. *International Journal of Human Resources Development and Management* 9(2–3), 162–79.
Settersten, R. and Mayer, K.-U. 1997. The measurement of age, age structuring, and the life-course. *Annual Review of Sociology* 23, 233–61.
Shaw, M., Bruna Galobardes, D.A., Lawlor, J.L. et al. 2007. *The Handbook of Inequality and Socioeconomic Position. Concepts and Measures*. Bristol: Policy Press.
Shorrocks, A. 2009. Spell incidence, spell duration and the measurement of unemployment. *Journal of Economic Inequality* 7(3), 295–310.
Stenfors-Hayes, T., Griffith, C. and Ogunleye, J. 2008. Lifelong learning for all? Policies, barriers and practical reality for a socially excluded group. *International Journal of Lifelong Education* 27(6), 625–40.
Suanet, B., Broese van Groenou, M. and Braam, A.W. 2009. Changes in volunteering among young old in the Netherlands between 1992 and 2002: The impact of religion, age-norms, and intergenerational transmission. *European Journal of Ageing* 6(3), 157–65.
Svallfors, S. 2008. The generational contract in Sweden: Age-specific attitudes to age-related policies. *Policy and Politics* 36(3), 381–96.
Trouw 2009. *Protest tegen verhoging van de AOW leeftijd* [Protest Against an Increase of the Retirement Age]. [Online, 20 September]. Available at: www.trouw.nl/nieuws/nederland/article2919886.ece/Protest_tegen_verhoging_van_de_AOW_leeftijd.html [accessed: 1 October 2010].
United Nations 2011a. Life expectancy at birth, both sexes combined. [Online, 25 August]. Available at: http://data.un.org/Data.aspx?q=life+expectancy&d=PopDiv&f=variableID%3a68 [accessed: 18 December 2011].
United Nations 2011b. Median age (years). [Online, 25 August]. Available at: http://data.un.org/Data.aspx?q=age&d=PopDiv&f=variableID%3a41 [accessed: 18 December 2011].
Van Dalen, H.P., Henkens, K. and Schippers, J. 2009. Dealing with older workers in Europe: A comparative survey of employers' attitudes and actions. *Journal of European Social Policy* 19(1), 47–60.

Chapter 11
Risky Business: Ageing as an Information Technology Worker

Emily Jovic and Julie McMullin

Ageing and Paid Work: The Case of Information Technology Employment

In this chapter we examine the juxtaposition of two important trends that are occurring in most developed, western countries: the emergence of new economies and workforce ageing. As we move further into the twenty-first century, the nature of paid work in developed countries is projected to change quite dramatically as the 'new economy' grows and evolves. The 'new economy' concept refers to the idea that economies are becoming more global with work more likely to be based on the commodification of knowledge and the proliferation of information than was true in the past (Castells 1996).

The emergence of new knowledge-based economies has corresponded with population and workforce ageing in many developed countries. Among the many challenges that have been linked to population ageing in these countries are the predicted productivity declines, labor force shortages, and pension shortfalls that are anticipated as a result of fewer younger workers entering the labor market relative to the number who are leaving as a result of retirement (McMullin 2011). This has led policy-makers and governments in western countries to modify the age at which 'normal' retirement benefits begin and to think more carefully about how to structure public policies with principles of the life course perspective in mind in an effort to retain older workers (Taylor 2008, Marshall and McMullin 2010, Bernard and McDaniel 2011). The question that still remains though is how will older workers fare in a knowledge economy that is quickly developing and in which the wide-spread, massive generation of information and information technology seems to be influencing not only the way we work but the way we think and the way we live? This chapter provides insights into this question by examining ageing and paid work within the Information Technology sector, an archetypical example of a new economy industrial sector in which work is based on the proliferation of information and new types of information technology.

Ageing processes and the accumulation of life events and responsibilities are integral parts of the passage of time and these things also influence the work experiences and career paths of individuals (Marshall, Craft, Morgan and Havilan, 2010). If a government policy aim, as noted above, is to retain older workers in the labor market, also critical are issues relating to retraining and the development of workplace policies and practices that capture the changing circumstances of workers as they age and creating an environment where workers can remain productive over the longer term. However, this is only possible in workplace environments where a certain value is attached to ageing and the resultant experience that comes with it. Yet, in industrial sectors that do not value experience or ones that place an overly positive emphasis on stereotypical characteristics of youth, the retention and retraining of older workers will no doubt be harder to attain. Moreover, such workplaces are likely not only designed with younger workers in mind, but predicated on it. As a result, the changing needs of workers as they age may not be taken into account and older workers may face additional barriers in workplace hiring, promotion and retention practices. Indeed, Sennett (1998: 91) points out a connection between ageing and feeling at risk in contemporary workplaces: 'It comes just from living into middle age. The current conditions of corporate life are full of prejudices against middle age, disposed to deny the worth of a person's past experience.' This, in turn, may influence how older workers view themselves and their productivity in relation to their own ageing process.

Past research on age bias in paid work has not explicitly considered the role that older workers play in perpetuating age-based stereotypes. Tangentially, however, McMullin and Marshall (2001), in a study of garment workers noted that older workers sometimes played a role perpetuating ageism by making statements about their ageing bodies in relation to their own productivity declines. The taken-for-granted assumption in these statements was that ageing processes were natural and universal, and workers did not question whether changes to the organization of work or the workplace might affect productivity as well. Similarly, McMullin and Shuey (2006) find that some workers interpret functional limitations as part of the normal ageing process (e.g., 'I'm just getting old'). As a result, they are less likely to seek workplace accommodation for the condition and are less likely to receive it, even if they did recognize a need for it. Importantly, this study supports the notion that people tend to conceptualize ageing as a natural process that produces functional limitations that are not recognized as needing workplace accommodation. There is thus a presumption that everyone's body 'deteriorates' and does so in more or less the same ways (McMullin and Shuey 2006: 843). This has the propensity to impact one's self-perception regarding ageing. As people age they begin to believe age-based stereotypes themselves, rendering them even more difficult to combat. As Sennett suggests, 'The middle aged can easily come to fear that they are eroding from within ... Social prejudice reinforces the internal fear of losing potency' (Sennett 1998: 91, 95).

In the research on ageing and paid work, there has been a focus on attitudes and stereotypes regarding older workers to the exclusion of attitudes and stereotypes about younger workers. Among other things, older workers are thought to not adapt well to new technology and to be resistant to change, although they are also thought to be reliable and productive (Taylor and Walker 1994, 1998, Marshall 1996, Duncan 2003, Henkens 2005). Because age is a relative term, including views about youth in analyses may add insight into assessments of 'old'.

Although there has been quite a lot of work on attitudes toward older workers, less research has considered how the characteristics of a particular occupational group or industrial sector might influence attitudes and negative stereotypes related to older workers and ageing in paid work. For instance, certain imperatives of IT work, such as remaining on the cutting edge of technology or working long hours, are seen to favor younger people (Sennett 1998, McMullin 2011). At the same time, younger workers may be more susceptible to exploitation because they are viewed to be highly efficient and can be paid less than older workers (Haviland, Marshall and McMullin 2011). Nonetheless, 'growing up' with technology stands in stark contrast to 'growing old' in a sector such as IT; knowledge and experience gained in youth seems to be prized over that accumulated later in the life course (McMullin and Duerden Comeau 2011). Age-based attributes and prejudices are difficult to transcend in an arena like the IT sector, where there is continual change and considerable pressure, coupled with some fairly enduring stereotypes. Indeed, there is evidence of a perceived link between age, exposure to technological innovations and level of expertise among both workers and employers in this sector, with younger workers mostly reaping the benefit of this association (McMullin, Duerden Comeau and Jovic 2007). In this context, the onetime valued advantages of seniority and experience are not entirely clear – there is some acknowledgement as to their benefit in terms of working smarter; yet, at the same time, workers do not wish to be seen as 'too experienced,' and therefore tied to outdated technology. Thus, in IT employment, general age stereotypes combined with related assessments of technical aptitude may place older workers at a heightened disadvantage. These ideas are taken up further in the results section below.

Method

The data for this chapter are drawn from the Canadian component of an international, comparative study of IT work, Workforce Aging in the New Economy (WANE). The larger study entails interviews and self-administered web-based surveys with IT workers as well as intensive ethnographic studies of selected IT firms in Australia, Canada, the European Union and the United States. Past research that has examined these data show negligible differences among the study countries (see McMullin and Marshall 2010, McMullin 2011). Rather than providing cross-country comparisons which, due to space limitations would only scratch the surface of the data, this chapter provides an in-depth assessment of the situation in Canada. Hence, the analysis is based on semi-structured, in-depth interviews with 135 IT workers in Canada who work for small firms that employ between 4 and 21 workers. Interview questions were largely open-ended and centered on experiences of IT employment and careers.

The analysis centers on interview data and the study sample reflects the profile of IT workers reported in Canadian national surveys (Wolfson 2004, Gunderson et al. 2005). The age of respondents ranged from 19 to 62 years, with an average of 37 years. The majority (79 percent) were men; about one-fifth (21 percent) were women. Over half (55 percent) had children and about two-thirds (65 percent) were married or living common-law. One-quarter (26 percent) were single/never married and 9 percent reported being separated or divorced. It was a relatively homogenous group; 7 percent were visible minorities.

The strategy underlying the analytical process presupposes that discourse is critical in making sense of the social world and that insight into social relations can be generated by taking into account individuals' interpretations of their experiences (Gubrium and Holstein 1997). In qualitative research, coding is an integral part of the analysis as raw data are brought up to a conceptual level (Corbin and Strauss 2008). Coding and analysis for this chapter was facilitated by a software package (NVivo) and proceeded in two phases: the organizational coding of interview transcripts (Lofland and Lofland 1995) and thematic coding and in-depth analysis of interview passages that centered on IT career trajectories, work experiences, and ageing.

One organizational code from the first phase, 'Age', was selected for further analytical coding. This category included interview content that dealt with ageing, age relations and generational aspects of IT work, spanning individual education and employment trajectories as well as personal history and opinions. A text search for terms related to age, including 'growing up/grew up', 'baby boomer' and 'generation X', generated additional interview segments for analysis.

The content of the 'Age' code and additional text search material was further organized into analytically meaningful subdivisions, sometimes using the respondent's age as a point of comparison. This process entailed looking for expected themes, patterns and differences as well as emergent ones, both within categories and among respondents. Analytical codes relating to a number of familiar age stereotypes (resistance to change, energy loss, etc.) as well as a few IT-specific ones (e.g., linking age, appearance and technical ability) became apparent in the data. As well, themes dealing with potential long-term employability challenges and truncated career trajectories in IT also emerged.

In this chapter, our focus is on the links between age and employability over the longer term, particularly how respondents describe ageing and older workers in IT and their speculation about a future in the field. The findings are organized thematically and data are presented in the form of illustrative quotations. To help contextualize respondents' words, select biographical information, such as gender, age and occupation, is provided for each passage.

Results

Images and Stereotypes of Ageing:
'Curmudgeons', 'COBOL Guys' and 'Cowboys'

Dominant images of ageing in the IT sector are generally not flattering and older workers are often ascribed with inauspicious qualities. In the data, there emerges a fairly consistent and disparaging image of 'old' in IT, which tends to tie together age, appearance (unkempt, hirsute), attitudes (stagnant, outmoded, non-progressive) and technology (COBOL, mainframes). Respondents draw on various combinations of these descriptors when speaking about older colleagues and acquaintances, and their choice of words helps reveal how ageing and older workers are perceived. Often such references are oblique, dropped into the conversation to explain a situation or illustrate a point; yet, they expose particular biases about ageing in IT.

For many in IT, inertia is about the worst fate that can befall anyone. Among respondents, older workers are the ones seen to be stagnant and immobile. One manager refers to a contractor he once met in a previous job, an 'old grizzled guy' stuck in a 'fairly brain-dead' role (1116045, early 40s). At the time, he regarded this individual, a consultant who had been in the same position with the same firm for 18 years, as a cautionary tale for getting out of that company, lest he turn out the same way. He asks, 'Oh my god, do I want to end up like him?'

Study participants commented openly about older workers, those they know or have known personally, and also more generally. For example, one programmer offers a vivid description of ageing in IT. While it is actually a portrayal of one person, the delivery renders the image archetypal: 'I've seen [it] in a lot of companies, and there's a guy that works in [client firm] that's exactly that' (1107133, woman, mid 40s). In her view, IT workers eventually become 'curmudgeons':

> They've been around since punch cards, they're still programmers and they're curmudgeons! [laughs] And they're sometimes fun to work with. They usually have the beard and the longish hair and haven't progressed probably past the '70s. But they're the people that just haven't seen any need to change or progress and they're happy working on COBOL.

This depiction brings together the elements of age (around a long time), appearance (hairy, disheveled), attitude (static yet amusing) and technology (punch cards, COBOL).

In fact, 'COBOL' and similar terms sometimes serve as synonyms or adjectives for old and outmoded, as a CEO demonstrates: 'My ex-brother-in-law is COBOL. COBOL's such an old technology' (1113016, man, early 40s). A manager similarly describes a former colleague, 'He was punch cards, the whole nine yards' (1110107, man, late 30s). These terms take on negative and derogatory tones as respondents refer to 'old mainframe guys' (1112068, man, early 30s) and the 'old COBOL attitude' (1108003, man, early 60s). This CEO maintains that anyone who 'holds on' to such attitudes and technologies 'is going to suffer terribly'.

Under these circumstances, ageing in IT is viewed as an accomplishment. It tends to be framed as something workers somehow manage to pull off; a feat that requires strategy and at least a little bit of luck. One CEO comments on a former employee, a 40-year-old 'who had managed to evolve out of the mainframe and through the PC era' in spite of being a 'socially incompetent, high strung beyond belief chain smoker' (1191016, man, mid 40s). Another recalls a colleague, an architect, who remained in the technical stream throughout her career:

> One of the ladies on our team is one of the senior architects and, yeah, she's five years or so from retirement and, yeah, she knows the latest network stuff and is one of the corporate architects. She's also someone who's managed to stay in technology, which is kind of cool, too. I'm amazed that she managed to do that her whole career. (1107133, woman, mid 40s)

Respondents generally regard these cases as exceptional, indicating that the odds are stacked against staying in IT over the longer term, particularly in highly technical occupations. Reports of exceptional cases – generally characterized as relatively rare and unique success stories – are relayed with a small degree of veneration, and more often, incredulity.

If 'old' takes on certain technological and attitudinal connotations in IT, so does 'young'. Cultural exemplars and popular representations of IT workers invoke varying degrees of prodigy, and related expressions are often age-imbued: whiz kid, hotshot, young turk, and the like. One respondent talks about the 'young dogs' and the 'fresh horses' who are new to the field and more willing to 'put up' with work demands (1112133, man, late 40s). Among respondents, such treatments are not as consistent or universal as the images of 'old' described above; however, they are typically more positive. Youth is similarly associated with certain attitudes (flexible, open, enthusiastic) and technologies (the latest and greatest), although physical descriptors are rare. Instead, comments about appearance tend to be used as counterpoint to emphasize what is seen as less appropriate for 'older' people: 'There's some contractors, they have the earrings and all that kind of stuff and the spiked hair, and the guy's 40 years old!' (1107029, man, late 50s). The most favorable and esteemed traits in IT – innovation, drive, risk-taking, speed, stamina and flexibility, for example – are largely associated with youth. A CEO offers his perspective on why younger workers may be preferred, arguing that they are inherently 'nimble':

> Young people are much more interactive and much more into play and they understand the concept of trial and error. They understand that if you go in this direction and it's not working, ok, you go in another one. People don't make those transitions at a more senior age. ... I find that IT, by virtue of the fact that

it changes so quickly and it is such a competitive industry, that you need to be nimble. And to be nimble right now is to be younger. (1110068, man, early 40s)

This explanation implies the notion that early exposure to computers engenders a natural inclination for technology (see also McMullin, Jovic and Duerden Comeau 2011). Yet, this association is taken further with the presumption that young people also hold innate aptitudes for the flexible work orientations and attitudes valued in IT.

A few respondents challenge the generally positive views of youth and young workers. One manager describes university graduates as 'the youngest and most naïve' (1107068, man, mid 40s). Another links youth 'all hot on technology' to the failure of some endeavors (1114084, man, mid 40s). A third manager notes that, 'A lot of the young people don't have the background or the history to truly appreciate some of the nuances of designing code' (1110003, man, early 40s). Even so, negative attributions are mild and images of younger workers are often somewhat flattering, even if the point being made is critical. For example, one CEO says 'I think there's a perception in the industry that a good, efficient, smart, innovative developer is a young kid. That's not true'. He uses the term 'cowboys' to draw attention to what he sees as a sometimes slapdash mentality among younger workers: 'And cowboys, the stuff we build is like [high security control and records systems] ... I mean, you can't be horsing around' (1107029, man, late 50s).

Indeed, very few respondents are overly optimistic about the prospects IT employment holds for workers as they age. Generally, many people will retire and leave the workplace well before they are actually physically or mentally unfit to work. And, in IT, as one CEO points out, 'Any skill that is retained becomes useless probably more quickly than your memory fading' (1105016, man, early 40s). Nevertheless, some respondents see physical processes of ageing as eventually becoming problematic, pushing them out of their line of work. One manager laments, 'I will be too old to program one day, not because I can't do it, but because my hands get too arthritic to type that much or my sight gets too poor to even see the code. That makes me sad' (1117032, man, early 30s). Another respondent reports the need to begin seeking out other career options as a result of ageing: 'I am just trying to find myself in other areas. What else can I do? I don't want to be a programmer 'til 65. ... Lots of sitting, lots of neck and back and hand' (1108068, woman, late 30s).

In the IT environment, the work and learning requirements generated by intense competition and rapid and constant changes in tools, techniques and platforms may over time lead to feelings of fatigue and burnout. A worker's personal life and the priorities or responsibilities he or she gains as life events stack up can also place considerable demands on time and resources previously allocated for work. In the words of one manager, 'I think there's a possibility of doing the aging but, um, I think something's gotta give' (1117149, man, early 30s).

Our data show that fatigue and reduced energy or stamina are attributable to age and relate to both work and learning requirements in IT. Descriptors invoking fatigue, such as 'mundane', 'monotonous', 'same old' and 'sick and tired', are pervasive. Such feelings are ascribed to working life more generally: 'They're just tired of the run, run, run. But that's not IT specific, it's just life in general' (1107094, woman, late 20s). However, the requisites of IT work are believed to be a key contributing factor, as one CEO explains, 'It's a stressful environment. It's a very dynamic environment. You need lots of energy. Have to say, as we get older, we do lose energy' (1105003, man, late 30s). A manager describes how cycles of learning and relearning eventually wear on workers:

> For a lot of it, hey, you just get tired of slogging. ... So even if you learned a new computer language or something, well guess what? I've learned five computer languages now and when I get the programming challenges, they're the same thing. (1115012, man, early 40s)

A programmer concurs with this sentiment: 'I've seen so many incarnations of software and stuff like that. It's just like, ah, not another thing I have to learn' (1114097, man, mid 40s).

In some cases, these characteristics are linked directly to older workers: 'I find the older people don't have the attention span or just the constitution to code for 16 or 20 hours at a go like a young person does' (1110003, man, early 40s). Although resistance to change is often imposed on older people, respondents of all ages are willing to claim fatigue for themselves. Many workers who have been in the field a while feel as though they have 'seen it all' and self-ascribe feelings of ennui:

> I feel like, I haven't seen it all maybe, but I've seen quite a bit. And when it comes right down to it, it's all doing the same thing to a certain degree. ... I don't know, I guess the stuff I am learning, I don't want to learn. I don't care. I don't care to learn. I mean, yeah, sure it's another technology – here today, gone tomorrow. If I don't learn it now, well, it'll be obsolete next year. (1107003, man, mid 40s)

Ongoing learning demands are often implicated: 'Getting a bit older, you know, I've learned and learned and learned and learned and learned and learned and I just don't want to learn that stuff anymore' (1110016, man, mid 40s). Even younger workers foresee over time that aspects of the work and the continual need to learn will start to become 'really monotonous' and 'a little boring' (1112107, man, late 20s).

There is some suggestion that fatigue is a primary explanation for the generally younger age composition of the IT sector:

> You don't get a lot of old technologists because normally you get so sick and tired of the technology after a while that you bail and you do, you know, your

pottery class. ... After dealing with it for a while, you get disillusioned with technology and then you think it's all BS anyways. (1116045, man, early 40s)

For many workers, staying in the development stream entails doing the same sorts of tasks repeatedly: 'And I suppose it's possible for a person to do it, if they have that kind of personality type. It's not possible for me or most normal people to do' (1115060, man, late 20s). The field seems to offer fewer technical paths and less opportunity to evolve as an IT practitioner.

Many workers claim a relatively early onset of fatigue and energy loss for themselves. This may or may not be related to age, but there is nevertheless a connection to length of time in IT and a sense of having 'seen it all'. Often, there is an explicit age association: 'As much as people like to think it's all new, maybe this is just age or something. ... I'm starting to see that there's a lot of what people are talking about is old wine in new bottles' (1114084, man, mid 40s). Similarly, another manager makes note of the changes he has experienced: 'I've certainly seen it even in my own life. When I was young, when I was in my 20s, I could easily work a 16-hour coding day and not have too much of a problem. ... As I started getting in my 30s, I realized that, no, you can't do that anymore, your brain shut down' (1110003, man, early 40s).

Fatigue and disillusionment appear to contribute to a desire to eventually leave the field. Developing software does a 'brain drain' on workers, as one programmer explains: 'A lot of the times, I go home just exhausted. Mental work I think is just as hard as physical work at times. And that's why I don't see myself as a programmer, because I don't want that feeling' (1191159, man, mid 20s). Another respondent draws on a treadmill metaphor for IT work and expresses his wish to slow down or get out: 'Everybody's on this treadmill and we've just kept turning the speed up and up and up and up. I want to just step off to one side' (1112133, man, late 40s).

From the foregoing, images of older workers are typically narrower and less flattering, conflating age with attitudes, abilities and technologies that are seen as detrimental to long-term success in sector. Ageing in IT is thus viewed as an achievement of sorts. At the same time, young people are ascribed favorable traits and the imagery tends to be less constricted and more positive. Criticisms are made somewhat grudgingly and most are fairly easily remediable through experience (though apparently not too much). It is possible that this influences self-perceptions and structure career trajectories in IT.

Age and Employability

Although the data do not tap the relationship between age and employability directly, interviews with employers and managers provide indication of such orientations within these study firms. This section examines how age might impact employer hiring and retention as well as how workers assess their employability and prospects in IT as they age.

Many of those charged with hiring are quite clear about their neutral views on age: 'Age? Nope, don't care' (1115006, woman, late 40s). A partner in a micro-sized firm similarly says: 'There is no age preference. Whoever gets a job to do something with us is going to fit the bill for what we need. Their age is irrelevant' (1109029, man, mid 50s). Nonetheless, these responses belie some of the attitudinal and structural barriers faced by certain groups of workers in IT. One manager says: 'We're not typically looking for really young, middle-aged or really old people. We look for specific skills' (1115012, man, early 40s). In theory, the skill sets can be attached to any individual; however, in reality, they are linked with training and certain demographic features, including age and gender.

'Fit' is an oft-cited qualification and one that has the propensity to marginalize workers. Many of the owners and managers use fit as a criterion for hiring and retention: 'We're big on fit' (1110068, man, early 40s). In some cases, this refers to technical skills and abilities or fiscal constraints within a firm; these are of less concern. It is less tangible applications, ones which draw on personality, attitudinal and cultural elements, which have greater potential to be exclusionary or even discriminatory.

When they hire, a lot of firms seek multiple types of fit: 'It's definitely about finding the person to fit the culture as well. So there's definitely skill fit as well as a culture fit' (1117149, man, early 30s). With an abundance of paper-qualified applicants, however, personal and cultural fit may be elevated in their importance: 'I've always hired more on a culture fit than a pure technical fit, even for technical resources. Technical skills can be trained. Basic things like work ethic, those can be trained, too' (1102003, man, late 20s). Where there is a good cultural fit, some firms may even try to fit the job to the individual: 'We'd rather say, "Oh here's a person who we know, who has some time and some skills, let's see how we can fit them in"' (1109003, woman, late 50s). Workers are aware of the primacy of fit. One respondent, who claims to have had no prior technical skills or training when he was hired, explains: 'I guess at that time [CEO] also knew I was maybe a little off beat and so he figured I'd fit in with the crew here' (1116071, man, mid 40s).

The significance of fit can be augmented in small firm environments: 'Whoever comes in has to fit into the social culture here. ... Things could fall apart real fast if we have major conflict' (1108003, man, early 60s). These businesses tend to lack formal organization and their employees often wear many hats and work closely together. Moreover, there are often few mechanisms for handling grievances and for companies that are fiscally stretched, replacing workers can be a costly and time-consuming endeavor. Another CEO says, 'I think it's very hard, especially in a small company. ... Skills aren't everything, let's just put it that way. It's more about, what is your personality? ... Are you going to fit in with our team?' (1106003, man, late 20s). To mitigate some of the risk involved in hiring, many employers hire primarily from social networks – their own and their employees': 'Being small, it's best to work off your own network if you can. ... You know what you're getting and not all of a sudden, 'Oh god, this one doesn't fit' (1112159, man, late 30s).

In evaluating potential hires, respondents admit to this elusive kind of fit sometimes trumping other indicators of qualification: 'Ah, in my opinion, a person's education and experience is secondary to how they fit into the culture' (1108003, man, early 60s). Appraising fit relies more on hunch, a common and useful but imperfect device: 'We know their skill set from their resume. The interview at that point is largely just kind of the intangibles, just the feeling you have about him' (1106016, man, late 20s). We might presume, then, that the characteristics and opinions of those doing the hiring may unduly influence assessments of fit, especially if they subscribe to particular stereotypes.

More subtly, it is a logical extension that employers seeking a cultural fit are likely to look for similarities to themselves in potential employees. Demographic features are an obvious start – and in a field numerically dominated by men and younger workers (Wolfson 2004, Gunderson et al. 2005), the end result can be the exclusion of some workers. A programmer from a demographically young firm says, 'We've had a couple older people who have applied and we're not discriminatory by any means. You give them their interviews and they just don't fit' (1106068, man, late 20s). Although such practices are not necessarily discriminatory, they have the potential to be so. In fact, one respondent suggests that age-related prejudice in hiring is linked to the age of those doing the hiring: 'I suppose if all three of us were just turned 19 years old and thought we knew everything, we'd probably have prejudices. But that simply wouldn't happen in our situation because, hey, we've already experienced this and some of us actually have learned things as we've gone through life' (1109029, man, mid 50s).

Some responses are more revealing and age is sometimes implicated in ways that other structured social relations, such as gender or race/ethnicity, are not. One CEO suggests, 'I'd look at older people who had the right experience and who were local and stable' (1116006, man, late 40s). Referring to new hires, another says, 'It depends on their attitude individually. Otherwise, I would hire an older person here, if he met our criteria' (1108003, man, early 60s). However, the same respondent continues: 'I love young blood. I like giving the opportunity for new people to come in and go with it'. Often, risks and failure are individualized, as blame is placed on older workers themselves for inertia and not keeping up:

> What I've seen often with older people in IT is that they are, some of them, who have essentially gotten stuck in a given set of skills. And they believe that that's what they know and they're not thinking about problem solving in general or they're not out there doing interesting things. (1117084, man, early 30s)

'New' and 'inexperienced' are frequently synonymous with 'young' in IT; however, this can leave later entrants in a somewhat tricky position in the labor market: they do not necessarily fit the mold of a new IT worker and they, too, are exposed to a bevy of age-related attributions. Moreover, many people are already preparing for retirement at the time some of these workers are making the transition to IT work in the first place. All of this is not lost on older respondents

– for example, one technician believes his current employer 'took a chance' by hiring him (1191133, man, late 40s).

The view of experience in the IT sector is somewhat complicated – some and recent is good; none, too much and too old are less so. Some respondents indicate that experience remains critical. There is some mention of the value of that comes with growing older in a given occupation or field: 'The older you get, I think the more your experiences will have taught you to work around things' (1107094, woman, late 20s). One CEO argues that in order to do high level IT work, maturity is critical. For him, this is mostly found in workers who are experienced and/or older:

> When you've done real work in a real way and been efficient, that to me is maturity. That can happen when you're 25. It can happen when you're 20. But most of the time, it happens when you're over 30, when you've got a few hard knocks and you have an opportunity to work with people who have done stuff. (1107029, man, late 50s)

Another CEO suggests that even with the creation of sophisticated tools that render many technical tasks much easier and less repetitive, elements of IT work have nonetheless become more intense: 'Unless you've got that ten years' worth of experience, you're not going to be able to grasp the very complex concepts' (1117175, man, mid 30s).

Among respondents, such views are mostly in the minority. Sennett (1998:94) maintains that prejudices against age send a powerful message to older workers in this regard: 'As a person's experience accumulates, it loses value'. Thus, ageist attitudes are occasionally couched in the language of 'too much experience', as a CEO explains: 'If you're able to come in at an early stage, then it's a lot easier than someone coming with 15 years' experience that has a certain way of doing things' (1106003, man, late 20s). According to another respondent, older workers face a dual dilemma of age and experience: 'When you see somebody with 20, 25 years' experience, they're in their 50s, late 40s, so when the client sees their resumes, he says ... "Why would he want to do this job? He's over-qualified, I'm not going to take him, or he's older"' (1113016, man, early 40s).

Even if respondents are content with their current firms and career trajectories, they are less certain about the attitudes of other employers. There is an awareness of the difficulties older workers face in the labor market. These challenges are not specific to high-tech fields: 'I think the older worker has always had that problem [finding another job], whether it's IT or anything else' (1109029, man, mid 50s). Nonetheless, one cannot help but speculate on the added influence of such strong age-based attributions of skill, ability and attitude found among IT workers: 'I think there are some problems in corporations of older people in IT trying to get another job' (1108003, man, early 60s).

The IT sector provides additional challenges for some respondents. One CEO who claims age is largely irrelevant in her own hiring decisions indicates with some confidence that this is certainly not the case for other firms: 'There will be a prejudice in a number of companies to ward against older people for sure' (1115006, woman, late 40s). In her view, the mercenary orientation of the venture capitalist funding may contribute to structural factors that will filter out older workers. She explains further: 'They're just looking for the exit strategy. ... I think the older workers, they would get discriminated out of those environments because they won't be seen as willing and or able to put in the hours that they perceive as being necessary.'

A lot of the information on which respondents draw is anecdotal, as one CEO relates in a description of the experience of a forty-something colleague: 'He's taken a drop in pay almost every year because there's less requirements for [what he does]. So he's going to take any job he can get. So he's getting older' (1113016, man, early 40s). These stories inform how workers assess and interpret their prospects and make work-related decisions, particularly given the inherent insecurity of IT work. A programmer is thus more dogmatic in his assessment: 'Later on [in life] if you lose a job, I don't think you can get another one. ... At 50 or something, there's no way' (1113172, man, late 30s).

Given the prevailing attitudes, workers also wonder about their own future employability and prospects: 'I think right now I am [marketable]. Yeah, that's a concern going ten years down the road, because, do you, 45 or 50, stack up to somebody that is my age right now?' (1107016, man, late 30s). Several of the 'older' respondents see themselves as otherwise unemployable, particularly by larger companies. Two work in the same firm, a very small and very insecure micro business. One of the technicians hopes to sell and get out, as he would never work for somebody else: 'I probably wouldn't be a good employee' (1109029, man, mid 50s). The other technician says: 'I'm pretty much resigned to the fact that I'll probably never work for another company, right? Even if I had to, I'm simply unhireable. ... I mean, certainly no large company would' (1109016, man, mid 40s). When pressed for why this might be the case, the respondent contends, ''Cause I'm not going to do stupid stuff, I'm not gonna listen to some moron. ... I certainly couldn't deal with the bureaucracies involved anymore. I just don't play that game'. Later on in the conversation, another reason emerges: 'Certainly having the certification would be for the fluff, right? ... Unfortunately, people buy crap like that. ... That's another reason why I'm probably not employable. I don't have high school.'

Together, the findings in this chapter paint a seemingly bleak picture of the situation for older and ageing workers in IT. Nonetheless, there are some encouraging perspectives. An analyst warns, 'There are things that will come back to haunt you if you just stay with the youth of it' (1115060, man, late 20s). One CEO argues for the stability of older workers and promotes a more progressive view of careers in IT: 'The younger folks ... say 20 year olds and so on, are unstable because they don't know what they want, which means they've got to try a lot of different things. ... I might as well just avoid the churn and work with people who know what they want' (1116006, man, late 40s). Another CEO highlights the value of age and experience for transferable skills: 'I've seen really good developers who have come in quote 'late' to the field. ... You know, they're older and in some ways it almost helps, as long as they've got the interpersonal skills' (1115006, woman, late 40s). Thus, there are prospects for older workers, even if they are undoubtedly influenced by the regimes constructed around age.

Nonetheless, challenges remain. One young programmer offers a reflection on ageing in IT that serves to highlight some of the complications workers may very well face in their career trajectories:

> If this is my career path, say I'm unfortunate when I'm 43, if I leave the company or get fired or laid off or whatever it is. Will I get another job? Or at that point, am I past my 30 age or something like this and after this I'm just too expensive. So I figure if you're a psychologist, you can still be 72 and be like a very seasoned psychologist, I guess, and someone with a lot of wisdom. Whereas I think there's a certain age in IT where after you hit it, unless you have friends and family in high places or people who are pulling for you, you just might not be that that attractive to the hiring team, unless you have the specific area. (1117019, man, mid 20s)

This narrative taps many of the key challenges raised here in regard to working and ageing in IT over the longer term: the volatility of the sector, the precarity of work in general, demands for worker flexibility, personal shouldering of risks, the exaltation of youth, age relativity among career fields and the significance of social networks and connections.

Discussion and Conclusion

In this chapter, we considered issues of age and ageing as part of the exploration of respondents' work experiences in IT. Age is shown to be a basis for explaining technical skill and ability as well as 'ideal' workers and 'normative' career paths in the IT sector. The nature of work and the field's age composition set up certain expectations about age and ageing, including particular stereotypes and affinities. For the most part, being older is associated with less favorable traits and outmoded technology; being younger is linked to preferred and admired qualities, such as innovation and drive, as well as the latest and greatest technological advances. Thus, among IT workers, age engenders judgments about ability and attitude.

Some of the concerns regarding ageing are linked to how seniority and experience are perceived in IT. Because technology changes quickly and frequently, the complex skill sets required by those who work in more technical occupations are not entirely additive. There are some foundational concepts upon which one can build; however, the overarching view is that technology is generational. There is the default position that new technology = new person and vice versa, and the resultant modus operandi is to replace old with new. This goes for people as well as equipment. Complexities of age also emerge from these findings; there are consistencies, concessions and contradictions. In IT, what is considered 'old' is actually not that old, chronologically. Even so, 'older' workers, some of whom are barely into their 30s, are believed to be less open to change, less willing and able to submit to the required learning and tire quickly. These are characteristics seen as essential in IT. Respondents invariably attribute resistance to change to workers older than themselves; however, they seem willing to own difficulties regarding learning and energy levels. These findings confirm Sennett (1998) suggestion that with the pervasiveness of age prejudice, it is quite easy for people to see stereotypes within themselves and others.

It is not a stretch to conclude that employers and employees take age perceptions into account when they are interpreting their experiences and making decisions. Insofar as less tangible forms of 'fit' are integral to hiring and retention, career trajectories may be impacted. There is some argument for personal orientations, but it is unclear whether this is simply an offshoot of a politically correct culture or a downplaying of reality. Cultural fit is not necessarily discriminatory; however, it can work for and against people in subtle ways. For example, in many IT firms, there is evidence of 'masculinist' regimes, management practices and workplace cultures. Although they do not exclude women per se, men, men's culture and men's careers are often advanced and endorsed (Duerden Comeau and Kemp 2007, Ranson and Dryburgh 2011). The same can be said for age. Age alone is not categorically implicated in the distribution of advantage and disadvantage; however, the evidence supports an association.

While these data cannot be used to make definitive causal connections, it is possible that views of ageing both contribute to and are consequences of the perception of truncated career trajectories in the technical stream of occupations in IT. Indeed, respondents believe (and national data shows) that there are comparatively few older workers in IT and thus there are not many exemplars of how to grow older in the field. Thus, ageing as an IT worker can be a risky business.

References

Bernard, P. and McDaniel, S. 2011. Life course as a policy lens: Challenges and Opportunities. *Canadian Public Policy* XXXVII(Supplement), S1–13.
Castells, M. 1996. *The Rise of the Network Society.* Cambridge, UK: Blackwell.
Corbin, J. and Strauss, A. 2008. *Basics of qualitative research: Techniques and procedures for developing grounded theory.* 3rd Edition. Los Angeles: Sage Publications.
Duerden Comeau, T. and Kemp, C.L. 2007. Intersections of age and masculinities in the information technology industry. *Ageing & Society* 27, 215–32.
Duncan, C. 2003. Assessing anti-ageism routes to older worker re-engagement. *Work, Employment, and Society* 17(1), 101–20.

Gubrium, J.F. and Holstein, J.A. 1997. *The New Language of Qualitative Method*. New York: Oxford University Press.

Gunderson, M., Jacobs, L. and Vaillancourt, F. 2005. *The Information Technology (IT) Labour Market in Canada: Results from the National Survey of IT Occupations*. Ottawa: Software Human Resource Council (SHRC).

Haviland, S., Marshall, V.W. and McMullin, J.A. 2011. Accommodations, Job Sorting, and Age Designations: A Structural Analysis of Age Relations at Work. Paper to the American Sociological Association Meetings: Las Vegas, Nevada, August 2011.

Haviland, S.B, Craft Morgan, J. and Marshall, V.W. 2010. New Careers in The New Economy: Redefining Career Development in a Post-internal Labor Market Industry in *Aging and Working in the New Economy*, edited by J. McMullin and V.W. Marshall. Camberley: Edward Elgar.

Henkens, K. 2005. Stereotyping older workers and retirement: The managers' point of view. *Canadian Journal on Aging* 24(4), 353–66.

Lofland, J. and Lofland, L. 1995. *Analyzing Social Settings: A Guide to Qualitative Observation and Analysis*. Belmont: Wadsworth.

Marshall, V.W. 1996. Issues of a workforce in a changing society: Cases and comparisons. Working Paper to the CARNET: The Canadian Aging Research Network, Toronto: University of Toronto Centre for Studies of Aging, 11 October 1996.

Marshall, V.W. and McMullin, J.A. 2010. The life course perspective and public policy formation: Observations on the Canadian case, in *Hrsg.: Grundzüge einer sozialen Lebenslaufpolitik*, edited by G. Naegele. Wiesbaden: VS Verlag für Sozialwissenschaften.

McMullin, J.A. 2011. *Age, Gender, and Work: Small Information Technology Firms in the New Economy* Kelowna: UBC Press.

McMullin, J.A. and Duerden Comeau, T. 2011. Aging and Age Discrimination in IT firms, in *Age, Gender, and Work: Small Information Technology Firms in the New Economy*, edited by J.A. McMullin. Kelowna: UBC Press.

McMullin, J.A., Duerden Comeau, T. and Jovic, E. 2007. Generational affinities and discourses of difference: a case study of highly skilled information technology workers. *British Journal of Sociology* 58(2), 297–316.

McMullin, J.A., Jovic, E. and Duerden Comeau, T. 2011. Generational discourse and information technology careers: An international comparison, in *Age, Gender, and Work: Small Information Technology Firms in the New Economy*, edited by J.A. McMullin. Kelowna: UBC Press.

Ranson, G. and Dryburgh, H. 2011. Firms as 'gender regimes': The experiences of women in IT workplaces, in *Age, Gender, and Work: Small Information Technology Firms in the New Economy*, edited by J.A. McMullin. Kelowna: UBC Press.

Sennett, R. 1998. *The Corrosion of Character: The Personal Consequences of Work in the New Capitalism*. New York: W.W. Norton & Company.

Taylor, P. (ed.) 2008. *Ageing Labour Forces: Promises and Prospects*. Camberley: Edward Elgar.

Taylor, P. and Walker, A. 1994. The ageing workforce: Employers' attitudes toward older workers. *Work, Employment, and Society* 15(4), 569–91.

Taylor, P. and Walker, A. 1998. Employers and older workers: Attitudes and employment practices. *Ageing and Society* 18, 641–58.

Wolfson, W.G. 2004. *Analysis of Labour Force Survey Data for the Information Technology Occupations 2000–2003* (Ottawa: Software Human Resource Council (SHRC)).

PART III:
Shifting Intergenerational Relations

Chapter 12
Gender, Marital Status and Intergenerational Relations in a Changing World

Sara Arber

The worldwide trend towards ageing of societies is well documented with extensive discussions of support and care needs for frail older people. There is less discussion of the implications of gender differences in later life for access to support in the event of frailty or disability. Although, marital status is fundamental to well-being in later life (Arber and Ginn 1991, 1995, Gaymu et al. 2008), there has been less appreciation of the scale of gender difference in marital status in later life, their variations between societies and their implications. It is important to consider the interaction between gender and marital status and the ways this may change over time (Arber 2004a, Arber 2004b, Manning and Brown 2011). The focus of this chapter is to examine the intersection of gender and marital status in later life across societies, how this links to inter-generational relations, and how global changes make it increasingly important to consider the implications of the gender-marital status interaction when studying access to caregivers and social support in later life.

Globalization and Changes Influencing Inter-generational Relations

Recent and rapidly accelerating societal changes associated with globalization and changing cultural norms are having a profound impact on inter-generational relations and the nature of flows between generations. Four changes are outlined. First, the global labor market results in international migration of young and mid-life adults to work in other countries, e.g. from the Philippines to work as maids in Singapore or nurses in the UK, from Poland and central European countries to work across the full spectrum of jobs in the UK, and from India and Pakistan to work in Saudi Arabia or the Gulf states (Isaksen et al. 2008). At the same time, the rapid industrialization of many emerging economies, such as China, India, and Mexico has witnessed vast migratory flows from rural to urban areas, with the older generation (and often also their children) left behind in rural settings. For example, there were 147 million Chinese rural-to-urban migration in 2005 (National Statistics Bureaus of China 2006, cited in Guo et al. 2009).

A second major change is the increased role that women now play in the paid labor force throughout the world. The expectation in northern European countries is that women with children will work full-time following periods of maternity leave (Saraceno 2008). Traditional family structures with women as full-time housewives and homemakers have sharply declined. Implications of this change relate to who provides care for children (during mothers' paid work), and who cares for frail or disabled older people, should they need care and support. A key debate in Europe is whether such care should be provided by the state through welfare services or by the family, particularly whether state provision 'crowds out' or 'substitutes for' care by the family, or whether state provision 'complements' family care provision (Keck 2008, Kunemund 2008).

A third change, which itself has been influenced by the previous two, is the decline in extended family co-residence, e.g. in three-generational households. The corollary of the growth of nuclear family residential patterns is that more older people live separately from younger relatives, either living together in couple-only households or living alone as a single person. In a traditional, rural region of China, Silverstein and colleagues (2006) found that only 23% of parents lived in three-generation families.

A final change, inter-connected with the other societal changes, relates to the decline in the birth rate and size of the family. Many countries have a birthrate that has been below replacement level for over two decades, e.g. Italy and Germany. China has had a 'one child' policy for over 30 years, and increasingly a child from a one child family marries another 'only' child, with the result that one couple potentially have four parents (or parents-in-law) to support should they become frail or disabled. In nearly all countries, the birth rate has tumbled, representing a sea change, as fewer children will be available to provide care or support to the growing older population. At the same time, there has been a substantial increase in childlessness, for example, in the UK, it is estimated that 30% of women who are currently 35 will remain childless. A key issue is who will provide care for the childless when they reach later life.

The demographic changes of declining fertility and decreased mortality have resulted in more vertically extended families of three or four generations, sometimes characterized as 'bean-pole' families. Hagestad (2006) discusses that 'top heavy' families are becoming increasingly common, with more grandparents than grandchildren, whereas in the past family structures were pyramidal, with a larger number of grandchildren and children, and smaller number of grandparents (Arber and Timonen 2012). In addition, there are more 'truncated' families with no generations below them (Hagestad and Herlofson 2005). Societies vary in the extent to which family structures are 'top heavy', 'bean pole' or 'pyramidal' in structure, as well as the prevalence of 'truncated' families. The shape of generational structures have implications for intergenerational relations, flows of resources between generations, and particularly for older women.

Inter-generational Flows (or transfers)

The so-called crisis of care for older people needs to be set within the wider context of inter-generational relations, which can be conceptualized as sets of upward and downward flows between the generations. Figure 12.1 provides a schematic representation of the nature of different types of intergenerational support between family members, which for illustrative purposes comprises four generations. The nature and extent of these flows are in rapid flux because of the sets of factors outlined in the previous section – migration, increases in women's labor force participation, decline in multi-generational households, and increase in one child families and childless adults.

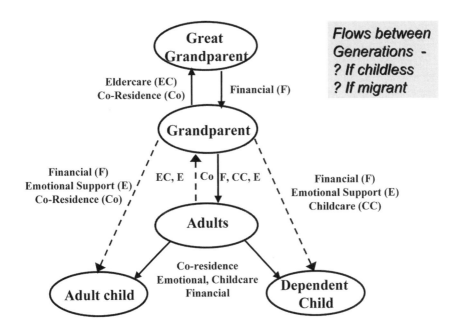

Figure 12.1 Nature of inter-generational transfers between generations
Note: F = Financial and material support; Co = Co-residence; CC = Childcare; EC = Eldercare; E = Emotional support.

There are four main types of intergenerational flows, namely: 1) Financial and material flows; 2) Co-residence; 3) Care or support for children; and 4) Care or support for frail, older people. The first two flows may occur in either direction, as upwards or downwards flows, while the final two are largely unidirectional. The prevalence of each of these inter-generational flows and their directionality are all inter-connected. The nature, volume and direction of these flows differ markedly between societies, particularly in concert with the nature of welfare state provision across societies (Saraceno 2008), as well as according to the factors outlined above. Each of these types of flows will be briefly considered:

Financial and Material Flows

Extensive research in Europe and North America has demonstrated that there are much greater downward financial flows from the grandparent (or great-grandparent) generation to the parent and grandchild generation (Attias-Donfut and Wolff 2000a, 2000b, Albertini et al. 2007). These downward *inter-vivos* flows may occur over lengthy periods, for example, providing financial assistance with education of the grandchild generation, buying an adult child's first house, and gifts, as well as major financial flows through inheritance. Such downward financial flows serve to increase inequality between social groups in society, while equalizing financial resources between generations (Hagestad and Herlofson 2005).

One key success of many welfare states and pension systems has been to enable older people to be financially independent of their adult children and to reside separately. Even in countries with low state pensions, such as the UK, although many older people may be technically defined as 'in poverty', their poverty level is rarely so great that they require financial support from family members in order to subsist. This contrasts with many emerging countries that have only rudimentary pension systems, where most older people live from their own resources, such as from paid employment, subsistence agriculture, or their own savings (if any). Where they have few personal financial or pension resources and are unable to work or earn money by any other means, older people are usually dependent on household or other family members, mainly their adult children (if they have any). For example, in China and countries with extensive rural-urban or transnational migration, adult children working in urban areas or other countries, may send substantial remittances back to the grandparent generation living in rural areas (Silverstein et al. 2006, Baker and Silverstein 2012). Thus, upward flows of financial resources from the parent to the grandparent (or great grandparent) generation occur mainly in countries that have limited pension systems or welfare support for older people.

Co-residence

Inter-generational relations and transfers tend to occur in a 'natural' (non-obvious and unacknowledged) way when more than one generation co-reside in the same household. In co-residence, where there is shared accommodation and generally shared meals, there is little concept of financial or material transfers between generations of family members living in the same household. However, once the household fissures and generations live separately, each separate unit must finance their separate housing, living costs and food. It is well-known that multi-generational or extended family living is less costly than living in separate households. Increasingly in many European countries, adult children are co-residing for longer in the parental home, representing a substantial downwards flow of financial, material and emotional support.

Living in a multi-generational household, generally occludes the possibility of assessing the value of material or financial transfers in both directions associated with co-residence. The care by parents for their children goes unremarked, not generally being seen as a transfer between generations. However, when the adult generation is missing because of working in an urban area or another country, this puts into sharp relief, normative care by parents (primarily mothers) for their children. Where a grandparent co-resides in the same household as the parent generation and/or the grandchild generation, there are likely to be multiple flows in both directions on an everyday basis. The frequency and complex interweaving of these flows of household labor, practical care, and emotional and social support mean they are largely invisible, and their importance only becomes apparent if one or more family members move to live in separate households, when these flows can be more easily recognized, 'named' and measured, as 'financial support', 'practical help', 'care' or simply 'visiting'.

Care for Children

It is obvious that young children need care on a 24-hour basis, with the nature of care for children changing as they grow older, from physical and practical (instrumental) care, to developmental care and emotional support. Where the parent generation or (in practice) the mother is absent completely, then grandparents (largely grandmothers) often take over the parental role (Arber and Timonen 2012). This occurs where the adult child dies (e.g. from AIDs in Africa) or is unable to perform the 'normative' mothering role (e.g. because of drug addiction in the US), in such cases the grandparents may take over the full role of the parents, co-residing with their grandchildren. Such (custodial) grandparents have been termed 'child savers' (Arber and Timonen 2012). In cases, of rural-urban migration or transnational migration of the parent generation, children are often 'left behind' in (or sent back to) the rural areas to live with their grandparents or other relatives. In China, the proportion of these 'skipped generation' families, comprising grandparents and grandchildren without the middle generation present, has increased rapidly in rural areas (Silverstein et al. 2006). Grandparents in these households are performing the parental role, and play a pivotal role in enabling their own adult children to work and earn money in urban areas, through care for their grandchildren on a full-time basis (Baker and Silverstein 2012).

Where women work full-time in societies with limited access to state provided childcare or day care, where childcare is expensive, or women command low or modest wages, the main option for women who wish to (or financially need to) work is for children to be cared for on a daily basis by one or both sets of grandparents. These grandparents could be seen as 'mother savers', since they enable the better financial wellbeing of the parent generation, as well as the well-being and development of grandchildren, but represent a substantial time, practical and emotional commitment by the grandparents (Arber and Timonen 2012).

Herlofson and Hagestad (2012) show that in the Nordic countries, despite grandparents not being involved in day to day childcare provision, they are generally the first 'port of call' in a 'crisis' or an emergency, when back-up childcare is needed, such as when a child is unwell, and are characterized as 'family savers'.

Care of children and grandchildren by definition represents a 'downward' inter-generational flow of caring resources. Although, flows from grandparents are often seen as gender-less, they are primarily transfers from older women to the parent generation, since the bulk of care for grandchildren is provided by grandmothers or other female relatives.

Care for Frail or Older Relatives

Should an older person become frail, disabled or mentally confused, they are likely to require support on a regular or daily basis to remain living in the community. The first port of call for such personal care and practical (instrumental) support is generally other household members. Where an older person is married, this support is likely to be provided by their spouse, unless the older couple co-reside in an extended multi-generational family, in which case the main carer for older women may be her daughter (or daughter-in-law). In the UK, when an older married person requires care, this is almost always provided by their spouse, irrespective of gender (Arber and Ginn 1991, 1992, Rose and Bruce 1995). However, in many patriarchal societies and those with more rigid gender divisions, there may be a weak or non-existent cultural norm for husbands to provide care for their wives.

In the UK, Europe and North America, only a tiny minority of older people co-reside with adult children. Following widowhood, most older people live alone, rather than live with their adult children, friends or other relatives. Older women and men who live alone therefore need to rely on support from either welfare state services, privately paid carers, or from family members or friends who live elsewhere. European states vary markedly in the extent of welfare state provision for older people demonstrating a clear North-South divide (Hagestad 2006). But even in the Nordic countries, with high welfare state provision, family members complement state support and provide extensive care for frail elderly parents. Most research indicates that the bulk of care for frail older people living alone is provided by daughters providing 'care at a distance'. Thus, by definition 'informal care' for frail older people is either provided by the same generation between spouses (or sometimes siblings or friends), or is an upward flow from the middle (or grandchild) generation.

Caregiving may be particularly problematic for 'truncated generations', where an older person has no children. As well as the rapid increase in childlessness and one child families, children may predecease their parents, including from AIDs (especially in Africa). The higher proportion in the future who reach late old age without children will have to rely on others, rather than children, to provide practical care and support when needed, which may be particularly problematic if they are widowed/divorced, and without a partner to provide such care. Childless people who become frail or disabled will therefore have to rely on the state for care, friends or more distant relatives, such as nieces or siblings. However, welfare state retrenchment means that the state's role in supporting older people is likely to diminish in the future (Estes and Wallace 2010).

Weighing Net Levels of Transfers of Resources between Generations

Extensive literature has assessed whether flows downwards from the grandparent generation to the parent (or grandchild) generation outweigh flows upwards from the middle to the grandparent generation (Attias-Donfut and Woolf 2000a, 2000b, Kohli et al. 2000), concluding that in European countries, there are much greater financial flows downwards than upwards. However, the valuation of financial flows are in principle easier to estimate than calculating the value of practical and caregiving support.

Despite these difficulties, the rhetoric about the rapid increase of the ageing population and the 'consequent burden' of paying for and/or caring for the frail older population focuses primarily on the 'unsustainable' nature of the required upwards flows. It rarely considers the downward flows of financial and caring contributions of older people to the middle and grandchild generations. Almost entirely neglected are valuations of the much more widespread general contributions to society of older people in terms of their role in community support, voluntary work, etc.

Societal changes, such as the growth of migration both transnationally and between rural-urban areas, mean that the nature of intergenerational transfers may change. Although, financial remittances can be transferred from the middle generation to the older generation living 'back home' (Silverstein et al. 2006, Baker and Silverstein 2012), it is generally much harder (or impossible) to provide everyday practical or personal care to a frail or disabled parent from hundreds of miles away. Thus, long distance migration potentially leaves a 'care gap' for the older generation who are 'left behind' in rural areas or in the 'home country'. The implications of these societal changes and changes in the nature of intergenerational relationships are likely to have greater adverse effects for older women's well-being in later life.

The Feminization of Later Life Cross-nationally

Because of the popular and policy focus on the 'burden' of older people and to what extent inter-generational relations can sustain/accommodate this growing 'burden' – the remainder of the chapter focuses on gender and care for older people. It addresses the gender and marital status of older people who are likely to 'need' such 'burdensome' care by society (in an era of welfare state retrenchment) or from family members or others.

Policy-related literature on ageing often conceptualizes older people who 'need' care in an undifferentiated way, as 'the elderly' or 'the old', and as genderless (Bould and Casaca 2011). This is despite extensive research by feminist scholars and others that has challenged earlier views of older people as homogenous, and documented inter-sectional differences associated with gender, class, race, ethnicity and sexuality (Arber and Ginn 1991, 1995, Calasanti and Slevin 2001, 2006, Mutchler and Burr 2011). In contrast, policy-makers and analysts have primarily been concerned about the 'social problems' of an ageing population. The vast majority of older people who 'need care' and thus potentially represent a 'burden' on other relatives or the state are older women, and these women are primarily widowed. This section focuses on the numerical predominance of older women, and the next section examines the likelihood of being a widow, while most older men can expect to die married.

Table 12.1 Expectation of life at birth and at age 65 by gender and country

	Expectation of life at birth			Expectation of life at 65		
	Male	Female	Male/Female difference	Male	Female	Male/Female difference
'High' Difference						
Canada – 2004	77.8	82.6	+5.8	17.7	21.0	+3.3
US – 2004	75.2	80.4	+5.2	17.1	20.0	+2.9
Japan – 2006	79.0	85.8	+6.8	18.5	23.4	+4.9
France – 2005	76.8	83.8	+7.0	17.7	22.0	+4.3
Finland – 2006	75.8	82.8	+7.0	16.8	20.9	+4.1
UK – 2000	75.3	80.1	+4.8	15.7	18.8	+3.1
Brazil – 2005	68.1	75.8	+7.7	16.0	18.6	+2.6
'Excess' Difference						
Russia – 2006	60.4	73.2	+12.8	11.4	15.6	+4.2
Belarus – 2006	63.6	75.5	+11.9	11.4	16.2	+4.8
Estonia – 2005	67.2	78.1	+10.9	13.1	18.0	+4.9
Modest difference						
China – 2000	69.6	73.3	+3.7	–	–	–
Singapore – 2005	77.9	81.6	+3.7	20.9	23.6	+2.7
Cuba – 2001–03	75.1	79.0	+3.9	17.7	21.0	+3.3
Zimbabwe – 2001–02	42.7	45.9	+3.2	12.5	14.5	+2.0
Abnormal low difference						
India – 2005	62.3	63.9	+1.6	13.5	15.3	+1.8
Pakistan – 2003	64.7	65.6	+0.9	15.4	15.4	0
Eqypt – 2001	65.6	67.4	+1.8	12.1	11.7	-0.4
Algeria – 2000	72.5	74.2	+1.7	16.1	16.6	+0.5

Source: United Nations (2008) *Demographic Yearbook 2006*. New York: United Nations. Derived from Table 22.

Gender Differences in Expectation of Life

In nearly all countries women outlive men. The gender differential in expectation of life at birth ranges from women living 12–13 years longer than men in Russia and some Eastern European countries to roughly equal life expectancy in Pakistan, India and Egypt (United Nations 2008), see Table 12.1. The high or 'conventional' gender difference in expectation of life, found in most European and other developed countries, is women living 5–7 years longer than men. However, there is considerable variation, for example from a difference in life expectancy of 7 years in France and Finland, reducing to 4.8 years in the UK. Some countries are experiencing a decreasing feminization of later life, because of faster improvements in male than female mortality, as in the UK over the last 30 years (Arber and Ginn 2005).

Some emerging countries, such as Brazil show a wide gender difference of 7.7 years in expectation of life. Whereas other emerging countries, such as China and Singapore, show a 'modest' gender difference of 3–4 years. It seems likely that these gender differences will become greater over time, and that more emerging countries in the future will have a gender difference in life expectancy similar to that of the 'high' difference countries of Europe.

Gender differences in mortality vary between societies for a range of reasons, including variation between men and women's roles in paid employment (including the danger, occupational hazards and stresses associated with types of employment); men and women's lifestyles and risk behaviors (men having more 'risky' lifestyles linked to smoking, alcohol consumption, motor accidents), and the cultural roles and valuation of women compared with men (Arber and Thomas 2001). The extent that changes in gender equality will lead to women taking on comparable roles to men in the workplace and similar levels of 'risky' behaviors, will tend to reduce gender differences in expectation of life in the future.

Countries with near gender equality in mortality (and expectation of life), such as Pakistan, are likely to be where women's social status is low, and women are more likely to have poor nutrition, less access to health care, are subject to frequent births, and have high maternal mortality (Doyal 1995, Santow 1995, Fuse and Crenshaw 2006). The gender difference in life expectancy is likely to be lower in societies where there is greater valuation of boy children and men, than girl children and women. As maternal mortality decreases in societies, and there is greater equality in the cultural valuation of the two sexes, this will tend to *increase* gender differences in expectation of life.

In some countries the life expectancy for women above 65 is the same or lower than that of men, such as in Egypt (Table 12.1). It is therefore important to consider what societal or cultural factors may disadvantage older women's survival in some societies, compared to the more 'conventional' pattern of women having a 3–5 year greater life expectancy at 65 than men. Improved health care and economic development in many emerging nations is likely to go hand-in-hand with a growing numerical predominance of older women among the ageing population. Thus, more emerging countries in the future are likely to have a sex difference in mortality similar to that of the 'high difference' countries of Europe.

Sex Ratios in Later Life

Gender differences in life expectancy are the main factor influencing sex ratios in later life. In nearly all societies, the proportion of women to men increases with advancing age. The greater the numerical predominance of older women at higher ages, the greater the relative proportion of older women than men that are likely to be frail or disabled and require care and support.

Figure 12.2 shows the degree of feminization of later life in a range of countries. In most European and western countries, there are 30–50% more women than men above age 65; this female 'excess' increases with advancing age. Figure 12.2(a) shows that for the UK, France and the US, there are over twice as many women aged 85–89 as men, which increases to three times as many aged 90–94, and over four times as many over age 95 in the UK and France. However, in countries with 'abnormally' high gender differences in life expectancy, the female predominance of older women over men is more stark. Figure 12.2(b) contrasts sex ratios in later life in Russia and Estonia compared with the UK, showing more than twice as many women as men in their late 70s in Russia and Estonia (compared to 41% more in UK), and four times as many women as men aged 85–89 (2.3 times more in the UK). Thus, in Russia and Eastern European countries, the vast majority of older people are women.

A different picture of how sex ratios change with ageing emerges in countries with a low gender difference in life expectancy. Figure 12.2(c) contrasts Pakistan and India with Cuba (which has a modest gender difference in life expectancy). India shows no evidence of more older women in each age group over 65, unlike in virtually all other countries. And in Pakistan there are more men than women in all ages above 60; falling to reach a sex ratio of only 74 women for every 100 men in their early 80s. The lack of feminization of later life in India, Pakistan and other countries with a negligible or low gender difference in life expectancy at age 65, is likely to reflect differential cultural valuations of older women and men, which may be manifest in a particularly precarious existence for older widows in these societies.

In conclusion, a greater feminization of later life in terms of more older women than men with advancing age, means the vast majority of older people who require care and support in later life are likely to be women. In addition, future societal changes may result in emerging countries having a greater predominance of women with advancing age than is evident at present.

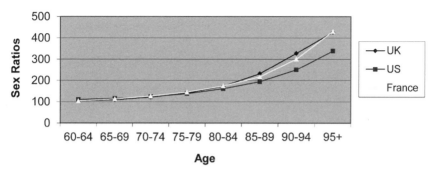

(a) UK, US and France

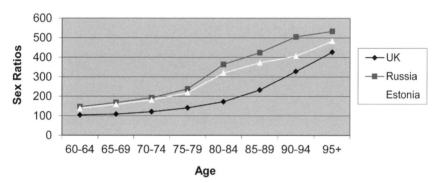

(b) Russia, Estonia and UK

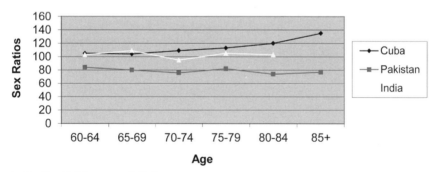

(c) India, Pakistan and Cuba

Figure 12.2 Sex ratios (female/male) for five year age groups above age 60 across countries

Source: United Nations (2008) *Demographic Yearbook 2006*. New York: United Nations. Derived from Table 7.

Older Women, Widowhood and the Provision of Care

Marital status is pivotal to the living arrangements, financial well-being, care-giving support and social relationships of older people, but in divergent ways for older women and men (Arber 2004a, 2004b). It is therefore important to examine how gender differences in marital status change with advancing age. Widowhood is a significant transition, often representing the loss of a partner of 40–50 years, who may have been their main source of companionship, support and care.

Gender differences in life expectancy and the increasingly divergent sex ratio with advancing age suggest a high proportion of older women will be living as widows. However, the proportion of widows in a society cannot be directly 'read off' gender differences in life expectancy and changing sex ratios. The relative number of older people who are married versus widowed also depends on gender differences in age of marriage. In most European and western societies, men are on average 2–3 years older than women at first marriage. For example, in France, if the gender gap in life expectancy of 7 years was added to a (first) marriage age gap of say 2–3 years, then a French woman could expect to live as a widow on average for 9–10 years. However, the marriage age gap is much larger in many emerging countries, as well as for remarriages.

Gender Differences in Marital Status in Later Life

Across all societies, the vast majority of older men are married, and therefore have a partner for domestic service support, companionship and for care should they become physically disabled, whereas this is the case for only a minority of older women. Figure 12.3 shows four contrasting societies, Canada, Japan, Singapore and Turkey; in each case over three-quarters of men over 65 are married (varying from 75% in Canada to 88% in Turkey). Even above age 80, two-thirds of men are married in each country. This contrasts with women over 65, where in each society under half of women are married (40–48%), and the likelihood of being married declines steeply with advancing age. Over age 80, only a small proportion of women are married, varying from 15% in Japan to 22% in Turkey.

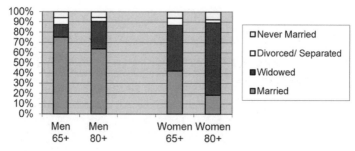

(a) Canada (2001)

Gender, Marital Status and Intergenerational Relations 227

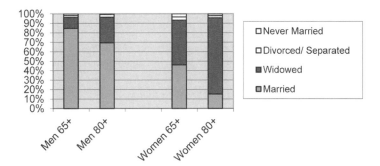

(b) Japan (2000)

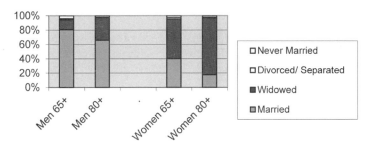

(c) Singapore (2000)

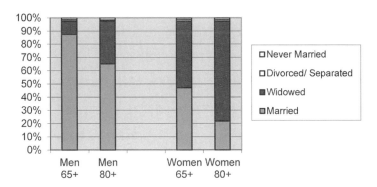

(d) Turkey (2000)

Figure 12.3 Marital status by gender for people aged 65+ and 80+ in four countries

Source: United Nations (2009) *Demographic Yearbook 2007*. Derived from Table 2.

In later life, being married is normative for older men and widowhood is normative for older women. More women over 65 are widowed than are married in each of these countries, and above age 80, over 80% are widowed. Despite the cultural and economic differences between these four societies, there is a remarkable consistency in the proportions of older men who are married and of women who are widowed. In contrast, more older people are divorced or never married in Canada, 13% (and in Europe and other western societies) than in Turkey, 0.8% (and in Asian and Middle Eastern societies), see Table 12.2(a). This has implications for intergenerational relationships and the likely need for care, since divorced and never married older people (particularly men) may have limited family support networks to provide care should they become frail or disabled (Arber and Ginn 1991, Arber 2004a, 2004b).

Table 12.2 Marital status distributions, and sex ratios of married and widowed, for aged 65+ and 80+, in Canada, France, Japan, Singapore and Turkey

	Canada 2001	France 1999	Japan 2000	Singapore 2000	Turkey 2000
(a) Marital status					
Age 65 and over					
Married	56.4	55.8	62.3	58.1	65.1
Widowed	30.7	32.1	32.1	36.8	34.1
Divorced + Never Married	12.9	12.1	5.4	5.1	0.8
Total	100%	100%	100%	100%	100%
N=	3,888,560	9,749,280	21,645,928	231,325	3,796,430
Age 80 and over					
Married	34.8	30.5	33.1	35.5	38.8
Widowed	56.1	58.8	62.8	61.6	58.9
Divorced + Never Married	9.1	10.7	4.1	2.9	2.4
Total	100%	100%	100%	100%	100%
N =	932,050	2,333,882	4,760,001	40,134	462,844
(b) Sex ratios					
Age 65 and over					
Sex Ratio (F/M)	1.34	1.46	1.39	1.22	1.25
Married ratio (F/M)	0.76	0.80	0.76	0.63	0.67
Widowed ratio (F/M)	4.82	5.50	5.59	5.06	4.61
Age 80 and over					
Sex Ratio (F/M)	1.93	2.17	2.05	1.69	1.54
Married ratio (F/M)	0.54	0.54	0.45	0.45	0.51
Widowed ratio (F/M)	4.93	5.53	6.15	4.32	3.60

Source: United Nations (2009) *Demographic Yearbook 2007*. New York: United Nations. Derived from Table 2.

Another way to highlight the fact that most older men are married, whereas older women are widowed, is to examine sex ratios *among* the married and *among* the widowed. For the five countries in Table 12.2(b), the preponderance of women age 65 and over compared with men is shown by the sex ratio, which varies from 1.22 in Singapore to 1.46 in France (146 women for every 100 men age 65 and over). But this modest numerical predominance of older women hides very different sex ratios among the married and among the widowed. In each society there are about five times more widows than widowers age 65 and over (sex ratios among the widowed vary from 4.6 in Turkey to 5.6 in Japan). The sex ratios among the married vary from 3 married men over 65 for every two married women in Singapore (sex ratio = 0.63) and Turkey (sex ratio = 0.67), to 5 married men to every 4 married women in Canada (sex ratio = 0.8). These sex ratios in widowhood and being married in later life are remarkably similar across these five contrasting countries.

At advanced ages (over 80), the sex ratios of being married become sharper, whereby about twice as many of the married are men than women in each of these countries (Table 12.2(b)). There is somewhat more variation in the sex ratio among the widowed across these five countries, varying from 3.6 more widows than widowers in Turkey to 6.15 more widows than widowers in Japan, reflecting cultural and mortality differences between these societies. The importance of the sex ratio among the widowed above age 80 is brought into sharp relief, given that about 60% of people over 80 across all five societies are widowed (Table 12.2(a)). Since most care and support is needed above age 80, not only are women the primary group in need of care, but they are predominantly widows. In contrast, men over age 80 are primarily married, so can rely on their wife for care and support should they require it.

Gender Differences in Late Marriage and Remarriage

The gender difference in 'being married' and in 'being widowed' is influenced not only by gender differences in life expectancy and age at first marriage, but also gender differences in rates of remarriage (following widowhood and divorce). Thus, an additional factor compounding the disproportionate number of widows compared with widowers is that widowers are more likely than widows to remarry including at very old ages. These higher remarriage rates of men reflect cultural norms and gender inequalities of power and status.

As little international comparative data is available on rates of remarriage by age and gender, Table 12.3 provides data on marriages above age 65 for men and women. The first column indicates the sex ratio of getting married above age 65, showing that in Canada and the UK twice as many men aged over 65 get married as women. However, in many societies this gender inequality is much greater, reaching around five times more men marrying above age 65 than women in Greece and Turkey, and over eight times more older men marrying than older women in Hong Kong.

Table 12.3 Marriages of men and women aged 65 and over by country

	Marriages age 65+ Male/Female Ratio	% of Men aged 65+, who marry a wife under age 50	% of Women aged 65+, who marry a husband under age 50
Canada – 2002	1.91	9.6%	1.3%
UK – 2002	2.05	14.4%	1.9%
France – 2006	2.17	15.8%	3.3%
Germany – 2006	2.37	16.5%	2.2%
Italy – 2005	4.32	32.6%	5.9%
Greece – 2006	5.05	28.3%	2.0%
Turkey – 2006	5.33	40.4%	0.9%
Brazil – 2006	3.79	36.6%	7.0%
Japan – 2006	2.42	18.6%	0.5%
Korea – 2006	3.18	16.1%	0.2%
Hong Kong – 2005	8.44	67.3%	2.8%

Source: United Nations (2009) *Demographic Yearbook 2007*. New York: United Nations. Derived from Table 24.

The gender inequality at older ages in 'being married' and 'being widowed' is even greater in societies where it is normative for the groom to be much older than the bride. Table 12.3 (second and third columns) shows among men and women who marry above age 65, what proportion marry a spouse who is under age 50. In each society, at least five times more older men marry a wife under 50, than older women marry a husband under 50. This gender asymmetry in marriage ages is very stark in many countries. Older men are over 30 times more likely to marry a woman under 50, than older women marry a man under 50, in Japan, Korea, Hong Kong and Turkey. In most countries, very small proportions (under 3%) of women over 65 marry a husband under age 50. In contrast, in Hong Kong, two-thirds of marriages of older men are to women under 50, and in Brazil and Turkey this is the case for over a third of older men's marriages. These large marriage age differentials reflect cultural traditions interlinked to broader gender inequalities and patriarchal ideologies in these societies. Thus, the greater the marriage age differential in a society, the greater the likelihood that men will be married even at very old ages, and the greater the likelihood that women will be widowed and live as a widow for more years of their life.

Discussion and Conclusions

The span of later life from age 65 upwards is increasing in all societies, and there is growing concern about whether intergenerational relationships can support the increasing needs for financial support and caregiving that will be required by the burgeoning older population. The chapter discussed four societal changes that are bringing these issues into sharper relief: the impact of transnational and rural-urban migration, the greater participation of women in paid work, decreasing co-residence in multi-generational households, and the fall in fertility and increase in childlessness. These changes have impacts on intergenerational flows of financial and caring support between generations. Thus, societal, cultural and economic changes globally mean that the nature of intergenerational relations is changing with consequences for elders, particularly older women. These societal trends simultaneously reduce availability of potential carers for frail elders, while increasing grandparents' role in childcare. They are likely to influence the availability of family caregivers for frail or disabled elders, with the greatest care gap likely to be experienced by older widows, who are particularly vulnerable in most societies in later life.

Policy-makers often treat the ageing population as if it is homogenous. This chapter focused on two sources of diversity among the older population, namely gender and marital status. (Although this focus does not deny other important sources of difference and disadvantage in later life.) Across nearly all societies, more women than men survive to advanced ages, and due to frailty, mental confusion or disability, often require care or support to remain living in the community.

Older married people in the UK, irrespective of gender, are highly advantaged in terms of their material resources, living circumstances, and access to caring support (Arber and Ginn 1991, 1995, Arber 2004a, 2004b). However, this gender similarity among the married must be tempered by the recognition that over three-quarters of older men are married, and most are married when they die. In contrast the advantages associated with marriage are the province of only a minority of older women. Research in western societies shows that widows are much more likely to live in poverty than widowers and than older married men and women (Ginn 2003, de Santis et al. 2008). Widows, constitute over half of all older women across most societies. More research is needed on the well-being and access to caring support for both widows and widowers in developing societies, especially where there is a lack of state health and welfare support for older adults.

Extensive research in the UK suggests that married older people who become disabled will be cared for by their spouse irrespective of gender (Arber and Ginn 1991, 1992, Rose and Bruce 1995). Across the societies considered in this chapter, since there are many more married older men than married older women, men are much more likely to receive care from their spouse. However, the smaller proportion of older married women may receive little caregiving support from their husbands in many societies. In Asia and other emerging economies, if older married women are frail and disabled, cultural norms may mean they cannot rely on receiving care from their husband, but may have to depend on daughters, daughters-in-law or other caregivers who, due to declines in co-residence, are increasingly likely to live elsewhere.

Marital status has a critical impact on older people's need for care and support from relatives or others living *outside* their household, and from state and private services. Global societal changes mean that older women are more likely in the future to live alone. Older women are likely to experience the disadvantages associated with living as a widow, which may be particularly poignant in societies with little welfare state provision and where there is welfare state retrenchment.

References

Albertini, M., Kohli, M. and Vogel, C. 2007. Intergenerational transfers of time and money in European families: Common themes – different regimes? *Journal of European Social Policy*, 17, 319–34.

Arber S. 2004a. Gender trajectories: How age and marital status influence patterns of gender inequality in later life, in *Ageing and Diversity: Multiple Pathways and Cultural Migrations*, edited by S. Olav Daatland and S. Biggs. Bristol: The Policy Press, 61–76.

Arber S. 2004b. Gender, marital status and ageing: Linking material, health and social resources. *Journal of Aging Studies*, 18(1), 91–108.

Arber, S. and Ginn, J. 1991. *Gender and Later Life: A Sociological Analysis of Resources and Constraints.* London: Sage.

Arber S. and Ginn, J. 1992. In sickness and in health: Caregiving, gender and the independence of elderly people, in *Families and Households: Divisions and Change*, edited by C. Marsh and S. Arber. London: Macmillan, 86–105.

Arber, S. and Ginn, J. (eds) 1995. *Connecting Gender and Ageing.* Buckingham: Open University Press.

Arber, S. and Ginn, J. 2005. Gender dimensions of the age shift, in *The Cambridge Handbook of Age and Ageing*, edited by M. Johnson. Cambridge: Cambridge University Press, 527–37.

Arber, S. and Thomas, H. 2001. From women's health to a gender analysis of health, in *The Blackwell Companion to Medical Sociology*, edited by W.C. Cockerham. Oxford: Blackwell, 94–113.

Arber, S. and Timonen, V. (eds) 2012. *Contemporary Grandparenting: Changing Family Relationships in Global Contexts.* Bristol: Policy Press.

Arber, S., Davidson, K. and Ginn, J. (eds) 2003. *Gender and Ageing: Changing Roles and Relationships.* Maidenhead: Open University Press.

Attias-Donfut, C. and Woolf, F.-C. 2000a. The redistributive effects of generational transfers, in *The Myth of Generational Conflict*, edited by S. Arber and C. Attias-Donfut. London: Routledge, 22–46.

Attias-Donfut, C. and Woolf, F.-C. 2000b. Complementarity between private and public transfers, in *The Myth of Generational Conflict*, edited by S. Arber and C. Attias-Donfut. London: Routledge, 47–68.

Baker, L. and Silverstein, M. 2012. The well-being of grandparents caring for grandchildren in rural China and the United States, in *Contemporary Grandparenting: Changing Family Relationships in Global Contexts*, edited by S. Arber and V. Timonen. Bristol: Policy Press, 51–70.

Bould, S. and Casaca, S.F. 2011. Aging populations, chronic diseases, gender and the risk of disability. SOCIUS Working Papers No. 02/2011. Lisbon: SOCIUS.

Calasanti, T.M. and Slevin, K.F. 2001. *Gender, Social Inequalities, and Aging*. Walnut Creek: AltaMira Press.

Calasanti, T.M. and Slevin, K.F. (eds) 2006. *Age Matters: Realigning Feminist Thinking*. New York: Routledge, 225–45.

De Santis, G., Seghieri, C. and Tanturri, M.L. 2008. Economic well-being in old age in Italy: Does having children make a difference? *Genus*, LXIV(1–2), 75–99.

Doyal, L. 1995. *What Makes Women Sick: Gender and the Political Economy of Health*. London: Macmillan.

Estes, C.L. 1999. Critical gerontology and the new political economy of aging, in *Critical Gerontology*, edited by M. Minkler and C.L. Estes. Amityville: Baywood.

Estes, C.L and Wallace, S.P. 2010. Globalisation, social policy, and ageing: A North American persepective, in *The Sage Handbook of Social Gerontology*, edited by D. Dannefer and C. Phillipson. New York: Sage.

Fuse, K. and Crenshaw, E.M. 2006. Gender imbalance in infant mortality: A cross-national study of social structure and female infanticide. *Social Science and Medicine*, 62(2), 360–74.

Gaymu, J., Festy, P., Poulain, M. and Beets, G. (eds) 2008. *Future Elderly Living Conditions in Europe*. Paris: INED, Les Cahiers de l'INED, 162.

Ginn, J. 2003. *Gender, Pensions and the Lifecourse: How Pensions Need to Adapt to Changing Family Forms*. Bristol: Policy Press.

Guo, M., Aranda, M.P. and Silverstein, M. 2009. The impact of out-migration in the inter-generational support and psychological wellbeing of adults in rural China. *Ageing and Society*, 29, 1085–104.

Hagestad, G. 2006. Transfers between grandparents and grandchildren: The importance of taking a three-generation perspective. *Zeitscrift fur Familienforschung*, 3, 315–32.

Hagestad, G. and Herlofson, K. 2005. Micro and macro perspectives on intergenerational relations and transfers in Europe. Report from United Nations Expert Group Meeting on Social and Economic Implications of Changing Population Age Structures. New York: United Nations Department of Economic and Social Affairs and Population Division.

Herlofson, K. and Hagestad, G. 2012. Transformations in the role of grandparents across welfare states, in *Contemporary Grandparenting: Changing Family Relationships in Global Contexts*, edited by S. Arber, and V. Timonen. Bristol: Policy Press, 27–49.

Isaksen, L.W., Devi, S.U. and Hochschild, A.R. 2008. Global care crisis: A problem of capital, care chain, or commons? *American Behavioural Scientist*, 52, 405–25.

Keck, W. 2008. The relationship between children and their frail elderly parents in different care regimes, in *Families, Ageing and Social Policy: Intergenerational*

Solidarity in European Welfare States, edited by C. Saraceno. Cheltenham: Edward Elgar.

Kohli, M., Kunemund, H., Motel, A. and Szydlik, M. 2000. Families apart? Intergenerational transfers in East and West Germany, in *The Myth of Generational Conflict*, edited by S. Arber and C. Attias-Donfut. London: Routledge, 88–99.

Kunemund, H. 2008. Intergenerational relations within the family and the state, in *Families, Ageing and Social Policy: Intergenerational Solidarity in European Welfare States*, edited by C. Saraceno. Cheltenham: Edward Elgar.

Manning, W.D. and Brown, S.L. 2011. The demography of unions among older Americans, 1980-present: A family change approach, in *Handbook of Sociology of Aging*, edited by R.A. Settersten Jr. and J.L. Angel. New York: Springer, 193–210.

Mutchler, J.E. and Burr, J.A. 2011. Race, ethnicity and aging, in *Handbook of Sociology of Aging*, edited by R.A. Settersten Jr. and J.L. Angel. New York: Springer, 83–102.

Rose, H. and Bruce, E. 1995. Mutual care but differential esteem: Caring between older couples, in *Connecting Gender and Ageing*, edited by S. Arber and J. Ginn. Milton Keynes: Open University Press, 114–28.

Santow, G. 1995. Social roles and physical health: The case of female disadvantage in poor countries. *Social Science and Medicine*, 40, 147–61.

Saraceno, C. (ed.) 2008. *Families, Ageing and Social Policy: Intergenerational Solidarity in European Welfare States*. Cheltenham: Edward Elgar.

Silverstein, M., Cong, Z. and Li, S. 2006. Intergenerational transfers and living arrangements of older people in rural China: Consequences for psychological well-being. *Journal of Gerontology*, 61B(5), S256–66.

United Nations (2008) *Demographic Yearbook 2006*. New York: United Nations.

United Nations (2009) *Demographic Yearbook 2007*. New York: United Nations.

Chapter 13

The Cultural Context of Social Cohesion and Social Capital: Exploring Filial Caregiving

Neena L. Chappell

It is well established that families in the West provide care to their elderly members when the need arises (Chappell 1992, 2003, Martin-Matthews and Campbell 1995, Pyke 2000). However, it is less clear that societal norms and personal values embrace the idea of providing care. That is, Western culture is more known for its political, economic and cultural focus on individualism and for ageism than it is for promoting respect and care for older adults. Cultures differ in this respect. Asia, and China in particular, is known for its explicit teachings of filial piety (care and respect for one's parents as they age) both through the family and political agendas (Ikels 2004). In modern times there has been considerable interest in the extent to which these traditional values have been changing (Whyte 2004). This chapter focuses on intergenerational caring across three cultural groups (Caucasian Canadians, Chinese Canadians and Hong Kong Chinese) examining the relationship between expressions of filial responsibility and caregiving behaviors. Viewing filial attitudes as social cohesion (expressed connectedness), and the provision of care as the parent's social capital (a resource), it explores the relationship between the two, within the three cultural groups. Do attitudes towards caring for one's parents vary across cultures? And, does the care provided vary across cultures? If so, how do these differ and how do we account for that difference?

Social Cohesion and Social Capital

Both Bourdieu (1991) and Coleman (1990) use social capital to refer to available resources accruing to individuals by virtue of their social ties. Adopting Carpiano's (2006) distinction, social cohesion refers to networks and trust while social capital is the actual or potential resource. Social cohesion and social capital are considered distinct concepts with social capital (resources) following from social cohesion. Filial responsibility therefore derives from norms and are part of the values and connectedness that are social cohesion. Filial responsibility is considered an aspect of the norm of familism. Any actual caregiving behavior that results from the filial responsibility is the resource and part of the parent's social capital. Borrowing from Putnam, this focus on intergenerational relations, is an aspect of bonding or localized social cohesion; it is the filial responsibility that potentially leads to the resource, the provision of care. The relationship between filial responsibility and behavioral caregiving is an example of Durkheim's 'value interjection' i.e. internalized values, norms and normal imperatives that influence individual actions (Portes 1995). It is not the task of this chapter to solve the many disputes within the social capital literature.[1] Rather, the intent is to explore the commonly held assumption that our attitudes and beliefs are related to, indeed lead to, certain behaviors. Further, this question is posed among three different cultural groups that can then be compared.

The East and the West

Social cohesion, evidenced in filial responsibility, differs historically between East and West. Social capital, evidenced in the provision of care, differs in form if not function. In the West, it would appear that, even though there have been numerous societal changes such as increased life expectancy, lower fertility, more women working for pay, geographic mobility, etc. adult children nevertheless continue to

---

1   Although the concept of social capital has received considerable attention, it is plagued with lack of conceptual clarity and measurement. Lynch et al. (2000) suggest that one of the reasons is that social capital has simply become a new label for what used to be called social support; Forrest and Kearns (2001) suggest the labels have changed but the questions have not. Friedkin (2004) suggests the confusion flows from the fact that the concept includes the reciprocal link between the individual and the group while Edmondson (2003) argues that the failure occurs because of the lack of taking context into account. Macinko and Starfield (2001) note that most approaches to measuring social capital do not distinguish between it as a resource, social product, and individual response. This is true of the major names associated with this concept, including Coleman, Bourdieu and Putnam. There is little consistency in the labels applied to the measures. The same can be said of the concept of social cohesion. As Friedkin (2004) notes, a main source of confusion is the proliferation of definitions of terms that do not cohere. These include, for example, for social cohesion: social networks and social capital, belonging and identity, social solidarity and wealth of equality, social order and social control, and common values and civic culture (Forrest and Kearns 2001); belonging in isolation, inclusion and exclusion, participation and non-participation, recognition and rejection, legitimacy and illegitimacy (Chan et al. 2006). Similar lists can be provided for the term social capital (empowerment, participation, associational activity and common purpose, supporting networks and reciprocity, norms and values, trust, safety, belonging) (Forrest and Kearns 2001). Furthermore, cohesion is sometimes defined as social capital, social capital is sometimes defined as social cohesion; the two are sometimes defined synonymously in terms of another term, such as trust or one is seen as one domain of the other (Kawachi et al. 1997, Dayton-Johnson 2000, Forrest and Kearns 2001, World Bank n.d.). Finally there is contested discourse over whether each concept is most appropriately conceptualized at the individual or collective level (or both) and whether it is most appropriately an independent, mediating or dependent variable (Beauvais and Jenson 2002, Carpiano 2006, Chappell and Funk 2010).

provide care for their parents when in need. This is despite values of individualism and independence that may be in opposition to familism. This provision of care, however, does not seem to come from strong values of filial responsibility. Indeed Fry (1996) argues that there is only an initial vague awareness of filial responsibility which Donorfio (1996) posits develops after a triggering event. Finch and Mason (1991) and Globerman (1995) argue that even though most children provide care, it is not unconditional or automatic. It varies depending on the child and the perceived deservedness of the parent. That is, a strong normative consensus does not exist. However, Dai and Dimond (1998) believe that filial piety is nevertheless an approved virtue referring to respect, care and love for our parents but without an emphasis on obedience and unlimited responsibility (also see in Dellmann-Jenkins and Brittain 2003).

Despite this lack of strong normative consensus in the West, research since the 1970s has revealed the provision of care by families (Pyke 2000, Chappell 2003). We know that spouses are the primary caregivers in old age, followed by daughters (Hong and Liu 2000, Montgomery et al. 2000). Sons tend to offer monetary assistance and supervision but step up given the unavailability of a daughter (Chappell 1992, Frederick and Fast 1999). We know further that the vast majority of care is in the form of assistance with instrumental activities of daily living (IADL) but increases as the need increases (Hollander et al. 2009). While there appears to be a clear gender difference in both the amount and types of care provided by sons and daughters (with sons typically helping with financial and management advice, heavy chores and shopping and daughters with more hands-on intensive instrumental and emotional assistance and daughters providing more assistance than sons), most attitudes of filial obligation in North America do not vary by gender (Hamon and Blieszner 1990).

China, on the other hand, has been undergoing major change with globalization which some believe is effecting the provision of care and potentially the value of filial piety. Traditionally, filial piety includes respect and care for elderly family members whereby sons, notably first born sons were culturally, morally, economically and legally favored. In return, they would provide care in old age (Ng et al. 2002). Daughters, on the other hand, were transferred to the husband's family upon marriage and were expected to assist the son in the care of her parents-in-law and not provide care to her own parents (Liu and Kendig 2000). Political, social and cultural change under Chairman Mao since the mid twentieth century undermined this traditional notion, with constitutional and legal changes that made the individual, not the lineage, legally entitled to civil rights. Love was emphasized as the foundation for marriage and children; women received the right of property and were civilly equal to men. Drastic measures were implemented to introduce family size and daughters were to share responsibility for their birth parents equally with sons. Indeed the notion of filial piety was officially attacked in the late 1970s (Ikels 2004, Miller 2004). It became embraced again by the late twentieth century, now viewed as a virtue to assist with the eldercare crisis at least partially created by the success of the one-child policy and the subsequent demise of the extended family. Children, notably women, were now to support their elderly parents in the absence of state welfare and public services and to do so out of gratitude (Hashimoto 2004, Wang 2004).

The extent to which filial piety as a personal value, and therefore social cohesion, has changed is contentious. Wang 2004, argues that it has not changed dramatically and Ikels (2004) argues that the core of understanding has not changed. However, Whyte (2004), reports that married Chinese daughters express as much support for filial obligations to their own parents as do married sons. Hendricks and Yoon (2006) argue that Asian beliefs are moving away from support for traditional values and towards more Westernized ideas of personal happiness and individualism (Ng et al. 2002).

And, there is evidence that the provision of social capital, i.e., the *practice* of care for parents in China is changing. Whyte (2004) finds that older adults' spouse and daughter are now providing more care than in the past and the daughter-in-law is providing less care to her husband's parents. This finding is supported in research by others (Yu et al. 2000, Chappell 2003). Some authors suggest that there is a new pattern emerging of 'networked families'. Here, elderly parents increasingly live apart from their adult children, but receive care when needed (Chen 1998, Whyte 2004, Zhang 2004). Nevertheless there are still differences from the West. For example, elderly parents are more likely to live with their children than in the West and there is a continuation of assisting parents who are older, but who are functionally independent, viewed as a continuation of the traditional belief that assistance before health fails demonstrates respect for one's parents (Yu et al. 2000). Sons continue to provide more assistance than is found in the West and they are still largely regarded as the primary source of assistance. Older adults themselves continue to express the desire to live with their children, especially sons (Lee et al. 2000, Kwok 2006).

Interest in this chapter lies in both a cross-cultural comparison of attitudes of filial responsibility (social cohesion) and a cross cultural comparison of caregiving behaviors (social capital) as well as an examination of the relationship between the two within these different cultures. A third group of diasporic Chinese Canadians have been added because they experience both cultures and are said to have a transnational identity (Van Ziegart 2002). Diasporic ethnic groups are particularly interesting because they can help us answer questions about the durability of historic family patterns of caregiving (in this case historic Asian patterns) given their experience of family disruption, a potential lack of family or resources for caring for older adults. Yet, as Blakemore (2000) notes, the impact of migration on the ageing process is seriously neglected in social gerontology. He studied South Asian migrants to the United Kingdom and concluded that, despite discrimination, social exclusion and disadvantage, traditional Asian family care patterns are 'surprisingly resilient'. This is so despite smaller households and increasingly separate living arrangements.

There is some research that supports the notion that caregiving among the diasporic Chinese reflects the blending of two cultures. Chappell and Kusch

(2007), find that the Chinese in Canada are more likely to live with their children than are other Canadians, but less so than in China. This occurs even when the spouse is still living, a practice more common in China than in Canada. Similarly the son and daughter-in-law unit is more involved in care than is found in Western culture, but daughters and spouses provide more care than is found in traditional Chinese society. Asian populations in other countries such as the US (Kauh 1999), New Zealand (Liu et al. 2000) and Australia (Lo and Russell 2007), also reveal possible modifications to beliefs and, in some instances, weaker support for filial obligations. However, Pinquart and Sorenson (2005) report that ethnic minority caregivers both provide more care and have stronger attitudes of filial obligation than Caucasian caregivers and Lai (2010) notes that their attitudes of filial responsibility are related to greater satisfaction in the role and easing the burden. Either way, ethnicity matters (Botsford et al. 2011).

In this chapter, the differential relationship between social cohesion (as reflected in the attitudes or values of filial responsibility) and social capital (for older parents as reflected in care provision) is examined cross-culturally among three different groups: Caucasian Canadians, Chinese Canadians, and Hong Kong Chinese.

Methodology

Data come from a recent study involving face-to-face interviews with filial caregivers among three groups: Caucasian Canadians, Chinese Canadians and Hong Kong Chinese. Interviews were conducted in Hong Kong in the fall and winter of 2007 and in Canada in the winter and summer of 2008. In Canada, data were collected in Victoria and Vancouver, British Columbia with interviews taking approximately 1.5 hours and all data collection taking place in English (the choice of all Chinese Canadians participating). The data collection in Hong Kong took place in Cantonese after the interview schedule had been translated into Chinese and then translated back. It consisted of measures that had been validated in both English and Chinese. Both Canadian samples were recruited as convenience samples through advertising and local papers, announcements at local meetings of caregiver networks and multi-cultural societies and through word of mouth. The Hong Kong sample consisted of caregivers to older adults aged 60+ who had originally been randomly selected from a list of households used for the regional government's general household survey. The Canadian data reported here therefore are not representative; the Hong Kong data are. In total, 316 caregivers were interviewed: 100 Caucasian Canadians; 92 Chinese Canadians; 124 Hong Kong Chinese.

Eligibility criteria included: a parent aged 60+ for whom an adult child was providing care for at least three hours a week (care or support refer to errands, phone calls, tending appointments, linking the parent to services, taking care of personal needs such as cooking and cleaning or providing emotional support), the parent was geographically proximate i.e. accessible by car; Caucasian was white or light skinned and ancestrally from Canada, England/Ireland/Scotland/Wales, United States, Scandinavian countries, Iceland, Europe; Chinese Canadians had to self-identify as Chinese and had descended from Hong Kong to ensure comparability with Chinese/China sample; those living in Hong Kong had to self-identify as Chinese.

The three cultural groups are analyzed separately; they have been analyzed as a group as a whole elsewhere (Chappell and Funk 2011). Two scales measure social cohesion (filial responsibility): the Filial Expectancy Scale (Lee and Sung 1997, Kim and Lee 2003) and the Filial Piety Measure (Liu et al. 2000). The Filial Expectancy Scale is used extensively, and has been validated both in North America and Asia (alphas range from .69–. 80). Consisting of five items such as, 'children should live close to their parents'; 'children should want a house with enough room for their parents to feel free to move in' and with Likert-style responses, Cronbach's alpha for the present study equals .81. The FilialPiety Measure contains six items such as, 'how much would you agree or disagree that, when it comes to elderly parents, adult Chinese have an obligation to ... look after them? assist them financially if needed? respect them?' This less extensively used measure also has a Likert-style response options and in a two generation of Chinese immigrant study in New Zealand had alphas reported from .81 to .88. In the present study, Cronbach's alpha equals .83.

Social capital (filial caregiving behaviors) refer to activities of daily living (both basic ADLs and instrumental IADLs), and emotional support (including companionship). The caregiver was asked whether they provided assistance with a list of activities that were then summed (ADL: bathing, dressing, using the toilet, feeding, getting in/out of bed, getting about the house; IADL: shopping, meal preparation, light housework, heavy housework, transportation, assistance with finances, negotiating service assistance). When both ADL and IADL items are combined, the alpha is .79. Emotional support was measured by asking: 'How well do you feel you meet your (mother's or father's) needs for emotional support on a scale where 1 represents "not at all" and 4 represents "very much so" (you can select any number between 0 and 4 in this scale to represent your feelings)?' The provision of companionship was measured based on responses to the question, 'How well do you feel that you meet your (mother's or father's) needs for companionship or visiting?' Response options were the same as for emotional support above. The two were combined: they meet the parent's need for neither emotional support nor companionship, they meet the parent's need for one but not the other; they meet the parent's need for both. A summative measure included assistance with ADL, IADL, emotional support, companionship and financial support.

Caregiver socio-demographic characteristics included: gender (male/female); age (coded continuously); education (coded continuously); employment status (full-time, part-time, not at all); income (in 13 categories); marital status (married, divorced/separated, not married); number of children (coded continuously); persons in household (coded continuously); lives with parent (yes/no); parent cared for (mother/father); geographic distance to receiving parent (minutes of travel time); and perceptions of personal health (excellent to bad). They were also asked, 'How enjoyable is the time you and your (mother/father) spend together (1 – not at all to 5 – very greatly)?' 'Lastly, to what extent can you confide in your (mother/father) (1 – not at all to 5 – greatly)?' Caregivers were also asked about the parent they cared for in terms of that parent's: gender (male/female); current marital status (married, widowed); need for assistance in ADL (none, some or total for each ADL noted above IADL and summed; short-term memory difficulties (yes/no); caregiver perception of parent's overall health (bad to excellent); and diagnosis of dementia or other forms of cognitive impairment (yes/no).

Analyses examined bivariate relationships between social capital and cultural group and between social cohesion and social capital within each cultural group. Then multiple regression analyses included three types of social capital as dependent variables: assistance with functioning, that is, the sum of both ADL and IADL; the provision of emotional support including companionship; and a sum of five separate caregiving behaviors: ADL, IADL, emotional support, companionship and financial support separated.[2]

Cultural Differences

As noted elsewhere (Chappell and Funk 2011), the total sample is almost three quarters female (73.7%). Few live alone (8.6%) reflecting their marital status in which fully 64.8% are married or common law. About half the samples have one parent who is still alive (47.6%) and three quarters (75.7%) are caring for their mother. Most are between the ages of 40 and 59 (63.5%); and most work for pay (55.9% work full-time; 15.6% work part-time).

All three groups reveal similar status in terms of their marital status and in terms of how close and how affectionate they feel they are to the parent to whom they are providing care. That is, closeness to parents is common across cultural groups. However, Caucasian Canadians included in this data set tend to be older, caring for a parent who is widowed, and not living with the care recipient when compared with the two Chinese groups. This is similar to other North American studies showing that daughters tend to become the caregiver after one parent is widowed, typically the mother who has cared for her husband until his death. (Chappell 1992, Montgomery et al. 2000). The fact that they are less likely to be

---

2 As reported elsewhere (Chappell 2011) the predictors of financial support also vary considerably by cultural group. Indeed within this dataset, there were no significant predictors of providing financial support among Caucasian Canadians. Among Chinese Canadians, however, those with greater social cohesion as well as those with less education and whose parents are in better health are more likely to provide more financial support. Among Hong Kong Chinese, those who are employed are also more likely to provide more financial support.

living with the parent reflects the greater tendency toward living with children in old age in the Chinese culture. The fact that Chinese Canadians are more likely to be caregiving sons and Hong Kong Chinese are more likely to be daughters, supports the current research showing that in China, women are now caring for their own parents rather than their parents-in-law (White 2004, Zhang 2004). However, the Chinese Canadians in this sample appear to be maintaining a more traditional cultural pattern of care. Chinese Canadians are also more likely to be employed than are either Hong Kong Chinese or Caucasian Canadians.

Turning first to the bivariate relationship between the provision of social capital and the three cultural groups, the results are shown in Table 13.1. All three measures of care provision show strong relationships with cultural groups. Caucasian Canadians are much more likely to be assisting with more ADL/IADL, indeed 69% assist with between 7 and 13 ADL/IADL (compared with 27.8% of Chinese Canadians and 31.2% of Hong Kong Chinese) and are the least likely to be helping with only 0–4 (10% compared with 36.7% of Chinese Canadians and 35.27% of Hong Kong Chinese). The two Chinese groups are similar in terms of assisting with ADL/IADL and are distributed fairly evenly from not helping with these activities to providing much help. In terms of emotional support, however, it is the Chinese Canadians who are most likely to provide this type of social capital 'very much' (60%) and Hong Kong Chinese are least likely to do so (25.6%); the figure is 47% among Caucasian Canadians. Indeed, just under half of the Hong Kong Chinese sample report providing none at all or only a little (46.4%) compared with 29% of Caucasian Canadians and 22.2% of Chinese Canadians. In terms of all types of social capital, there is a variation by cultural group but over three fourths of all groups are helping with at least three of the five discrete types. Hong Kong Chinese most likely help with all five (24/8% compared with only 4% of Caucasian Canadians and 1.1% of Chinese Canadians). The majority of Chinese Canadians (58.9%), however, help with four of the areas whereas the Caucasian Canadians are most likely to help with three (44% compared with 22.2% for the Chinese Canadians and 34.4% among Hong Kong Chinese).

Although Caucasian Canadians are much more likely to be providing more assistance with ADL/IADL than the two Chinese groups, the latter are much more likely to be providing help with four or all five of the different types of discrete caregiving behaviors. That is, it is important to include various types of caregiving because a focus on only one or two results in an incomplete picture.

Table 13.2 shows the correlations between social cohesion and social capital within each cultural group. Among Caucasian Canadians, there is no significant correlation between either filial expectancy or filial piety and the provision of help with ADL, emotional support, or the total behavior variable that is, between social cohesion and social capital. However, among Chinese Canadians there is a significant relationship between both measures of social cohesion and two types of social capital (emotional support and the total number of behaviors). Indeed the only social capital measure that is not related to social cohesion is help with ADL/IADL. The strongest relationships are with total behaviors for both of the social cohesion measures. Among Hong Kong Chinese, both social cohesion measures are also related to emotional support and the number of behaviors, although the relationships are weaker. In all instances, the stronger the attitude toward helping parents, the more likely the child is helping, that is, the stronger the social cohesion the more social capital.

These findings not only point to the cultural relativity of the importance of attitudes for behaviors but also to 1) a serious questioning of the assumption that attitudes of filial piety are the basis from which caregiving behavior stems (the correlation is not as strong as expected and not at all significant for ADL/IADL – the most standard of caregiving behaviors); and 2) the behavior-specific relevance of social cohesion (it is not related to ADL/IADL among any of the three groups even at this bivariate level).

Now, turning to the within-group multivariate analyses (Table 13.3), it is evident that social cohesion is unrelated to any social capital among Caucasian Canadians. Rather, education of the caregiver is related to providing emotional support, with those having less formal education providing more support. Not being in paid employment is predictive of providing all of these types of social capital. And those who have a parent who is in worse health are more likely to provide assistance with ADL/IADL and to provide assistance in more areas.

Among Canadian Chinese, social cohesion does result in social capital for the parent even when controlling for other factors. More specifically, an attitudinal measure is significantly related to all three measures of caring behaviors (filial expectancy is related to assistance with ADL/IADL and the provision of emotional support, filial piety is related to the total measure). In addition, caregivers who are older are providing more assistance with ADL/IDL and those whose parent is in better health also receive more such assistance. However, those with parents who are in *better* health, receive more emotional support. Those with less education are helping in more areas; as are those who are in better health themselves.

Among the Hong Kong Chinese, social cohesion is sometimes related to social capital, filial expectancy is related to the provision of emotional support and to helping in more areas; filial piety is also related to helping in more areas. It is caregivers who are older who provide more assistance with ADL/IADL and who provide more emotional support. Parents who are in worse health receive more assistance with ADL/IADL but those whose parents are in better health receive more emotional support.

The multivariate analyses tell us whether the bivariate relationships remain after taking a variety of other factors into account. When controlling for socio-demographic and health characteristics, social cohesion emerges as less important for social capital than was evident in the bivariate analyses although among Chinese Canadians it becomes a strong predictor of ADL/IADL. Parental ill health is the only factor related to care among all three groups, that is, it is important cross-culturally. The inverse relationship with education and employment is interesting – suggesting time availability might be a critical factor here.

Discussion and Conclusions

This chapter has examined the relationship between filial attitudes of responsibility towards their parents in old age as a measure of connectedness, bonding or social cohesion and the care provided to the parent, as the actual resource or the parents' social capital. Interestingly, the findings suggest this particular type of social cohesion is important to a certain extent for the Chinese groups but is unimportant in terms of social capital among Caucasian Canadians. That is, in this instance, attitudes whether positive or negative towards providing care to one's parents are unrelated to what Caucasian Canadians do for their parents. In other words, whether or not social cohesion translates into social capital, is culturally dependent, at least in terms of certain types of social cohesion and certain types of social capital. Furthermore, among the two Chinese groups, social cohesion appears to be more important for translation into actual support among the Canadian Chinese group than among the Hong Kong Chinese group even when controlling for other factors such as health of the parent and health of the caregiver, socio-economic status, living arrangements and various demographic characteristics. This was not expected, given that the diasporic Chinese were viewed as less entrenched within traditional Chinese culture than those in Hong Kong. Perhaps the diasporic group is more committed to the cultural ideal as they move further away culturally, whereas those in Hong Kong are immersed in the ongoing change of their own cultures? This calls for further research. Otherwise, the relationships are in the expected direction.

Among Caucasian Canadians, it is those with less education and those who are not in paid employment who are more likely to provide more assistance. These two, of course, may be correlated, but they are not multi-collinear within this data set. Among the Canadian Chinese, those who are older, with less education, and in better health provide more care than those whose parent is in worse health in terms of ADL/IADL. Among Hong Kong Chinese, those who are older also provide more assistance.

The relationship with parental health varies by the type of social capital provided. Whenever parent's health is related either to assistance with ADL/IADL or the total care measure, the worse the parent's health the more care is provided. However, in terms of emotional support and companionship, it is opposite. It is parents with better health who receive more emotional support. This might reflect the fact that parents in better health are more able to engage emotionally and therefore the child can give more such social capital.

These findings support the argument that cultural differences are profound and important when examining the caregiving area. In the West, ageist attitudes and emphases on individualism and independence do not lead to lack of care for our parents, but rather are irrelevant. Within a culture, such as China, where there are deep historical roots and explicit teachings to care for and respect one's parents, the adoption of these attitudes at the personal level does matter, at least for some caregiving behaviors. In other words, whether social cohesion is relevant for certain types of social capital appears to be culturally specific, supporting Edmondson's admonition that context matters, here we would specify that cultural context matters.

Table 13.1 Care provision by cultural group

#ADL/IADL

	Caucasian	Chinese Canadian	Hong Kong Chinese
0–4	10%	36.7%	35.2%
5–6	21.0%	35.6%	33.6%
7–13	69.0%	27.8%	31.2%

Note: $x^2 = 45.68$; d.f. = 4; $p<.000$.

Emotional

	Caucasian	Chinese Canadian	Hong Kong Chinese
Not at all/a little	29.0%	22.2%	46.4%
Yes	24.0%	17.8%	28.0%
Very much	47.0%	60.0%	25.6%

Note: $x^2 = 27.83$; d.f. = 4; $p<.000$.

Total help

	Caucasian	Chinese Canadian	Hong Kong Chinese
1 of 5	3%	5.6%	3.2%
2 of 5	15%	12.2%	11.2%
3 of 5	44%	22.2%	34.4%
4 of 5	34%	58.9%	26.4%
5 of 5	4%	1.1%	24.8%

Note: $x^2 = 28.10$; d.f. = 8; $p<.000$.

Table 13.2 Within group correlations between attitudes and behaviors

Caucasian Canadians

	Filial expectancy	Filial piety
ADL/IADL	ns	ns
Emotional	ns	ns
Total behavior	ns	ns

Table 13.2 continued

Chinese Canadians

ADL/IADL	ns	ns
Emotional	.33**	.26*
Total behavior	.46**	.42**

Hong Kong Chinese

ADL/IADL	ns	ns
Emotional	.26**	.19*
Total behavior	.22*	.20*

Note: * p<.05; ** p<.01.

Table 13.3 Multivariate analyses

A) Caucasian Canadians

	ADL/IADL[1]	Emotional/ companionship[2]	Total behaviors[3]
CG Education		-.31**	
CG Employment	-.24*	-.23*	-.35***
Parent ill health	.52***		.29**

Note: [1] $R^2 = .28$; F = 17.04; d.f. = 2 + 89; p<.000; [2] $R^2 = .23$; F = 9.45; d.f. = 3 + 96; p<.000; [3] $R^2 = .16$; F = 8.76; d.f. = 2 + 89; p<.000.

B) Chinese Canadian

	ADL/IADL[1]	Emotional/ companionship[2]	Total behaviors[3]
CG Age	.42***		
CG Education			-.32**
CG ill health			-.21*
Filial piety			.18*
Filial expectancy	.32***	.25*	
Parent ill health	.26**	-.36**	

Note: [1] $R^2 = .43$; F = 20.72; d.f. = 3 + 84; p<.000; [2] $R^2 = .26$; F = 15.12; d.f. = 2 + 86; p<.000; [3] $R^2 = .30$; F = 12.16; d.f. = 3 + 85; p<.000.

Table 13.3 continued

C) Hong Kong Chinese

	ADL/IADL[1]	Emotional/ companionship[2]	Total behaviors[3]
CG Age	.21*	.25**	
(Filial piety)			(.20*)
Filial expectancy		.26**	.22**
Parent ill health	.38***	-.24*	

Note: [1] $R^2 = .21$; $F = 10.55$; d.f. $= 3 + 120$; $p<.000$; [2] $R^2 = .19$; $F = 9.12$; d.f. $= 3 + 120$; $p<.000$; [3] $R^2 = .05$; $F = 6.08$; d.f. $= 1 + 123$; $p<.02$; * $p<.05$; ** $p<.01$; *** $p<.001$.

Acknowledgement

Financial support for the data reported here came from the Social Sciences and Humanities Research Council of Canada to Chappell, Chou and Funk.

References

Beauvais, C. and Jenson, J. 2002. Social Cohesion: Updating the State of the Research. Canadian Policy Research Networks Discussion Paper, No. F/22.

Blakemore, K. 2000. Care and social support – The example of ageing migrants, in *Who Should Care for the Elderly? An East-West Value Divide*, edited by W.T. Liu and H. Kendig. Singapore: Singapore University Press.

Botsford, J., Clarke, C.L. and Gibb, C.E. 2011. Research and dementia, caring and ethnicity: A review of the literature. *Journal of Research in Nursing* 16(5), 437–49.

Bourdieu, P. 1991. The forms of capital, in *Handbook of Theory and Research for the Sociology of Education*, edited by J.G. Richardson. New York: Greenwood, 241–58.

Carpiano, R.M. 2006. Toward a neighbourhood resource-based theory of social capital for health: Can Bourdieu and sociology help? *Social Science and Medicine* 62, 165–75.

Chan, J., To, H.-P. and Chan, E. 2006. Reconsidering Social Cohesion: Developing a Definition and Analytical Framework for Empirical Research. *Social Indicators Research* 75, 273–302.

Chappell, N.L. 1992. *Social Support and Aging*. Toronto: Butterworths.

Chappell, N.L. 2003. Correcting cross-cultural stereotypes: Aging in Shanghai and Canada. *Journal of Cross-Cultural Gerontology* 17(2), 127–47.

Chappell, N.L. and Funk, L.M. 2010. Social capital: Does it add to the health inequalities debate? *Social Indicators Research* 99(3), 357–73.

Chappell, N.L. and Funk, L.M. 2011. Filial caregivers: Diasporic Chinese compared with homeland and hostland caregivers. *Journal of Cross-Cultural Gerontology* 26(4), 315–29.

Chappell, N.L. and Kusch, K. 2007. The gendered nature of filial piety – A Study among Chinese Canadians. *Journal of Cross-Cultural Gerontology* 22, 29–45.

Chen, Y. 1998. An analysis of living arrangements and environment of rural elderly: A case study of a Guangdong rural community. *Northwest Population Journal* 72, 36–8.

Coleman, J.S. 1990. *Foundations of Social Theory.* Cambridge, MA: Harvard University Press.

Dai, Y.T. and Dimond, M.F. 1998. Filial piety: A cross-cultural comparison and its implications for the well-being of older parents. *Journal of Gerontological Nursing* 24(3), 13–18.

Dayton-Johnson, J. 2000. What Does Social Cohesion Contribute to the Rural Economy? A Take of Four Countries. Paper prepared for the Canadian Employment Research Forum (CERF) Conference on Rural/Urban Differences in Economic Development, 8–9 September. Laurentian University, Sudbury, Ontario.

Dellmann-Jenkins, M. and Brittain, L. 2003. Young adults' attitudes toward filial responsibility and actual assistance to elderly family members. *Journal of Applied Gerontology* 22(2), 214–29.

Donorfio, L.M. 1996. Filial responsibility: Widowed mothers and their caregiving daughters, a qualitative grounded theory approach. *Dissertation Abstracts International Section A: Humanities and Social Sciences.* US, University Microfilms International, 56 (UMI No. 9629785).

Edmondson, R. 2003. Social capital: A strategy for enhancing health? *Social Science and Medicine* 57, 2729–42.

Finch, J. and Mason, J. 1991. Obligations of kinship in contemporary Britain: Is there normative agreement? *British Journal of Sociology* 42(3), 345–67.

Forrest, R. and Kearns, A. 2001. Social Cohesion, Social Capital and the Neighbourhood. *Urban Studies* 38(12), 2125–43.

Frederick, J. and Fast, J. 1999. Eldercare in Canada: Who does how much? *Canadian Social Trends* (54), 26–30 (Ottawa: Statistics Canada, cat. No. 11-008).

Friedkin, N.E. 2004. Social Cohesion. *Annual Review of Sociology* 30, 409–25.

Fry, C.L. 1996. Age, Aging and Culture, in *Handbook of Aging and the Social Sciences*, edited by R.H. Binstock and L.K. George, 4th ed. San Diego: Academic Press, Inc., 117–36.

Globerman, J. 1995. The Unencumbered Child: Family reputations and responsibilities in the care of relatives with Alzheimer's disease. *Family Process* 34(1), 87–99.

Hamon, R.R. and Blieszner, R. 1990. Filial responsibility expectations among adult child-older parent pairs. *Journal of Gerontology* 45(3), 110–12.

Hashimoto, A. 2004. Culture, Power, and the Discourse of Filial Piety in Japan: The Disempowerment of Youth and Its Social Consequences, in *Filial Piety, practice and discourse in contemporary East Asia*, edited by C. Ikels. Stanford: Stanford University Press, 182–97.

Hendricks, J. and Yoon, H. 2006. Foreword: Mapping Intersections in the Atlas of Asian Aging, in *Handbook of Asian Aging*, edited by J. Hendricks and H. Yoon. New York: Baywood Publishing.

Hollander, M.J., Liu, G. and Chappell, N.L. 2009. Who Cares and How Much? The Imputed Economic Contribution to the Canadian Health Care System of Middle Aged and Older Unpaid Caregivers Providing Care to the Elderly. *Health Care Quarterly* 12(2), 42–9.

Hong, Y. and Liu, W.T. 2000. The social psychological perspective of elderly care, in *Who Should Care for the Elderly: An East-West Value Divide*, edited by W.T. Liu and H. Kendig. Singapore: Singapore University Press, 165–82.

Ikels, C. 2004. *Filial piety: Practice and discourse in contemporary East Asia*. Palo Alto: Stanford University Press.

Kauh, T.O. 1999. Changing status and roles of older Korean immigrants in the United States. *International Journal of Aging and Human Development* 49(3), 213–29.

Kawachi, I.B., Kennedy, B. and Lochner, K. 1997. Long live community: Social capital as public health. *American Prospect* (November-December), 56–9.

Kim, J.-S. and Lee, E.-H. 2003. Cultural and non-cultural predictors of health outcomes in Korean daughter and daughter-in-law caregivers. *Public Health Nursing* 20, 111–19.

Kwok, H.-K. 2006. The son also acts as a major caregiver to elderly parents: A study of the sandwich generation in Hong Kong. *Current Sociology* 54(2), 257–72.

Lai, W.L. 2010. Filial piety, caregiving appraisal, and caregiving burden. *Research on Aging* 32(2), 200–23.

Lee, R.P.L., Lee, J.-J., Yu, E.S.H. et al. 2000. Living Arrangements and Elderly Care: The Case of Hong Kong, in *Who Should Care for the Elderly? An East-West Value Divide*, edited by W.T. Liu and H. Kendig. Singapore: Singapore University Press.

Lee, Y.R. and Sung, K.T. 1997. Cultural differences in caregiving motivations for demented parents: Korean caregivers versus American caregivers. *International Journal of Aging and Human Development* 44(2), 115–27.

Liu, W.T. and Kendig, H. 2000. *Who should care for the elderly? An East-West value divide*. Singapore: Singapore University Press.

Liu, J.H., Ng, S.H., Weatherall, A. and Loong, C. 2000. Filial piety, acculturation and intergenerational communication among New Zealand Chinese. *Basic and Applied Social Psychology* 22(3), 213–23.

Lo, M. and Russell, C. 2007. Family care: An exploratory study of experience and expectations among older Chinese immigrants in Australia. *Contemporary Nurse* 25(1–2), 31–8.

Lynch, J., Due, P., Muntaner, C. and Davey Smith, G. 2000. Social Capital: Is it a Good Investment Strategy for Public Health? *Journal of Epidemiology and Community Health* 54, 404–408.

Macinko, J. and Starfield, B. 2001. The Utility of Social Capital in Research on Health Determinants. *Millbank Quarterly* 79(3), 387–427.

Martin-Matthews, A. and Campbell, L. 1995. Gender Roles, Employment and Informal Care, in *Connecting Gender and Aging: a Sociological Analysis*, edited by S. Arber and J. Ginn. Buckingham: Open University Press, 129–43.

Miller, E.T. 2004. Filial daughters, filial sons: Comparisons from rural North China, in *Filial piety: Practice and discourse in contemporary East Asia*, edited by C. Ikels. Stanford: Stanford University Press, 34–52.

Montgomery, R.J.V., Borgatta, E.F. and Borgatta, M.L. 2000. Societal and family change in the burden of care, in *Who Should Care for the Elderly: An East-West Value Divide*, edited by W.T. Liu and H. Kendig. Singapore: Singapore University Press, 27–54.

Ng, A.C.Y, Phillips, D.R. and Lee, W.K. 2002. Persistence and challenges to filial piety and informal support of older persons in a modern Chinese society: A case study. *Journal of Aging Studies* 16, 135–53.

Pyke, K. 2000. 'Normal American family' as an interpretive structure of family life among grown children of Korean and Vietnamese immigrants. *Journal of Marriage and the Family* 62(1), 240–55.

Pinquart, M. and Sorenson, S. 2005. Ethnic differences in stressors, resources, and psychological outcomes of family caregiving: A meta-analysis. *The Gerontologist* 45(1), 90–106.

Portes, A. 1995. The Economic Sociology of Immigration: A Conceptual Overview, in *The Economic Sociology of Immigration: Essays on Networks, Ethnicity, and Entrepreneurship*. New York: Russell Sage.

Van Ziegart, S. 2002. Global spaces of Chinese culture: A transnational comparison of diasporic Chinese communities in the United States and Germany. PhD Dissertation. Houston: Rice University.

Wang, D. 2004. Ritualistic coresidence and the weakening of filial practice in rural China, in *Filial piety: Practice and discourse in contemporary East Asia*, edited by C. Ikels. Stanford: Stanford University Press, 106–27.

Whyte, M.K. 2004. Filial obligations in Chinese families: Paradoxes of modernization, in *Filial piety: Practice and discourse in contemporary East Asia*, edited by C. Ikels. Stanford: Stanford University Press, 106–27.

World Bank. n.d. What is Social Capital? http://www.worldbank.org/poverty/scapital/whatsc.htm [accessed June 2010].

Yu, E., Shilong, L., Zehuai, W. and Lie, W.T. 2000. Caregiving survey in Guangzhou: A preliminary report, in *Who Should Care for the Elderly: An East-West Value Divide*, edited by W.T. Liu and H. Kendig. Singapore: Singapore University Press, 322–38.

Zhang, H. 2004. 'Living alone' and the rural elderly: Strategy and agency in post-Mao rural China, in *Filial Piety: Practice and discourse in contemporary East Asia*, edited by C. Ikels. Stanford: Stanford University Press, 63–87.

Chapter 14
Generational Differences in Caregiving and its Consequences

Janet Fast

Caregiving is fast becoming a normative experience. Over the past five years, the proportion of Canadians over age 45 who are caregivers has grown by nearly 10%, but their numbers have increased by 65% (Fast, Dosman and Lero 2012). In 2007, 28.9% or 3.8 million Canadians aged 45 or older provided assistance to someone with a long term health condition or physical limitation, an increase of 9.4%, or nearly 1.7 million individuals, since 2002. However, it is an even more normative experience when caregiving across the life course is examined: 62.2% of women and 48.8% of men report having provided such care at some time since the age of 15 (Fast, et al 2012).

While some caregivers are assisting a spouse, sibling or age-peer, much of the care is provided by one generation to another. With population ageing comes an increasing demand for care and a shrinking pool of potential family care providers, hence a higher likelihood that any one child will care for parents, grandparents, aunts, uncles or older friends and neighbors (Carriére et al. 2008, Keefe 2011). At the same time, higher rates of disability at all ages mean that more parents are caring for children with lifelong or long term disability (Statistics Canada 2008).

Caring for family members and friends also has been shown to have both positive and negative consequences for those providing the care. Negative consequences include economic costs, such as those arising from care-related employment accommodations, out-of-pocket expenses and direct labor costs, and non-economic costs such as those related to physical, mental and social health and well-being (Lero et al. 2007). About three-quarters of caregivers age 45 to 64 are employed and most are employed full time (Fast et al. 2012). It's no surprise, then, that employment consequences, including missing full or part days of work, working fewer hours for pay, changing work schedules, and even quitting or retiring early from a job, are common among caregivers (Fast et al. 2012). Duncan et al. (2011) similarly demonstrate that many caregivers (41% of men and 59% of women) age 45 and over make care-related out-of-pocket expenditures, most commonly on items such as household goods, food and meals, travel and transportation and medical care. In 2007 high proportions of caregivers age 45 and over reported experiencing social consequences such as reduced time for social activities (40% of women, 30% men) and disrupted holiday plans (23% of women, 18% of men) (Fletcher and Fast 2011). Many also reported that it affected their relationships with close family members by restricting the amount of time they were able to spend with spouses (31% of women, 22% of men) or children (23% of women, 18% of men). Health consequences also are reported by a substantial minority of caregivers (almost 20% of women and 8% of men age 45 and over in 2007) (Fletcher and Fast 2011).

Family and friend care and its consequences are tremendously diverse. One important source of variation relates to the nature of the relationships involved and the stage in the life course when caregiving episodes occur, though the evidence as to which caregivers experience more severe consequences is mixed (Lero et al. 2007). For example, older caregivers are likely to have more health limitations and less physical strength than younger caregivers and are likely at higher risk of retiring early from their jobs and jeopardizing their pension income (Evandrou and Glazer 2004). In contrast, some studies suggest that older caregivers and spouse caregivers may experience less psychological distress than younger caregivers (Edwards et al. 2002). Yet other research indicates that younger caregivers may experience longer-term impacts on employment and more distress at being confined by caregiving responsibilities, especially if caring alone. Seltzer and Wailing (2000) hypothesized that the higher salience of the wife versus daughter role accounted for their finding that wives were more likely to experience negative care-related outcomes than daughters, while Chumbler et al. (2003) found that adult daughter caregivers had similar caregiver burden scores to wives, sons and husbands. The high cost of raising children with disabilities has been shown to leave many families living in poverty with less time and financial resources for vacations, leisure activities and even basic necessities (Parish and Cloud 2006).

As the body of research on caregiving matures, more attention is being paid to studying the experiences of specific groups of caregivers. Among these, children caring for older parents and parents caring for children with disabilities feature prominently. Yet there has been little research of a comparative nature focusing on *differences* in experiences of specific groups. Indeed, research, policy and practice regarding care to different generations (non-senior adults, older adults and children with disabilities) seem to have evolved quite separately (Arksey et al. 2007). This chapter draws on findings from a recent nationally representative survey of Canadian caregivers that highlight diversity in caregiving and its consequences across generations.

Methods

Data were drawn from Statistics Canada's 2007 General Social Survey (GSS) on Family, Social Support and Retirement. Data were collected over a twelve month period from the non-institutionalized population age 45 and over living in private households in the 10 Canadian provinces. The survey employed random digit dialing to select a sample (with the exception of the Cycle 20 respondents who were re-interviewed for Cycle 21) and Computer Assisted Telephone Interviewing

(CATI) to collect the data. Thus persons living in the northern Territories, those without telephones and those living in institutional settings were omitted from the sample. Several modules of the survey focused on caregiving, which was defined as providing assistance with at least one of a specified set of care tasks, to at least one family member or friend with a long term health or physical limitation. Care tasks included transportation, meal preparation, house cleaning, outdoor work/ house maintenance, personal care, medical treatment, scheduling or coordinating services and appointments.

From the original sample of 23,404, sub-samples were drawn comprising 4,701 respondents who were caring for a senior (age 65+) and 1,797 who were caring for a non-senior (age <65), corresponding to some 3,646,686 caregivers age 45 and over in the population in 2007. These samples were further split by age to obtain four groups: those caring for older age peers; those caring for younger age peers; those caring for someone from an older generation; and those caring for someone from a younger generation.

Descriptive analyses provide a profile of the sample and sub-samples while multivariate analyses, including OLS regression and logistic regression, identified characteristics that predict hours of care work performed by respondents, participation in selected care tasks, and the likelihood of experiencing selected consequences of care. Multivariate analyses were split by age (<65 and 65+) so as to determine whether predictors of involvement in care and its consequences are different for younger and older caregivers.

Findings

Generational Care

As Figure 14.1 illustrates, most of the caregivers in the sample were under the age of 65, whether caring for a senior (75.4%) or a non-senior (84.6%), but a substantial minority were themselves seniors (24.6% of eldercare providers and 15.4% of those caring for a non-senior).

Figure 14.2 further illustrates that most care is provided to a family member or friend of a different generation from the caregiver. Of respondents caring for a senior, 61.9% were caring for a parent though and 1% were caring for a child age 65 or over. Similarly, among respondents caring for a non-senior, 20.3% were caring for a child with a long term health or physical limitation and 39.3% for older distant kin and friends. Care to age-peers was not uncommon, however. Almost 7% of eldercare providers and 20.8% of respondents caring for a non-senior reported caring for a spouse. It should be noted, though, that it is likely that these data under-estimate spousal care among seniors. It is likely that caring for an older spouse is considered normative behavior – part of everyday life and an expected component of the marital relationship in later life – so doing the specified tasks for one's spouse may not be reported as being the result of the spouse's

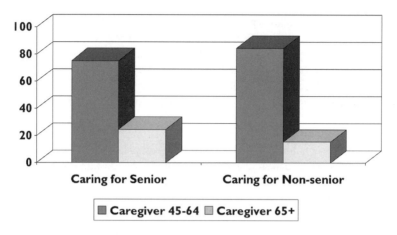

Figure 14.1 Distribution of care providers by age of caregiver and care receiver
Note: Most caregivers are <65, but higher % of eldercare providers are seniors themselves.

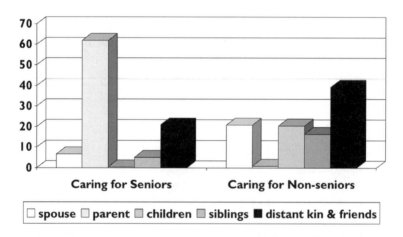

Figure 14.2 Distribution of caregivers by generation and relationship
Note: Most eldercare is intergenerational; most non-senior care is same generation.

long term illness or disability. Since it is less likely to be considered normative to do such tasks for a younger spouse, it is more likely to be attributed to health problems and disability and so to be captured as care in the survey. A substantial minority of respondents caring for non-seniors also reported caring for a sibling (16.4%), compared to only 5.1% of eldercare providers.

Type and Amount of Care Provided

There were few differences between those caring for seniors and non-seniors with respect to the types of care provided, though there was a two hour per week difference in time spent on care tasks: 9 hours per week for eldercare providers compared with 11 hours per week for those caring for non-seniors. However, as Figure 14.3 shows, the differences between those caring for seniors and non-seniors with respect to the types care-related consequences they experienced were small and statistically insignificant for all of the selected consequences except extra expenses and health consequences. Higher proportions of respondents caring for non-seniors than seniors reported experiencing health consequences and making extra care-related expenditures.

Predictors of Care Time and Tasks

While age was not a significant predictor of how much time caregivers spent on care tasks, regardless of whether they were providing eldercare or caring for a non-senior, relationship was an important factor (see Table 14.1). Generally speaking, respondents caring for a family member spent more time on care tasks than those caring for friends and neighbors. However, the magnitude of the relationship tells a more important story about generational differences in caregiving. Respondents caring for a spouse spent a great deal more time on care tasks than those caring for friends and neighbors, but the effect was much bigger for eldercare providers than for those caring for non-seniors. Eldercare providers spent in excess of 30 additional hours each week on care tasks for their spouse than did their counterparts caring for non-kin, whereas those caring for a non-senior spouse spent 'only' 12 additional hours per week performing care tasks compared to those caring for friends or neighbors. In contrast, caregivers to non-seniors spent more than 13 additional hours on care tasks if caring for a child with a long term illness or disability relative to those caring for non-kin, while caring for a child had no significant effect on care time for eldercare providers.

Predictors of Participation in Care Tasks

Table 14.2 shows findings from logistic regression models in which the predictors of the probability of participating in selected care tasks were examined. For eldercare providers increasing age was associated with a decline in the likelihood of providing help with housekeeping tasks, with the impact increasing with age: respondents age 55–64 were only 84% as likely, respondents age 65–74 55% as likely, and respondents age 75 and over only 33% as likely as eldercare providers age 45–54 to provide help with housekeeping. In contrast, eldercare providers age 55–64 were 32% more likely to participate in care management than their counterparts age 45 to 54 while caregivers to non-seniors age 65 and over were between 45% and 80% less likely to participate in care management tasks compared

Table 14.1 Predictors of time spent on care tasks (hours/week of care: OLS regression coefficients)

	Caring for senior	Caring for non-senior
Age (45–54 reference category)		
Age 55–64	0.745	0.487
Age 65–74	0.223	-2.36
Age 75+	-1.75	-1.95
Sex (female reference category)		
Male	-2.29***	-2.81**
Marital status (single, never married reference category)		
Married	-6.48***	-4.53*
Widowed, divorced, separated	-2.53*	-1.93
Education (less than high school completion reference category		
University	-4.02***	-6.04***
Diploma	-0.91	-5.82***
Secondary school completion	-0.84	-3.57*
Employment status (not employed reference category)		
Employed full time	-3.49***	-7.19**
Employed part time	-1.98*	-3.85*
Relationship to care recipient (friend reference category)		
Spouse	31.21***	12.36***
Parent	6.73***	10.72*
Sibling	1.47	1.48
Child	6.55	13.35***
Distant kin	4.50***	8.10**
Type of disability (mental/cognitive disability only reference category)		
Physical disability only	-0.72	1.13
Both mental/cognitive and physical disability	2.20	3.45*
Constant	13.03***	18.00***

Note: * = significant at .05; ** = significant at .01; *** = significant at .001.

to their younger counterparts. Caregivers age 75 and over also were less likely to provide personal care than their younger counterparts, regardless of the age of the person for whom they cared. Eldercare providers age 75+ were 69% as likely and caregivers to non-seniors 45% as likely as younger care providers to be performing personal care tasks. This likely reflects a higher likelihood that caregivers in this oldest group face their own health and functional status challenges.

Relationship was an important predictor of the probability of participating in care tasks as well as care time. Once again respondents caring for relatives were generally more likely to participate in all of the selected care tasks than those caring for friends and neighbors, but the magnitude of the relationship varies widely and systematically. Eldercare providers were almost 13 times more likely to participate in housekeeping or personal care tasks and more than 10 times more likely to participate in care management if caring for a spouse as compared to caring for a friend or neighbor. Respondents caring for a non-senior were similarly more likely to participate in these tasks if caring for a spouse than for non-kin, but the magnitude of the relationship is much smaller: 6.5, 4.8 and 5.7 times more likely to do housekeeping, personal care and care management tasks respectively. That said, the magnitude of the relationship was greatest for spousal care for these caregivers as well. Caregivers to non-senior spouses were 6.5, 4.8 and 5.7 times more likely to be participating in housekeeping, personal care and care management tasks respectively than if they were caring for other family members and friends. Caring for a parent had the second biggest impact on the likelihood that eldercare providers will participate in personal care or care management tasks (more than three and six times more likely respectively compared to caring for non-kin) while caring for a child had the second biggest impact on the likelihood that eldercare providers would assist with housekeeping tasks (4.6 times more likely than if caring for non-kin). Similarly, for caregivers to non-seniors caring for an ill or disabled child had the second biggest impact on the likelihood that they would participate in housekeeping and personal care tasks (in both cases about three times more likely than those caring for a friend or neighbor) while caring for a parent had the second biggest impact on the likelihood that they would be doing care management (3.23 times more likely than if caring for non-kin). The fact that the magnitude of the effect of caring for an ill or disabled child is smaller than that of caring for a parent for respondents caring for non-seniors may be a function of the behavior being more normative when caring for one's child than one's parent, the reverse of the case with spousal care noted above.

Eldercare providers also were more likely to help a parent or sibling with housekeeping (2.67 and 1.55 times more likely respectively than if caring for non-kin), to help a sibling or distant family member with personal care (1.7 and 1.64 times more likely respectively) and care management (2.72 times and 2.31 times more likely) relative to caring for friends and neighbors. Respondents caring for non-seniors also were more likely to perform housekeeping tasks (2.1 times more likely) and personal care (3.22 times more likely) for distant relatives, personal care (1.5 times more likely) and care management (2.13 times more likely) for siblings, and care management for children (3.17 times more likely) than for friends and neighbors.

Predictors of Health and Social Consequences

While age was unrelated to the likelihood that a caregiver will find that their social participation has been affected by their care responsibilities, it was a significant predictor of their own health status (see Table 14.3). The likelihood that a caregiver's health was compromised by their care responsibilities declined with advancing age. Eldercare providers were 71% as likely to report that care has affected their health at age 55–64 as at age 45–54, 65% as likely at age 65–74 and

Table 14.2 Predictors of likelihood of participation in care tasks (logistic regression odds ratios)

	Housekeeping		Personal care		Care management	
	Caring for senior	Caring for non-senior	Caring for senior	Caring for non-senior	Caring for senior	Caring for non-senior
Age (45–54 reference category)						
Age 55–64	0.84*	1.00	0.99	.083	1.32***	1.08
Age 65–74	0.55***	0.84	0.78	0.78	1.18	0.55**
Age 75+	0.33***	0.63	0.69*	0.45*	1.14	0.20***
Sex (female reference category)						
Male	0.41***	0.32***	0.45***	0.53***	0.72***	0.72**
Marital status (single, never married reference category)						
Married	0.64***	0.90	0.93	0.83	0.92	0.73
Widowed, divorced, separated	0.79	0.89	1.18	0.89	0.99	0.77
Education (less than high school completion reference category)						
University	0.98	1.11	1.43***	1.02	1.84***	1.52*
Diploma	0.98	1.38	1.26*	1.09	1.44***	0.99
Secondary school completion	0.97	1.05	1.14	1.07	1.34**	1.06
Employment status (not employed reference category)						
Employed full time	0.72***	0.79	0.93	1.01	0.92	0.58***
Employed part time	1.01	1.10	0.95	1.28	0.92	0.82
Relationship to care recipient (friend reference category)						
Spouse	12.95***	6.54***	12.80***	4.79***	10.21***	5.72***
Parent	2.67***	2.25	3.24***	0.97	6.41***	3.23**
Sibling	1.55**	1.14	1.70**	1.50*	2.31***	2.13***
Child	4.65***	2.88***	1.90	3.17***	1.84	3.17***
Distant kin	1.27	2.10*	1.64**	3.22***	2.72***	0.94
Type of disability (mental/cognitive disability only reference category)						
Physical disability only	1.47*	1.61**	0.79	0.97	0.61***	0.51***
Both mental/cognitive and physical disability	1.52**	1.66**	1.23	1.55*	1.46*	1.24
Constant	1.01	0.86	0.35***	0.43**	0.23***	0.82

Note: * = significant at .05; ** = significant at .01; *** = significant at .001.

40% as likely once they were over the age of 75. For caregivers to non-seniors the decline in the likelihood that caregiving will impact the caregiver's health was more pronounced: at age 55–64 they were 71% as likely as those age 45–64 to report care-related health consequences, just as eldercare providers were, but at age 65–74 they were only 45% as likely and at 75 years or over they were only 18% as likely.

Relationship was once again an important predictor of the probability that respondents experienced care-related health and social consequences. Eldercare providers had the highest probability of reporting both health and social consequences if caring for a spouse. They were almost 5.6 times more likely to report health consequences and almost 7.5 times more likely to report social consequences as those caring for friends and neighbors. Like eldercare providers, respondents caring for non-seniors spouses were most likely to report social consequences (4.3 times more likely to do so than those caring for non-kin), but for these caregivers it was caring for ill or disabled children that had the most profound impact on care-related health consequences, increasing the likelihood that they would report such consequences almost three-fold relative to those caring for friends and neighbors. For eldercare providers it was caring for ailing parents that had the second greatest impact on the odds of experiencing both health and social consequences, increasing the odds 2.73 and 4.65 times respectively. Eldercare providers also were more likely to report that providing care had compromised their health if caring for a sibling or distant relative (2.24 times and 2.13 times more likely respectively) than if caring for a friend or neighbor, and were more likely to report social consequences if caring for a child (3.41 times more likely) a distant relative (2.96 times more likely) or a sibling (1.97 times more likely) than if caring for non-kin.

For caregivers to non-seniors it was caring for a spouse that resulted in the second the greatest increase in the likelihood that they would experience care-related health consequences (2.53 times more likely) and caring for a child that had the second biggest impact on the likelihood that they would experience social consequences (2.34 times more likely), relative to caring for friends and neighbors.

Predictors of Economic Consequences

Among the economic consequences examined, age was related only to the likelihood that caregivers to non-seniors would report incurring additional expenses because of their care responsibilities: those who were themselves seniors were about half as likely as those under age 65 to report making extra care-related expenditures. These oldest caregivers on limited fixed incomes are less likely to have the financial wherewithal to incur such added expenses. Once again, however, relationship is a significant predictor of economic consequences. Generally speaking, those caring for relatives were more likely to report economic consequences than those caring for friends and neighbors. Eldercare providers were most likely to report incurring extra expenses if caring for a spouse (3 times

Table 14.3 Predictors of care-related health and social consequences (logistic regression odds ratios)

	Health consequences		Social consequences	
	Caring for senior	Caring for non-senior	Caring for senior	Caring for non-senior
Age (45–54 reference category)				
Age 55–64	0.71**	0.71*	0.95	1.03
Age 65–74	0.65*	0.45*	1.07	0.63
Age 75+	0.40**	0.18***	0.68	0.55
Sex (female reference category)				
Male	0.58***	0.40***	0.82**	0.80
Marital status (single, never married reference category)				
Married	0.57**	0.60	0.78	0.56*
Widowed, divorced, separated	0.81	0.77	1.04	0.53*
Education (less than high school completion reference category)				
University	0.96	1.26	2.13***	2.23***
Diploma	1.11	1.30	1.94***	1.83**
Secondary school completion	0.90	0.88	1.65***	1.35
Employment status (not employed reference category)				
Employed full time	0.59***	0.76	1.10	1.41*
Employed part time	0.76	0.84	0.92	0.99
Relationship to care recipient (friend reference category)				
Spouse	5.59***	2.53***	7.48***	4.30***
Parent	2.73***	1.06	4.65***	1.64
Sibling	2.24**	1.17	1.97**	1.34
Child	0.00	2.94***	3.41***	2.34***
Distant kin	2.13**	1.12	2.96***	0.90
Type of disability (mental/cognitive disability only reference category)				
Physical disability only	0.56**	0.48***	1.04	0.77
Both mental/cognitive and physical disability	1.30	1.13	1.81***	1.52*
Personal care	1.79***	1.60**	2.07***	1.92***
Hours/week of care	1.02***	1.01***	1.03***	1.03***
Constant	0.175***	0.38*	0.70***	0.28***

Note: * = significant at .05; ** = significant at .01; *** = significant at .001.

more likely to do so than those caring for friends and neighbors), but most likely to report employment consequences if caring for an older child (4.5 times more likely to report missing days of paid work and 8.6 times more likely to reduce paid work hours than those caring for non-kin). Eldercare providers also were more likely to incur extra expenses if caring for a parent (2.75 times more likely), a sibling (2.16 times more likely) or more distant relative (2.13 times more likely) than if caring for friends and neighbors; were more likely to report missing days of work if caring for a parent, spouse or more distant kin (3.9 times more likely if caring for a parent, three times more likely if caring for a spouse and twice as likely if caring for more distant relatives than those caring for non-kin respectively); and were more likely to reduce their hours of paid work if caring for a spouse (6.34 times more likely), a parent (3.87 times more likely) or more distant kin (3.2 times more likely) than if caring for non-kin.

Like eldercare providers, caregivers to non-seniors also were most likely to report incurring extra expenses if caring for a spouse (almost three times more likely than those caring for non-kin), but they also were most likely to report missing days of work (almost nine times more likely than those caring for friends and neighbors). Caregivers to non-seniors also were much more likely to report extra care-related expenditures if caring for a child (2.57 times more likely) or sibling (1.78 times more likely) than if caring for friends and neighbors, and more likely to report missing days of work if caring for distant kin (6.41 times more likely), children (6.23 times more likely), a parent (5.6 times more likely) or a sibling (3.6 times more likely) relative to caring for non-kin. They were similarly more likely to report reducing their hours of work if caring for a spouse or child (2.5 times more likely and 2.39 times more likely than if caring for friends and relatives respectively).

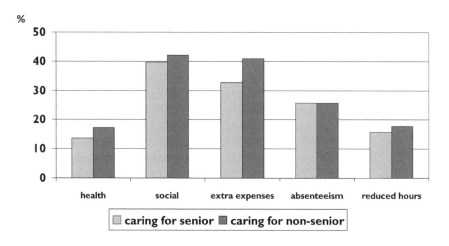

Figure 14.3 Consequences of caregiving

Discussion and Implications

As observed above, most eldercare is inter-generational while most care provided to non-seniors was provided to someone who is the same generation as the caregiver. Caring for a parent was especially prevalent among eldercare providers but rare among those caring for non-seniors, while caring for older distant relatives or friends, a disabled child or a spouse was most common among caregivers to non-seniors.

Spouse caregivers spent more time on care tasks than those caring for non-kin, especially among eldercare providers, and also were more likely to participate in all of the care tasks examined (housekeeping, personal care and care management). Caregivers for non-seniors spent the most time caring for children with disabilities. These caregivers also were more likely to incur extra expenses and, if caring for a non-senior, to experience high impact employment consequences. Age did not predict time spent on care, but it did predict some consequences, especially health consequences.

Caring for a parent has figured prominently in the extant literature on caregiving. Interestingly, while parent care was more 'costly', both in terms of time spent on care tasks and in terms of negative health, social and economic consequences, than caring for non-kin, it was not the most impactful caregiving relationship.

Caring for a spouse was much less costly in terms of care time to younger than to older spouse caregivers, and somewhat less costly to younger spouse caregivers than to parents of non-senior ill or disabled children. It also was somewhat less costly in terms of health consequences and hours of paid work, but it was more costly with respect to social consequences and absenteeism for younger spouse caregivers compared to older spousal caregivers. Caring for a non-senior spouse also was more costly than caring for a non-senior child with a long term health condition or disability, with the exception of health consequences.

In sum then, same-generation caregiving appears to have a bigger impact on caregivers than cross-generation caregiving whether caring for a senior or not, but caring for an ill or disabled child also has important implications for those caring for non-seniors. Yet programs, policies and services vary considerably according to the age and relationship between caregiver and care receiver, which may account in part for the differential outcomes across the types of caregivers studied here. Further research that is even more nuanced than the current study with respect to age and relationship is needed to fully understand the unique experiences and needs of caregivers.

References

Arksey, H., Beresford, B., Glendinning, C. et al. 2007. *Outcomes for parents with disabled children and carers of disabled or older adults: Similarities, differences and the implications for assessment practice.* York: Social Policy Research Unit, University of York.

Carriére, Y., Keefe, J., Légaré, J. et al. 2008. *Projecting the future availability of the informal support network of the elderly population and assessing its impact on home care services.* Ottawa: Statistics Canada.

Chumbler, N.R., Grimm, J.W., Cody, M. and Beck, C. 2003. Gender, kinship and caregiver burden: the case of community-dwelling memory impaired seniors. *International Journal of Geriatric Psychiatry*, 18, 722–32.

Duncan, K., Shooshtari, S., Roger, K. and Fast, J. 2011. Care-related out-of-pocket expenses. Paper to the Canadian Research Data Centre Network Conference: Edmonton, AB.

Edwards, A.B., Zarit, S.H., Stephens, M.A.P. and Townsend, A. 2002. Employed family caregivers of cognitively impaired elderly: An examination of role strain and depressive symptoms. *Aging & Mental Health*, 61, 55–61.

Evandrou, M. and Glaser, K. 2004. Family, work and quality of life: Changing economic and social roles through the lifecourse. *Ageing & Society*, 24, 771–91.

Fast, J., Dosman, D. and Lero, D. 2012. The intersection of caregiving and employment. Final report to Human Resources and Skills Development Canada, Gatineau, PQ.

Fletcher, S. and Fast, J. 2011. *FACTS: The social and health consequences of family/friend caregiving.* Edmonton, Canada: Research on Aging, Policies and Practice.

Keating. N., Lero, D., Fast, J. and Lucas, S. 2011. A framework and literature review on the economic costs of care. Final report to Human Resources and Skills Development Canada: Gatineau, Canada.

Keefe, J. 2011. *Supporting caregivers and caregiving in an aging Canada.* Ottawa, Canada: Institute for Research on Public Policy.

Lero, D., Keating, N., Fast, J. et al. 2007. The Interplay of Risk Factors Associated with Negative Outcomes among Family Caregivers: A Synthesis of the Literature. Final Report to Human Resources and Skills Development Canada: Ottawa, Canada.

Parish, S.L. and Cloud, J.M. 2006. Financial well-being of young children with disabilities and their families. *Social Work*, 51(3), 223–32.

Seltzer, M.M. and Wailing, L.L. 2000. The dynamics of caregiving: Transitions during a three-year prospective study. *The Gerontologist*, 40(2), 165–78.

Statistics Canada 2008. Participation and Activity Limitation Survey 2006: A profile of education for children with disabilities in Canada, Statistics Canada, Ottawa, 2008. Available at: http://www.statcan.gc.ca/pub/89-628-x/89-628-x2007001-eng.htm.

Chapter 15
Family Relations and the Experience of Loneliness among Older Adults in Eastern Europe

Kim Korinek

It is widely observed that age associated transitions (linked to widowhood, worsening health, and retirement) alter the quality and quantity of social relationships and thus tend to heighten loneliness in older adulthood (Lopata 1995, Fees et al. 1999, Pinquart 2003, Dykstra et al. 2005). Importantly, feelings of loneliness are indicative of more than negative affect. Loneliness correlates with heightened risks of mental illness and suicide in older adults (Peplau and Perlman 1982), and weak social relationships more generally are among the most central predictors of mortality and morbidity in older adulthood (Dykstra 1995, 2009). In Eastern Europe, and Russia in particular, scholars have noted that circles of friendship and other informal associations have served to help make ends meet in times of economic insecurity and insulate citizens' everyday lives from negative effects of the state (Rose 1995). Macro level social and demographic conditions prevailing in many of the former Eastern bloc countries, specifically their very low fertility levels, rates of steady emigration among working-age adults, and eroded socialist era employment and welfare guarantees, may be behind the particularly high levels of older adult loneliness witnessed in the region (de Jong Gierveld 2008, de Jong Gierveld et al. 2011).

In this chapter I analyze the individual and family structural determinants of loneliness among older adults in Russia and Bulgaria, two post-socialist societies recently experiencing myriad, far-reaching economic, demographic and social transitions. Not only do the 'demographic catastrophes' underway in Russia and Bulgaria, brought about especially by declining male life expectancy in Russia and significant out-migration from Bulgaria, threaten population loss (Demko et al. 1999, Vassilev 2005). They also threaten to strain traditional bonds and obligations of support to aged family members. Threats to older adult wellbeing are also intertwined with economic changes wrought in the transition to market economy, namely vast reductions of social welfare provisions and precipitous declines in pension values.

How widespread is loneliness among older adults in Russia and Bulgaria? And to what extent is it associated with family structure, i.e., marital status, and the number and co-residence status of children and grandchildren? Given gendered social roles in family and economic life, and differential experiences of widowhood, are men and women differently susceptible to loneliness in old age? These are among the questions I address in analyses of the Generations and Gender Surveys (GGS), conducted in Russia and Bulgaria in 2004. The state of economy, demography and civil society in formerly Soviet Eastern Europe following the collapse of many institutions that ensured older adult welfare suggest that the chances that older adults will experience social relational *gains* in late life will be quite limited. An important exception may be those older adults who, despite historically low fertility rates, form relationships with grandchildren. By examining the determinants of loneliness in these contexts, I aim to provide theoretical and policy insights into the social costs, as represented by elevated risks of loneliness and social isolation, of the demographic and family structural changes underway in post-socialist Eastern Europe.

Previous Research on Loneliness and Family Relations

Recent research conducted in Western European settings (e.g., the Netherlands and United Kingdom) provides little evidence to suggest that the advance of population ageing has brought an increase in older adult loneliness. Rather, these studies indicate that rates of older adult loneliness have held steady, or even declined, during recent decades (Victor et al. 2002, Dykstra 2009). This is somewhat paradoxical for a number of reasons, for instance the increase in loneliness observed with advancing age (Dykstra et al. 2005), and the increasing share of older adults who are widowed, living alone, and/or facing old age with relatively few living children. Further empirical and theoretical work points toward cultural and structural factors that underlie older adult loneliness, or its relative absence, in particular settings. For instance, Van Tilburg and colleagues (1998) highlight older adults' degrees of social integration as an explanation for the somewhat unexpected finding that elderly Tuscans' loneliness exceeds that of the Dutch. This pattern is attributed to Tuscans' relatively limited extent of extra-familial social integration in older adulthood. Others highlight normative perceptions to explain why living alone results in differing degrees of loneliness. Johnson and Mullins (1987) and Jylha and Jokela (1990) observe that 'loneliness thresholds' depend on context and culture, and that living alone breeds loneliness where it is the exception rather than the rule.

What might be the situation and risk factors for older adult loneliness in Bulgaria and Russia, two nations whose trajectories of rapid population decline have been described as portending demographic 'collapse' and 'catastrophe'? (Demko et al. 1999, Vassilev 2005). Social scientists have only begun to answer these questions in the former Eastern bloc societies. Decades of below replacement fertility (both countries experienced a total fertility rate of 1.4 in 2010), coupled with steady emigration (Bulgaria) and declining male life expectancy (Russia), place future cohorts of Russian and Bulgarian elderly men and women in vulnerable positions *vis-à-vis* the marital and intergenerational supports and co-resident arrangements thought to ward off loneliness. Co-residence with children has been found to be a more significant antidote to older adult loneliness in settings, including Eastern Europe, where such living arrangements are consistent with normative ideas about family cohesiveness and intergenerational responsibility (de Jong Gierveld and van Tilburg 1999, de Jong Gierveld et al. 2011). One must question, then, how current and future cohorts of older adults will fare in Bulgaria and Russia, where demographic changes will seriously undermine the supply of kin available for support and proximate or co-residential living arrangements.

Because it represents the loss of one of life's most salient, primary ties, widowhood is a crucial life course stage to examine in analyses of older adult emotional wellbeing, especially in settings like Russia where the life expectancy gap markedly favors women. The importance of contact with children, siblings, neighbors and friends to allay loneliness varies according to older adults' marital status. Pinquart's (2003) analysis of German older adults indicates that contact with friends, neighbors, children and siblings was more likely to alleviate loneliness in currently unmarried older adults (i.e., widowed, divorced, and never married) than in those with a spouse. Pinquart reasons that, in the German setting, spouses most often meet needs for intimacy, closeness and sharing, and the absence of a spouse thus is associated with greater loneliness and greater importance of other familial and extra-familial contacts. In Russia, and to a lesser extent Bulgaria, gender life expectancy gaps are such that sizable proportions of older women will send numerous years of later life as widows. I question whether children and grandchildren, especially if they find themselves in economically and socially precarious positions, will provide the close and supportive ties to their widowed mothers, and smaller populations of widowed fathers, to keep deep feelings of social isolation at bay.

While relationships beyond the spousal and parent-child tie, such as those with siblings and neighbors, are considered in many analytical frameworks, few have considered the role of grandchildren in shaping older adults' wellbeing and experiences of loneliness. There are many reasons to believe that the grandparent-grandchild tie is pertinent. First, as Hayslip and Kaminski (2005) note in their overview of custodial grandparents, although grandparent caregiving is associated with numerous stressors, it can also enhance one's pleasure, sense of purpose, and provide activities that form the basis of active ageing (Giarrusso et al. 2000, Geurts et al. 2009). In analysis of multigenerational families in Bulgaria, Botcheva and Feldman (2004) found that the presence of grandparents served to buffer stress in the younger generations and minimize 'harsh parenting' in households facing economic adversity. While this and other research on multigenerational families is often focused on benefits to grandchildren, I reason that grandparents who invest in, and experience proximity to, grandchildren, are likely to experience unique psychosocial benefits, especially when other segments of their social relationship networks have grown thin.

In the former Eastern bloc countries, research has been hampered, until quite recently, by a dearth of data on objective and subjective measures of social relationship quality (Dykstra 2009). In the early period of transition, scholars suggest there was a renewed tendency toward reliance on kin and informal networks simply to ensure survival in lieu of government sponsored institutions (Sik and Wellman 1999). However, at the same time, increased life stress and mobility tended to fracture social networks, leaving many, older adults in particular, with a heightened sense of alienation and isolation (Goodwin 2006, Kraus et al. 1998). Iecovich and colleagues' (2004) analysis of elderly Jews in Russia and Ukraine found that many exhibit intense levels of loneliness, an experience linked to thin social networks and network holes created not only through contemporary emigration and diminished social services, but also through deaths and displacements in the Holocaust. Transition to the new era was a particularly difficult, and experienced as a loss for older adults, as one study participant (Iecovich et al. 2004: 313) indicated: 'For us, elderly people, the former regime provided everything and we felt secure, but now we feel abandoned and neglected.' Where social services provided by the state were summarily abolished in Bulgaria and Russia, family members were expected to turn to one another to address the social and economic costs of market reforms (Botcheva and Feldman 2004: 160). Accordingly, it is important to consider whether the structural characteristics of families, as shaped by unique economic and demographic strains, are pertinent to older adults' experiences of loneliness and emotional wellbeing more generally.

Contexts of Study: Russia and Bulgaria

In absolute and relative terms, Eastern Europe's population is in a state of decline (Demeny 2005). The remaining population is growing older, such that in the future older adults will be supported by smaller cohorts of workers in the labor force and smaller cohorts of children and grandchildren in their families. To date, growth of the oldest-old population in the East has been held at bay, as compared to Western European nations, due to slowing gains, and even declines, in life expectancy. This halting of life expectancy gain has recovered in most of Eastern Europe, with the notable exception of Russian, and especially Russian male, life expectancy (Schoenmaeckers and Vanderleyden 2006). Although growth of the elderly share of population in the region has slowed since the 1990s, very low fertility in recent cohorts promises to produce rapid population ageing in decades to come (Garilova and Gavrilov 2009). In-migration from outside of the region is one of the few possible demographic correctives for this transition which has powerful momentum and is already well underway (Coleman 2006).

On some measures, demographic trends are even bleaker in Bulgaria than in Russia. With a negative population growth rate that even outpaces that of Russia, conditions have led observers to warn of a severe looming demographic crisis for Bulgaria (Georgiev 2008). A key contributor to Bulgaria's population decline is emigration, which, drawing from professionals and laborers in their prime working ages, stands to greatly diminish native-born workforce and care-giving resources (Rangelova and Vladimirova 2004). The consequences of net emigration for Bulgaria's elderly are neither well documented nor understood.

The elderly have proven to be among the most vulnerable groups in Eastern Europe's 'third transition,' as the previous certainties of communist social and economic organization were undermined by rapid social change and their ways of living and communities were dismantled by radical social reorganization (Goodwin 2006). Many older adults find themselves coping with 'multiple deprivations' produced, in part, by the collapse of socialism and failed welfare, health care, and other institutions (Tchernina and Tchernin 2002). Many older Russians' and Bulgarians' stresses have socioeconomic origins, as payments to pensioners have frequently fallen below legal minimum levels, while inflation has soared, leading to poverty, indebtedness, and often desperate attempts to find employment in informal and black market economies (BAGSO 2001, Botcheva and Feldman 2004). Surveys of Russian pensioners note that many struggle to subsist solely on their pension payments, leaving female, unemployed pensioners, in particular, one of the most vulnerable social groups, evolving adaptive means of survival that still result in precarious situations (Karyukhin 2008).

Changes in policy, in addition to empirical research, suggest that experiences of isolation and exclusion among the elderly have risen during market and demographic transitions in the former Eastern bloc nations. Soviet era social services to disadvantaged elderly have all but disappeared, leaving older adults lonelier and more isolated (Iecovich et al. 2004). More than in Soviet times, 'age exclusion', or the reduction of economically active life through retirement and other policies, is seen as a potential threat, not only in terms of economic outcomes, but social and psychological ones (Rantanen 2002). Diminished formal institutional welfare supports mean that, in Russia, and Bulgaria to a similar extent, 'there is no longer a welfare state, medical and personal care services have been annihilated, and societal welfare shocks have evolved haphazard, often marginal, day-to-day strategies of survival' (Tchernin and Tchernina 2002: 545). These trends suggest that rising long term care demands will fall heavily upon informal caregivers, likely the spouses and children of older adults who have experienced loss of functioning and other forms of dependency (Ovseiko 2008). Scholars have pointed to the arrival of a 'new intergenerational balance' weighing upon smaller cohorts of children as larger cohorts of older adults are living longer and often with lengthier durations of compromised functional health (European Commission 2006). How families will withstand these demographic shifts, and whether older adult quality of life will be buoyed upon support provided by children and grandchildren, remains to be seen.

Gender in the Post-Soviet Context

In Eastern Europe, as elsewhere, gender is an important factor delineating quality of life and relationships in older adulthood. Within Eastern Europe, Schwarzer and colleagues (1994) found that women reported significantly greater received and perceived support than their male counterparts. By extension, loneliness, which reflects perceptions of social relational deficits, also ought to be a gendered experience. Gender disparities in older adult loneliness have been observed in a range of settings, and are often attributed to men's and women's different degrees of contact with children, siblings and friends, not to mention the greater share of older adult women who experience the death of a spouse (e.g., Kaufman and Uhlenberg 1998, Pinquart 2003).

In the case of Russia, older adults' living situations, as well as their relations with grown children, are likely to be sharply gendered due in part to the very wide life expectancy gap between men and women. Gendered differences in survival among the current generation of elderly are a by-product not only of men's currently high levels of chronic disease and other causes of death, but also are a legacy of high levels of male mortality during the WWII era (Velkoff and Kinsella 2000). Recent data indicates that Russian male life expectancy falls around 60 years of age, while for Russian females the figure is 73 years, a gender gap of 13 years. Given this disparity, Russian women are more likely to lose a spouse than their counterparts elsewhere in the region. Bulgarian life expectancies significantly exceed Russians', with a gender gap that is wide (77 years for women, and 70 years for men), but only approximately half of that separating Russian men and women. Both Russia and Bulgaria require earlier retirement for women than men, policies that raises questions about the economic and social vulnerability of older Russian and Bulgarian women, widows in particular.

Aside from the divergence in longevity across men and women, which is especially stark in Russia, there are also distinctive, gendered social and familial roles with implications for the experience of loneliness in late adulthood. As Ashwin and Lytkina (2004) observe, men's lesser involvement in family and household affairs has compromised their ability to cope with losses related to labor market experience. Men were essentially 'estranged' from domestic and caring work under the patriarchal mode of the Soviet family, making 'the frailty of men's presence and position in the family ... a constant ingredient in the everyday knowledge of the Soviet people' (Rotkirch 2000: 11, Ashwin and Lytkina 2004). Ashwin and Lytkina further suggest that because men's status, and especially Russian men's status in the household is defined by their fulfillment of the breadwinner role, then loss of this role – as through retirement, disability, or other changes, will be particularly challenging to social and emotional wellbeing.

Research Questions

In order to gain an understanding of the social relational elements that underlie older adult loneliness in post-Soviet Russia and Bulgaria, I pose the following set of questions: First, do numbers of children and child co-residence impact older adults' experiences of loneliness? Second, what impact does widowhood have on older adults' loneliness and does the effect diverge by gender? Next, to consider relationships beyond the husband-wife, and parent-child dyad, I ask, does having and co-residing with grandchildren alleviate loneliness in older adulthood?

Data and Study Design

I draw upon the Generations and Gender Survey (GGS), a cross-national, comparative, and multidisciplinary study of 'the dynamics of family relationships in contemporary industrialized countries' to characterize older adults' living arrangements, family structure and experiences of loneliness in Bulgaria and Russia (Vikat et al. 2005). The choice of these two nations for comparative investigation is in part data driven, but it is also allows insights into the situations faced by older adults in countries that share many elements of historical experience and demographic structure, as indicated in Table 15.1 by nearly identical fertility rates, negative population growth rates, and a moderate-to-high share of population over the age of 65.

Table 15.1 Basic demographic characteristics of the Bulgarian and Russian populations (2009)

	Bulgaria	Russia
% 65 and Older	18%	14%
Population growth rate	-.8%	-.5%
TFR	1.4	1.4
Net migration rate	-3.1	.28
Sex ratio, Age 65 (M/F)	.68	.44
Life expectancy at birth (M/F)	70/77	59/73

Source: CIA World Factbook.

I utilize the baseline survey of the GGS, conducted in 2004 by the Population Activities Unit of the United Nations Economic Commission of Europe (UNECE), to analyze living arrangements, family structure and other predictors of older adult loneliness in Russia and Bulgaria. The GGS features a probability sample representing the study country's non-institutional population of 18 to 79 year olds.

Data were collected through computer assisted, face to face interviews. To allow for cross-national, comparative research, the same survey design, questionnaire, and instructions were adapted across countries.

While representative of national populations and extensive in its coverage, the GGS was not designed as a survey of the elderly. Use of a household roster tool means that basic demographic information (e.g., age, sex, employment status) is available for all household members, irrespective of their age. The most extensive, detailed information in the survey is provided by, and with reference to, the head of household. The analyses that follow are limited, given this data collection strategy. First, in analyzing older adults' experiences of loneliness I must delimit the sample in a way that may limit the study's generalizability. Specifically, in multivariate analyses the analytical sample consists of heads of household only, as only heads of household were asked questions about loneliness and most other questions beyond basic demographic characteristics. The analytical sample is not representative of all older adults in either Russia or Bulgaria, but rather heads of household. Second, while subsequent waves of data collection are planned, at this point the GGS data remain cross-sectional. As a result, I am limited in commenting on the causal relationship between older adults' family relationships, changes therein, and the experience of loneliness.

Variables and Measurement

Loneliness is the dependent variable in the following analyses. A working definition for loneliness is: 'an unpleasant feeling of dissatisfaction with existing social relationships, a perceived lack of intimacy, and a feeling of exclusion from social relationships that is influenced by some form of social relationship deficit' (Iecovich et al. 2004: 308). This is similar to other definitions (e.g., Young 1982) which point to psychological distress deriving from absence of satisfying social relationships, as well as perceived social isolation (Koropeckyj-Cox 1998). de Jong Gierveld and colleagues (2006) further note that loneliness is a subjective, negative experience, the opposite of which is a feeling of embeddedness or belongingness.

I develop an index of loneliness by aggregating GGS participants' responses to a series of six questions assessing current life experience. The six statements are derived from the De Jong Gierveld Loneliness scale (de Jong Gierveld and Kamphuis 1985). A Rasch-type scale, the De Jong Gierveld scale is highly correlated with other loneliness scales, such as the UCLA Loneliness Scale (Pinquart 2003). Specifically, respondents were asked to indicate a yes, more or less, or no response to the following six statements: There are plenty of people that I can lean on in case of trouble; I experience a general sense of emptiness; I miss having people around; There are many people that I can count on completely; Often, I feel rejected; and, There are enough people that I feel close to. Items two, three and five were reverse coded such that, in the resultant index (with maximum score of 18 and minimum score of six) high values indicate high degrees of loneliness.

There are three focal independent variables in the models which tap into older adults' family structures and living arrangements. First, I consider current marital status, or whether the older adult was currently married, or currently unmarried, at the time of the survey. Those currently cohabiting, a relatively small fraction of older adults, are grouped with the currently married. Unfortunately, the phrasing of the question in the GGS does not allow for a straight-forward separation of the unmarried category into widowed, divorced, and never married persons. Nevertheless, given the age of the cohorts and divorce trends in the countries, I surmise that the vast majority in this category are, indeed, widows and widowers. Second, I jointly assess number of children and living arrangements in a variable that delineates numbers of living adult children, and for older adults with living children, whether any child currently co-resides in the same dwelling unit. The modal category, having two or more children but none co-residing, is the omitted, reference category in the models. This status is juxtaposed with the following categories: having no living children; having one, non-co-resident child; having one, co-resident child; and having two or more children with at least one co-resident. Finally, to assess the role of grandchildren in older adults' loneliness assessments, I measure whether older adults: a) have no grandchildren; b) have grandchildren, but none co-resident; or c) have grandchildren, some of whom co-reside in the same household.

Control variables in the models tap into a set of individual level characteristics shown to correlate with loneliness in previous research. Age is included in the model as an interval variable. Controlling for age is essential, given the different age distributions across gender and other categories in the model, and also given that previous research finds loneliness increases with age. For the reasons discussed above, gender of the older adult is included and critically examined in the models. Whether an older adult is currently retired, or still in the labor force, is controlled in the model, so as to consider whether retirement may involve severing social ties or otherwise generating social exclusion, and thereby, loneliness. The place of residence, whether it is urban or rural, is also included as a control variable in the model, as social structures with implications for loneliness are likely to diverge across types of place.

As previous assessments of loneliness (e.g., Fees et al. 1999) maintain, deterioration in physical health associates with loneliness for several reasons, for instance due to the lessened ability to maintain and interact in stimulating relationships. Thus, I include two measures which capture dimensions of health – a global measure of self-reported health (i.e., health rated on a five-point scale from very bad to very good); and a dummy variable indicating the respondent's functional health (i.e., whether the older adult reports having a disability which limits one's ability to carry out normal, everyday activities).

Finally, economic circumstances also pertain to the experience of loneliness and other dimensions of quality of life. Due to the difficulty of assessing income and wealth through the GGS, I rely instead on a single measure which asked heads of household to provide a subjective estimation of their household's economic situation. In particular, they were asked to assess, given their average level of monthly income, the level of difficulty encountered in 'making ends meet'. Difficulty was scored in one of six categories, ranging from 'with great difficulty' to 'very easily'.

Results

A descriptive picture of the GGS sample of older adults, both the broader sample of older adults surveyed, and the sample of household heads featured in the multivariate analyses, is provided in Table 15.2. By way of summary, it is important to note that in both countries, but especially Russia, as reflective of its gender life expectancy gap, women outnumber men in the GGS elderly sample. In both countries the vast majority of persons over age 60 are retired, and between 8 and 10% report having a disability that limits daily functioning. Reflecting the long history of low fertility in Eastern Europe, the mean number of living children in both countries is below two. And, given this, and other aspects of familial and social relations, it is the minority experience among older adults in Bulgaria and Russia (i.e., 25–35%) to co-reside with one or more adult children. Aside from the distributions by gender and marital status, the samples in Russia and Bulgaria are characterized more by similarity than by striking difference.

It also bears mentioning that the multivariate analytical sample differs from the full sample of older adults in key ways. For instance, the head of household sample is younger on average, more likely to be married, and less likely to be co-residing with children (in part because living with children often means moving into a grown child's home where that child is head of household). It is important to take these sample characteristics into account when considering the analytical sample's generalizability to the Russian and Bulgarian populations in general.

To provide additional description of older adults' expressed loneliness in Russia and Bulgaria, I provide unadjusted mean loneliness scale scores for elderly male and female household heads in Bulgaria and Russia across key covariates in the study. Results presented in Table 15.3 are quite consistent with previous empirical work and theorizing on loneliness in older adulthood. Specifically, in terms of bivariate association, and among both Russian and Bulgarian heads of household, mean scores for loneliness are significantly greater among the widowed, those with no living children, those with no grandchildren, the more aged, the disabled, those with poorer self-assessed health and in more needy economic circumstances. Prior to controlling for social and demographic characteristics such as marital status, I observe that loneliness is greater, on average, among elderly Russian and Bulgarian women as compared to their male counterparts. Being retired is associated with greater loneliness, but only among Russians, whereas rural residents are more lonely only in Bulgaria.

Table 15.2 Summary statistics for Bulgarian and Russian older adult heads of household, age 60 and older, 2004

	Bulgaria				Russia			
	Heads of household, spouses of household heads & parents of household heads		Heads of household only		Heads of household, spouses of household heads & parents of household heads		Heads of household only	
	Percent/N		Percent/N		Percent/N		Percent/N	
Male	47.3	2,930	50.2	1,257	35.5	1795	30.6	864
Female	52.7	3,265	49.8	1,249	64.6	3268	69.4	1963
Age: 60–69	59.5	3,688	58.5	1,466	56.2	2847	57.5	1625
Age: 70–79	35.7	2,209	40.9	1,025	38.7	1961	42.4	1199
Age: 80+	4.8	298	0.6	15	5.0	255	0.1	3
Not currently married	55.5	3,435	33.4	838	70.6	3573	57.4	1623
Currently married	44.4	2,748	66.1	1,656	29.4	1490	42.6	1204
Missing data on marital status	0.2	12	0.5	12	0.0	0	0.0	0
Total Children: 0	4.2	251	7.2	180	6.9	350	9.2	261
Total Children: 1	22.9	1,381	24.9	624	23.9	1209	29.5	835
Total Children: 2	57.3	3,456	55.0	1,379	42.6	2156	42.7	1206
Total Children: 3+	15.2	942	12.9	323	21.8	1101	18.6	525
Total Children: Indeterminate	2.7	165	0.0	0	4.9	247	0.0	0
No coresident children	63.5	3,931	72.4	1,815	71.6	3627	78.0	2208
One or more coresident children	36.5	2,264	27.6	691	28.4	1436	22.0	619
Has a disability that limits work	9.9	611	10.0	251	8.9	448	6.8	192
No disability	90.1	5,584	90.0	2,255	4615.0	4615	93.2	2635
Currently working	8.0	495	7.0	174	11.8	599	12.8	361
Retired	92.0	5,700	93.1	2,332	88.2	4464	87.2	2466
Head of household	40.5	2,506	100.0	2,560	55.9	2827	100.0	2827
Spouse of head	26.6	1,649	0.0	0	24.1	1218	0.0	0
Parent of head	32.9	2,040	0.0	0	20.1	1018	0.0	0
Rural	40.5	3,686	40.5	1,014	67.1	3396	66.0	1866
Urban	59.5	2,509	59.5	1,492	32.9	1667	34.0	961

Source: Generations and Gender Survey.

Table 15.3 Mean loneliness scale scores for Russian and Bulgarian heads of household, 60 and older, by sex, family structure and sociodemographic characteristics

	Russia						Bulgaria					
	Men			Women			Men			Women		
	Mean loneliness scale score	N	Mean diff. test	Mean loneliness scale score	N	Mean diff. test	Mean loneliness scale score	N	Mean diff. test	Mean loneliness scale score	N	Mean diff. test
Marital Status												
Not currently married	10.7	230	***	10.3	1380	***	12.6	207	***	12	617	***
Currently married	9	631		9	566		9.8	1032		9.7	617	
Status of Children												
No living children	10.2	70	**	11	190	***	12	91	***	12	89	***
1 noncoresident child	10	182		10.1	450		10.8	189		11.1	207	
1 coresident child	9.4	54		9.7	206		10.2	146		10.3	168	
2+ children, none coresident	9.3	515		9.7	1032		10	772		10.7	728	
2+ children, 1+ coresident	9.6	40		9.5	68		9.6	48		10.9	47	
Status of Grandchildren												
No grandchildren	10.4	113	***	10.8	316	***	11.3	196	***	11.4	151	***
1+ grandchildren, none coresident	9.4	651		9.7	1357		10.2	916		10.9	882	
1+ grandchildren, 1+ coresident	8.9	92		9.6	273		9.2	134		10.1	206	
Age												
Age 60–74	9.4	697	ns	9.8	1546	***	10.1	1007	***	10.6	1098	***
Age 75+	9.7	164		10.4	400		10.8	239		12.1	141	
Has a Disability												
No disability	9.3	162	***	9.6	1539	***	9.9	1048	***	10.6	1013	***

	%	N	sig	%	N	sig	%	N	sig	%	N	sig
Yes	10.4	698		11	404		11.8	195		11.8	221	
Self Reported Health												
Very good or good	9.2	81	***	8.9	64	***	9.5	429	***	9.6	278	***
Fair	9.1	463		9.1	838		10.1	531		10.5	556	
Bad	9.9	268		10.4	865		11.4	218		11.8	335	
Very bad	11.4	48		11.5	179		12.5	66		13.1	70	
Difficulty Meeting Ends Meet												
Great difficulty	10.3	195	**	10.8	696	***	11.2	476	***	11.6	580	***
Difficulty	9.7	285		9.8	638		9	373		10.6	368	
Some difficulty	8.8	307		8.9	488		9.3	317		9.4	238	
Fairly easily	9	56		9	92		9.6	31		8.6	20	
Easily or very easily	10.2	18		8.7	31		9	26		8.9	17	
Employment Status												
Retired	9.6	707	***	10	1740	***	10.3	1117	ns	10.8	1195	ns
Working	8.9	154		9.1	206		10	129		10.5	44	
Rural/Urban Status												
Rural	9.5	563	ns	9.9	1288	ns	10.5	507	**	11	501	*
Urban	9.4	298		10	658		10	739		10.7	738	
Total Sample	9.5	861	***	9.9	1946	***	10.2	1246	***	10.8	1239	***

Source: Generations and Gender Survey, 2004.

Multivariate Results

I use Ordinary Least Squares (OLS) regression to model older adult loneliness among heads of household age 60 and older in Russia and Bulgaria. As mentioned above, the GGS was designed for comparability across survey countries, thereby allowing for side-by-side comparative analyses. Nested OLS Regression results (unstandardized regression coefficients) for the Bulgarian and Russian samples are shown in Table 15.4. Before discussing the family relationship variables of interest, I will note associations for the social/demographic control variables in the models. First, age has a positive association with loneliness, such that expressed loneliness increases with age. Disability, too, exhibits this positive association with loneliness, but the relationship only reaches statistical significance among Russian older adults. In both Russia and Bulgaria there is a strong, negative relationship between physical health, economic wellbeing, and loneliness, such that those in poorer health and poorer economic situations also experience greater levels of loneliness. Last, and notably, when accounting for marital status and other variables in the model, men in both Russia and Bulgaria have levels of loneliness significantly greater than those of their female counterparts. As elaborated below, it is the experience of widowhood, far more common among women, which is a key dimension influencing older adult loneliness in the Bulgarian, and especially the Russian, context.

Table 15.4 OLS regression analysis: Predictors of loneliness in Russian and Bulgarian heads of household, age 60 and older, 2004

VARIABLES	Russia			Bulgaria		
	Model A	Model B	Model C	Model A	Model B	Model C
Not currently married (ref: currently married)	1.03*** (0.119)	0.98*** (0.119)	1.52*** (0.216)	2.12*** (0.130)	2.13*** (0.129)	2.44*** (0.213)
No living children (ref: 2+ noncoresident children)	1.00*** (0.187)	0.25 (0.255)	0.26 (0.255)	0.90*** (0.221)	0.51** (0.245)	0.48* (0.245)
1 noncoresident child (ref: 2+ noncoresident children)	0.57*** (0.131)	0.49*** (0.132)	0.51*** (0.132)	0.57*** (0.157)	0.48*** (0.157)	0.46*** (0.157)
1 coresident child (ref: 2+ noncoresident children)	0.23 (0.188)	0.01 (0.202)	0.03 (0.202)	-0.05 (0.171)	-0.10 (0.192)	-0.09 (0.192)
2+ coresident children (ref: 2+ noncoresident children)	-0.47* (0.276)	-0.49* (0.278)	-0.44 (0.278)	-0.40 (0.292)	-0.15 (0.298)	-0.14 (0.298)
No grandchildren (ref: 1+ grandchildren, none coreside)		0.88*** (0.205)	0.87*** (0.205)		0.57*** (0.193)	0.54*** (0.193)

VARIABLES	Russia			Bulgaria		
	Model A	Model B	Model C	Model A	Model B	Model C
1+ coresident grandchildren (ref: 1+ grandchildren, none coreside)		0.07 (0.168)	0.06 (0.168)		-0.63*** (0.177)	-0.62*** (0.177)
Age in years	0.03** (0.011)	0.03*** (0.011)	0.03*** (0.011)	0.02* (0.011)	0.02* (0.011)	0.02* (0.011)
Female (ref: Male)	-0.42*** (0.127)	-0.39*** (0.127)	-0.08 (0.163)	-0.37*** (0.121)	-0.32*** (0.121)	-0.19 (0.142)
Retired (ref: Currently working)	0.07 (0.168)	0.08 (0.167)	0.03 (0.168)	-0.02 (0.228)	0.06 (0.227)	0.04 (0.227)
Disability that limits daily activity (ref: No disability)	0.60*** (0.141)	0.60*** (0.140)	0.60*** (0.140)	0.27 (0.175)	0.26 (0.174)	0.26 (0.174)
Fair self-reported health (ref: Good or very good SRH)	-0.12 (0.245)	-0.17 (0.245)	-0.20 (0.245)	0.47*** (0.135)	0.45*** (0.134)	0.45*** (0.134)
Poor self-reported health (ref: Good or very good SRH)	0.67*** (0.255)	0.64** (0.255)	0.61** (0.254)	1.35*** (0.178)	1.35*** (0.177)	1.35*** (0.177)
Very poor self reported health (ref: Good or very good SRH)	1.39*** (0.314)	1.34*** (0.313)	1.33*** (0.313)	2.24*** (0.295)	2.23*** (0.293)	2.23*** (0.293)
Difficult to make ends meet (ref: Very difficult)	-0.69*** (0.132)	-0.70*** (0.131)	-0.72*** (0.131)	-0.68*** (0.133)	-0.66*** (0.132)	-0.66*** (0.132)
Some difficulty making ends meet (ref: Very difficult)	-1.36*** (0.140)	-1.36*** (0.140)	-1.40*** (0.141)	-1.31*** (0.148)	-1.27*** (0.148)	-1.28*** (0.148)
Fairly easy to make ends meet (ref: Very difficult)	-1.42*** (0.251)	-1.45*** (0.250)	-1.51*** (0.251)	-1.54*** (0.394)	-1.57*** (0.392)	-1.60*** (0.392)
Easy or very easy to make ends meet (ref: Very difficult)	-1.13*** (0.409)	-1.09*** (0.408)	-1.22*** (0.409)	-1.84*** (0.424)	-1.78*** (0.422)	-1.80*** (0.422)
Urban area residence (ref: Rural residence)	0.13 (0.111)	0.13 (0.111)	0.12 (0.111)	-0.19* (0.115)	-0.19 (0.115)	-0.18 (0.115)
Female * Not currently married			-0.77*** (0.259)			-0.48* (0.262)
Constant	7.64*** (0.737)	7.49*** (0.738)	7.28*** (0.741)	8.64*** (0.735)	8.51*** (0.737)	8.44*** (0.738)
Observations	2,801	2,796	2,796	2,424	2,424	2,424
R-squared	0.156	0.161	0.164	0.249	0.258	0.259

Note: Standard errors in parentheses *** p<0.01, ** p<0.05, * p<0.1.
Source: Generations and Gender Survey, 2004.

The family relationship variables – marital status, children and child co-residence, and status of grandchildren – each exhibit statistically significant associations with older adult loneliness in Bulgaria and Russia. In both settings, the widowed express much higher degrees of loneliness than their married counterparts. This result meshes with much previous research indicating that the marital tie, which usually features most prominently in day to day activity and emotional life, is pivotal to satisfaction with one's social relationships.

In addition to marriage, numbers of living children, which reflect both completed fertility as well as the survival of children, as well as children's residential locations, are also highly relevant to older adults' social relationship satisfaction. Specifically, it is found that, in terms of family structure, the loneliest of older adults in Russia and Bulgaria are those with no living children, followed by those with just one, non-co-resident child. These groups are lonelier than the reference, modal category of elders with two or more children, none of whom co-reside. Co-residing with children, while in the direction of reducing the experience of loneliness, does not have a statistically significant association, except in the case of Russian older adults co-residing with two or more adult children. These results suggest that relationships with children have significant, lasting impacts upon the quality of life of older adults. Child co-residence cannot be easily interpreted as indicating support and interpersonal closeness, as some co-resident arrangements may be driven more strongly by need and dependence, and hence may not allay loneliness. Acknowledging this, the presence of children may offer a buffer against feelings of social isolation in such settings where social integration through employment and state-sponsored programs have declined in the post-Soviet era.

Perhaps the most interesting results, and telling for advancing understanding older adult wellbeing, are those illustrating the relationship between having grandchildren, grandchild co-residence, and the experience of loneliness. To demonstrate how the consideration of grandchildren mediates the relationship between own children and loneliness, the grandchildren and grandchild co-residence categorical variables are added in Model B. A comparison of Models A and B reveals that grandchildren, in part, mediate the effect of own children on loneliness. Having grown children not only means that older adults may receive social and economic support and regular contacts with children that stave off loneliness, it also often means that they may have grandchildren involved in their lives and in their homes. In both settings, older adults with grandchildren exhibit significantly lower levels of loneliness than their grandchild-less counterparts. In Bulgaria, but not Russia, living together with at least one grandchild brings an even greater reduction in the degree of loneliness. This pattern suggests a role for multigenerational, extended family in enhancing older adults' quality of life and emotional wellbeing, especially in a society like Bulgaria where patterns of emigration are creating many transnational families whose separations may create gulfs in parent-child relationships.

Finally, in Model C, the gendering of loneliness and the marital relationship is examined through an interactive model, specifically introduction of a statistical interaction between gender and marital status. The results in Model C suggest that, net of other variables, older adult male widowers experience greater levels of loneliness than their female counterparts. The significant interaction terms suggest that the exacerbation of loneliness associated with widowhood is greater for men than for women. While there are several possible explanations for this relationship, one likely explanation is that, especially in Russia, women are protected from loneliness through a wider range of relationships than the spousal one, such as those to children, extended kin, friends and neighbors. For men, on the other hand, given their lifelong emphasis on the economic provider role, their ties to children, extended family and others may by fewer and weaker, leaving them more susceptible to loneliness when faced with the loss of a spouse.

Discussion

Loneliness is one of several quality of life disadvantages facing older adults in Eastern Europe as the region undergoes a difficult transition from 'red to grey'. Previous research (in particular de Jong Gierveld 2008) reveals that older adult loneliness is significantly higher in Eastern European nations than in Western European nations such as France and Germany. The current chapter delves further into the correlates of loneliness in older adulthood, finding that in Russia and Bulgaria loneliness is quite commonplace, especially among elderly men, and rises with age. Loneliness is found to correlate positively not only with widowhood, small family size and limited extended family relations, but also with economic deprivation and poor health. These findings are relevant for a host of policy related considerations, not least of which are the implications of poor relationship quality for mortality and morbidity in late adulthood.

It is significant that in Russia and Bulgaria, as elsewhere, loneliness is not simply a byproduct of small families and weak family ties. Rather, the threat of 'multiple deprivations' is apparent as loneliness is strongly, positively correlated with other quality of life impairments – economic insecurity, ill health, and disability. In other words, poor quality of life on one dimension appears to reinforce poor quality of life on other dimensions. This joint experience of myriad hardships, which are then reflected in older adults' dissatisfaction with their personal relationships, is consistent with the so-called 'litany of suffering' expressed by older Russians as a means to articulate the insecurities they have incurred in the transition to capitalism (Pietilä and Ryktönen 2008).

Importantly, family structure appears to matter in exacerbating, and possibly, buffering older adults from experiences of loneliness in these post-Soviet states. Being married, having several children, and notably, having and (in Bulgaria) living together with grandchildren correlate with relatively positive assessments of one's social relationships. While having numerous children diminishes loneliness, co-residing together with them has limited additional effect in either country. Possible explanations for this pattern are that independent living is preferred in the post-Soviet era, or that co-residence does not necessarily imply greater socio-emotional support, but may, in many cases, be a product of economic need and dependency in both the older and younger generation. The findings about own children and grandchildren in holding loneliness at bay raise some concern given the steep fertility declines in Eastern Europe which promise to create even smaller families and more tenuous structures of family-based support in the future.

The analyses also indicate that loneliness is another dimension of older adulthood that is highly gendered. While it is important to acknowledge that older women are far more likely to endure years of widowhood, a life stage that is particularly likely to be accompanied by increased loneliness, it is also important to note that, controlling for widowhood, family structure and other characteristics, both Russian and Bulgarian women express significantly less loneliness than their male counterparts. There are numerous possible explanations for this gender gap, most of which are tied to men's and women's different orientations to the family, household and workforce in the post-Soviet era. For one, as elsewhere, women's greater investment in social reproduction and 'kin keeping' activities generates greater embeddedness in family networks, both immediate and extended families, and extra-familial ties to neighbors and other significant others. That men's sense of relational satisfaction, versus loneliness, is more contingent on their marital status than is the case for women is also apparent in Russia, where loneliness is exacerbated more so in widowhood for men than for women. For men, not only does their heavy investment in the economic provider role mean lesser investment in developing kinship ties over the life course, it also means that the social exclusion wrought by retirement likely weighs more heavily upon them than it does upon women. And, added to this, experienced at the micro-level, the low life expectancy of males, especially in Russia, means that men will be more likely to see their personal, nonfamily networks eroded through friends' and coworkers' early deaths. In many ways, then, the patriarchal definitions of masculinity that held sway under the communist system in Russia and elsewhere in the Soviet bloc continue to bear out in the experience of loneliness among elderly men in the current, transitional era.

This research has several limitations which warrant mentioning and suggest further investigation. To begin, in its current state the GGS remains a cross-sectional survey. Lacking a longitudinal design it is difficult to parse out causality, and our assertions about the causal factors of loneliness must remain tentative, and phrased in terms of correlation. The absence of an extended time series also prevents our understanding the extent to which living arrangements and family relations changed in Russia and Bulgaria under the new social and economic regime. Time series data would assist in placing current family and living arrangements, and their consequences for social isolation and loneliness, in context.

This chapter only addresses the experience of loneliness as reported by heads of household. Sensitivity analyses indicate that heads of household do differ in some key ways from the broader group of all older adults. For instance, a greater share of household heads is married as compared to the full population of older adults. Thus, caution must be exercised in generalizing these results to the full population of older adults. Furthermore, the featured analyses consider relations with family – spouses, children, and grandchildren – as they relate to the experience of loneliness. While instructive, much information is lacking about the nature and scope of older adults' social networks. For one, I do not assess the quality of parent-child relations, or the extent of solidarity across generations in the survey. Additionally, the question of ties to friends, neighbors, and other non-kin, as well involvement in organizations such as churches and community groups, is not addressed here. Although the GGS provides little information on these sorts of social ties and associations, they are likely critical to older adults' satisfaction with their social relationships.

Conclusion

The fates of older adults in Eastern Europe are tied to the difficult economic, social and demographic transitions unfolding since the Soviet Union collapse in the 1990s. In myriad ways the 'transition from red to grey' has entailed social, demographic and functional obstacles to rewarding social involvements for CEE older adults (de Jong Gierveld et al. 2011). Older adults in Russia and Bulgaria exhibit levels of loneliness that far exceed those of their younger counterparts. The age-related decline in older adult social relationship satisfaction is associated with increasingly precarious economic positions and impaired functional and physical health. Lost and strained spousal and intergenerational relationships brought on by widowhood, declining fertility, and migration out of the region, each the product of post-Soviet demographic trends, further threaten social relationship satisfaction. The long-standing trend of very low, below replacement fertility, coupled with a low life expectancy for Russian and Bulgarian men, equates with a sizable segment of older adults who have no, or very few, living family members. Having children and grandchildren, and having them in close proximity, appears as a bulwark against older adult loneliness. Especially in Bulgaria, where persistent emigration places many adult children of older adults at great distances, multigenerational ties between grandchildren and grandparents may prove to be pivotal to the wellbeing of both older adults and children in coming decades,

The World Health Organization has observed that programs promoting social connectedness are as vital for older adult wellbeing as those improving physical health (WHO 2002). Looking forward with CEE demographic realities in mind, social planners may well consider programs and resources to buttress the support relationships that will link members of smaller extended families, as well as efforts to enhance older adults' participation in community and civic associations that might build intra- and inter-generational supports beyond the boundaries of family.

References

Abbott, P.A., Turmov, S. and Wallace, C. 2006. Health World Views of Post-Soviet Citizens. *Social Science & Medicine* 62(1), 228–38.

Ashwin, S. and Lytkina, T. 2004. Men in Crisis in Russia: The Role of Domestic Marginalization. *Gender and Society* 18(2), 189–206.

BAGSO. 2001. *Aging in Eastern Europe*. Seniorenreport. Bundesarbeitgemainschaft der Senioren-Organisationen (BAGSO).

Bezrukov, V.V. and Verzhikovskaya, N. 1994. Status Report from Ukraine. *Aging International* 21, 54–61.

Botcheva, L.B. and Feldman, S.S. 2004. Grandparents as family stabilizers during economic hardship in Bulgaria. *International Journal of Psychology* 39(3), 157–68.

CIA World Factbook 2009. [Online: 14 September] Available at: https://www.cia.gov/library/publications/the-world-factbook/ [accessed: 14 September 2009].

Coleman, D. 2006. Europe's demographic future: Determinants, dimensions, and challenges. *Population and Development Review* 32, 52–95.

de Jong Gierveld, J. 2008. Intergenerational relationships and transfers between older adults and their co-resident and not co-resident children. Paper to the 2008 European Population Conference: Barcelona, July 2009.

de Jong Gierveld, J. and Kamphuis, F. 1985. The development of a Rasch-type loneliness scale. *Applied Psychological Measurement* 9, 289–99.

de Jong Gierveld, J. and van Tilburg, T. 1999. Living arrangements of older adults in the Netherlands and Italy: Co-residence values and behaviour and their consequences for loneliness. *Journal of Cross-Cultural Gerontology* 14(1), 1–24.

de Jong Gierveld, J., Dykstra, P.A. and Schenk, N. 2011. *Living Arrangements, Intergenerational Support Types and Older Adult Loneliness in Eastern and Western Europe*. Multilinks Report. [Online] Available at: http://multilinksproject.eu/uploads/papers/0000/0041/Multilinks_deliverable_D2.3.pdf [accessed: 26 October 2011].

Demeny, P. 2005. Policy challenges of Europe's demographic changes: From past perspectives to future prospects, in *The New Demographic Regime, Population Challenges and Policy Responses*, edited by M. Macura et al. New York: United Nations, 1–9.

Demko, G.J., Ioffe, G. and Zayonchkovskaya, J. 1999. *Population Under Duress: The Geodemography of Post-Soviet Russia*. Oxford: Westview Press.

Dykstra, P.A. 1995. Loneliness among the never and formerly married: The importance of supportive friendships and a desire for independence. *Journal of Gerontology* 50B, S321–9.

Dykstra, P.A. 2009. Older adult loneliness: Myths and realities. *European Journal of Aging* 6(2), 91–100.

Dykstra, P.A., van Tilburg, T.G. and de Jong Gierveld, J. 2005. Changes in older adult loneliness: Results from a seven-year longitudinal survey. *Research on Aging* 27, 725–47.

European Commission 2006. The Social Situation in the European Union 2005–2006: The Balance between Generations in an Ageing Europe. [Online: Directorate-General for Employment, Social Affairs and Equal Opportunities, Unit E.1, Eurostat – Unit F.3] Available at: ec.europa.eu/employment_social/social_situation/docs/ssr2005_2006_en.pdf [accessed: 3 November 2011].

Fees, B.S., Martin, P. and Poon, L.W. 1999. A model of loneliness in older adults. *Journal of Gerontology: Psychological Sciences* 54B, P231–9.

Gachter, A. 2002. The Ambiguities of Emigration: Bulgaria since 1988. International Migration Paper No. 139, Geneva, Switzerland: The International Labour Office.

Garilova, N.S. and Gavrilov, L.A. 2009. Rapidly aging populations: Russia/Eastern Europe, in *International Handbook of Population Aging*, Volume 1. Netherlands: Springer, 113–31.

Georgiev, Y. 2008. Immigration to Bulgaria – preconditions and possible developments, in *The Implication of EU Membership on Immigration Trends and Immigrant Integration Policies for the Bulgarian Labor Market*. Sofia: Economic Policy Institute, 9–24.

Geurts, T., Poortman, A-R., van Tilburg, T. and Dykstra, P.A. 2009. Contact between grandchildren and their grandparents in early adulthood. *Journal of Family Issues* 20(10), 1–16.

Giarrusso, R., Silverstein, M. and Feng, D. 2000. Psychological costs and benefits of raising grandchildren: Evidence from a national survey of grandparents, in *To Grandmother's House We Go and Stay: Perspectives on Custodial Grandparents*, edited by C. Cox. New York: Springer, 71–90.

Goodwin, R. 2006. Age and social support perception in Eastern Europe: social change and support in four rapidly changing countries. *British Journal of Social Psychology* 45, 799–815.

Hayslip, B. Jr. and Kaminski, P.L. 2005. Grandparents raising their grandchildren: A review of the literature and suggestions for practice. *The Gerontologist* 45(2), 262–9.

Iecovich, E., Barasch, M., Mirsky, J. et al. 2004. Social support networks and loneliness among elderly Jews in Russia and Ukraine. *Journal of Marriage and Family* 66, 306–17.

Johnson, D.P. and Mullins, L.C. 1987. Growing old and lonely in different societies: Toward a comparative perspective. *Journal of Cross Cultural Gerontology* 2, 257–75.

Jylhä, M. and Jokela, J. 1990. Individual experiences as cultural: A cross-cultural study on loneliness among the elderly. *Aging and Society* 10, 295–315.

Karyukhin, E. 2008. Country Report: Limited Opportunities for the Employment of Elderly People in Russia. Paper to the International Sociology Association, RC11 meetings: First ISA World Forum of Sociology, Barcelona, Spain, 6–8 September 2008.

Kaufman, G. and Uhlenberg, P. 1998. Effects of life course transitions on the quality of relationships between adult children and their parents. *Journal of Marriage and Family* 60(4), 924–38.

Koropeckyyj-Cox, T. 1998. Loneliness and depression in middle and old age: Are the childless more vulnerable? *Journal of Gerontology: Social Sciences* 53B, S303–12.

Kraus, N., Liang, J. and Gu, S. 1998. Financial strain, received support, anticipated support, and depressive symptoms in the Peoples' Republic of China. *Psychology and Aging* 13, 58–68.

Long, M.V. and Martin, P. 2000. Personality, relationship closeness, and loneliness of oldest old adults and their children. *Journal of Gerontology: Psychological Sciences* 55B, P311–19.

Lopata, M. 1995. Loneliness, in *The Encyclopedia of Aging*, edited by G.L. Maddos et al. New York: Springer, 571–2.

Ovseiko, P. 2008. Ageing emerging economies in Eastern Europe and Central Asia. *Ageing Horizons Brief*. Oxford Institute of Ageing, Oxford, UK.

Peplau, L.A. and Perlman, D. 1982. *Loneliness: A Sourcebook of Current Theory, Research, and Therapy*. New York: John Wiley and Sons.

Pietila, I. and Rytkonen, M. 2008. Coping with stress and by stress: Russian men and women talking about transition, stress and health. *Social Science and Medicine* 66, 327–38.

Pinquart, M. 2003. Loneliness in married, widowed, divorced and never-married older adults. *Journal of Social and Personal Relationships* 20, 31–53.

Rangelova, R. and Vladimirova, K. 2004. Migration from central and eastern Europe: The case of Bulgaria. *South-East Europe Review for Labour and Social Affairs* 3, 7–30.

Rantanen, J. 2002. *Work in the Global Village*. Helsinki: Finnish Institute of Occupational Health.

Rose, R. 1995. Russia as an hour-glass society: A constitution without citizens. *East European Constitutional Review* 4(3), 34–42.

Rotkirch, A. 2000. *The Man Question: Loves and Lives in Late 20th Century Russia*. Helsinki: University of Helsinki.

Schoenmaeckers, R.C. and Vanderleyden, L. 2006. *Intergenerational Solidarity, the Elderly and Aging*. Population Policy Acceptance Study, 2006, No. 8. Wiesbaden: Federal Institute for Population Research.

Sik, E. and Wellman, B. 1999. Network capital in capitalist, communist, and postcommunist countries, in *Networks in the Global Village: Life in Contemporary Communities*, edited by B. Wellman. Boulder: Westview Press, 225–54.

Tchernina, N.V. and Tchernin, E.A. 2002. Older people in Russia's transitional society: Multiple deprivation and coping responses. *Aging & Society* 22, 543–62.

Van Tilburg, T., de Jong Gierveld, J., Lecchini, L. and Marsiglia, D. 1998. Social integration and loneliness: A comparative study among older adults in the Netherlands and Tuscany, Italy. *Journal of Social and Personal Relationships* 15(6), 740–54.

Vassilev, R. 2005. Bulgaria's demographic crisis: Underlying causes and some short-term implications. *Southeast European Politics* VI(1), 14–27.

Velkoff, V.A. and Kinsella, K. 2000. *An Aging World*. Washington, DC: US Census Bureau.

Victor, C.R., Scrambler, S.J., Shah, S.G. et al. 2002. Has loneliness amongst older people increased? An investigation into variations between cohorts. *Ageing & Society* 22, 585–97.

Vikat, A., Beets, G., Billari, F. et al. 2005. Wave 1 Questionnaire Manual. [Online: Generations and Gender Programme Survey Instruments, Population Activities Unit, United Nations Economic Commission for Europe] Available at: www.unece.org/pau/_docs/ggp/GGP_QuestW1Manual.pdf [accessed: 12 December 2011].

Walker, A. 1993. *Age and Attitudes: Main Results from a Eurobarometer Survey*. Brussels: Commission of the European Communities.

World Health Organization 2002. *The World Health Report 2002: Reducing Risks, Promoting Healthy Life*. Geneva: World Health Organization.

Young, J.E. 1982. Loneliness, depression and cognitive therapy: Theory and applications, in *Loneliness: A Sourcebook of Current Theory, Research and Therapy*, edited by L.A. Peplau and D. Perlman. New York: Wiley, 379–405.

Chapter 16
Levels of Welfarism and Intergenerational Transfers within the Family: Evidence from the Global Ageing Survey (GLAS)

George W. Leeson and Hafiz T.A. Khan

The twentieth century was one of dramatic individual and population ageing in most developed countries with significant increases in the proportion of the population aged 65 years and over and in life expectancies at all ages. The twenty-first century is expected to see this ageing continue and to emerge elsewhere around the world, particularly in Asia. Population ageing will truly become a global phenomenon (Leeson and Harper 2006, 2007, 2007a, 2008). The family has always played a significant role in terms of support, particularly to dependent older people, but it can be hypothesized that increasing levels of societal welfare provision *crowd out* the family in respect of its supportive role for older people (Motel-Klingebiel et al. 2005, Leeson 2009). The demographics of support for older people are often expressed crudely in the form of the so-called old age dependency ratio (the arithmetic ratio of the absolute number of persons aged 65 and over to the number of persons aged 15–64 years), and this ratio is expected to increase steadily (even dramatically) in all 21 economies covered by this chapter in the first half of the twenty-first century. These crude demographics alone will likely pressure families, individuals and societies and consequently the supportive role of the family may take on new forms.

Filial piety – the practice of respecting and caring for one's parents in old age based on moral obligation (Hashimoto and Ikels 2005) – is under challenge in Asia (Schroder-Butterfill 2003), and children's obligation in adulthood towards their parents is increasingly developing to become one of shared familial intergenerational responsibilities as part of the natural progression of life interdependencies (Harper 1992). Intergenerational familial transfers are of importance to family members, but they can also be regarded as significant familial supplements to societal provision both financially and practically, and the transfer of financial resources in particular has a bearing on socioeconomic development (Attias-Donfut and Lapierre 2000, Attias-Donfut and Wolff 2000, Arrondel and Masson 2001, Attias-Donfut et al. 2005, Leeson 2005, 2009). Children are variously valued as demand and utility functions and as old age risk insurance, which supports the idea that levels of fertility in countries with low welfare provision would be and thereby reflect concern for old age support (Datta and Nugent 1984, Cain 1990, Schultz

1997). On the other hand, low levels of fertility are regarded as an outcome of rapid socioeconomic development, modernization and high welfare provision, and higher fertility is associated often with lower socioeconomic status of people and is regarded as being linked positively to old age social security (Cain 1991, Khan and Raeside 1994).

Fertility decline in some parts of Asia has been extremely dramatic and it is therefore pertinent to consider the consequences for intergenerational familial support in old age as families of the future shrink (Asis et al. 1995).

The slow but certain decline in the co-residency between older parents and adult children has raised additional concerns about intergenerational familial transfers in countries such as the Philippines, Thailand, Indonesia and Bangladesh – concerns which are conceivably valid elsewhere (Knodel and Ofstedal 2002, Schroder-Butterfill 2003). Intergenerational transfers – be they financial, emotional or instrumental – may have a more pronounced effect on older family members in rural areas, where filial piety is generally stronger and where family support systems are more institutionalized (Davis-Friedmann 1991). However, the demographic, social and ideological changes in recent decades have given rise to increasing concerns about the ability and willingness of families to support older family members (Leeson and Harper 2007, 2007a).

In developing countries, much of the research has focused on the support provided by children to older parents, but some research has focused on transfers down through the generations, and the role of older people as providers (rather than recipients) of support in the family and the community is acknowledged increasingly (Schroder-Butterfill 2003, Leeson and Harper 2007, 2007a). For example, grandparents provide valuable child care in families, with the role of grandfathers also attracting research attention (Chen et al. 2000, Mann and Leeson 2010).

Research has examined the determinants of intergenerational proximity and contacts between older parents and their children in a number of European countries and in the United States, and research in Asia reveals that co-residence with an adult child effects the size and frequency of upward flows of intergenerational familial support (Lawton et al. 1994, Greenwell and Bengtson 1997, Cameron 2000, Keasberry 2001, Leeson 2005, 2009, Hank 2007). While large numbers of older people in developing countries live with children or other family members, urbanization and poverty threaten the supporting role of families, and in addition, increasing female labor force participation may also pressure the supply of informal care (Sokolovsky 2000).

In Europe, interest in the effects of welfare regime on family dynamics has been intense. Esping-Andersen (1990, 1999) identified three types of welfare state regime ranging from comprehensive and (near) universal state provision of high-level benefits and services to reliance on family and self. As pointed out, the final decades of the twentieth century witnessed comprehensive changes in the structure and role of the traditional family and in the division of supportive labor between the family and the welfare state (Hagestad 1988, Bengtson et al. 1990, Kiernan and Mueller 1999, Harper 2004).

It has traditionally been assumed in the sociology of the family that the roles of family and the welfare state are substitutive (see Parsons 1943). This led to the development of the crowding out theory (Cox 1987, Costa 1996). This theory is, however, challengeable on the basis of the complexity of the relationship between the family and the welfare state in respect of support for older people (Kunemund and Rein 1999). Both aspects of the theory give rise to interesting policy issues with regard to the capability and willingness of the family to take on an increasing share of the supportive role for older people as welfare state provision is under pressure.

Regardless of the type of welfare state regime, societies are experiencing an *ageing of some life-transitions*, which when combined with the shift from a high-mortality/high-fertility to a low-mortality/low-fertility society have significant implications for both family structure and kinship roles (Farkas and Hogan 1995, Harper 2004). In an ageing population, the child-parent relationship moves from one of dependency to one of adult relationship. The common experience for many parents and children is moving towards one of around 60 years of joint life, with less than a third of this time spent in a traditional parent/dependent-child relationship (Riley 1983). Time spent as the daughter of a parent over 65 now exceeds the time spent as the parent of a child under 18, but this should be viewed against the situation that while a high proportion of these persons aged 65 years and over previously were dependent to some degree on others, this is less the case (Watkins et al. 1987). Dependence on children for help with daily living activities is now most likely to occur after age 80 (Ulhenburg 1995). The growing significance and length of old age, however, places other and additional demands on the roles and relationships of adult women in particular (Zeilig and Harper 2000).

As family structures change, an older person in need of familial support may be faced with a complex of potential providers of support, and the role of reconstituted or step families in caring for older adults is then a central issue. There is only limited research, which elucidates these phenomena, but the suggestion is that the complexities of the ensuing relationships do not lend themselves to any particular pattern or structure of care (Haskey 1998). The dominant care relationship of blood-related daughter for mother, found within non-reconstituted families, seems to remain central. Whilst there is a growing awareness of the possibilities of looser-knit, divorce-extended families, when it comes to 'the crunch' the availability of care will usually depend on access to close 'blood ties' (Dimmock et al. 2004). In addition, the child-parent dyad becomes one not of dependency but of mutual adult relationships (Riley 1983). Family structures have verticalized during the twentieth century leading to inter-generational contraction and an increase in inter-generational extension with all the implications this may have for support in later life (Bengtson et al. 1990).

It is claimed that intergenerational ties in some cases strengthened towards the last decades of the twentieth century (Dirn 1990). Intergenerational relations in respect of ageing are quite central to the social contract, which is in turn central to the survival of the social-democratic welfare state regime (Bengtson 1993). The question of intergenerational equity in relation to a redistribution of resources is thus equally central (Guillemard 1996).

Thus, for a variety of socioeconomic and demographic reasons, family structures and dynamics are being transformed and restructured, but how may this development affect intergenerational familial transfers, and how may the increasing levels of welfarism affect these transfers? These questions are pertinent in both the more developed and the emerging economies of our ageing world.

Data and Methods

This chapter utilizes data for 21 economies from the third wave of the Global Ageing Survey (GLAS), a cross-sectional survey carried out in 2004–05, 2005–06 and 2006–07 to investigate a variety of attitudes and behaviors in relation to later life, including intergenerational familial transfers (Leeson and Harper 2006, 2007, 2008).

The third wave has focused on pre- and post-retirement generations and a total of 21,233 respondents aged between 40 and 79 years were successfully interviewed in the selected economies. These economies represent significantly different welfare regimes.

The Samples

The sample framework comprised two pre- and two post-retirement generations aged 40–49, 50–59, 60–69 and 70–79 years respectively, with samples being generationally representative. If there is more than one valid respondent in the same generation in the household contacted, the person with the next birthday is interviewed. Interviews were conducted either by telephone with respondents identified via random digit dialing (including mobile telephone numbers) or face-to-face. Interview length was 20–30 minutes depending on the language. The framework ensured at least 250 completed responses in each of the four generations in each economy. In the emerging economies, samples are predominantly from urban populations.

The Instrument

The GLAS questionnaire has modules relating to socio-demographic variables (for example, educational level, occupational status and household income), subjective health and functional ability (ADLs), family structures and proximity, intergenerational and intra-familial support transfers, subjective quality of life and control, and aspirations and expectations around late life work and retirement and financial security in old age. In addition, most important sources of retirement income are categorized (government, employer, family or self).

Educational level is measured using information on completed education (primary, secondary or tertiary). Occupational status is classified by primary chief occupation comprising 11 categories of occupation. Income is measured as household income from all sources before tax and other deductions.

Variables and their Measurements

Age, gender, household size, self-appraisal of health, educational level, occupational status, marital status, and contact with parents or children respectively over the previous six months are identified as independent variables, and the effects of these variables on intergenerational familial transfers is analyzed. Four dependent intergenerational familial transfer variables are defined:

1. The receipt of financial support during the previous six months;
2. The provision of financial support during the previous six months;
3. The receipt of practical help in the home (for example, cleaning, shopping, cooking) or personal care (for example, nursing, bathing, dressing) during the previous six months; and
4. The provision of practical help in the home during the previous six months.

The survey actually asks separate questions on the receipt and provision respectively of practical help and personal care respectively, but the data reveal limited personal care transfers so in this analysis the two types of support are merged. The definition, measurement and classification of variables for the total survey group are shown in Table 16.1.

Analytical Methods

A logistic regression analysis has been used to determine the independent variables contributing to either receiving or providing transfers. This approach enables us to identify the significant predictors of the dependent variable. Odds ratios (OR) explain the effect of a particular variable compared to its corresponding reference group, and they are commonly used to explain the contribution of covariates.

Table 16.1 List of variables selected for the study

Variables	Classification and measurement	Category	Percent
Independent variables:			
Gender	Male = 0	Reference	46.4
	Female = 1		53.6
Age cohort	40–49 years = 1	Reference	25.0
	50–59 years = 2		25.1
	60–69 years = 3		25.1
	70–79 years = 4		24.8
Household size	Live alone = 1	Reference	11.7
	Live with 1 other person = 2		28.7
	Live with more than 1 other person = 3		59.6
Self-reported health	Very good = 1	Reference	22.8
	Good = 2		37.3
	Fair = 3		29.7
	Poor and very poor = 4		10.2
Education	Primary or less = 1	Reference	36.2
	Secondary = 2		33.8
	Tertiary and higher = 3		30.1
Occupation	White collar job = 1	Reference	21.8
	Blue collar job = 2		36.9
	Other jobs = 3		22.6
	Unemployed = 4		18.7
Marital status	Single = 1	Reference	5.4
	Married and long term partner = 2		71.5
	Widowed and divorced, separated = 3		23.1
Generation contact	Contact with parent's generation = 0	Reference	5.8
	Contact with children's generation = 1		94.2
Dependent variables:			
Received financial support	No = 0		79.4
	Yes = 1		20.6
Provided financial support	No = 0		62.8
	Yes = 1		37.2
Received help and care support	No = 0		72.7
	Yes = 1		27.3
Provided help and care support	No = 0		65.8
	Yes = 1		34.2

Note: Total number of respondents N = 21,233 (roughly 1000 drawn from each country).

Cross Economy Analyses of Transfers

The cross economy results are shown in Tables 16.2 and 16.3. Only significant values of the odds ratios are tabulated. Let us firstly consider the independent variables and their effects on the provision and receipt of intergenerational familial transfers.

Gender is a significant variable determining intergenerational transfers in a number of economies. Thus, as appears from the data, females are more likely to receive financial transfers in the United States, the United Kingdom, Russia, Brazil, Mexico, South Korea, Malaysia, the Philippines and South Africa, while they are more likely to receive practical and care transfers in the United Kingdom, Russia, Mexico, Hong Kong, India, South Korea, Malaysia, Taiwan, Turkey and Saudi Arabia. Females are more likely to provide financial transfers in France and the Philippines but less likely in Malaysia. In respect of providing practical and care transfers, females are more likely to provide in most of the surveyed economies, particularly in Saudi Arabia where females are almost five times more likely than males to provide these transfers to other family members.

Age is naturally and expectedly of interest. Generally speaking in the more developed economies of the survey, increasing age implies a decreasing likelihood to receive financial transfers, whilst the reverse age effect is observed in the emerging economies of the survey. This may reflect on the one hand an increasing reliance on state financial support with increasing age in the more developed economies of the survey, which relieves family members of providing transfers, and on the other hand the absence of significant state financial support in emerging economies, which increases reliance on family transfers as people age and become less able to support themselves, for example through paid work. It is also the case that increasing age increases the likelihood to receive practical and care transfers from family members. In South Africa, for example, older people aged 70–79 and 60–69 years are 2.137 times and 1.492 times respectively more likely than those of the youngest age cohort to receive practical and care transfers. In the more developed economies of Canada, the United Kingdom, France Germany, Denmark and Japan older generations of the survey are more likely to provide financial transfers to family members relative to the youngest surveyed generation. However, in the emerging economies, the pattern is more or less the opposite with the likelihood to provide such financial transfers decreasing with increasing age. It is interesting to note that across economies the likelihood to provide practical and care transfers gradually declines with increasing age, where there is a significant effect, albeit with varying intensity. So compared with the 40–49 year old reference group, the likelihood of those aged 70–79 years to provide practical and care transfers decreases to 0.511 times the likelihood in the United States, 0.312 times in the United Kingdom, 0.448 times in Russia, 0.222 in Mexico, 0.429 in China, 0.548 in the Philippines, 0.431 in Taiwan, 0.322 in Turkey, and 0.392 in Saudi Arabia.

Household size has a significant positive effect on the likelihood to receive financial transfers in Denmark, Hong Kong and South Africa so that increasing household size increases the likelihood to receive financial transfers. The same household composition effect is found with regard to the likelihood to receive practical and care transfers. For example, in South Korea someone living in a

Table 16.2 Odds ratios of significant parameters for the receipt of support by economy

	USA	Canada	UK	France	Germany	Denmark	Russia	Brazil	Mexico	China	Hong Kong	India	Korea	Japan	Malaysia	Singapore	Philippines	Taiwan	Turkey	Saudi Arabia	South Africa
Received financial support																					
Female	3.131		2.168				1.631	2.427	1.513				11.553		1.792		1.699				1.73
Age 50–59	0.500	0.409						0.528				1.389							0.551		
Age 60–69	0.199	0.317	0.290	0.170					1.624		2.269	1.509	2.423			2.001	1.614		0.488		1.689
Age 70–79	0.193	0.198	0.135	0.073	0.143				1.751		3.248	1.792	4.15			3.218	2.063				2.216
Live with 1 person											4.001										
Live with > 1 person						3.968					4.512										2.084
Good health	3.991		2.128															2.982		1.418	1.781
Fair health	5.363	2.694	3.085												1.756			4.454			2.398
Poor or very poor health	15.118	9.357	3.713						2.647			1.547				3.100		8.057			1.746
Secondary education															0.361	0.530		0.317		0.549	
Tertiary	7.503				2.673						0.390				0.312	0.361	1.805	0.126		0.382	0.601
Blue collar															2.203						
Other jobs							1.655					2.142			2.708						
Unemployed			6.648				2.455				0.541	2.625	1.789		2.950		1.820	0.282			
Married/long term partner	0.243	0.192																0.070			0.524
Widowed/divorced/separated									2.648									0.115			0.533
Children generation						0.232			0.473	0.348	11.53	2.76								0.375	

	USA	Canada	UK	France	Germany	Denmark	Russia	Brazil	Mexico	China	Hong Kong	India	Korea	Japan	Malaysia	Singapore	Philippines	Taiwan	Turkey	Saudi Arabia	South Africa
Received practical and care support																					
Female			1.752	0.076	1.682		2.475		1.776		0.429	0.731	0.089		0.538			1.863	2.134	0.623	
Age 50–59			0.646			0.496	0.682														
Age 60–69			0.289										2.356			3.247			2.237	2.171	1.492
Age 70–79				0.208			0.630			1.790		1.530	2.746					2.544	1.687	2.177	2.137
Live with 1 person	2.091		2.163								3.123	5.159							1.729		
Live with > 1 person	2.806		2.598				2.465						12.111								1.854
Good health	4.233	2.136	1.636					0.534				1.430	1.756		2.096		0.722				
Fair health			4.944			1.751				1.982		1.472			3.120		0.675	1.795			1.969
Poor or very poor health	20.743	5.338	10.156	8.715	3.477	4.018				3.189		2.142		3.934	5.360			5.556		4.526	3.170
Secondary education			2.111										0.589		0.367	0.503		0.477		0.428	
Tertiary	2.673		1.649			1.804	1.604				0.213				0.287	0.601				0.242	
Blue collar											0.390	1.370			1.995	1.849					0.620
Other jobs			0.460									1.896			2.746					0.523	
Unemployed			3.079								0.361	1.831			2.231						
Married/long term partner	0.387																				
Widowed/divorced/separated											3.926		3.620								
Children generation												2.257	0.303							2.217	

Note: Figures are at least significant at the 5% level.

Table 16.3 Odds ratios of significant parameters for the provision of support by economy

	USA	Canada	UK	France	Germany	Denmark	Russia	Brazil	Mexico	China	Hong Kong	India	Korea	Japan	Malaysia	Singapore	Philippines	Taiwan	Turkey	Saudi Arabia	South Africa
Provided financial support																					
Female			1.404																		
Age 50–59	1.707	1.411													0.491		1.293				
Age 60–69		1.542			1.547				1.384		0.594					0.360					
Age 70–79									0.418	0.558	0.279			0.258	1.879	0.548	0.371	0.464	0.306	0.342	
Live with 1 person						0.407		3.357					0.410			0.243		0.228			2.821
Live with > 1 person					0.494	0.470		4.078						0.255							3.603
Good health			1.344							0.602	1.699										
Fair health			1.585	0.585						0.579	0.471								0.435		1.589
Poor or very poor health		0.292								0.352	0.358					0.330		0.410	0.335	2.278	
Secondary education			1.615								1.621	3.394									
Tertiary	2.141	1.386	2.541	1.470	1.480	2.176			1.443			2.222		1.647		2.166		1.552	1.655	2.448	1.878
Blue collar		0.694					0.678	0.328	1.738	0.540	0.425		0.364		0.594	0.499	0.259				
Other jobs	0.721		1.445				0.605	0.428			0.478					0.551	0.338				1.707
Unemployed							0.579	0.275		0.254	0.286		0.257			0.264	0.220			0.553	
Married/long term partner			2.446				5.231									8.259				14.53	0.629
Widowed/divorced/separated			3.255				4.092							0.217		4.102				10.42	0.601
Children generation	2.745	1.712		3.677	3.093	2.088			0.388			4.975		3.509		0.423				0.345	

	USA	Canada	UK	France	Germany	Denmark	Russia	Brazil	Mexico	China	Hong Kong	India	Korea	Japan	Malaysia	Singapore	Philippines	Taiwan	Turkey	Saudi Arabia	South Africa
Provided practical and care support																					
Female	1.319			1.625				2.053	2.599	1.908	1.689	1.396	1.746	1.731	1.936		1.973	2.206		5.049	1.87
Age 50–59				1.86		1.515										0.671			0.525		
Age 60–69									0.562					1.850					0.472		
Age 70–79	0.511		0.312				0.448		0.222	0.429							0.548	0.431	0.322	0.392	
Live with 1 person	1.605							8.080	3.355			11.951				3.459			3.342		2.313
Live with > 1 person	1.925					1.956	1.596	11.747	3.379			8.646							2.651		
Good health										0.567										0.618	
Fair health						0.642					0.499	0.644		0.489		0.560				0.348	
Poor or very poor health		0.469		0.206	0.501					0.321	0.283		0.479							0.101	
Secondary education				1.668	1.445						1.693	1.587				0.665			1.715	0.346	
Tertiary				1.797								1.521									
Blue collar											0.643		0.529			0.629	0.386			0.571	
Other jobs			0.681									1.921			2.587		0.488			0.434	
Unemployed					0.387				0.483		0.568	2.687	0.478		2.216	0.570		0.369			
Married/long term partner				2.410						0.162				0.182		3.903				8.101	
Widowed/divorced/separated														0.454		5.539					
Children generation					0.447											0.426					0.567

Note: Figures are at least significant at the 5% level.

household with one other person is 5.159 times more likely to receive practical and care transfers than someone living alone and someone living in a household with at least two other people is 12.111 times more likely. Similar patterns of household size effect are found in the United States, the United Kingdom, Russia, Hong Kong and South Africa. In terms of providing financial transfers, the analyses reveal an almost stereotypical pattern with the likelihood to provide financial transfers decreasing with increasing household size in the developed economies of Germany, Denmark, and Japan (but interestingly also in Singapore and the Philippines), but increasing with increasing household size in emerging economies such as Brazil and South Africa. What it indicates is that the lager household size the greater the likelihood of providing financial supports to other members and relatives. This may be due to strong kinship structure in those countries. Where household size significantly affects the likelihood to provide practical and care transfers (in the United States, Denmark, Russia, Brazil, Mexico, South Korea and Turkey) the effect generally is one of increasing likelihood with increasing household size, which would possibly indicate transfers within the household.

Health and the likelihood to receive or provide transfers are related much as one would expect, so that those in poor health are more likely to receive transfers and less likely to provide them than those in better health across the surveyed economies. This is particularly so in respect of practical and care transfers, where those in poor health are significantly more likely to receive such transfers in almost all surveyed economies, the exceptions being Russia, Brazil, Mexico, Hong Kong, South Korea, Singapore, the Philippines and turkey where health does not significant affect the likelihood. The increased likelihood of those in poor health to receive practical and care transfers ranges from 20.743 times (the United States) greater than those in very good health to 2.142 times (India). On the other hand, the likelihood of people in poor health to provide practical and care transfers ranges from 0.101 times less (Saudi Arabia) to 0.501 (Germany).

Education has interesting significant effects on the receipt of transfers in some of the emerging economies of the survey, where higher education is associated with a significantly lower likelihood to receive financial as well as practical and care transfers. However, the likelihood to provide financial transfers increases with increasing levels of education.

The effect of occupation on the receipt and provision of transfers does reflect some economy-specific patterns. So, for example, unemployed people have a significantly greater likelihood to receive financial transfers in the United Kingdom, Russia, India, Korea and Malaysia, but a significantly lower likelihood in Hong Kong and Taiwan. Likewise, they have a significantly higher likelihood to receive practical and care transfers in (again) the United Kingdom, India and Malaysia, but a significantly lower likelihood in (again) Hong Kong. Where it has a significant effect, unemployed people are less likely to provide financial transfers in all surveyed emerging economies except Mexico, India, Malaysia, Taiwan and Turkey, while the pattern for the provision of practical and care transfers is more fragmented.

The relationship between marital status and transfers is significant in only a limited number of economies. In Hong Kong and India, those in contact with their children are more likely to receive financial transfers than those in contact with their parents (in-law), while they have significantly lower likelihood in Denmark, Mexico, China and Saudi Arabia. However, contact with children does have a significantly positive effect on the receipt of practical and care transfers in India and Saudi Arabia. Interestingly – and perhaps not surprisingly – contact with children has a significantly positive effect on the provision of financial transfers in the United States, Canada, France, Germany, Denmark, Korea and Japan, while it has negative effect in Mexico, Singapore and Saudi Arabia. Contact with children has limited significant effects on the provision of practical and care transfers – namely negative in Denmark and Singapore.

Discussion and Conclusion

While there are limitations to cross-sectional studies of transfers as they do not necessarily capture a continuity of transfer, for example, the findings of this study reveal how intergenerational familial transfers involving people aged 40–79 years are influenced by selected socioeconomic, demographic and cultural variables in individual economies and across economies. These findings may indicate how social and demographic developments impact on the nature of intergenerational transfers.

What is clear from the findings is that older people (aged 60–79 years) are not simply recipients of intergenerational familial transfers. Indeed, they are also providers of both financial and practical and care transfers, so that there is a climate of what could be called on-going reciprocity and not just reciprocity based on the transfers of contemporary older people within the family when they were younger.

While the study does reveal interesting – even surprising – differences between emerging and developed economies in the survey, which in many ways do reflect the traditional welfare regime hypotheses, they also underline that the welfare regime hypothesis is extremely complex and not simply a question of high welfare (state) provision equaling low familial provision. For example, in terms of financial transfers, the presence of universal, attractive state pension provision in the welfare states of Europe and North America does not eliminate transfers from recipients of these benefits, something which should be borne in mind by governments in emerging economies when considering the development of their own state pension schemes.

Some of the stereotypical expectations are confirmed by the findings. Females are more likely to provide practical and care transfers in the family and the better-educated are more likely to provide financial transfers, and in the emerging economies disadvantaged older people are more likely to receive – but they do also provide transfers within the family although they are less likely to do so than their more advantaged fellow citizens. As we have revealed above, *gender* is an interesting, significant variable, which determines intergenerational transfers in a number of economies. We see both within and across economies with different cultures that females are more likely to receive financial transfers, for example in the United States, the United Kingdom, Russia, Brazil, Mexico, South Korea, Malaysia, the Philippines and South Africa. In some but not all of these economies, females are also more likely to receive practical and care transfers, for example in the United Kingdom, Russia, Mexico, South Korea, and Malaysia. In other cultures, namely Hong Kong, India, Taiwan, Turkey and Saudi Arabia, females are only likely to receive practical and care transfers. Elsewhere, there is no gender significance in the receipt of either financial or practical transfers. Interestingly, gender significance in respect of providing transfers is much more restricted, so females are more likely to provide financial transfers in France and the Philippines but less likely in Malaysia, and in respect of providing practical and care transfers, females are more likely to provide in most of the surveyed economies, particularly in Saudi Arabia where females are almost five times more likely than males to provide these transfers to other family members.

Clearly, the support – both financial and practical – of older people is likely to become an area of increasing political importance as populations across the globe age and as individuals themselves experience increasing longevity. Given that the family is fundamentally important in terms of support, it will be imperative that governments across the globe implement and strengthen policies that will enable families to fulfill this supportive role.

Globally, the issue of universal pension provision is much debated and it is clearly necessary in the emerging economies in particular that the presence of intergenerational financial transfers should not be seen as a reason not to develop and introduce such production. Rather state provision should be seen as just one of a number of financial support possibilities in an increasingly long old age.

Acknowledgement

The authors wish to acknowledge the financial support of HSBC Insurance for the Global Ageing Survey.

References

Arrondel, L. and Masson, A. 2001. Family transfers involving three generations. *Scandinavians Journal of Economics* 103, 415–43.

Asis, M.M.B., Domingo, L., Knoedel, J. and Mehta, K. 1995. Living arrangements in four Asian countries: A comparative perspective. *Journal of Cross-Cultural Gerontology*, 10, 145–62.

Attias-Donfut, C. and Lapierre, N. 2000. Three generations in Guadeloupean society, in *The history of the family*. New York: Elsevier Science Inc.

Attias-Donfut, C. and Wolff, F.C. 2000. The redistributive effects of generational transfers, in *The Myth of Generational Conflict, The Family and State in Ageing Societies*, edited by S. Arber and C. Attias-Donfut. London: Routledge, 22–46.

Attias-Donfut, C., Ogg, J. and Wolff, F. 2005. European patterns of intergenerational financial and time transfers. *European Journal on Ageing* 2, 161–73.

Bengston, V. 1993. Is the 'contract across generations' changing? Effects of population aging on obligations and expectations across age groups, in *The Changing Contract across Generations*, edited by V. Bengtson and W.A. Achenbaum. New York: Aldine de Gruyter, 3–23.

Bengtson, V., Rosenthal, C. and Burton, L. 1990. Families and aging: Diversity and heterogeneity, in R.H. Binstock and L.K. George (eds), *Handbook of aging and the social sciences* (3rd ed.). San Diego: Academic Press, pp. 263–87.

Cain, M. 1990. Risk and fertility in a semi-feudal context: The case of rural Madhya Pradesh. Population Council Research Division. Working Paper 19. New York.

Cain, M. 1991. Widows, sons, and old-age security in rural Maharashtra: A comment on Vlassoff. *Population Studies* 453, 519–35.

Cameron, L. 2000. The residency decision of elderly Indonesians: A nested logit analysis. *Demography* 371, 17–27.

Chen, F., Short, S.E. and Entwistle, B. 2000. Impact of grandparental proximity on maternal childcare in China. *Population Research and Policy Review* 19, 571–90.

Costa, D.L. 1996. Displacing the family: Union army pension and the elderly's living arrangements. Working Paper 5429. Cambridge: National Bureau of Economic Research.

Cox, D. 1987. Motives for private income transfers. *Journal of Political Economy* 95, 508–46.

Datta, S.K. and Nugent, J. 1984. Are old-age security and utility of children in rural India really unimportant? *Population Studies* 38, 507–509.

Davis-Friedmann, D. 1991. *Long lives: Chinese elderly and the communist revolution*, 2nd ed. Cambridge: Harvard University Press.

Dimmock, B., Bornat, J., Peace, S. and Jones, D. 2004. Intergenerational relationships among UK stepfamilies, in *Families in Ageing Societies*, edited by S. Harper. Oxford: Oxford University Press.

Dirn, L. 1990. *La societe francaise en tendens*. Paris: Puf.

Esping-Andersen, G. 1990. *The Three Worlds of Welfare Capitalism*. Princeton: Princeton University Press.

Esping-Andersen, G. 1999. *Social Foundations of Postindustrial Economics*. Oxford: Oxford University Press.

Farkas, J. and Hogan, D. 1995. The demography of changing intergenerational relationships, in *Adult Intergenerational Relations*, edited by V. Bengtson et al. New York: Springer, 1–18.

Greenwell, L. and Bengtson, V.L. 1997. Geographic distance contact between middle-aged children and their parents: The effects of social class over 20 years. *Journal of Gerontology and Social Sciences* 52B, S13–26.

Guillemard, A.M. 1996. Equity between generations in ageing societies, the problem of assessing public policies, in *Aging and Generational Relations*, edited by T.K. Hareven. New York: Aldine de Gruyter, 157–76.

Hagestad, G.O. 1988. Demographic change and the life course: Some emerging trends in the family realm. *Family Relations* 37(4), 405–10.

Hank, K. 2007. Proximity contacts between older parents and their children: A European comparison. *Journal of Marriage and Family* 69, 157–73.

Harper, S. 1992. Caring for China's ageing population: The residential option – a case study Shanghai. *Ageing Society*, 12, 157–84.

Harper, S. 2004. Changing Families as European Societies Age. *European Journal of Sociology*, XLIV(2), 155–84.

Hashimoto, A. and Ikels, C. 2005. Filial piety in changing Asian societies, in *The Handbook of Age and Ageing*, edited by M.L. Johnson. Cambridge, Cambridge University Press.

Haskey, J. 1998. Families: Their historical context and recent trends in the factors influencing their formation and dissolution, in *The Fragmenting Family, Does It Matter?* edited by M. David. London: Institute of Economic Affairs.

Keasberry, I.N. 2001. Elder care and intergenerational relationships in rural Yogyakarta, Indonesia. *Ageing and Society* 21(5), 641–65.

Khan, H.T.A. and Raeside, R. 1994. Urban and rural fertility in Bangladesh, a causal approach. *Social Biology*, 41, 240.

Kiernan, K. and Mueller, G. 1999. Who divorces? in *Changing Britain, Families and Households in the 1990s*, edited by S. McRea. Oxford: Oxford University Press.

Knodel, J. and Ofstedal, M.B. 2002. Patterns and determinants of living arrangements, in *Well-being of the elderly in Asia: A Four Country Comparative Study*, edited by A.I. Hermalin. Ann Arbor: University of Michigan Press, 143–84.

Kunemund, H. and Rein, M. 1999. There is more to receiving than needing: Theoretical arguments and empirical explorations of crowding in and crowding out. *Ageing & Society* 19, 93–121.

Lawton, L., Silverstein, M. and Bengtson, V. 1994. Affection, social contact, and geographic distance between adult children and their parents. *Journal of Marriage and Family* 56, 57–68.

Leeson, G.W. 2005. Changing patterns of contact with and attitudes to the family in Denmark. *Journal of Intergenerational Relationships* 3(3), 25–45.

Leeson, G.W. 2009. The myth of welfarism crowding out family in old age: The Danish experience. *Hallym International Journal of Aging* 1, 33–47.

Leeson, G.W. and Harper, S. 2006. *The Global Ageing Survey (GLAS) – Attitudes to Ageing and Later Life*. Research report 106. Oxford: Oxford Institute of Ageing, University of Ageing.

Leeson, G.W. and Harper, S. 2007. *The Global Ageing Survey (GLAS) – Ageing and Later Life, United Kingdom*. Research report 107. Oxford: Oxford Institute of Ageing, University of Ageing.

Leeson, G.W. and Harper, S. 2007a. *The Global Ageing Survey (GLAS) – Ageing and Later Life, the Americas*. Research report 207. Oxford Institute of Ageing, University of Ageing, Oxford.

Leeson, G.W. and Harper, S. 2008. *Some descriptive findings from the Global Ageing Survey (GLAS) – Investing in Later Life*. Research report 108. Oxford: Oxford Institute of Ageing, University of Ageing.

Mann, R. and Leeson, G.W. 2010. Grandfathers in contemporary families in Britain: evidence from qualitative research. *Journal of Intergenerational Relations* 8(3), 234–48.

Motel-Klingebiel, A., Tesch-Roemer, C. and von Kondratovitz, H.-J. 2005. Welfare states do not crowd out the family: Evidence for mixed responsibility from comparative analyses. *Ageing & Society* 25, 863–82.

Parsons, T. 1943. The kinship system of the contemporary United States. *American Anthropologist* 45, 22–38.

Riley, M. 1983. The family in an ageing society: A matrix of latent relationships. *Journal of Family Issues* 4, 439–54.

Schroder-Butterfill, E. 2003. Pillars of the family: Support provided by the elderly in Indonesia. Working paper WP303, Oxford: Oxford Institute of Ageing.

Schultz, T.P. 1997. Demand for children in low income countries, in *Handbook of Population and Family Economics*, edited by M.R. Rosenzweig and O. Stark. Amsterdam: Elsevier Science Publishers, 349–430.

Sokolovsky, J. 2000. Living arrangement of older persons and family support in less developed countries. [Online] Available at: http://www.un.org/esa/population/publications/bulletin42../sokolovsky.pdf [accessed: 2 November 2011].

Uhlenberg, P. 1995. Demographic influences on intergenerational relationships, in *Adult Intergenerational Relations*, edited by V. Bengston, K.W. Schaie and L. Burton, New York: Springer, 19–25.

Watkins, S., Menken, J. and Bongaarts, J. 1987. Demographic foundations of family change. *American Sociological Review* 52, 346–58.

Zeilig, H. and Harper, S. 2000. Locating Grandparents. Working Paper WP3/00, Oxford Centre on Population Ageing, University of Oxford.

Chapter 17

Conclusion: Global Ageing in the Twenty-First Century – Where to From Here?

Susan McDaniel and Zachary Zimmer

Global ageing, about which much has been said and written, is both welcomed and feared. It is welcomed as a societal good, an indication that quality of life is sufficiently good in increasing numbers of countries and regions of the world that people do not die as often in infancy or youth, but more have the opportunity to live long and healthy lives. Global ageing is also an indication of peoples' control over childbearing, so that they more completely approximate having the number of children they want and can afford. Even in societies with very low birthrates (some of which are currently oldest demographically), however, there is never complete control of fertility. Global ageing is also feared and fretted about by policy-makers who are concerned with possible labor shortages, increased health care costs, and how to care for more elders who may be disabled and/or have chronic health problems.

Population ageing is often characterized as a challenge of the global North, the more economically developed part of the world. Often, population challenges in some of the less developed regions of the world, or the global South, are thought to center around high birthrates, in essence, too little demographic ageing. Both have been the subject of public and policy debate and discussion, the latter often in the context of food security, drought and other crises, and the idea that population growth may burden economic growth or the environment. Population ageing in the more developed world has become almost a daily mantra, with worries of all kinds expressed from loss of productivity to health care burdens. At times, population ageing is perceived as a problem to be solved, possibly by immigration of younger people, incentives to increase the birthrate, or increasing taxes/decreasing benefits to old people. Most so-called demographic solutions to population ageing have been revealed by research as non-viable, and ageing, although not without challenges, may not be as much of a crisis for public purse as some think.

In this volume, we have examined population ageing in various ways and in many contexts across the globe. No single volume, of course, can be comprehensively global, as we noted in our introduction. Population ageing clearly poses opportunities and challenges for societies and policies, but neither the opportunities nor the challenges are uniform worldwide. Dynamic factors are at work impacting how population ageing is influencing, and will influence, people and places. Here, we have focused on three overarching themes that we see as critical to understanding of global ageing in this early quarter of the twenty-first century: healthy ageing and health care; ageing workforce, retirement and the provisions of pensions; and shifting intergenerational relations. In some of the chapters, multi-country comparisons are made; in others, the focus is on one region or country. All contribute in vital and important ways to understanding global ageing and to pointing out what lies ahead.

Population ageing, even apart from its global context, is a complex, multi-layered process, as the Héran chapter shows. At least four factors are known to contribute, although not all to the same degree. First, there is the rise in life expectancy, which although not universal across the globe, is nonetheless a dominant narrative of modernity. Russia is a notable exception to this secular trend, with its precipitous drop in life expectancy, mainly male, in recent decades. A second and significant factor is declining birthrates, as outlined both in our introductory chapter. A third, related factor is differential cohort size as the large generations such as the post-World War II baby boom, characteristic of some western countries, moves into the older years. And lastly, an increasingly important factor is the outmigration from some countries of younger people. This may particularly characterize the less developed countries, but also has been true for countries such as those of the former Eastern Bloc and the Middle East.

Although it is the case that the demographically oldest countries tend to be in the more economically developed parts of the world, Japan and some countries in Europe, the less developed countries are becoming demographically old at a very fast pace. This has led some to pronounce that these countries are the 'new old' whereas the more developed countries are the 'old old' (AARP 2003). Population ageing, particularly if rapid, along with economic globalization, are major forces shaping the world, including the balance of prosperity and opportunities across the world. To this point, most research has been directed to comparisons among countries, with attention to the relative degrees of population ageing in less developed countries compared to more developed. Going forward, however, it is anticipated that the focus will shift dramatically since ageing will pose much more serious challenges for the new old countries. In essence, the new old regions of the world will be old before becoming well off. It was the opposite sequence for the 'old old' regions. And there was more time to anticipate the implications population ageing posed for more developed countries.

Our Volume

This volume focuses on three particular challenges of global ageing: health, health care and wellbeing; ageing workforce, retirement and pensions; and shifting intergenerational relations. In each of the three sections, insights and analyses from different parts of the world are offered.

Prior to the chapters in the thematic sections, the chapter by Héran offers an overview of the population ageing processes in global comparative perspective.

With examples taken from various parts of the world, he shows how complex the population ageing process is. He also reveals the folly of some policy proposals, such as dramatically increasing the birth rates through various incentives, or increasing immigration to counter population ageing. Héran ends with his insights on the essential paradox of demography and demographic change: between the inexorable march of age structures over time, and of human agency in choosing what is best at the individual and familial levels.

Opening the section on healthy ageing and health care, Alam shows that in India, population is ageing and posing policy challenges, despite the image of India as a young country with high birthrates. He points out that even in India, there has been a sustained decline in birthrates and a rapid growth in the older population, posing challenges both present and future to policies. Given that the fastest growing elder population in India, as elsewhere, is women, the challenges are more severe given that women are more often in poorer socio-economic groups, have more frailty in old age including more multiple disabilities, and less strength on standardized tests. Widows in Delhi, according to Alam's findings from a small scale study that measures functional abilities, are significantly worse off on all counts than other women, and certainly worse off than men. The challenges for the future are great as India works to assist older populations.

Ajrouch and colleagues look at ageing and health in a part of the world about which little is known, the Middle East. It is presumed by some that the Middle East, with higher than global average birth rates, is not ageing, but in fact, it is. Arab countries, according to Ajrouch and colleagues, follow the overall trend in less developed countries toward ageing, with the added challenge that political instability and conflict create unusual conditions for the well-being of older adults whose life courses may have been much affected over time. This examination of Algeria, Lebanon and Palestine finds that a marked epidemiological transition has occurred with chronic diseases rapidly replacing infectious illnesses as the primary causes of death. Family care and provisioning matters to older people in the Arab world, particularly older women, in the absence of welfare states and other options for family support. A striking number of older women, particularly in Palestine, live alone. This analysis offers a baseline, but reveals that more and better data are needed as well as policies that could address the ageing challenges of the Arab world.

The Crimmins et al. analysis of comparative physiological changes with ageing relies on unique data sources from various countries and sub-national populations that include biomarker measurements. The accumulated harmonized data includes countries that are both now demographically old(er) and rapidly ageing. What is really fascinating about this innovative first-time analysis of comparative biomarkers is the finding that many markers are not correlated at all with ageing across the various countries. This means that there is little that is physiologically consistent with ageing across societies. Even biomarkers that vary with socio-economic status are not found to vary across societies consistently. For both future research and policy on global ageing, these findings are highly significant.

The connection of religion to healthy ageing has been shown, but primarily in western countries. It has been found that part of the effect is social, in that religious practice and participation in western religions tends to be a socially interactive experience. In Asian religions, however, religious is much more of an individual activity, less focused on meetings and social interactions. The question asked by Hidajat, Zimmer and Hurng in their chapter is whether religion, as practiced in Taiwan, has the same salutary effect among the aged as it does in western societies. Taiwan is an interesting case study since it is one of the most rapidly ageing societies in the world. The findings, based on analysis of the Taiwan Survey of Health and Living Status of the Middle Aged and Elderly, are that religious activities do have some positive associations with healthy ageing, lowering risks of disability onset and death, and increasing likelihood of recovery from disability. In essence, there are few differences in effects of religion on health with ageing, in Taiwan and in the west. In Taiwan, however, those who are more religious experience better transitions to improved health states, whether or not they practice their religion publicly. Pathways other than the social support aspect of religion, found in studies of western countries, may be operative in Asian contexts. For example, meditative activities may be equally beneficial for health.

Sub-Saharan Africa has been little studied with respect to population ageing, in part because this region has not been thought to be ageing. Aboderin's chapter addresses the policy challenges facing sub-Saharan African countries associated with the health of ageing populations. She highlights the impasse on policy action resulting from a combination of lack of political will and lack of clarity over what programs should be developed. Her conclusion is that policy action is warranted on several fronts.

Jonathan Swift, the eighteenth-century Irish satirist, wrote about being careful in wishing for a longer life. In *Gulliver's Travels*, he 'encounters' the Struldbrugs in the land of Luggnagg, who are immortal; they do not die but continue ageing perpetually. The chapter by Deeg could be said to build on Swift's insights. Based on data from the Longitudinal Aging Study of Amsterdam, she explores three prominent beliefs about ageing societies: that increasing longevity means living longer healthy; that it implies ageing with fewer chronic diseases and mobility limitations; and that future cohorts will be healthier than current older cohorts. Deeg finds that the Amsterdam longitudinal data do not support these myths. However, she suggests that her findings do not necessarily mean that the myths will not find support in other countries. She reports that the notion that all older people experience similar declines is not supported by her data. This is consistent, of course, with Crimmins and colleagues' analyses. In fact, socially advantaged elders with higher education and a partner, do much better with healthy ageing trajectories.

The volume turns next to labor market issues in global ageing. The Rada chapter takes a wide lens look at economic challenges of global ageing in both more and less developed countries. The chapter's historical overview reveals that dependency ratios, which really do not capture actual dependencies since all those of working age are never all working and all those 65+ are not economically dependent, may not be a good guide for policy in rethinking public pensions. In fact, Rada points out economies around the world have weathered high demographic 'dependency' ratios in the past. She finds, based on excellent international data, that population ageing will not create labor constraints as large as those predicted. Most countries have significant labor reserves on which to draw, and with increased life expectancies, the interest in working longer is likely, aided perhaps by policy incentives. Lastly, and very importantly, Rada concludes that dealing successfully with any economic challenges posed by global ageing, is best done by stimulating innovation and productivity growth.

While global ageing is occurring, meanings of old age are changing. The chapter by Komp looks at these changes in Europe. She argues that the previous image of older people is one of frailty and earned inactivity in retirement. It is being replaced by concepts of older people being an untapped labor source, and by active ageing. Mandatory retirement in Europe provides Europeans with a sense of entitlement to retirement and pensions that they feel they have earned by contributing to the economy and society. Policies intended to keep people in the labor market longer have been met with protests in some countries of Europe. Komp seems to laud the possibility of return to the image of older people as frail and entitled to a period of inactivity, in that it could decrease intergenerational tensions. Time will tell.

Jovic and McMullin juxtapose global ageing trends with the emergence of new economies based on global reach, use of information and knowledge. The question is: how will older workers fare as they are encouraged to work longer in a knowledge economy? They focus on the information technology (IT) sector in Canada as a case study, relying on intensive qualitative interviews. The analysis is part of a large international comparative study of IT work, *Workforce Aging in the New Economy*. The findings are striking. The IT sector is volatile, precarious and focused on youth, flexibility and risk-taking. The prevalent image of youth teaching elders about technology comes to mind. The IT sector workers tend to see people as 'old' much earlier than what society sees as old. Older workers, some as young as their 30s, are seen as less open to change, less willing to learn and prone to fatigue. Young IT workers do, however, see the stereotypes in themselves. Ageing as an IT worker in the new economy, can be risky.

The last set of chapters focus on intergenerational aspects of global ageing. Gender and marital status are known to matter to global ageing, particularly to policy. Arber's chapter looks closely at four societal changes that impact intergenerational flows of caring and financial support: transnational and rural-urban migration; increased women's labor market participation; decreasing intergenerational co-residence; and declining fertility. She particularly addresses the realities that older populations tend toward having more women and more widows than younger populations, with implications that intersect with all four of the changes above. Older women without partners are more likely than other older persons to be poor, without co-resident family, and with smaller numbers of children than women had in the past. They are more likely to experience welfare state retrenchment on their skins as they need more supports and services.

Filial obligations are often presumed to be cultural. In Chappell's chapter, we find a study of three cultural groups: Caucasian Canadians, Chinese Canadians and Hong Kong Chinese. Based on in-depth interviews, Chappell examines the relationship between filial attitudes toward ageing parents as an indicator of bonding/social cohesion, or of social capital – an actual resource. Attitudes among Caucasian Canadians toward parental care have little bearing on whether offspring provide care. For the Canadian Chinese, social beliefs matter more for care provision than for the Hong Kong group, a finding that remains even with controls for health of both the caregiver and care recipient, socio-economic status and various demographic variables. Cultural differences in intergenerational attitudes matter but contexts matter too. Even without filial attitudes, care is provided by non-Chinese to ageing relatives.

Fast's chapter focuses specifically on caregiving for elders, which she describes as becoming normative. Most eldercare, she finds based on Canada-wide data, is intergenerational, with caring for an ageing parent being the most common. Spouses also provide a significant amount of care to ailing spouses. That said, caring for non-seniors, is found to have the biggest impact on caregivers, something policy should consider.

Korinek looks at the interesting question of loneliness of older people in a part of world that has experienced population decline, Eastern Europe. In particular, she examines the situation of elders in Russia and Bulgaria in contexts of unique economic and demographic strains. She finds in what she terms the transition from 'red to grey' a great deal of loneliness and social isolation, accompanied by impaired health and precarious economic security. Bulgaria, in particular, faces a bleak future as youth migrate, weakening intergenerational ties.

Leeson and Khan rely on the Oxford University *Global Ageing Survey*, a survey of 21 economies on five continents that taps into attitudes and behaviors in later life, including on intergenerational matters. They find differences between emerging and developed countries in intergenerational familial transfers. For example, in more developed countries, older generations are more likely to provide financial transfers to younger family members. In less developed countries, however, the opposite is found: financial transfers in families decrease with age. Overall, it is found that older people are not simply recipients of intergenerational transfers, but also providers of transfers. What is revealed clearly is that the relationship between welfare state provision of supports and familial transfers is far more complex than the 'crowding out' concept believes. 'Crowding out', a popular notion in the European research on welfare states and ageing, suggests that state provision of benefits crowds out familial supports. Here, however, it is apparent that availability of universal pensions does not eliminate intergenerational transfers, an important policy consideration.

Global Ageing from Here

Population ageing will not end, or even subside, in the future. People whose lives come more and more under their control, tend to exert their preferences for smaller families and better quality lives, including better sanitation, better food and better access to good health care. All of these propel the globe into ever more aged societies. Is this a challenge? Yes, particularly in the anticipation and transition. Is it an opportunity? By all means! Few of us would chose not to have control over our family sizes, or to die young of various infectious and chronic illnesses.

The focus on global ageing is relatively new both in population studies and in interdisciplinary research on ageing. What do we see as the issues arising in global ageing research as we go forward? We see three sets of compelling challenges for scholars/researchers. The first is to connect the insights and theories of globalization scholars to global ageing. Questions here would include how demographic forces and factors interconnect with social and economic globalizing forces to shape not only the ageing experience, but the processes by which ageing is seen and analyzed. The second challenge to scholars of global ageing going forward is to continue the development of comparable data. Excellent data exists in countries such as the United States with its 14 National Institute of Aging centers (Scheoni and Ofstedal 2011), and in Europe with the Survey of Health Aging and Retirement in Europe (SHARE) We should continue to collect comparable data and work towards ways of harmonizing and making more usable data already collected for cross-national comparisons. And topic-specific international networks exist. That said, much of the data and certainly the analyses needed to understand ageing globally, is either not there in many less developed countries or inaccurate, incomplete or particularly focused, even though the latter are ageing more rapidly and will have many more older people than in more developed countries in the near future. Demographic data may exist but lacking is the sense of ageing as experienced by older people and the kinds of analyses necessary to develop solid policy and planning. The third challenge is the absence of serious conceptual frames for analyzing ageing on a global scale, to which we now turn.

The chapters in this volume have shown much about the contours of ageing globally and dispelled many myths and misunderstandings. No volume, no matter how lengthy, can include all dimensions of a topic as large as global ageing. This volume is no exception. If a significant dimension is missing in global ageing, it would be theoretical framing. Age as a structural yet changing feature of societies, around which privileges and responsibilities are allocated, has been theorized by classical social theorists ranging from Talcott Parsons and Robert Merton (structural functionalism), Gerald Lenski and Ralph Dahrendorf (social conflict), Georg Simmel and George Homans (social exchange), George Herbert Mead and Irving Goffman (symbolic interactionism), and Alfred Schütz and Peter Berger (social constructivism). Micro perspectives on ageing have been theorized most notably by disengagement theory (Cumming and Henry 1961) and, in parallel, activity theory (Burgess 1960). Both focus on individuals as they age with an eye toward the societal context with its norms, expectations and constraints. Disengagement theory focuses on older people taking a more passive role as they age when their societal participation may no longer be so highly valued. Activity theory, on the other hand, sees older people as assuming new roles and activities as they age and continue to lead productive lives.

Life course theory has been fundamentally important in research in the more developed regions, with Elder's pioneering study of *Children of the Great Depression* (1974) leading the way. Data have been developed over years and decades with a longitudinal frame that enable the following of individuals over time as social and economic conditions change. Similar analyses are not possible with comparable data in the less developed global regions, however, where lives may be even more marked by historical events occurring at crucial life course stages. These life course markings may be independent of processes of ageing but have implications for later life. Much more can be learned about global ageing through a life course lens.

There are other aspects of global ageing in need of infusing with a theoretical frame. One is the question of inequality and imbalance on a global scale. Thus, looking at countries as case studies, or even in comparative perspective at one point in time misses the dynamics of global migration, which often has an age and skills component. Youth tend to be mobile, globally as well as regionally. Regionally, globalization and changing economic and social dynamics that come with it is leading younger aged adults to migrate out of rural areas for the prospect of jobs and a better life in urban areas across many developing countries. Many are moving toward the bright lights of cities, while their older relatives remain behind in rural areas. Since the current generation of older adults in developing countries still has large families, this does not necessarily mean they are left alone. But it does mean that intergenerational relations are taking on new forms, and we are in need of both data and frameworks that can help us understand the long-term impacts on older persons. Globally, immigration policies of more developed countries increasingly seek the skills of youth, but block immigration of older relatives. This may have little impact on overall demographic ageing of any given country, but can have significant implications for families and for care demands, as well as possibly for labor demands in the countries of emigration. It can also have an unintended effect on family sizes as the older relatives who are often the child minders in immigrant families, may not be there to help, thereby constraining birth rates even more.

Further, there can be counter-intuitive effects of the inequalities of migration on global ageing. One such is found in research by Hazan and Zoabi (2011). The fact of higher birth rates in the United States where there are few public options for childcare and minimal policy supports for having children has long puzzled researchers. Hazan and Zoabi find the answer, or at least a possible answer in the large inequalities found in the US between immigrant women, often Hispanic, and middle and upper class Americans. It is the supply of cheap marketized caregivers that seems to drive educated American women to substitute inexpensive and readily available market childcare services for their own time, enabling them to have larger families. It is an explanation for higher birthrates in the American south when slavery was common (Glenn 2010).

What do we see as the issues arising in global ageing policy going forward? It is important to have acknowledgement by policy-makers, both in countries and globally, that population ageing is already upon the world not only in the more developed countries, but also in the less developed countries. That penny has not yet dropped in many policy circles. The focus of much international population aid programming remains on lowering birthrates that are already falling without policy intervention. Key for international programs is shifting their focus to the challenges that ageing populations may pose for less developed countries for whom population ageing has happened very rapidly. These countries often lack the resources to deal with increased numbers and proportions of elders in their populations.

There are important lessons here for policy. There is a dual image of ageing societies: either that we will all age well and happily, or that ageing populations will be the doom of social programs and societal cohesion. What we have seen in the chapters of this volume is that there is some truth and some falsity in both of these images. There are clearly risks to the image of happy and contented ageing, with growing tendencies toward poverty or income challenges in the older years, particularly for women and even more so for widows, increasing probability of chronic illnesses, isolation and lack of family support. That said, we are overall living into the later years in a healthier state. Policy discourse on population ageing may need to attend to the diversity of ageing and that older people are as often contributors to society, through work, taxes, and provision of care and voluntary services as they are dependent on societal services and transfers.

Tackling of ageism may be a crucial theme in addressing the challenges of population ageing both in more and less developed countries. Seeing older people as dependent may be completely inaccurate as more people 65 and above, continue to work in the paid labor force, continue to contribute to their families through transfers of wealth and caregiving, and continue to be active in their communities. No matter what the age is for becoming or being seen as 'old', for it varies widely across societies, older people more often remain contributing members of societies. Smart policy in both more and less developed countries as well as international policy, would recognize these contributions and build on them.

Lastly, in the realm of policy challenges for future, connections matter. In a global world, we are not isolates. Families increasingly connect between more and less developed countries. Market forces cannot address the challenges of population ageing, despite rhetoric to the contrary. Ageing remains a social policy challenge, exacerbated by growing income inequalities in societies and across societies. The concept of retirement is changing in all regions of the world. As a middle class develop in emerging economies and in the less developed countries, flexibility in working life course and in the concept and timing of retirement is likely to be under discussion. As well, as the knowledge and embodied wisdom of workplaces becomes more valued in all parts of the world, the notion of glorified youth is likely to lessen. Youth will be less sought after as consumers and workers as what older workers can offer becomes more apparent and valued.

We need to remain cognizant that the number of people that will be old and have health issues, such as disabilities and chronic disorders, is going to grow quickly into the future. Policy must anticipate their needs and build programs to support them. Norms about caring for older relatives in families are being challenged by globalization of families, of work and of concepts of what families can and should do. Policy can no longer automatically assume that families, and particularly women within families, will be able to provide needed care. Long held notions regarding caregiving will require testing as population ageing advances and family sizes decline. Targeting people by life style choices made eons ago in a different era is to punish people for living long.

Challenges remain for understanding and addressing global ageing in the future. There is, however, a solid base of knowledge and insights from which to build. We hope that this volume in its breadth and depth of coverage illustrates that base. We are hopeful that the chapters here provide a kind of intellectual and policy trampoline from which we can spring into a bright future where people and societies age well and with dignity and respect.

References

AARP 2003. The New Old World: Challenges and Opportunities of Aging Populations. [Online: American Association of Retired People] Available at: http://www.aarp.org/about-aarp/press-center/info-2003/thenewoldworld.html [accessed: 23 January 2012].
Burgess, E.W. 1960. *Aging in Western Societies*. Chicago: University of Chicago Press.
Cumming, E. and Henry, W.E. 1961. *Growing Old: The Processes of Disengagement*. New York: Basic Books.
Elder, G.H. Jr. 1974. *Children of the Great Depression*, 2nd ed. Chicago: University of Chicago Press.
Glenn, E.N. 2010. *Forced to Care: Coercion and Caregiving in America*. Cambridge, MA: Harvard University Press.
Hazan, M. and Zoabi, H. 2011. Do Highly Educated Women Choose Smaller Families? Discussion Paper No. 8590, Centre for Economic Policy Research.
Higa, M. and Williamson, J. B. 2011. Global aging, in *Handbook of Sociology of Aging*, edited by R. A. Settersten and J. Angel. New York: Springer, 117–30.
Schoeni, R.F. and Ofstedal, M.B. 2010. Key Themes in Research on the Demography of Aging. *Demography*, 47(Suppl 1), S5–15.

Index

Aboderin, I. 9, 312
absolute age 24, 25, 26
ADLs (activities of daily living) 67–68
    caregiving 240, 241, 242–43, 244, **245–47**
    India 35–37, **38**, 38–41, **39**, **40–41**, 43
    religious activities 107, 110, 112–14, **113**
Africa **5**, 6, **7**, 7, 8, *20*, 24, 160, 297
age structure 1, 2–3, 4, 8, 21–22, 24, 26, 33, 311
ageing 11, 79, 149
ageing populations 4, 7–8, 139, 221, 222, 231, 293, 317
ageing process 13–15, *15*, 17–18, 19–21, 25–26, 27, 79–80, 159, 160–62, 195–96, 238, 310–11
Ajrouch, K.J. 9, 311
Alam, M. 9, 311
Algeria *25*, 50, **51**, 53, 56, 57, 70, 311
    family structure 57, 58, **60**, 62, **62**, 63, 69
    fertility rates 24, 54
    health 60, **61**, 67, **68**
    life expectancy **51**, 53, **222**
    social relations 58, **60–61**, 63, 64, **65**, 66, 69
    socio-economic status 59, **61**, 66–67, **67**, 70
Arber, S. 10–11, 313
Ashwin, S. and Lytkina, T. 272
Australia 3, **5**, **7**, 239

baby boom 3, 13–14, 16, 17–18, 22
biomarkers 79, 81–82, 97–98, 311
    blood pressure 79, 80, 81, 82–83, *84*, *85*, *86*, **95**, 97, 98
    body mass index 80, 87, *88*, **142**
    cholesterol 79, 80, 81, 89, *90*, *91*, *92*, 94, **95**, 95, 96, 97, 98

glycosylated hemoglobin *93*, 94, 97, 98
birth rates 24, 216, 309, 311, 316–17
blood pressure 79, 80, 81, 82–83, *84*, *85*, *86*, **95**, 97, 98
body mass index (BMI) 80, 87, *88*, **142**
Brazil **7**, 8, *23*, *25*, **164**, 297, 302, 304
    fertility rates 3, **5**
    life expectancy **222**, 223
    marital status 230, **230**
Bulgaria 267, 268, 270–71, 272, **273**, 273, **277**, 285, 314
    intergenerational relations 269, 270, 276, 282–83, 284, 285
    loneliness 267, 268–69, 276, **278–79**, 280–83, **280–81**, 284, 285

Canada 3, **222**, 238–39, 303
    caregiving 240, 241–43, 244–45, **245–46**, 253–54
    Caucasian Chinese 239, 240, 242, 243, 244, **245**, 246, 314
    Chinese 239, 240, 241–42, 243, 244, **245**, 246, 314
    marital status *226*, 226, **228**, 228, 229, **230**
caregiving 10, 220–21, 255–56, *256*, 257–63, **258**, **260**, **262**, *263*, 264, 269, 314, 316–17, 318
    ADLs 240, 241, 242–43, 244, **245–47**
    Canada 240, 241–43, 244–45, **245–46**, 253–54
    filial responsibility 235–36, 237, 238–39, 240, 243, 244, 314
Caucasian Chinese, Canada 239, 240, 242, 243, 244, **245**, 246, 314
CDM (count data model) **42**, 43, **45**, **46**
Chappell, N.L. 10, 239–40, 314
childcare 219–20, 231, 292, 316–17
China 3–4, **7**, 8, *20*, 20–21, 22, 27, 79, 80, 98, 216

blood pressure 83, *84*, *85*, *86*
body mass index 87, *88*
cholesterol 89, *90*, *91*, *92*
fertility rates 3–4, **5**
filial piety 235, 237–38
glycosylated hemoglobin *93*, 94
grandparents 218, 219
life expectancy 80, *81*, **222**, 223
Chinese Canadians 239, 240, 241–42, 243, 244, **245**, **246**, 314
cholesterol 79, 80, 81, 89, *90*, *91*, *92*, 94, **95**, 95, 96, 97, 98
chronic diseases 9, 96, 125, 143–44, *144*, *145*, 145, 146–47, 148, 151
CNCD (chronic non-communicable diseases) 122, 123, 124, 130, 131
co-residence
　intergenerational relations 69, 216, 217, *217*, 218–19, 231, 269, 292, 313–14
　loneliness 275, 282, 283
Cowgill, D.O. and Holmes, L.D. 10
Crimmins, E. 9, 311, 312
crowding out theory 293, 314
Cuba **222**, 224, *225*

DBP (diastolic blood pressure) 81, 82, 83, *85*, **95**, 97, 98
Deeg, D.J.H. 9, 312
Delhi, India 9, 34, 37, 43, 311
　ADLs **38**, 38–41, **39**, **40–41**
demographic indicators 24, 27, 28
demographic projections 15–16, 26–28, 33, 43, 121, 160, 315
demographic windows 21–22, 24, 26
dependency rates 21, 161–62, 188, 312–13
　economic rates 162, 164–65, *165*, 172
　old-age rates 159, 162, *163*, **164**, 169, 171, 291
disabilities 33, 146, 253, 254, 264, 280
　chronic diseases 143–44, *144*, 145, 146–47, 148
　functional decline 149–51, **150**

Eastern Europe 7, **161**, **162**, **164**, 179, 180, 270–71, 285
　fertility rates 3, **5**, 6
　life expectancy 160, 223

loneliness 10, 267–68, 269, 270, 272, 283, 314
economic dependency rates 162, 164–65, *165*, 172
eldercare providers *217*, 217–18, 220–21, 237–38, 255–63, *256*, **258**, **260**, **262**, *263*, 264, 314
emigration 14, 22, 57, 66, 70, 270–71, 285
England 79, 80
　blood pressure 83, 97, 98
　body mass index 87, 98
　cholesterol 89
　glycosylated hemoglobin 94
Europe 2, 8, 175, 176, 177, 180–83, 184–87, 188–89, 292–93
　labor force **166**, 166–67, 215–16
　retirement 176, 177, 180, 183–84, **184**
　retirement age *178*, 178–80, **180**, 183, 186, 188, 313
　working-age population 176, *181*, 182–83

family structure 10, 34, 51–52, 62–63, 216, *217*, 217–19, 292–94
　Algeria 57, 58, **60**, 62, **62**, 63, 69
　Lebanon 53, 54–55, 57, 58, **60**, 62, **62**, 69
　Palestine 52, 57, 58, **60**, 62, **62**, 63, 69
Fast, J. 10, 314
fertility rates 1, 2–6, **5**, 14, 16–17, 18, 21, 24, 54, 291–92
　replacement rates 5–6, 13, 16, 216
Filial Expectancy Scale 240
filial piety 10, 235, 237–38, 243, 291, 292, 314
Filial Piety Measure 240
filial responsibility 235–36, 237, 238–39, 240, 243, 244, 314
financial flows 58, 63–65, 218, 219, 221, 304
financial transfers 297–303, **298–99**, **300–301**, 302, 304, 314
France 7, 8, *17*, **164**, 297, 303, 304
　fertility rates **5**, 16, 18
　life expectancy **222**, 223, 224, *225*, 226
　marital status **228**, 229, **230**
　working-age population 21–22, *181*
functional decline 149–51, **150**, 196

functional disabilities 67–68
    caregiving 240, 241, 242–43, 244, **245–47**
    India 35–37, **38**, 38–41, **39**, **40–41**, 43
    religious activities 107, 110, 112–14, **113**

Germany 14–15, *15*, 16–17, 18, **164**, 167, 269, 297, 303
    productivity growth 169, **170**, 170
    retirement age 180, 183
    working-age population *181*, 182
GGS (Generations and Gender Surveys) 268, 273–74, 275, 276, 280, 284, 285
GLAS (Global Ageing Survey) 11, 294–95, **296**, 296–303, **298–99**, **300–301**, 314
global ageing 309, 315–16
global population 1, 2–3, 4, 6–8, **7**, 159
glycosylated hemoglobin (HbA1c) *93*, 94, 97, 98
grandparents 216, 218, 219–20, 221, 269, 292

Hazan, M. and Zoabi, H. 316
health 8–9, 33–34, 56, 60, **61**, 67–68, **68**, 70, 311
health care 8–9, 44, 96–97, 140, 146, 223–24, 309
    SSA 124–25, 126–28, 129–30, 133
Héran, F. 8, 310–11
Hidajat, M.M., Zimmer, Z. and Hurng, B.-S. 9, 312
Hong Kong 22, 229, 230, **230**, 297, 302, 303, 304
Hong Kong Chinese 239–40, 241n2, 242, 243, 244, **245–46**, **247**, 314

income 53, 59, 66–67, **67**, 70, 168–69, 176, 177, 183–84, **184**
    pensions 9–10, 59, 159, 162, 166–67, 177, 180, 182, 218, 271
India **5**, **7**, 8, 21, 24, 33–34, 43, **164**, 215, 302, 303, 311
    ADLs 35–37, **38**, 38–41, **39**, **40–41**, 43
    life expectancy **222**, 223, 224, *225*
    productivity growth 169–70, **170**

Indonesia **5**, **7**, 8, 24, 79, 80, 292
    blood pressure 83, *84*, *85*, *86*, 98
    body mass index 87, *88*, 98
    cholesterol 89, *90*, *91*, *92*
    glycosylated hemoglobin *93*, 94
information technology employment 195, 197–98, 199–203, 204–9, 313
inter-generational flows *217*, 217–21, 221
intergenerational relations 10–11, 58–59, 63–66, 69, 215–16, *217*, 217–21, 228, 292–94, 313–14
    Bulgaria 269, 270, 276, 282–83, 284, 285
    caregiving 230–32, 235–36, 255–56, *256*, 264
intergenerational transfers 297–303, **298–99**, **300–301**, 303–4
Italy **7**, 8, 16, **164**, 167, 169, **170**, 170, 181, **230**
    fertility rates **5**, 6
    productivity growth 169, 170, **170**

Japan 2, 6, **7**, 7–8, 79, 80, 98, 108, 162, **164**
    blood pressure 83, *84*, *85*, *86*, 97, 98
    body mass index 87, *88*, 98
    cholesterol 89, *90*, *91*, *92*
    glycosylated hemoglobin *93*, 94
    life expectancy 4, 80, *227*
    marital status 226, *227*, **228**, 229, 230, **230**
    productivity growth 169, **170**, 170
Joseph, S. 55
Jovic, E. and McMullin, J. 10, 313

Kant, I. 28
Kenya 3, 124, 125
Komp, K. 10, 313
Korinek, K. 10, 314

labor force 160, 161, 165–68, **166**, *167*, *168*, 171–72, 189, 317–18
    productivity growth 10, 159, 168–71, **170**, 172, 313
LASA *see* Longitudinal Aging Study Amsterdam
Lebanon 50, **51**, 51–52, 54, 56, 57, 69, 70, 311

family structure 53, 54–55, 57, 58, **60**, 62, **62**, 69
health 60, **61**, 67, **68**
life expectancy **51**, 53
social relations 58–59, **60–61**, 64, **65**, 66, 69
socio-economic status 59, **61**, 66–67, **67**, 70
Leeson, G.W. and Khan, H.T.A. 11, 314
life expectancy 4, 17–18, 21, 80, *81*, 94–95, **95**, 160, 175, **222**, 223–24, 226, 310
Algeria **51**, 53, **222**
Lebanon **51**, 53
Netherlands *140*, 140–42, *141*, 143, *145*, 145–46, 148, 151
Russia 18, **222**, 223, 269, 272, 276
literacy 53, 59, 66, 70
loneliness 267–70, 272, 274, 275, 283–85, 314
Bulgaria 267, 268–69, 276, **278–79**, **280–81**, 280–83, 284, 285
Eastern Europe 10, 267–68, 269, 270, 272, 283, 314
Russia 267, 268–69, **273**, 273, 276, **278–79**, **280–81**, 280–83, 284
Longitudinal Aging Study Amsterdam (LASA) 9, 142–43, 145, 147, 150–51, 312

marital status 215, 226, *226*, *227*, **228**, 228–30, **230**, 231–32
men 160–61, 221–24, *225*
functional disabilities **38**, **39**, 42, 68, **68**
labor force **166**, 166–68, *168*
life expectancy *81*, **95**, 95, **222**, 223–24
marital status 226, *226*, *227*, **228**, 228–30, **230**, 231–32
MENA (Middle Eastern and North African) countries 49, 53, 54, 55–56, 62–63, 66, 67–68, 69, 70, 311
Mexico 79, 80, 96, 98, 297, 302, 303, 304
blood pressure 83, *84*, *85*, *86*, 98
body mass index 87, *88*, 98
cholesterol 89, *90*, *91*, *92*
glycosylated hemoglobin *93*, 94
migration 2, 3, 15, 16, 17, 159, 215, 221, 238, 316

mortality rates 1, 3–4, 6, 15, 87, 106–7, 108, 216

Netherlands 139, 143, 147, 148–49, **149**, 151
body mass index **142**, 142
chronic diseases 143, *144*, *145*, 145–46, 148
disabilities *144*, 144–45, 146–47
functional decline **150**, 150–51
life expectancy *140*, 140–42, *141*, 143, *145*, 145–46, 148, 151

old-age dependency rates 159, 162, *163*, **164**, 169, 171, 291

Pakistan **222**, 223, 224, *225*
Palestine 50, **51**, 52, 53, 54, 56, 57, 311
family structure 52, 57, 58, **60**, **62**, 62, 63, 69
health 60, **61**, 67, **68**
social relations 58, 59, **60–61**, 64, **65**, 65, 66, 69
socio-economic status 59, **61**, 66–67, **67**, 70
PAPFAM (Pan Arab Project for Family Health) 57
patriarchal connectivity 54–55, 56
pensions 9–10, 59, 159, 162, 166–67, 177, 180, 182, 218, 271
Pinquart, M. 269
population ageing 1–2, 6–8, **7**, 18–21, *19*, *20*, 49, 159, 160–61, 291, 309–10
Population Division (UN) 14–15, *15*, 16–17, 21, *23*
population growth rates 160, **161**
PP (pulse pressure) 81, 82, 83, *86*, **95**, 95, 97
productivity growth 10, 159, 168–71, **170**, 172, 313

Rada, C. 10, 312–13
relative age 25–26
religious activities 9, 105, 106–7, 108, 109, 110–11, **111**, 112–14, **113**, 115–16, 312
replacement rates 5–6, 13, 16, 27
retirement 9–10, 139, 162, 176–77, 180, 183–84, **184**, *185*, 185–86, 189, 317

retirement age 166, 167, *178*, 178–80, **180**, 183, 186, 188, 195, 313
Russia 18, *19*, 224, *225*, 270, 271, 276, **277**, 285, 314
  life expectancy 18, **222**, 223, 269, 272, 276
  loneliness 267, 268–69, **273**, 273, 276, **278–79**, 280–83, **280–81**, 284

SBP (systolic blood pressure) 81, 82, 83, *84*, 95, **95**, 97, 98
Sennett, R. 196, 206, 209
SES *see* socio-economic status
Singapore 22, *23*, *25*, **222**, 223, 303
  marital status 226, *227*, **228**, 229
social capital 235, 236–37, 238–39, 240–41, 242–43, 244–45, **245–47**, 314
social cohesion 10, 187, 235–36, 238, 240, 242–43, 244–45, **245–47**, 314
social relations
  Algeria 58, **60–61**, 63, 64, **65**, 66, 69
  Lebanon 58–59, **60–61**, 64, **65**, 66, 69
  Palestine 58, 59, **60–61**, 64, 65, **65**, 66, 69
socio-economic status (SES) 41–42, **42**, 70, 122
  Algeria 59, **61**, 66–67, **67**, 70
  Lebanon 59, **61**, 66–67, **67**, 70
  Palestine 59, **61**, 66–67, **67**, 70
SSA (sub-Saharan Africa) 9, 21, 24, 121–23, 126–28, 132–33, **161**, **162**, **164**, 312
  health care 124–25, 126–28, 129–30, 133

Taiwan 79, 80, 105–6
  blood pressure 83, *84*, *85*, *86*
  body mass index 87, *88*, 98
  cholesterol 89, *90*, *91*, *92*
  glycosylated hemoglobin *93*, 94
  religious activities 107–8, 109–11, **111**, 112–14, **113**, 116, 312
TFR (Total Fertility Rate) 4–6, **5**, **51**, 54, 105
Thailand **5**, 6, **7**, 8
tripartite life course model 176, 177, 180, 182, 184–86, *185*, 188

Tsimane, Bolivia 79, 80, 98
  blood pressure 83, *84*, *85*, *86*, 97
  body mass index 87, *88*
  cholesterol 89, *90*, *91*, *92*
  glycosylated hemoglobin *93*, 94
Turkey 24, **184**, 297, 302, 304
  marital status 226, *227*, **228**, 228, 229, **230**, 230

UK (United Kingdom) 18, 21–22, 80, 98, 171, 216
  blood pressure 83, *84*, *85*, *86*, 97
  body mass index 87, *88*
  cholesterol 89, *90*, *91*, *92*
  glycosylated hemoglobin *93*, 94
  life expectancy 80, *81*, **222**, 223, 224, *225*
Ukraine 3, **184**, 270
unemployment 49, **51**, 53, 65
  Europe 166–67, 170, **170**, 179, 180, *181*, 182
US (United States) 3, **5**, 6, 18, *19*, 54, 79, 80, 96, 148, 316–17
  blood pressure 83, *84*, *85*, *86*, 97
  body mass index 87, *88*, 98
  cholesterol 89, *90*, *91*, *92*, 98
  glycosylated hemoglobin *93*, 94, 97
  life expectancy 18, 80, *81*, **222**, 224, *225*
  productivity growth 169, 170, **170**
  working-age population 22, *23*

Vallin, J. 21, 24

WANE (Workforce Aging in the New Economy) 197–98
WHO (World Health Organization) 122, 128, 129, 285
women 70, 160–61, **162**, 215–16, 221–24, *225*
  functional disabilities 37, **38**, **39**, 42, 43, 67, **68**
  labor force **166**, 166–68, *168*
  life expectancy 4, *81*, **95**, 95, **222**, 223–24
  marital status *226*, 226, *227*, **228**, 228–30, **230**, 231–32
work societies 176

working-age population 21–22, *23*, 24, *25*, 160–61, 164, 165–68, 171–72, 176–77, *181*

young-age population 160
young old population 185–87
youth 176, 196, 197, 200, 201, 313, 316, 318
youth migration 52, 53, 57, 314, 316